SOFT

GOODBYE DESPAIR

TRANSLATION BY JACKIE MCCLURE

LETTERING AND TOUCHUP BY JOHN CLARK

EDITED BY CARL GUSTAV HORN

SPECIAL THANKS TO ARIANNE ADVINCULA AND
MIMI SAITO AT SPIKE CHUNSOFT

1

DR2:

CONTENTS

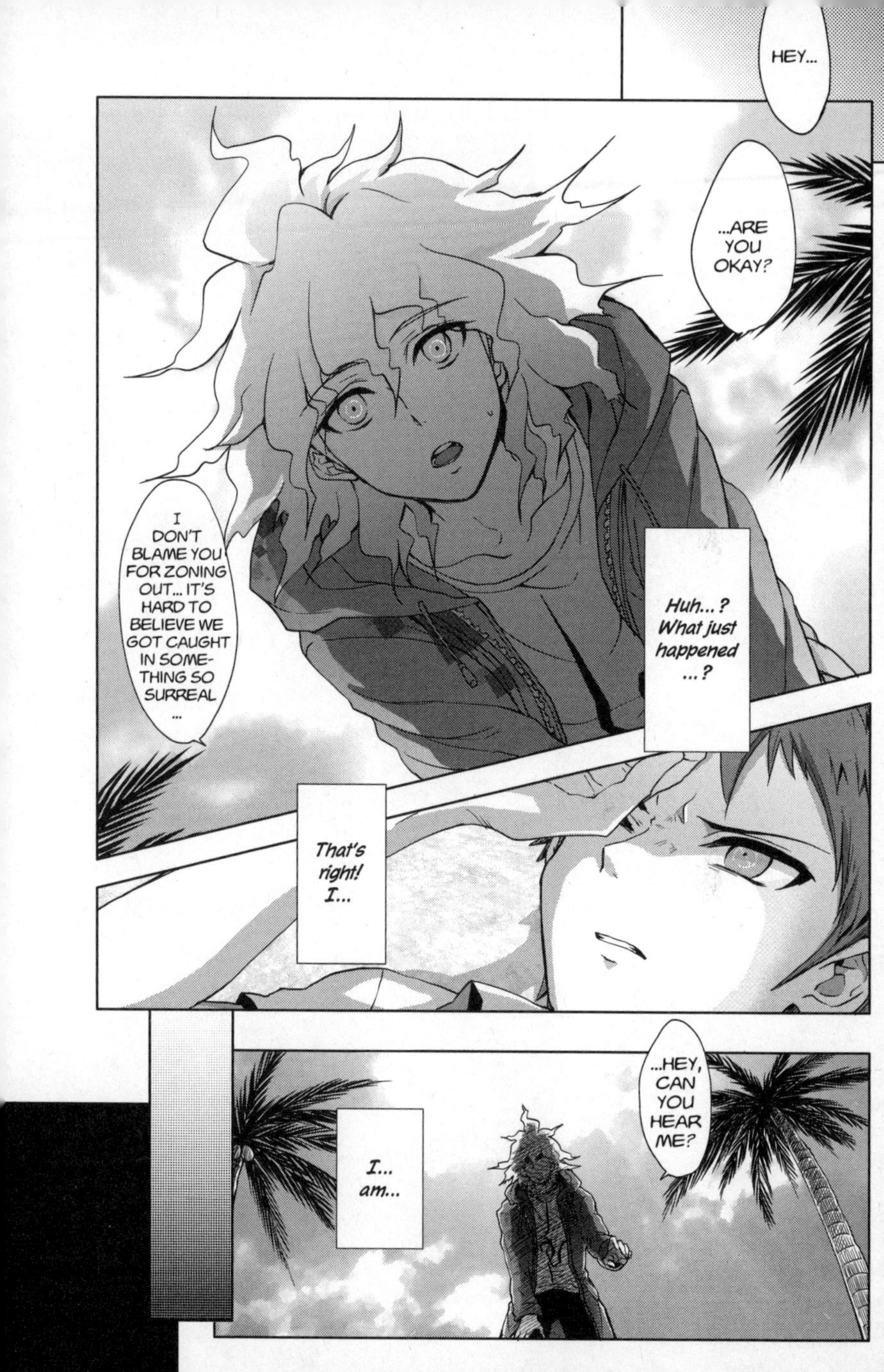
HEY...
...ARE YOU OKAY?
Huh...? What just happened...?
I DON'T BLAME YOU FOR ZONING OUT... IT'S HARD TO BELIEVE WE GOT CAUGHT IN SOME-THING SO SURREAL...
That's right! I...
...HEY, CAN YOU HEAR ME?
I... am...

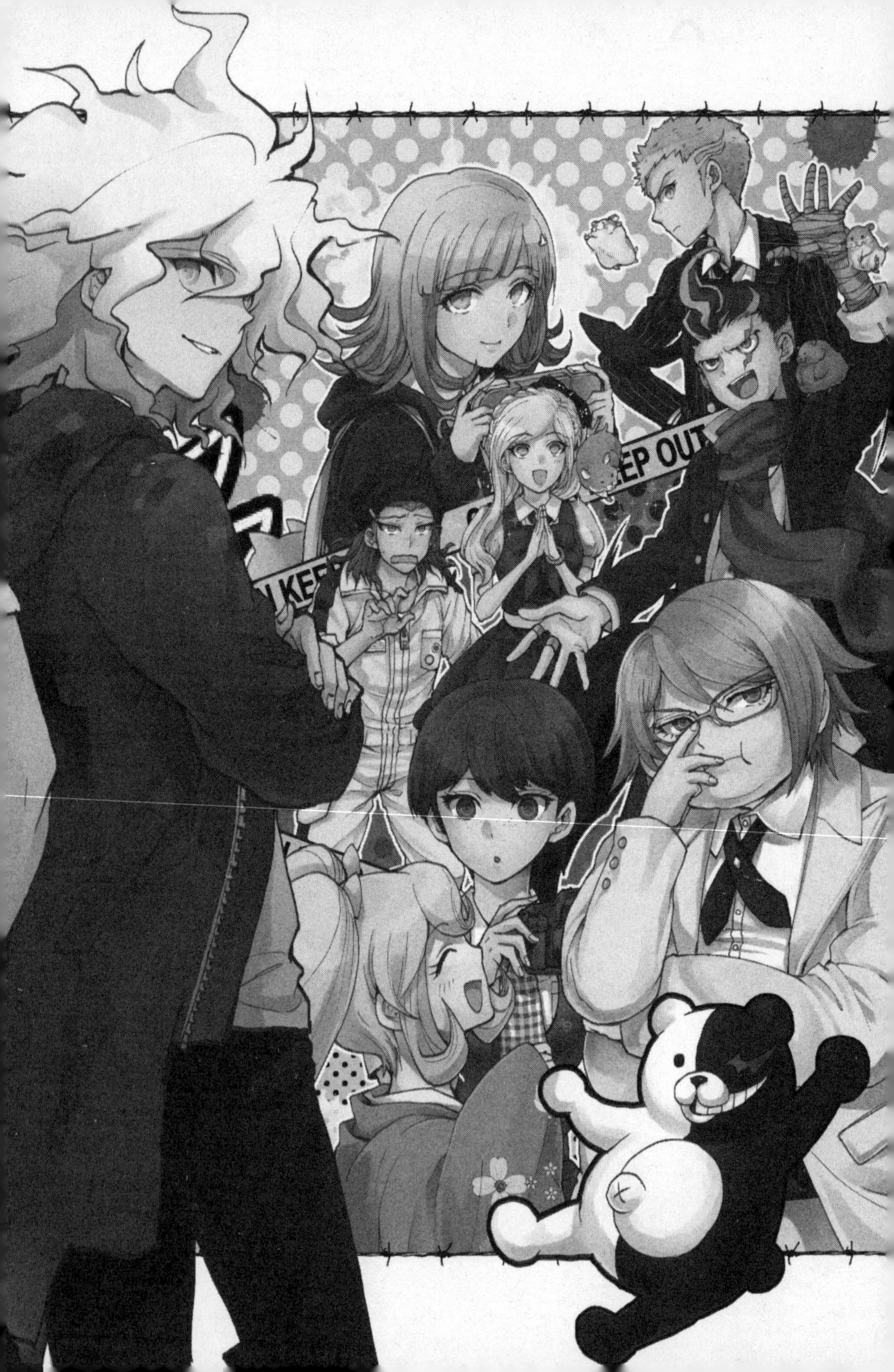
EP OUT

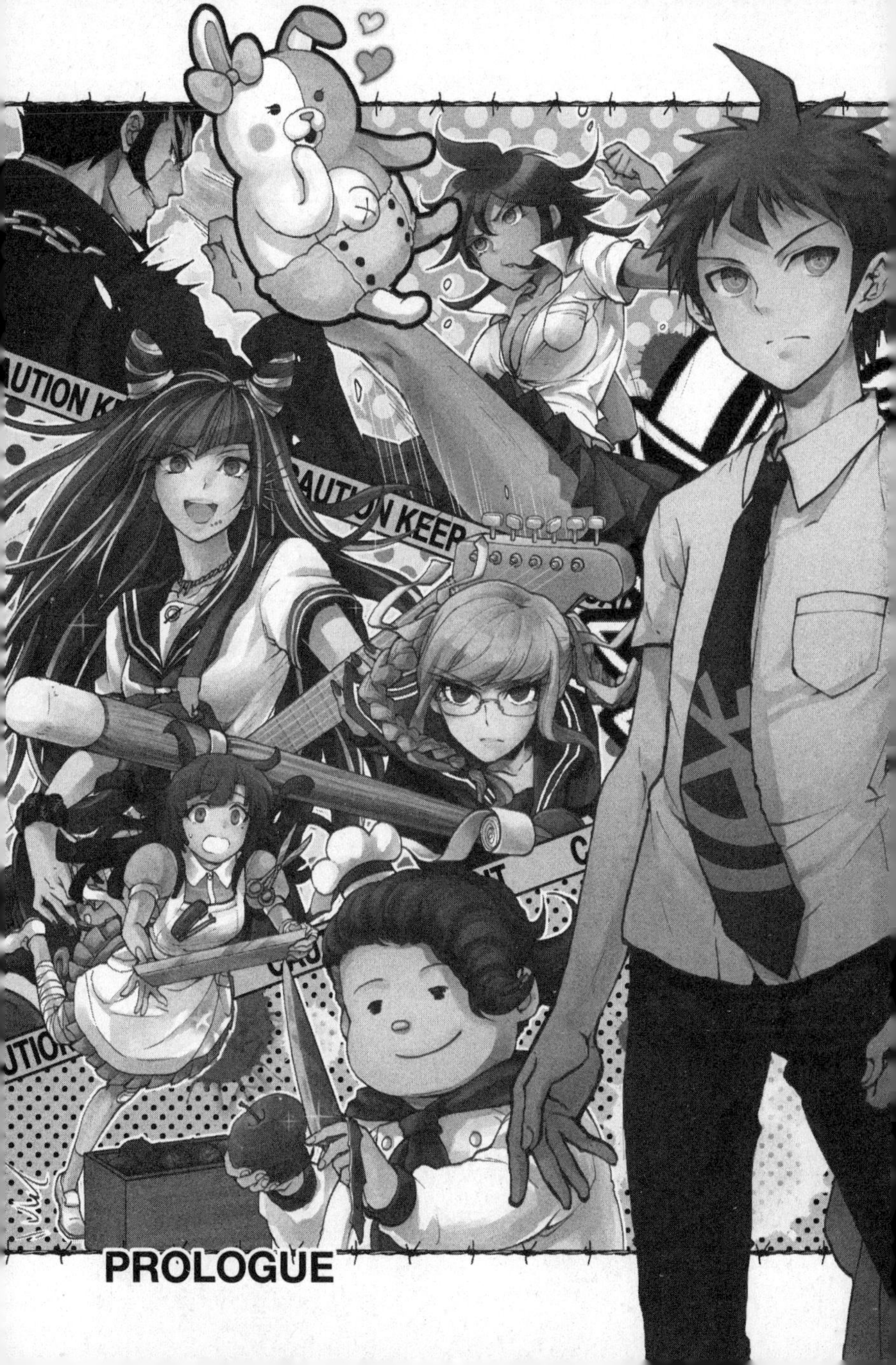

PROLOGUE

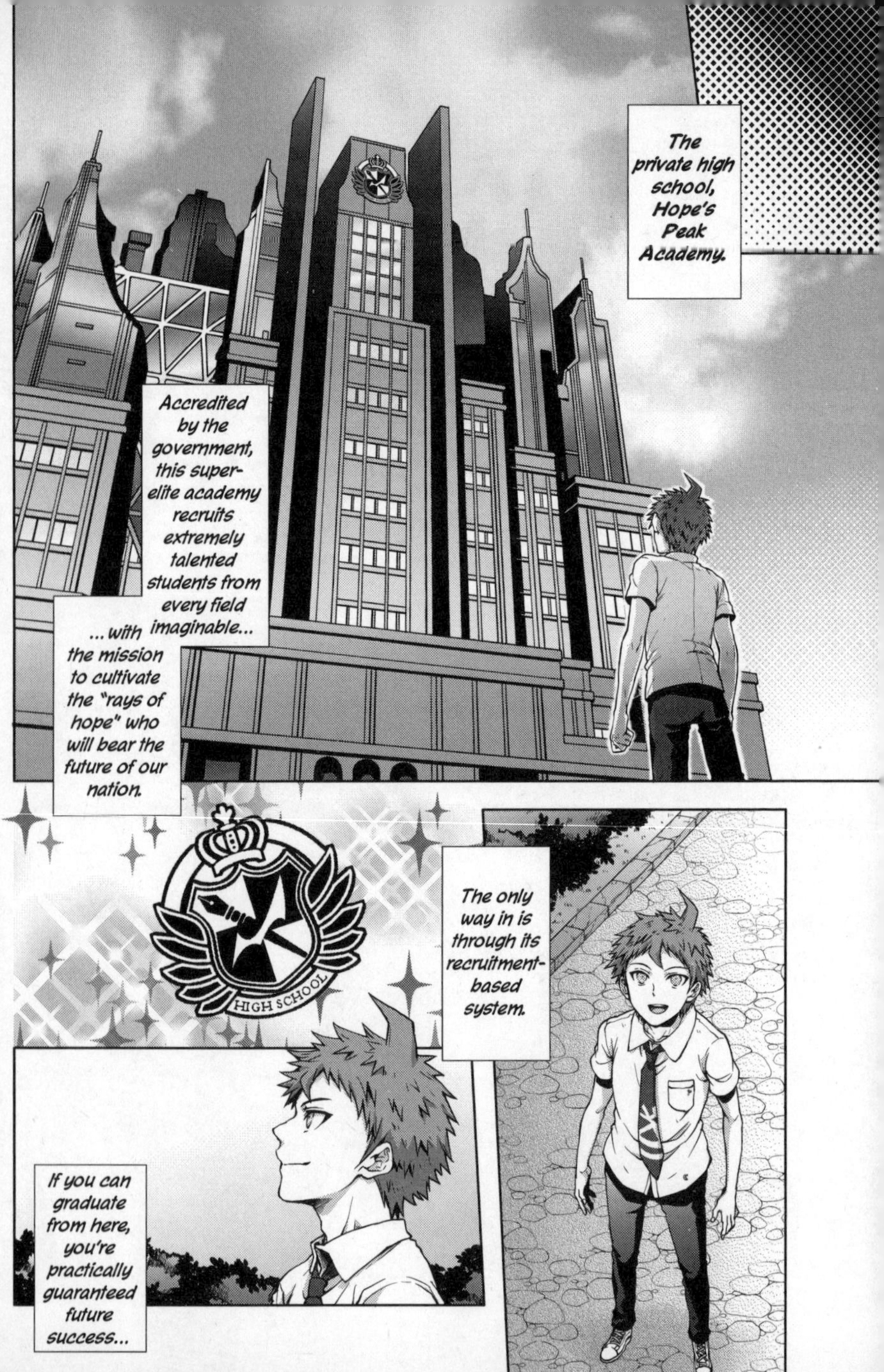
The private high school, Hope's Peak Academy.
Accredited by the government, this super-elite academy recruits extremely talented students from every field imaginable...
...with the mission to cultivate the "rays of hope" who will bear the future of our nation.
The only way in is through its recruitment-based system.
HIGH SCHOOL
If you can graduate from here, you're practically guaranteed future success...

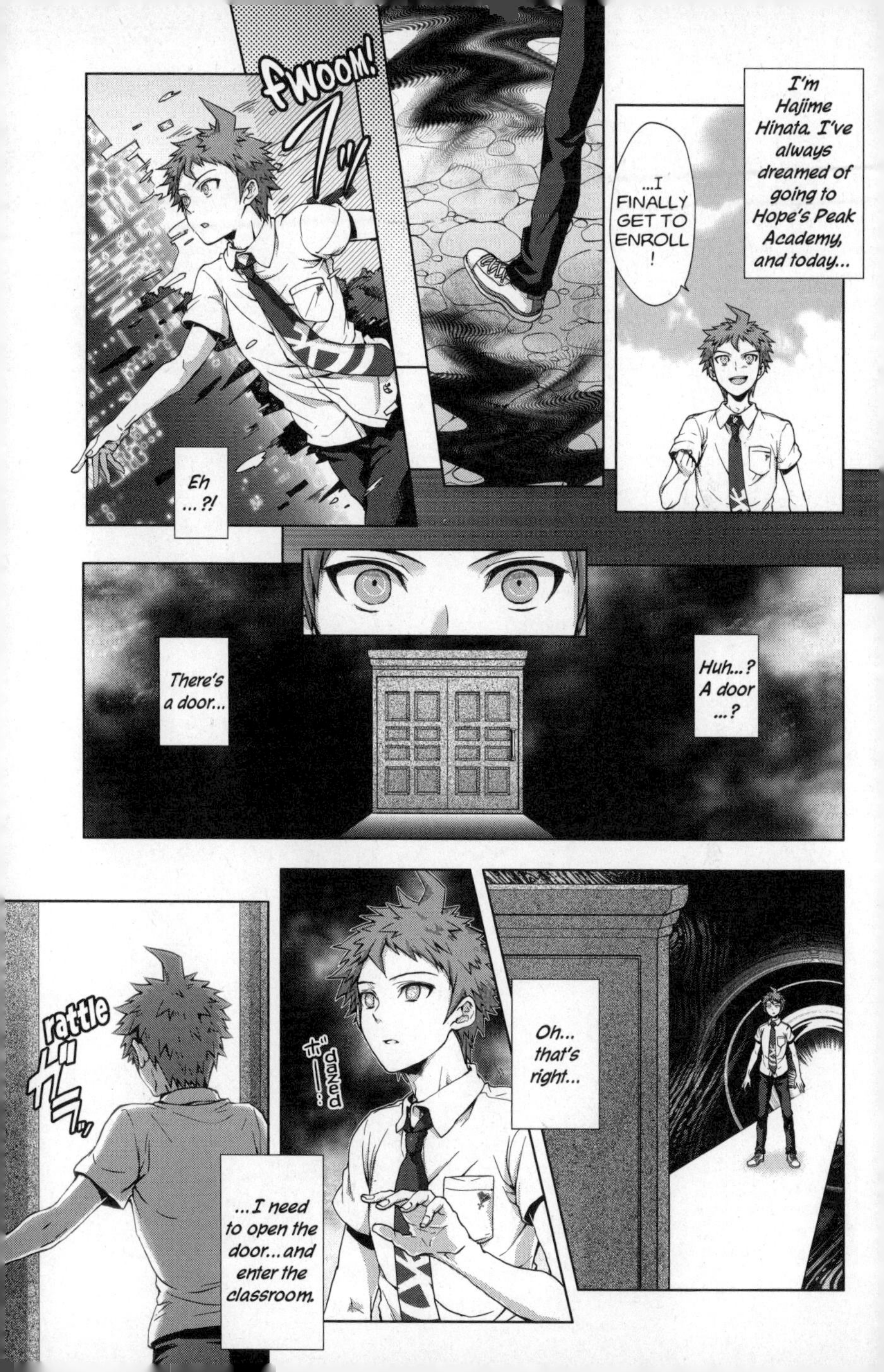
I'm Hajime Hinata. I've always dreamed of going to Hope's Peak Academy, and today...
...I FINALLY GET TO ENROLL!
FWOOM!
Eh ...?!
Huh...? A door ...?
There's a door...
Oh... that's right...
dazed
...I need to open the door... and enter the classroom.
rattle

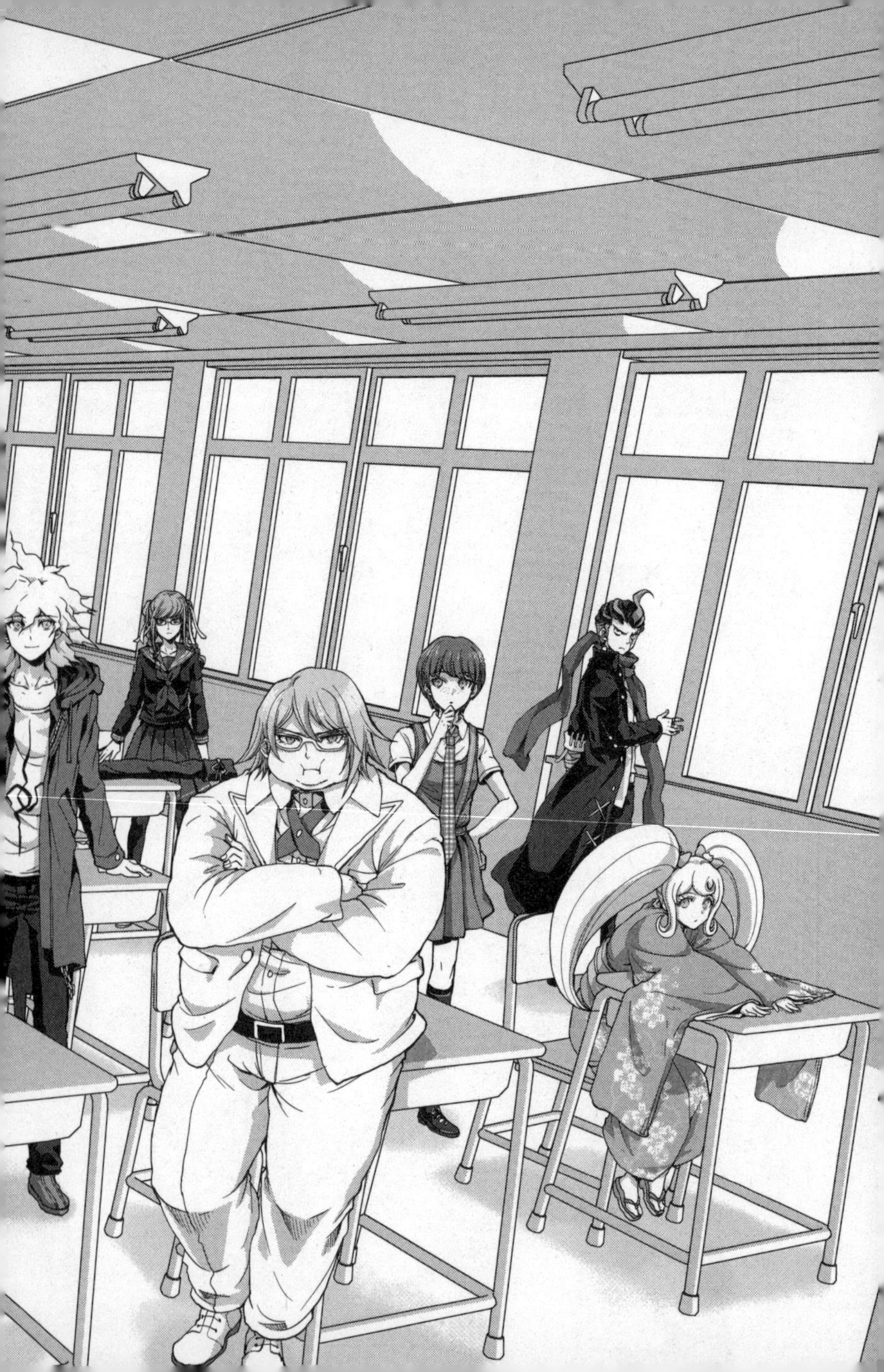

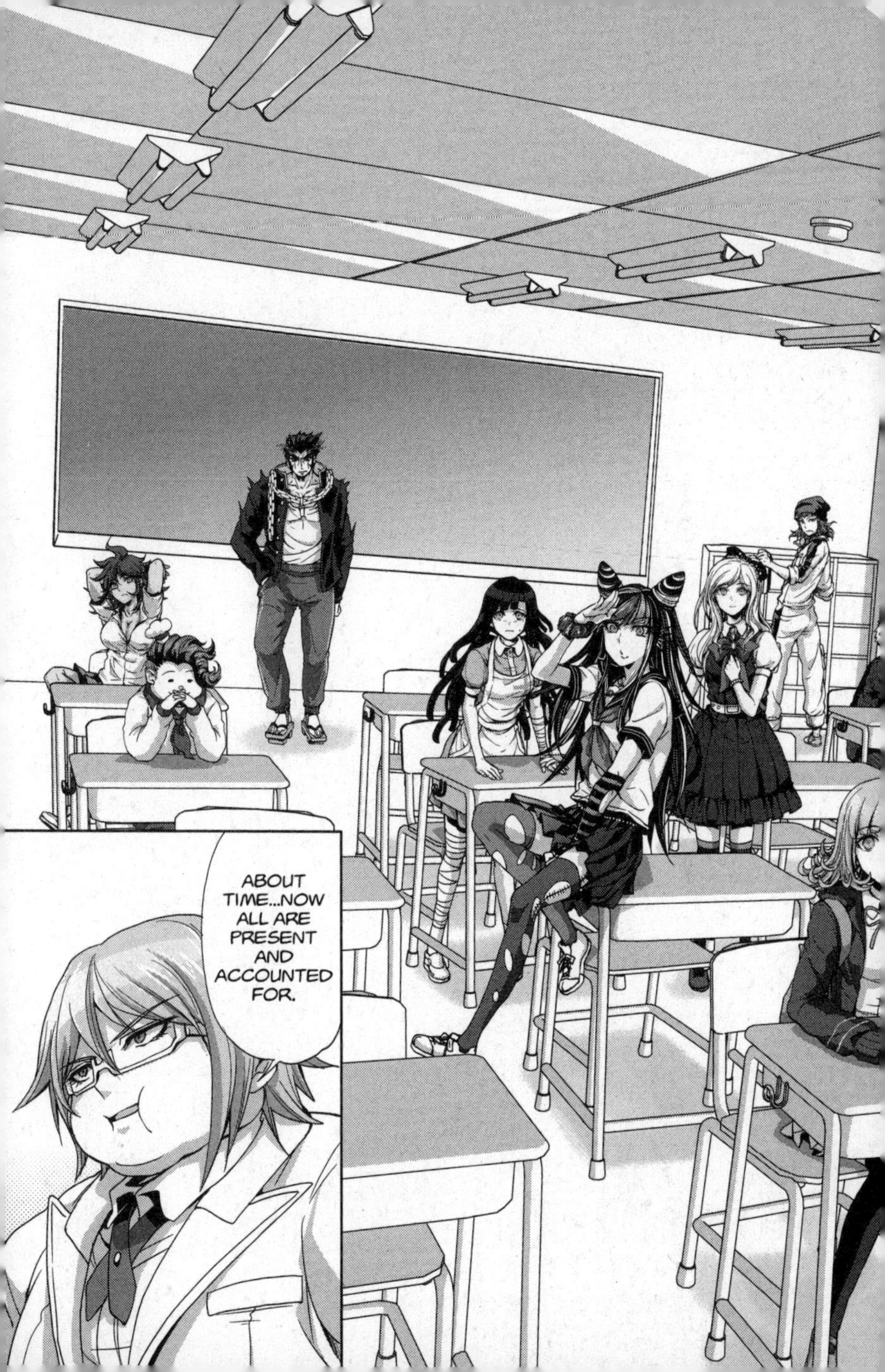
ABOUT TIME...NOW ALL ARE PRESENT AND ACCOUNTED FOR.

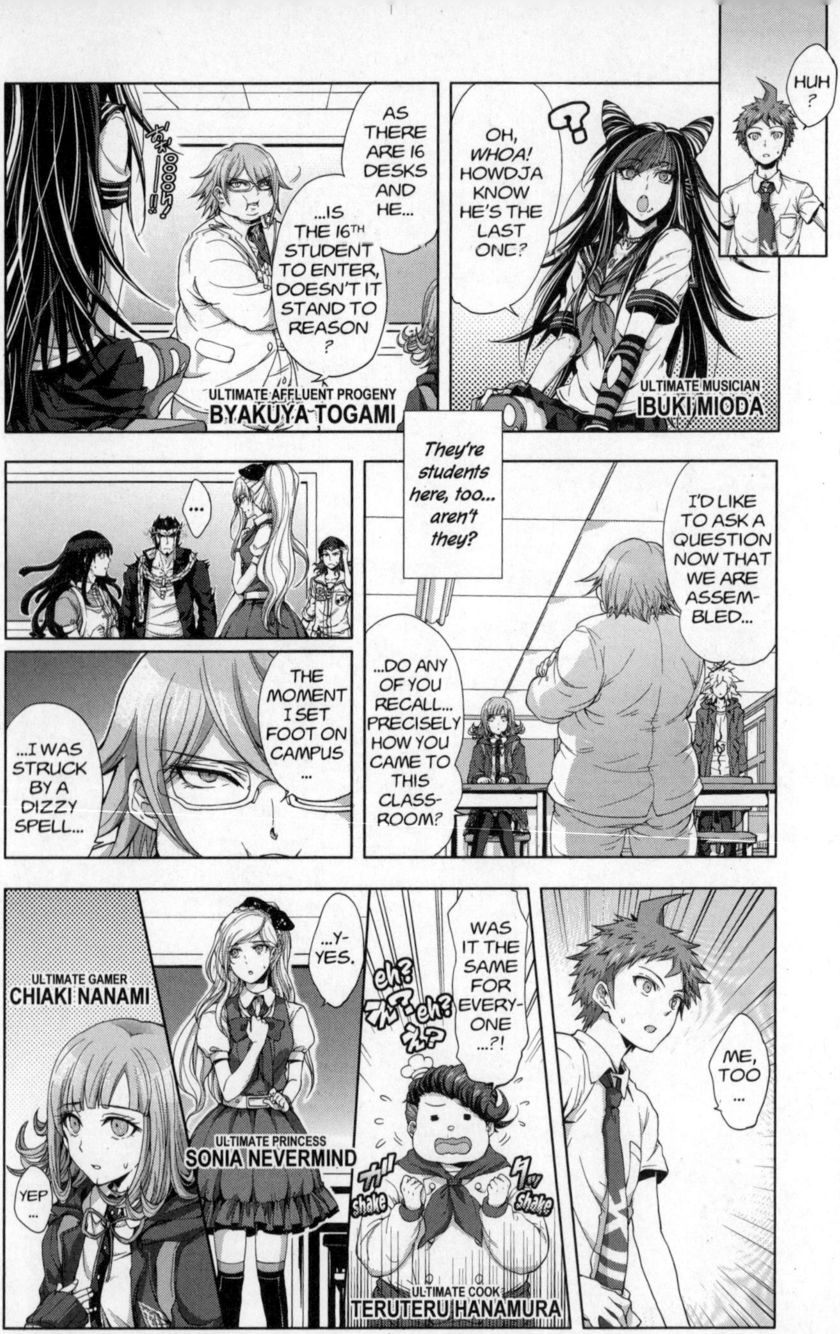
HUH?
OH, WHOA! HOWDJA KNOW HE'S THE LAST ONE?
ULTIMATE MUSICIAN
IBUKI MIODA
AS THERE ARE 16 DESKS AND HE...
...IS THE 16TH STUDENT TO ENTER, DOESN'T IT STAND TO REASON?
OOOOH!!
ULTIMATE AFFLUENT PROGENY
BYAKUYA TOGAMI
They're students here, too... aren't they?
I'D LIKE TO ASK A QUESTION NOW THAT WE ARE ASSEMBLED...
...DO ANY OF YOU RECALL... PRECISELY HOW YOU CAME TO THIS CLASSROOM?
...
THE MOMENT I SET FOOT ON CAMPUS...
...I WAS STRUCK BY A DIZZY SPELL...
ME, TOO...
WAS IT THE SAME FOR EVERYONE...?!
eh? eh?
shake shake
ULTIMATE COOK
TERUTERU HANAMURA
...Y-YES.
ULTIMATE PRINCESS
SONIA NEVERMIND
ULTIMATE GAMER
CHIAKI NANAMI
YEP...

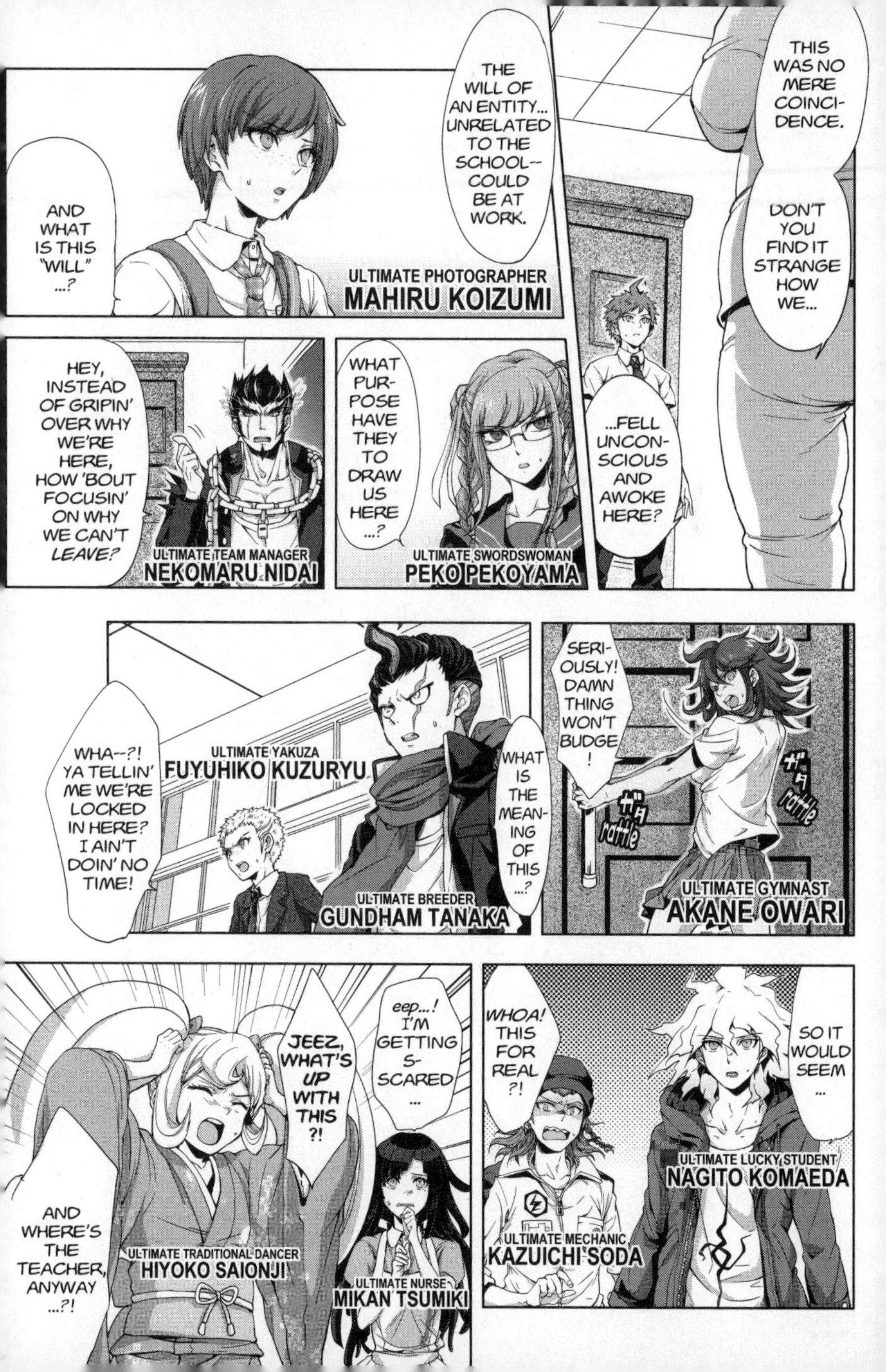
THIS WAS NO MERE COINCIDENCE.
DON'T YOU FIND IT STRANGE HOW WE...
...FELL UNCONSCIOUS AND AWOKE HERE?
THE WILL OF AN ENTITY... UNRELATED TO THE SCHOOL-- COULD BE AT WORK.
AND WHAT IS THIS "WILL" ...?
ULTIMATE PHOTOGRAPHER
MAHIRU KOIZUMI
WHAT PURPOSE HAVE THEY TO DRAW US HERE ...?
ULTIMATE SWORDSWOMAN
PEKO PEKOYAMA
HEY, INSTEAD OF GRIPIN' OVER WHY WE'RE HERE, HOW 'BOUT FOCUSIN' ON WHY WE CAN'T *LEAVE?*
ULTIMATE TEAM MANAGER
NEKOMARU NIDAI
SERIOUSLY! DAMN THING WON'T BUDGE!
ガタ rattle
ガタ rattle
ULTIMATE GYMNAST
AKANE OWARI
WHAT IS THE MEANING OF THIS ...?
ULTIMATE BREEDER
GUNDHAM TANAKA
WHA--?! YA TELLIN' ME WE'RE LOCKED IN HERE? I AIN'T DOIN' NO TIME!
ULTIMATE YAKUZA
FUYUHIKO KUZURYU
SO IT WOULD SEEM ...
ULTIMATE LUCKY STUDENT
NAGITO KOMAEDA
WHOA! THIS FOR REAL ?!
ULTIMATE MECHANIC
KAZUICHI SODA
eep...! I'M GETTING S-SCARED ...
ULTIMATE NURSE
MIKAN TSUMIKI
JEEZ, WHAT'S *UP* WITH THIS ?!
AND WHERE'S THE TEACHER, ANYWAY ...?!
ULTIMATE TRADITIONAL DANCER
HIYOKO SAIONJI

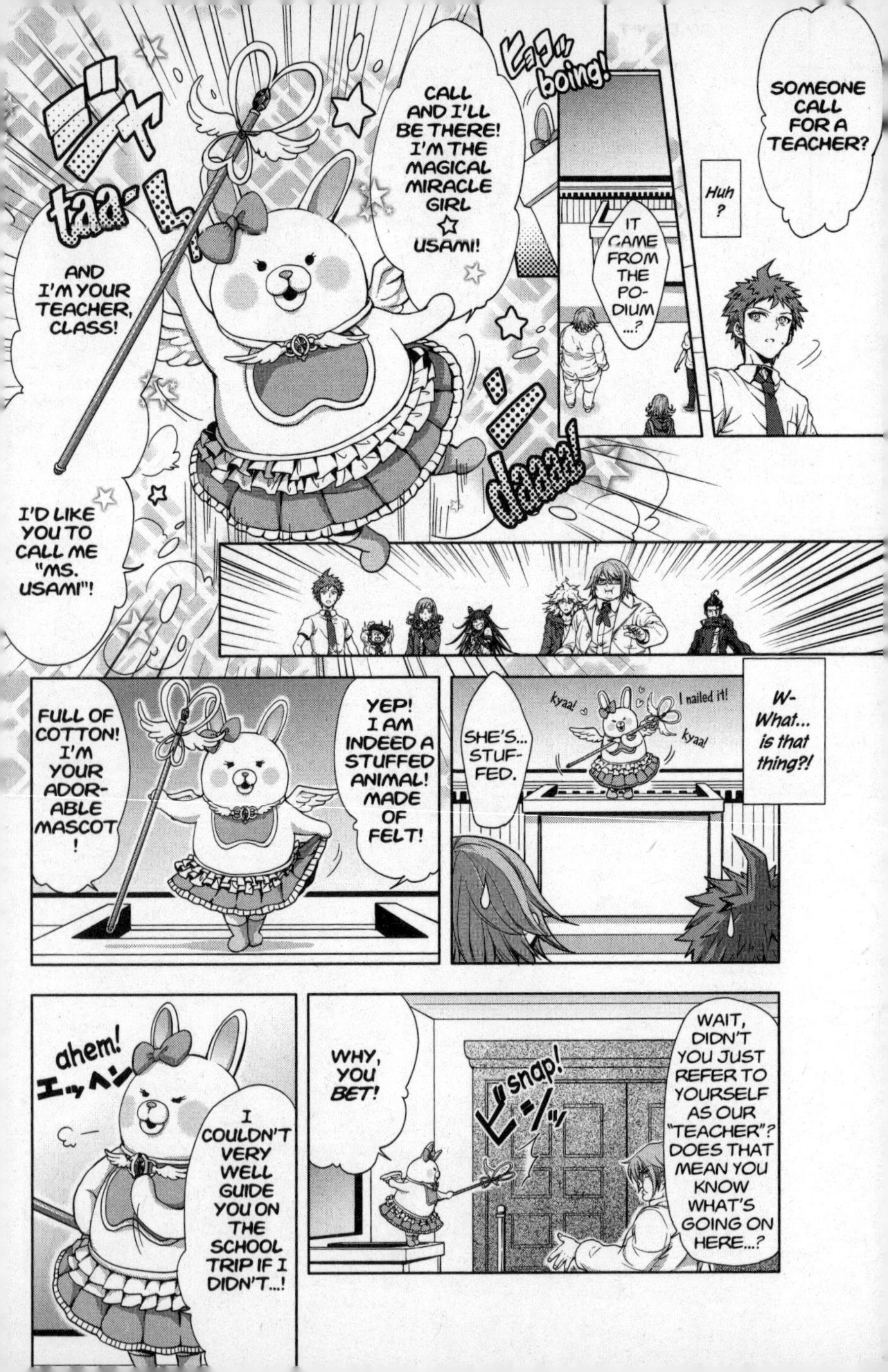
SOMEONE CALL FOR A TEACHER?
Huh?
IT CAME FROM THE PO-DIUM ...?
boing!
CALL AND I'LL BE THERE! I'M THE MAGICAL MIRACLE GIRL ☆ USAMI!
taa-
AND I'M YOUR TEACHER, CLASS!
I'D LIKE YOU TO CALL ME "MS. USAMI"!
W-What... is that thing?!
I nailed it!
kyaa!
kyaa!
SHE'S... STUFF-FED.
YEP! I AM INDEED A STUFFED ANIMAL! MADE OF FELT!
FULL OF COTTON! I'M YOUR ADOR-ABLE MASCOT!
WAIT, DIDN'T YOU JUST REFER TO YOURSELF AS OUR "TEACHER"? DOES THAT MEAN YOU KNOW WHAT'S GOING ON HERE...?
snap!
WHY, YOU BET!
ahem!
I COULDN'T VERY WELL GUIDE YOU ON THE SCHOOL TRIP IF I DIDN'T...!

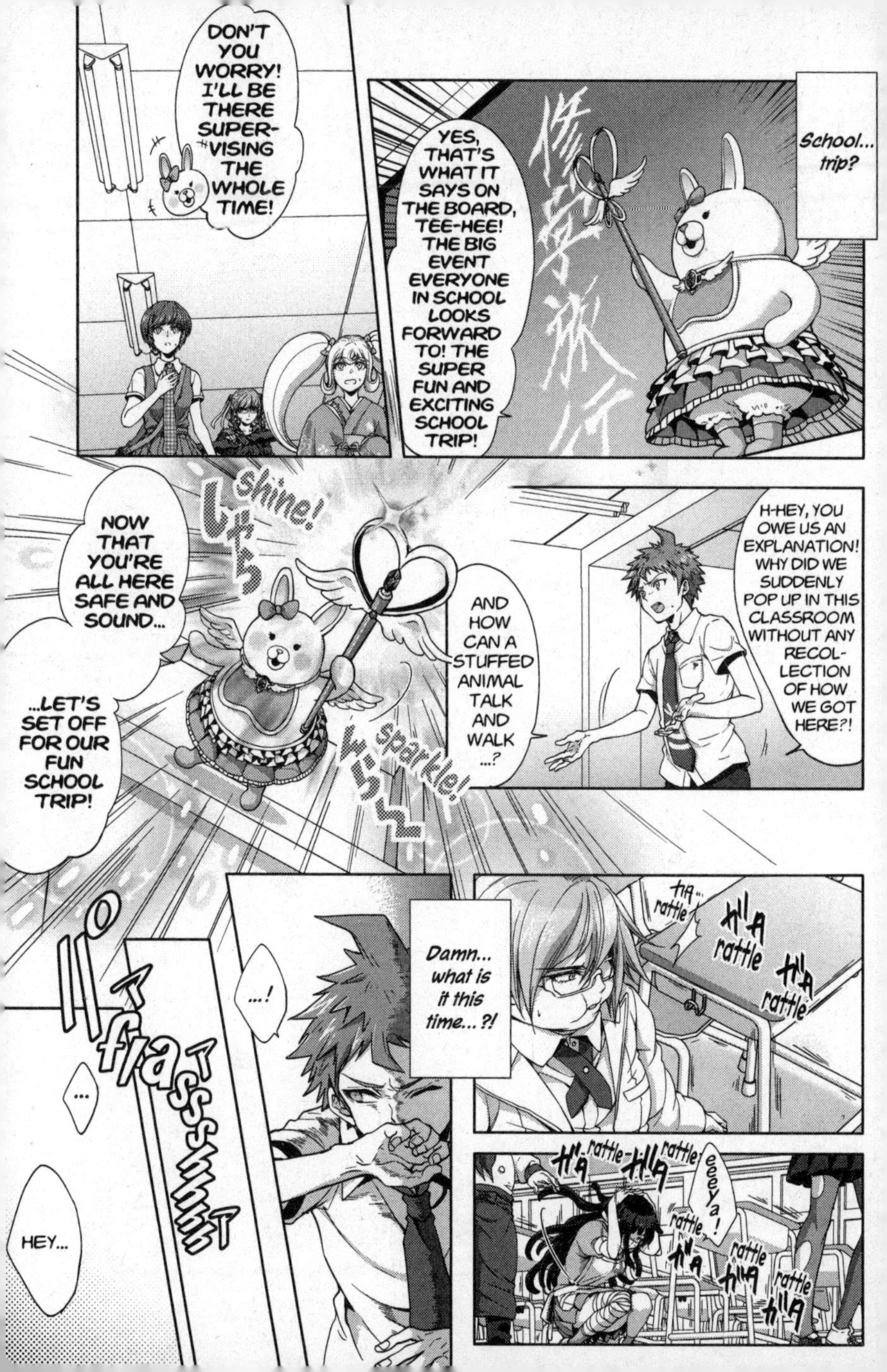
School... trip?
YES, THAT'S WHAT IT SAYS ON THE BOARD, TEE-HEE! THE BIG EVENT EVERYONE IN SCHOOL LOOKS FORWARD TO! THE SUPER FUN AND EXCITING SCHOOL TRIP!
DON'T YOU WORRY! I'LL BE THERE SUPER-VISING THE WHOLE TIME!
H-HEY, YOU OWE US AN EXPLANATION! WHY DID WE SUDDENLY POP UP IN THIS CLASSROOM WITHOUT ANY RECOL-LECTION OF HOW WE GOT HERE?!
AND HOW CAN A STUFFED ANIMAL TALK AND WALK ...?
shine!
NOW THAT YOU'RE ALL HERE SAFE AND SOUND...
...LET'S SET OFF FOR OUR FUN SCHOOL TRIP!
sparkle!
rattle...
rattle
rattle
rattle
rattle
eeeya!
rattle
rattle
rattle
Damn... what is it this time...?!
...!
flassshhh
...
HEY...

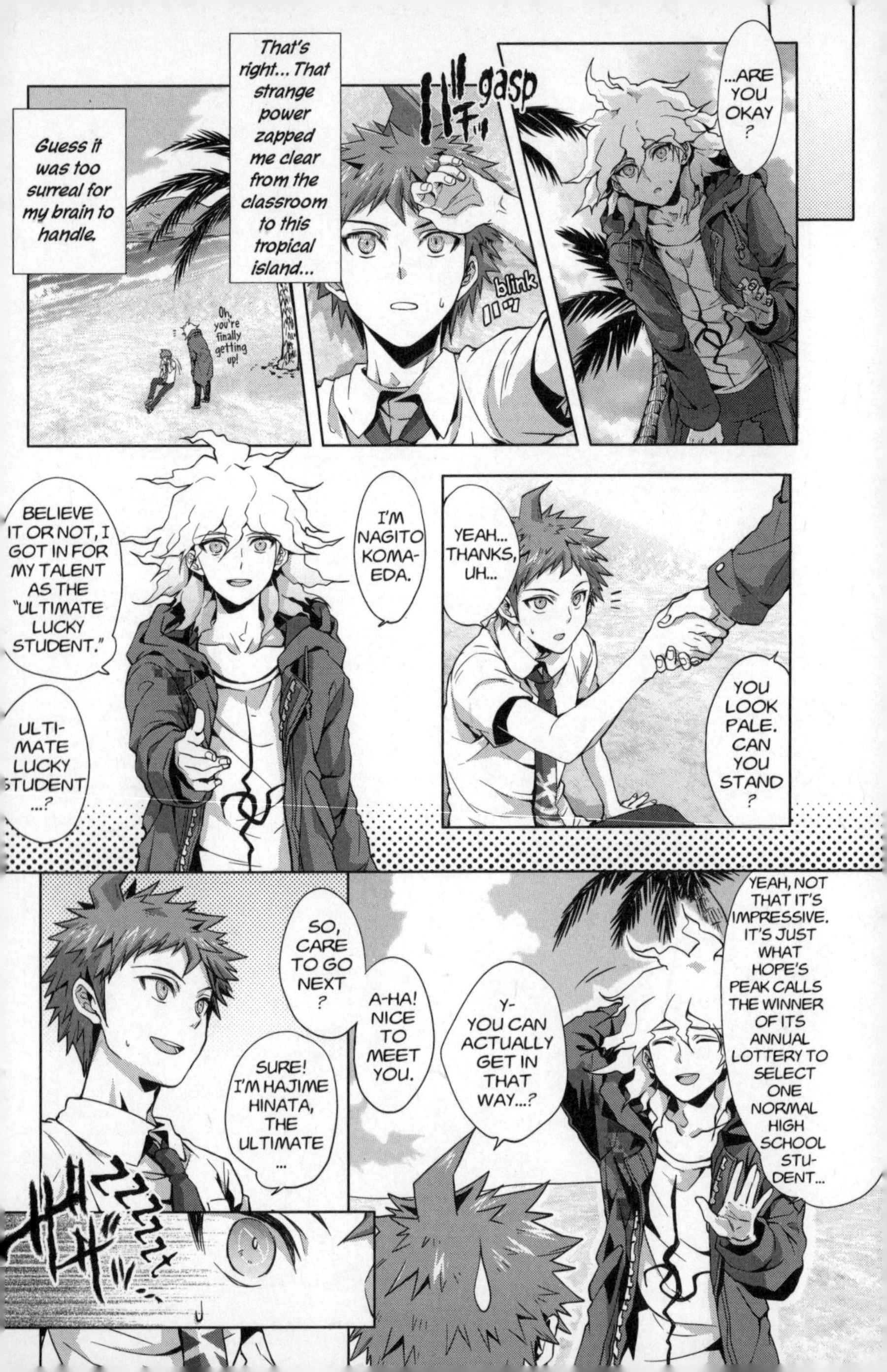
...ARE YOU OKAY?
gasp
That's right... That strange power zapped me clear from the classroom to this tropical island...
blink
Guess it was too surreal for my brain to handle.
Oh, you're finally getting up!
YEAH... THANKS, UH...
YOU LOOK PALE. CAN YOU STAND?
I'M NAGITO KOMAEDA.
BELIEVE IT OR NOT, I GOT IN FOR MY TALENT AS THE "ULTIMATE LUCKY STUDENT."
ULTIMATE LUCKY STUDENT...?
YEAH, NOT THAT IT'S IMPRESSIVE. IT'S JUST WHAT HOPE'S PEAK CALLS THE WINNER OF ITS ANNUAL LOTTERY TO SELECT ONE NORMAL HIGH SCHOOL STUDENT...
Y-YOU CAN ACTUALLY GET IN THAT WAY...?
A-HA! NICE TO MEET YOU.
SO, CARE TO GO NEXT?
SURE! I'M HAJIME HINATA, THE ULTIMATE...
zzzzzt

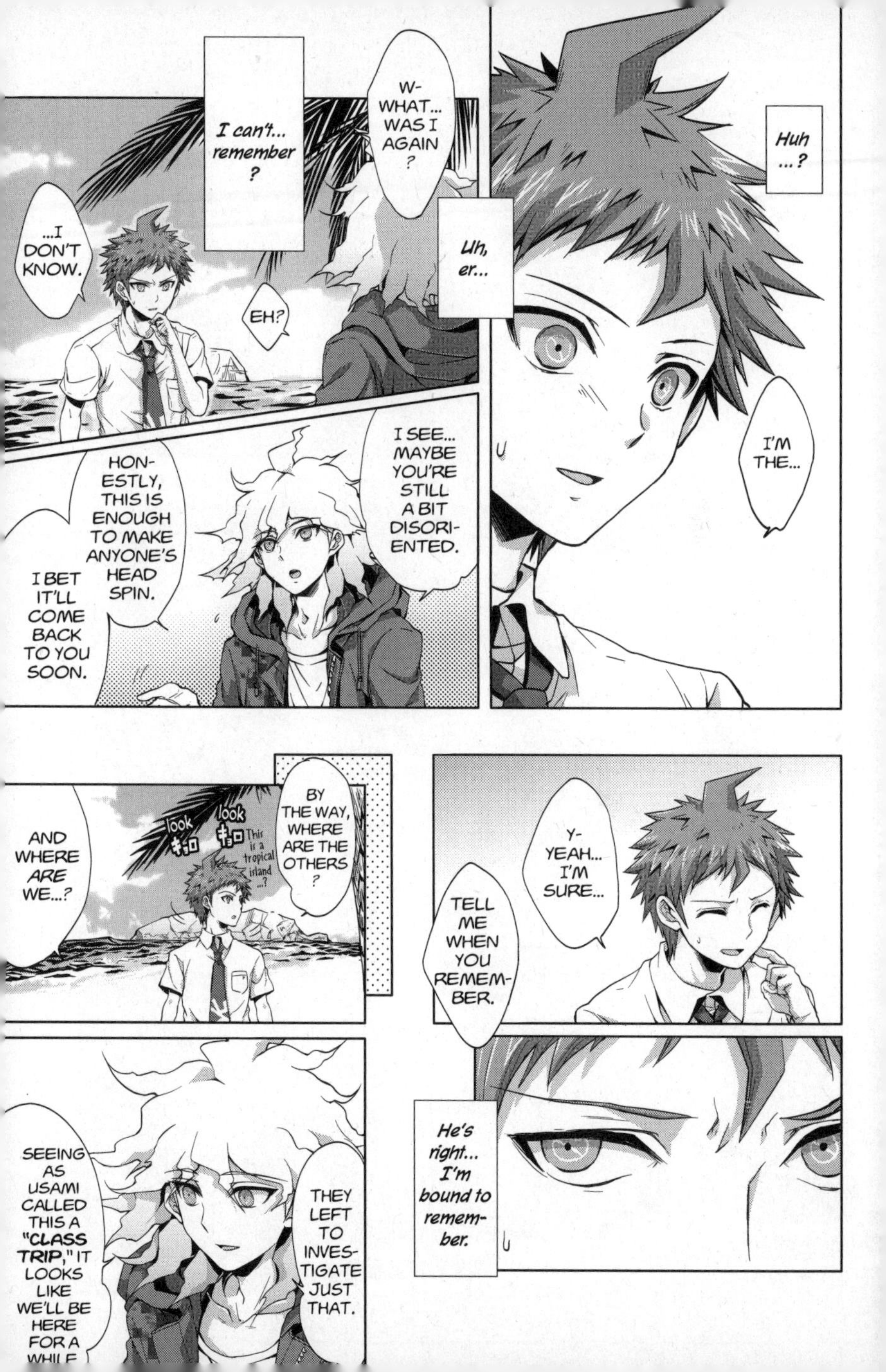
Huh ...?
Uh, er...
I'M THE...
W-WHAT... WAS I AGAIN?
I can't... remember?
EH?
...I DON'T KNOW.
I SEE... MAYBE YOU'RE STILL A BIT DISORIENTED.
HONESTLY, THIS IS ENOUGH TO MAKE ANYONE'S HEAD SPIN.
I BET IT'LL COME BACK TO YOU SOON.
Y-YEAH... I'M SURE...
TELL ME WHEN YOU REMEMBER.
BY THE WAY, WHERE ARE THE OTHERS?
look キョロ
look キョロ
This is a tropical island ...?
AND WHERE ARE WE...?
He's right... I'm bound to remember.
THEY LEFT TO INVESTIGATE JUST THAT.
SEEING AS USAMI CALLED THIS A "CLASS TRIP," IT LOOKS LIKE WE'LL BE HERE FOR A WHILE

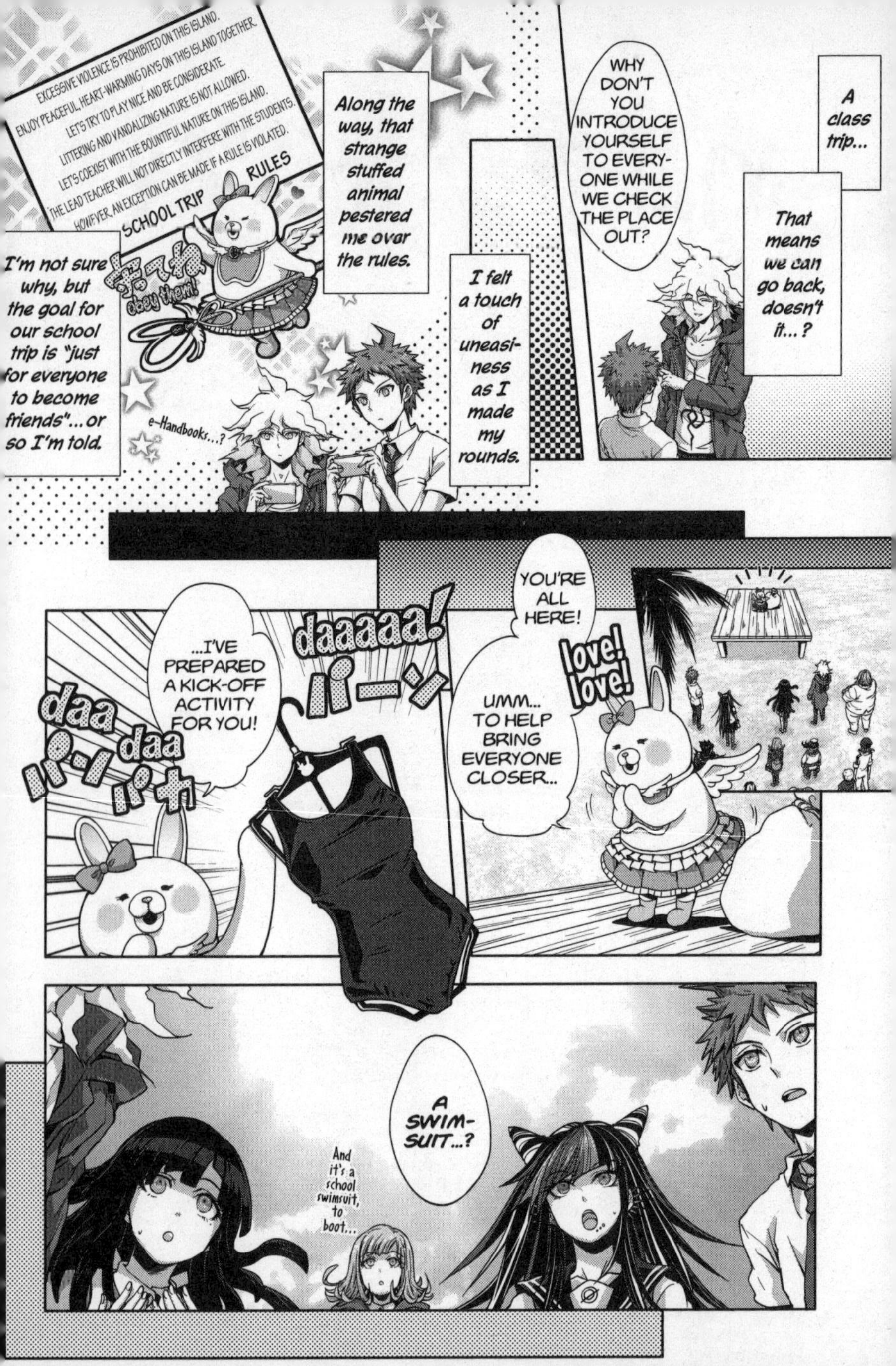
A class trip...
That means we can go back, doesn't it...?
WHY DON'T YOU INTRODUCE YOURSELF TO EVERYONE WHILE WE CHECK THE PLACE OUT?
I felt a touch of uneasiness as I made my rounds.
Along the way, that strange stuffed animal pestered me over the rules.
SCHOOL TRIP RULES
EXCESSIVE VIOLENCE IS PROHIBITED ON THIS ISLAND.
ENJOY PEACEFUL, HEART-WARMING DAYS ON THIS ISLAND TOGETHER.
LET'S TRY TO PLAY NICE AND BE CONSIDERATE.
LITTERING AND VANDALIZING NATURE IS NOT ALLOWED.
LET'S COEXIST WITH THE BOUNTIFUL NATURE ON THIS ISLAND.
THE LEAD TEACHER WILL NOT DIRECTLY INTERFERE WITH THE STUDENTS.
HOWEVER, AN EXCEPTION CAN BE MADE IF A RULE IS VIOLATED.
obey them!
I'm not sure why, but the goal for our school trip is "just for everyone to become friends"...or so I'm told.
e-Handbooks...?
YOU'RE ALL HERE!
UMM... TO HELP BRING EVERYONE CLOSER...
love! love!
...I'VE PREPARED A KICK-OFF ACTIVITY FOR YOU!
daaaaa!
daa daa
A SWIM-SUIT...?
And it's a school swimsuit, to boot...

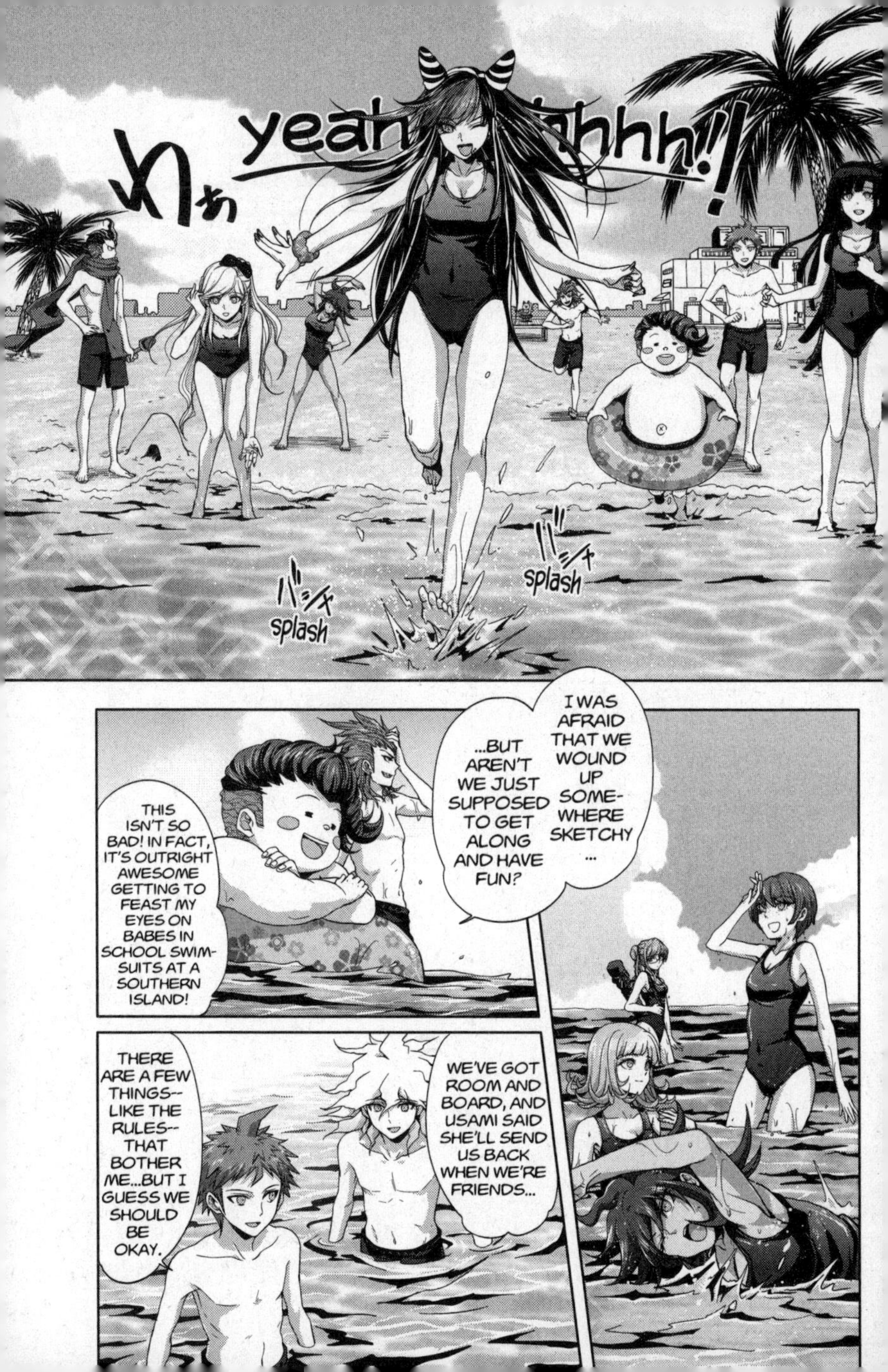
めぁ
yeah hhhh!!
バシャ
splash
バシャ
splash
I WAS AFRAID THAT WE WOUND UP SOMEWHERE SKETCHY...
...BUT AREN'T WE JUST SUPPOSED TO GET ALONG AND HAVE FUN?
THIS ISN'T SO BAD! IN FACT, IT'S OUTRIGHT AWESOME GETTING TO FEAST MY EYES ON BABES IN SCHOOL SWIMSUITS AT A SOUTHERN ISLAND!
WE'VE GOT ROOM AND BOARD, AND USAMI SAID SHE'LL SEND US BACK WHEN WE'RE FRIENDS...
THERE ARE A FEW THINGS--LIKE THE RULES--THAT BOTHER ME...BUT I GUESS WE SHOULD BE OKAY.

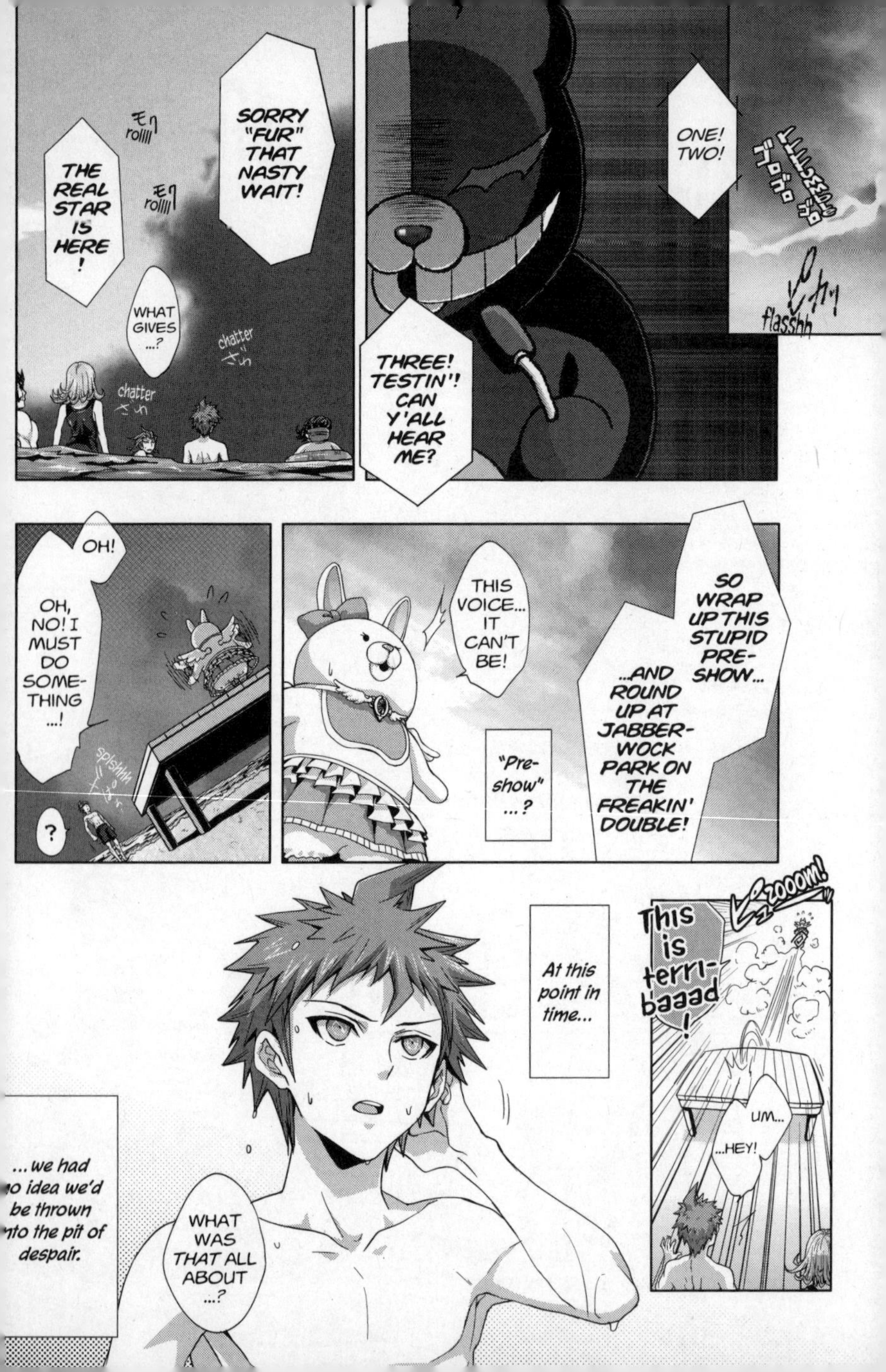

ONE! TWO!
ゴロゴロ
ピカッ
flasshh
THREE! TESTIN'! CAN Y'ALL HEAR ME?
SORRY "FUR" THAT NASTY WAIT!
THE REAL STAR IS HERE!
roll
roll
WHAT GIVES...?
chatter
chatter
SO WRAP UP THIS STUPID PRE-SHOW...
...AND ROUND UP AT JABBERWOCK PARK ON THE FREAKIN' DOUBLE!
THIS VOICE... IT CAN'T BE!
"Pre-show"...?
OH!
OH, NO! I MUST DO SOMETHING...!
splshhh
?
zooom!
This is terri-baaad!
UM...
...HEY!
At this point in time...
WHAT WAS THAT ALL ABOUT...?
...we had no idea we'd be thrown into the pit of despair.

DANGAN
RONPA 2
GOODBYE
DESPAIR

DANGAN
RONPA 2

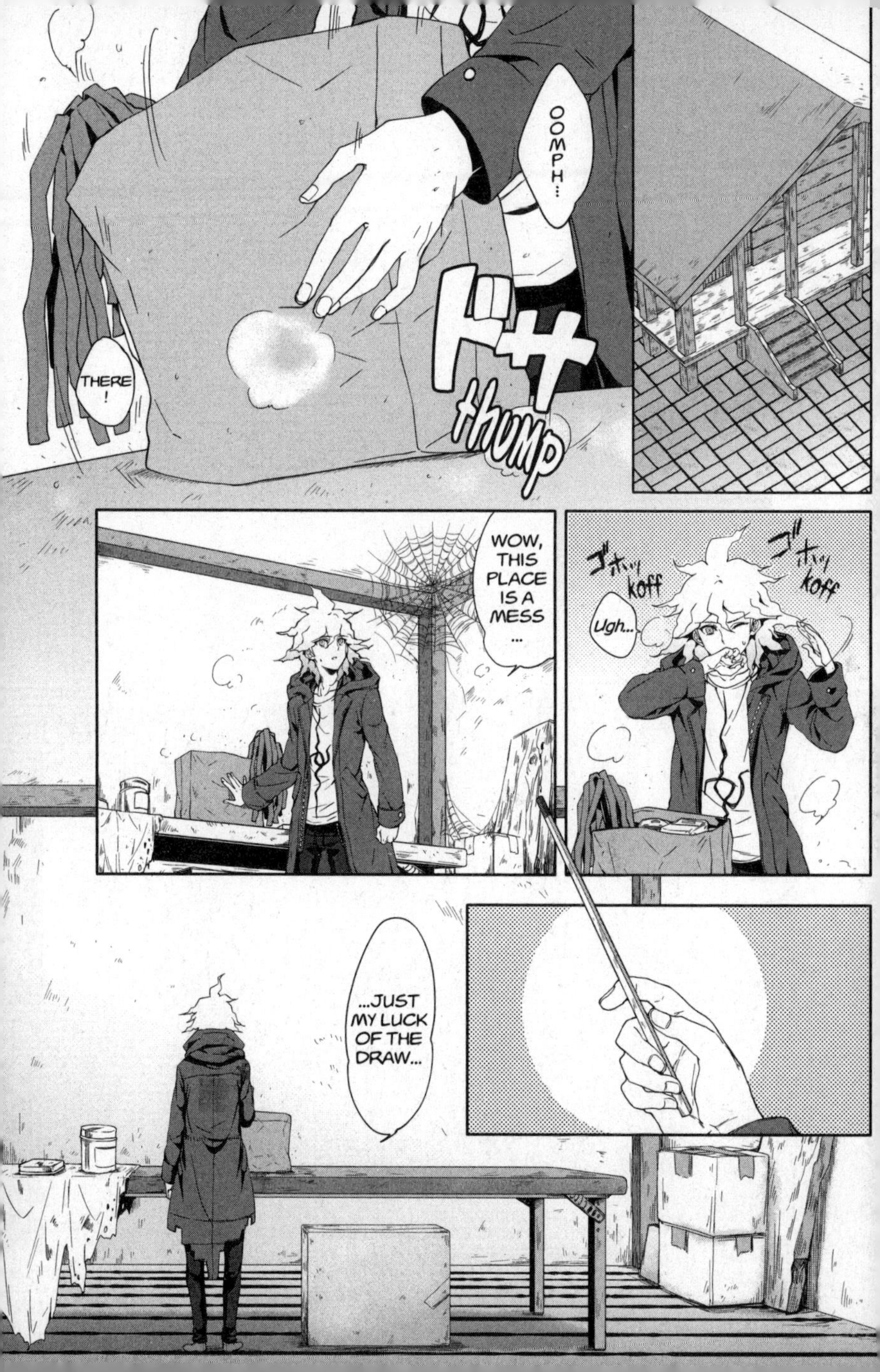
OOMPH...
ドサ
thump
THERE!
ゴホッ koff
ゴホッ koff
Ugh...
WOW, THIS PLACE IS A MESS...
...JUST MY LUCK OF THE DRAW...

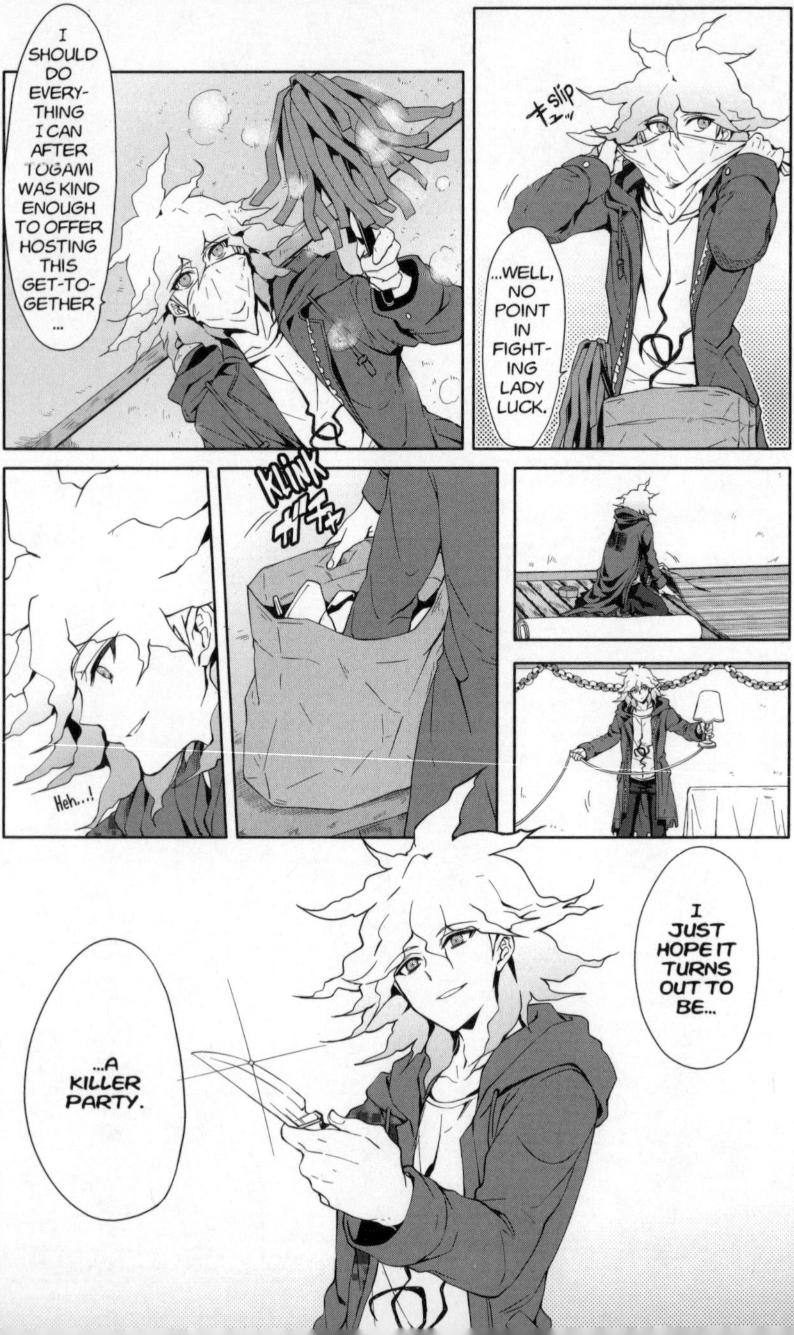
slip
キュッ
...WELL, NO POINT IN FIGHTING LADY LUCK.
I SHOULD DO EVERYTHING I CAN AFTER TOGAMI WAS KIND ENOUGH TO OFFER HOSTING THIS GET-TO-GETHER ...
KLINK
ガチャ
Heh...!
I JUST HOPE IT TURNS OUT TO BE...
...A KILLER PARTY.

CHAPTER 1: CURTAIN RISES ON THE KILLING SCHOOL TRIP

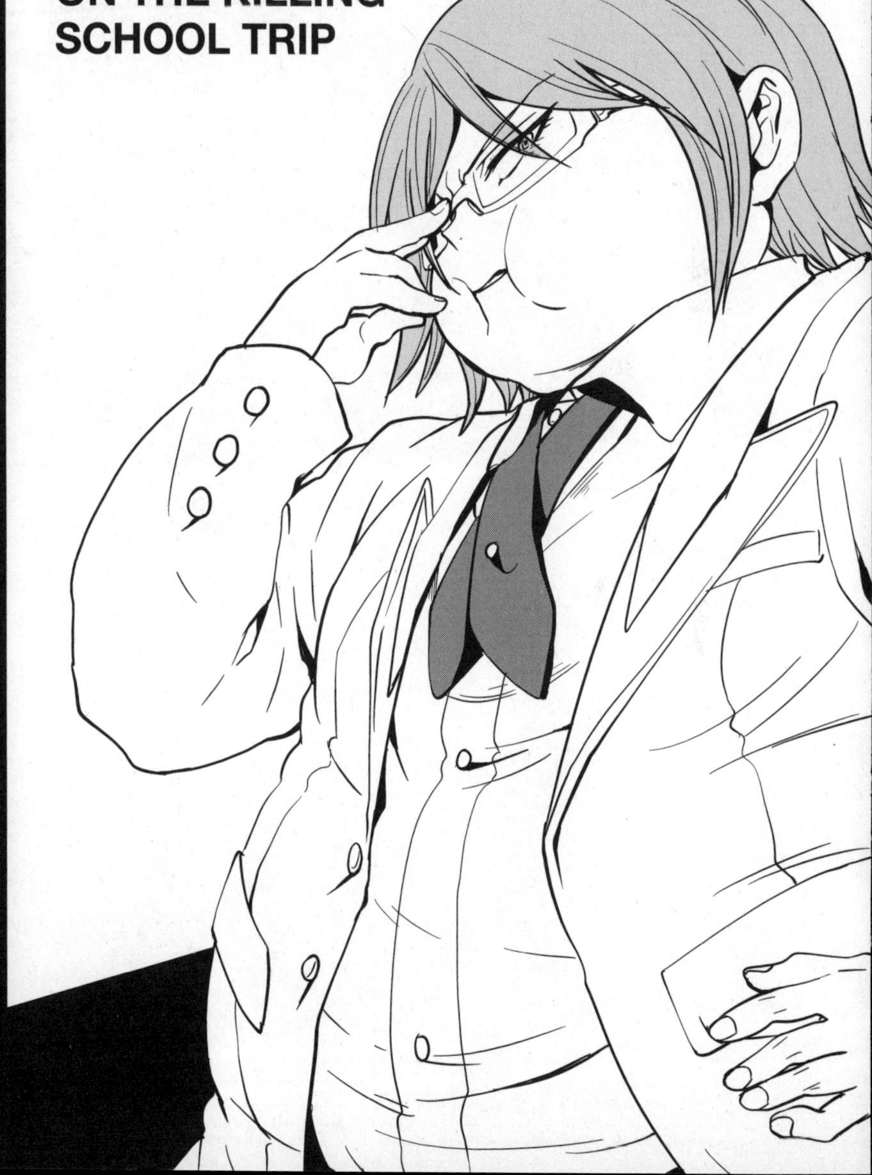

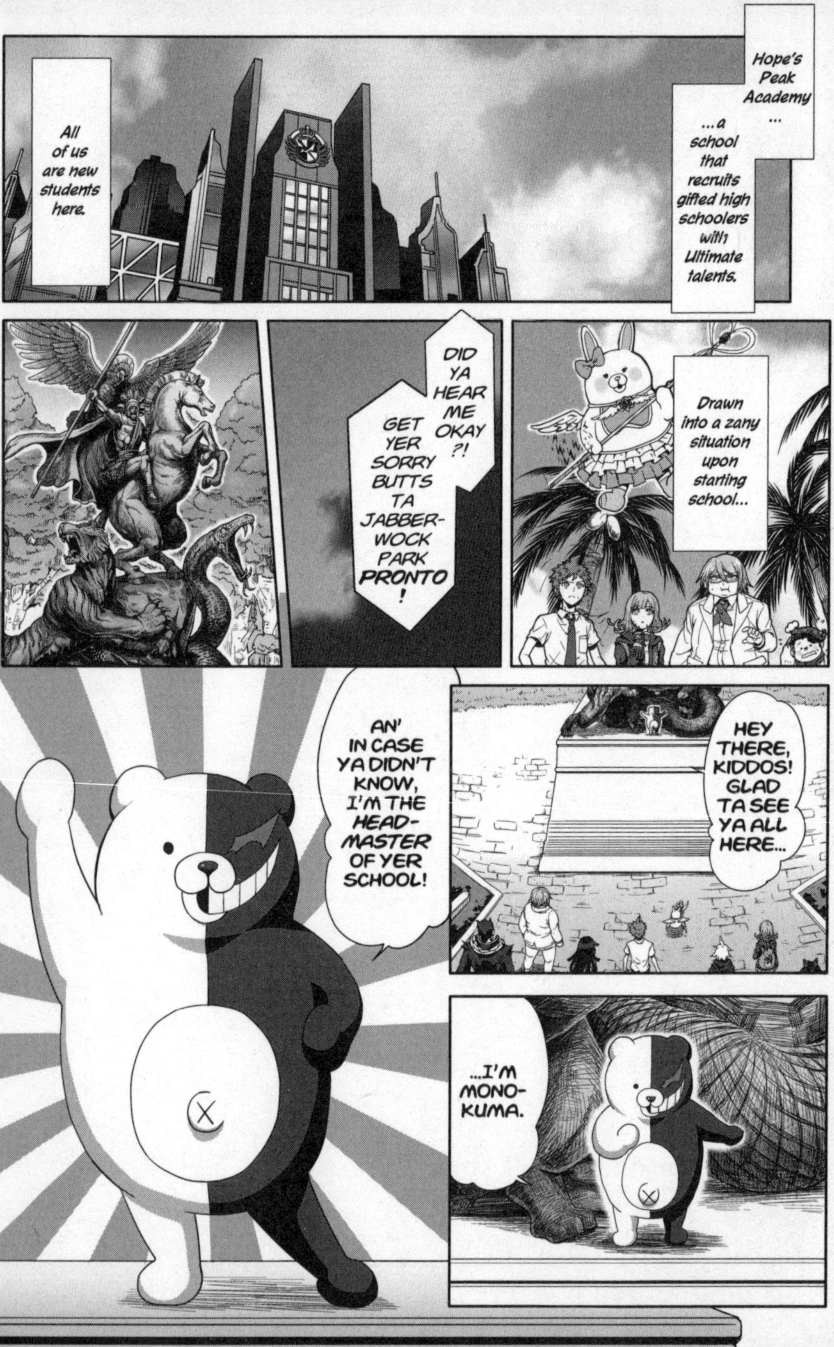
Hope's Peak Academy...
...a school that recruits gifted high schoolers with Ultimate talents.
All of us are new students here.
Drawn into a zany situation upon starting school...
DID YA HEAR ME OKAY?!
GET YER SORRY BUTTS TA JABBER-WOCK PARK PRONTO!
HEY THERE, KIDDOS! GLAD TA SEE YA ALL HERE...
...I'M MONO-KUMA.
AN' IN CASE YA DIDN'T KNOW, I'M THE HEAD-MASTER OF YER SCHOOL!

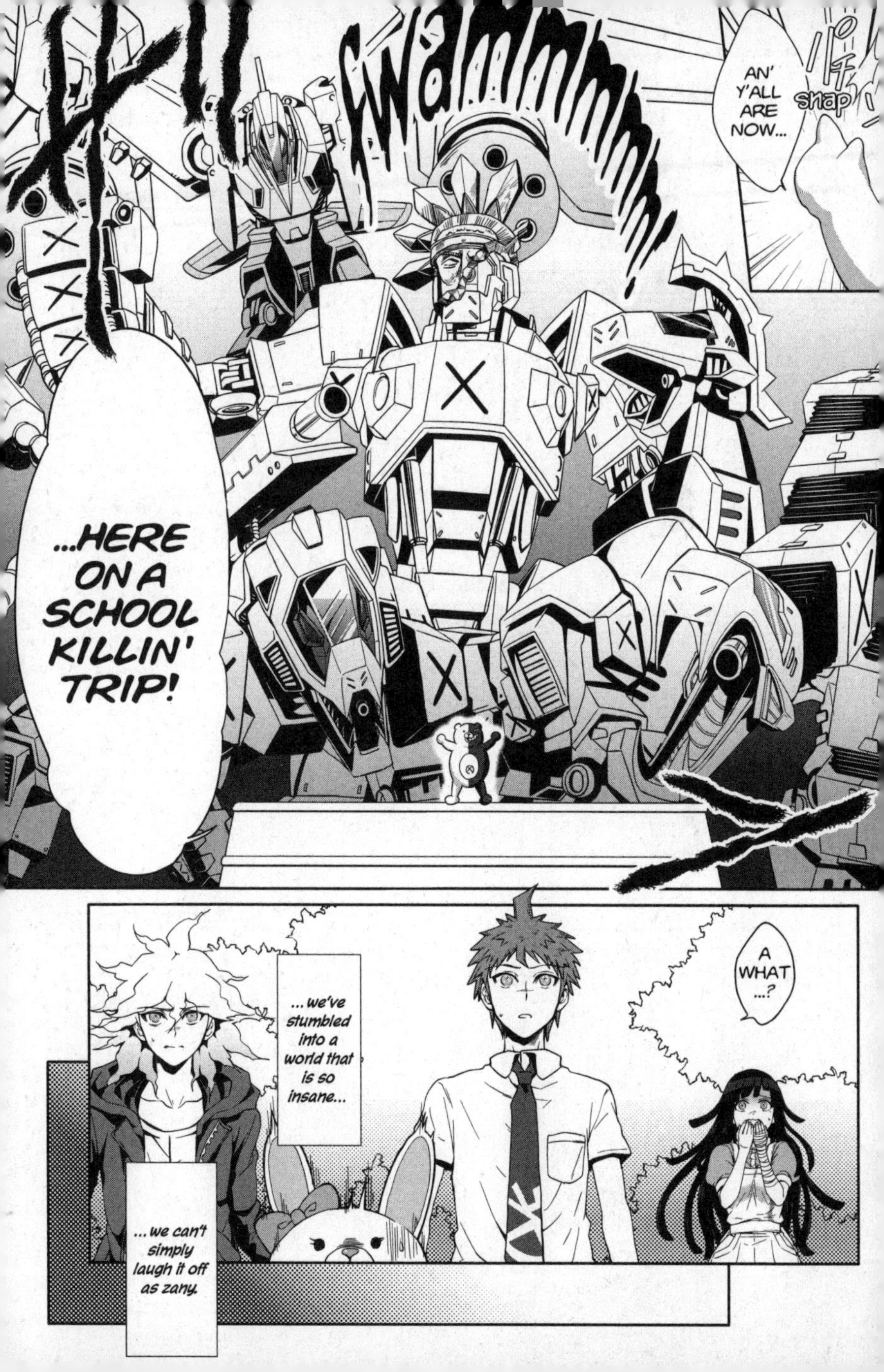
AN' Y'ALL ARE NOW...
snap
FWAMMMM
...HERE ON A SCHOOL KILLIN' TRIP!
A WHAT ...?
...we've stumbled into a world that is so insane...
...we can't simply laugh it off as zany.

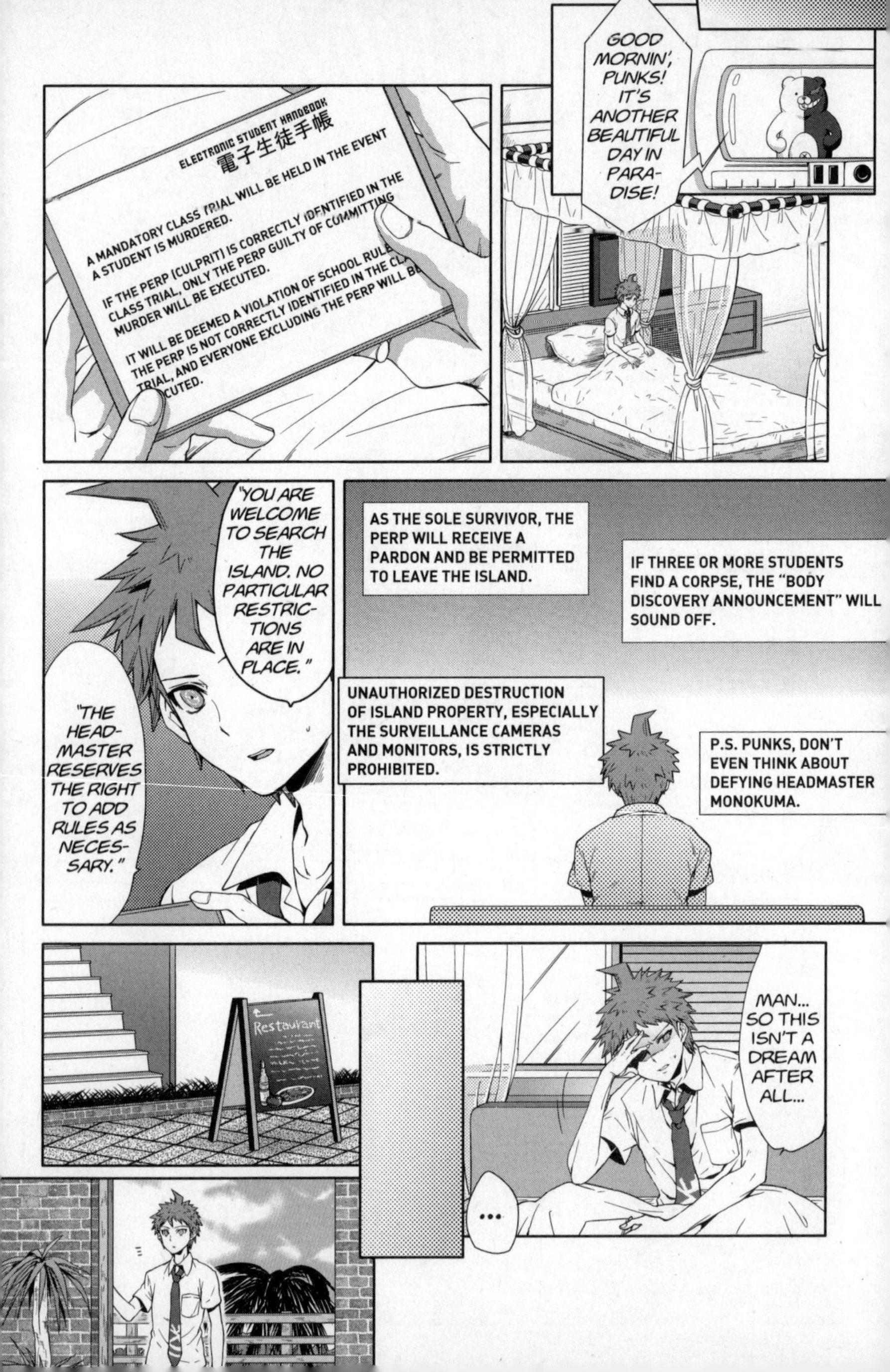
GOOD MORNIN', PUNKS! IT'S ANOTHER BEAUTIFUL DAY IN PARA-DISE!
ELECTRONIC STUDENT HANDBOOK
電子生徒手帳
A MANDATORY CLASS TRIAL WILL BE HELD IN THE EVENT A STUDENT IS MURDERED.
IF THE PERP (CULPRIT) IS CORRECTLY IDENTIFIED IN THE CLASS TRIAL, ONLY THE PERP GUILTY OF COMMITTING MURDER WILL BE EXECUTED.
IT WILL BE DEEMED A VIOLATION OF SCHOOL RUL
THE PERP IS NOT CORRECTLY IDENTIFIED IN THE CL
TRIAL, AND EVERYONE EXCLUDING THE PERP WILL B
CUTED.
AS THE SOLE SURVIVOR, THE PERP WILL RECEIVE A PARDON AND BE PERMITTED TO LEAVE THE ISLAND.
IF THREE OR MORE STUDENTS FIND A CORPSE, THE "BODY DISCOVERY ANNOUNCEMENT" WILL SOUND OFF.
UNAUTHORIZED DESTRUCTION OF ISLAND PROPERTY, ESPECIALLY THE SURVEILLANCE CAMERAS AND MONITORS, IS STRICTLY PROHIBITED.
P.S. PUNKS, DON'T EVEN THINK ABOUT DEFYING HEADMASTER MONOKUMA.
"YOU ARE WELCOME TO SEARCH THE ISLAND. NO PARTICULAR RESTRIC-TIONS ARE IN PLACE."
"THE HEAD-MASTER RESERVES THE RIGHT TO ADD RULES AS NECES-SARY."
MAN... SO THIS ISN'T A DREAM AFTER ALL...
...
Restaurant

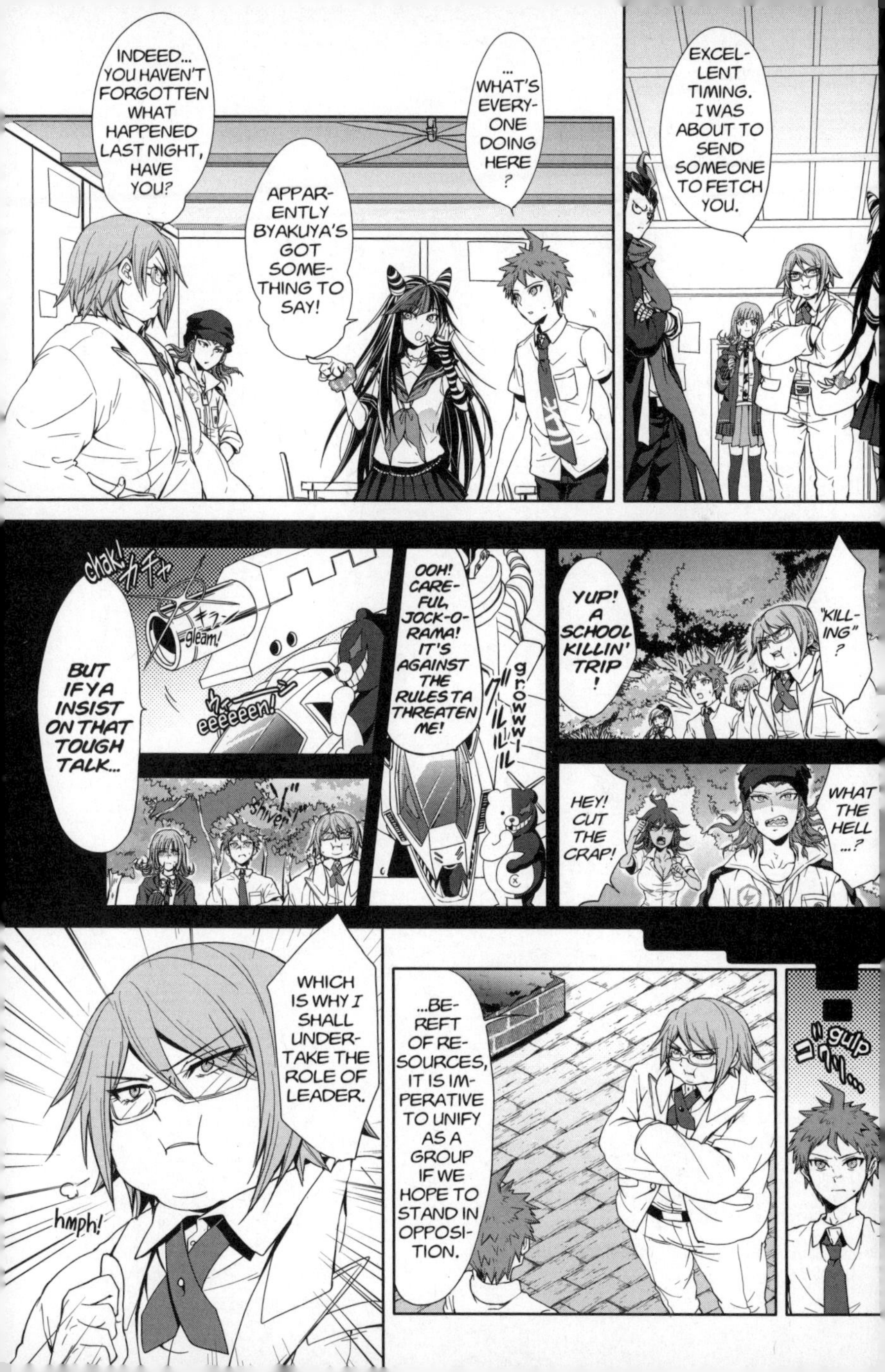
EXCELLENT TIMING. I WAS ABOUT TO SEND SOMEONE TO FETCH YOU.
...WHAT'S EVERYONE DOING HERE?
APPARENTLY BYAKUYA'S GOT SOMETHING TO SAY!
INDEED... YOU HAVEN'T FORGOTTEN WHAT HAPPENED LAST NIGHT, HAVE YOU?
"KILLING"?
YUP! A SCHOOL KILLIN' TRIP!
WHAT THE HELL...?
HEY! CUT THE CRAP!
growwl
OOH! CAREFUL, JOCK-O-RAMA! IT'S AGAINST THE RULES TA THREATEN ME!
chak!
gleam!
eeeeeen!
BUT IF YA INSIST ON THAT TOUGH TALK...
shiver
gulp
...BEREFT OF RESOURCES, IT IS IMPERATIVE TO UNIFY AS A GROUP IF WE HOPE TO STAND IN OPPOSITION.
WHICH IS WHY I SHALL UNDERTAKE THE ROLE OF LEADER.
hmph!

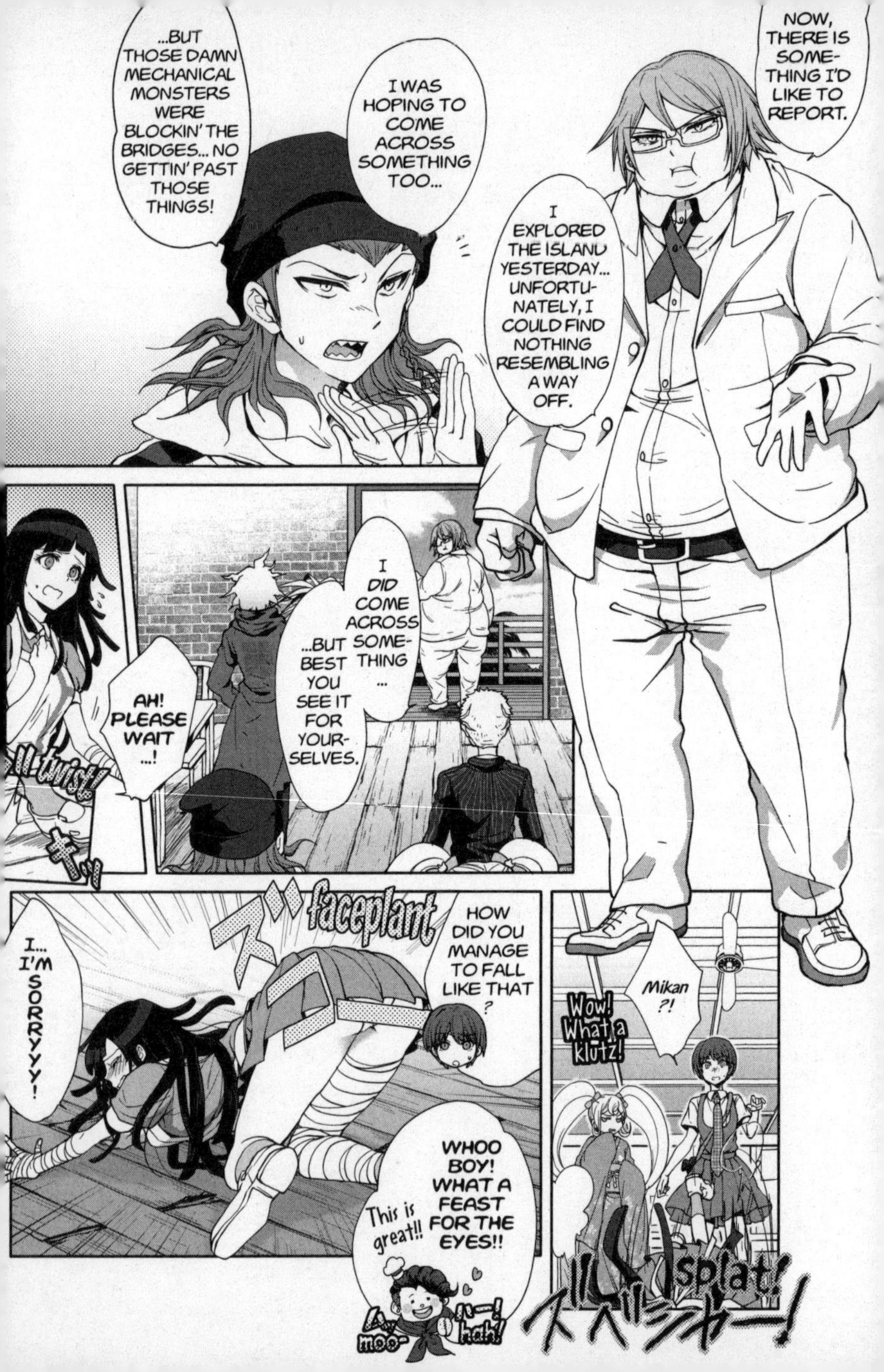
NOW, THERE IS SOME-THING I'D LIKE TO REPORT.
I EXPLORED THE ISLAND YESTERDAY... UNFORTU-NATELY, I COULD FIND NOTHING RESEMBLING A WAY OFF.
I WAS HOPING TO COME ACROSS SOMETHING TOO...
...BUT THOSE DAMN MECHANICAL MONSTERS WERE BLOCKIN' THE BRIDGES... NO GETTIN' PAST THOSE THINGS!
I DID COME ACROSS SOME-THING ...
...BUT BEST YOU SEE IT FOR YOUR-SELVES.
AH! PLEASE WAIT ...!
twist!
Mikan ?!
Wow! What a klutz!
splat!
faceplant
HOW DID YOU MANAGE TO FALL LIKE THAT ?
I... I'M SORRYYY!
WHOO BOY! WHAT A FEAST FOR THE EYES!!
This is great!!
moo-
hah!

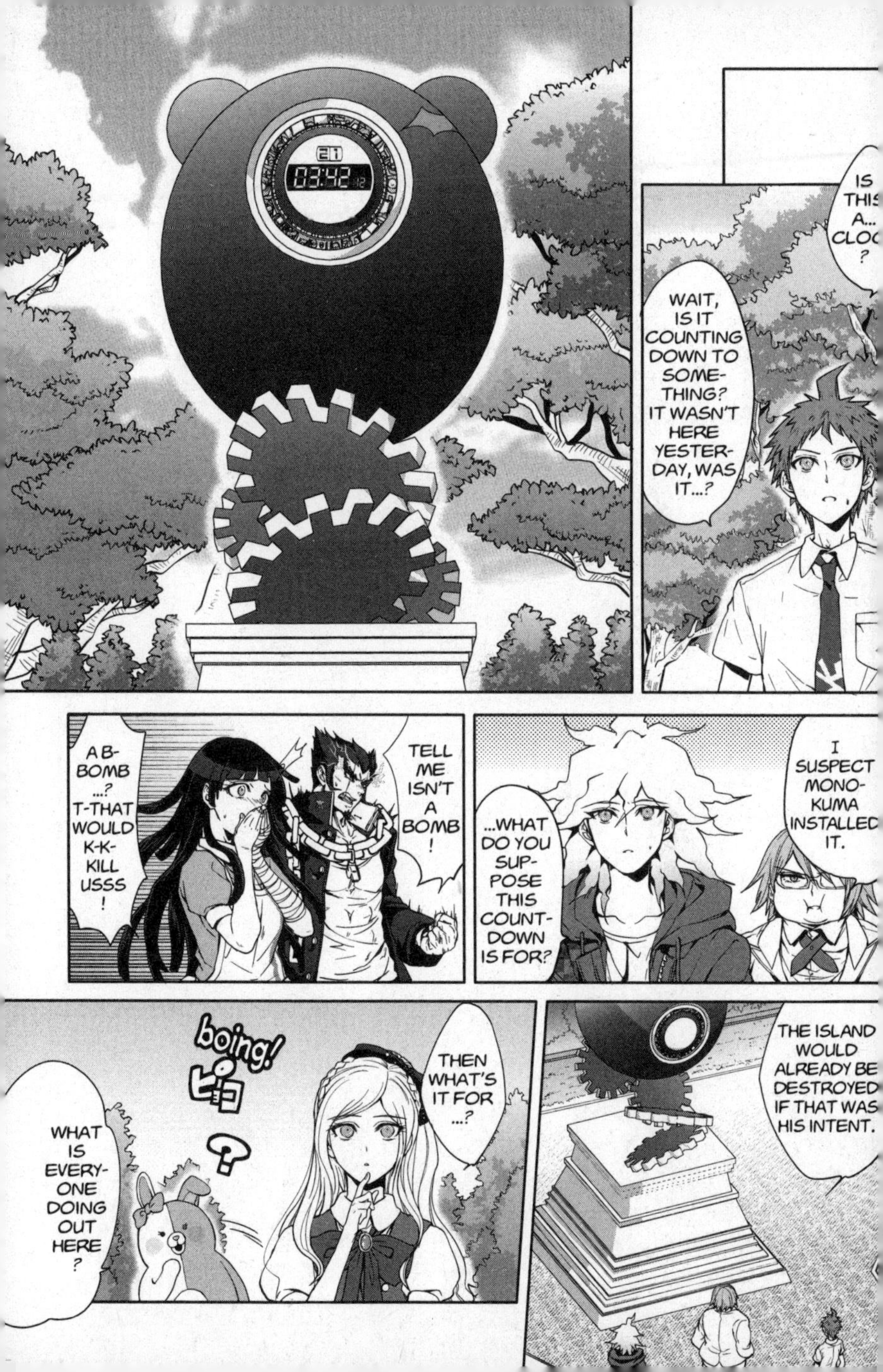
IS THIS A... CLOC?
WAIT, IS IT COUNTING DOWN TO SOME-THING? IT WASN'T HERE YESTER-DAY, WAS IT...?
21
03:42 12
I SUSPECT MONO-KUMA INSTALLED IT.
...WHAT DO YOU SUP-POSE THIS COUNT-DOWN IS FOR?
TELL ME ISN'T A BOMB!
A B-BOMB...? T-THAT WOULD K-K-KILL USSS!
THE ISLAND WOULD ALREADY BE DESTROYED IF THAT WAS HIS INTENT.
THEN WHAT'S IT FOR...?
boing! ピョコ
?
WHAT IS EVERY-ONE DOING OUT HERE?

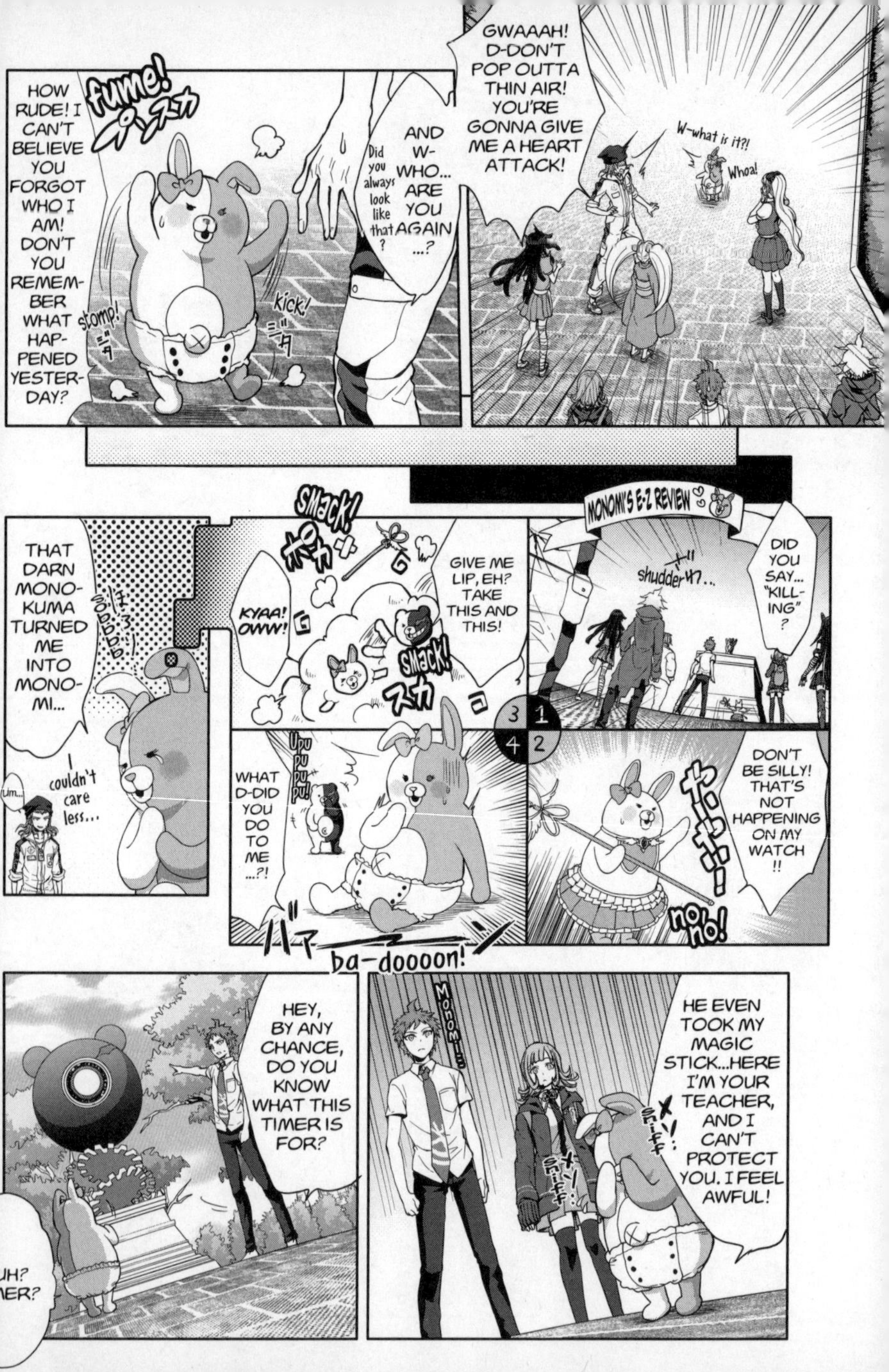
GWAAAH! D-DON'T POP OUTTA THIN AIR! YOU'RE GONNA GIVE ME A HEART ATTACK!
W-what is it?!
Whoa!
AND W-WHO... ARE YOU AGAIN ...?
Did you always look like that?
HOW RUDE! I CAN'T BELIEVE YOU FORGOT WHO I AM! DON'T YOU REMEMBER WHAT HAPPENED YESTERDAY?
fume!
stomp!
kick!
MONOMI'S E-Z REVIEW
DID YOU SAY... "KILLING"?
shudder
DON'T BE SILLY! THAT'S NOT HAPPENING ON MY WATCH!!
no no!
GIVE ME LIP, EH? TAKE THIS AND THIS!
KYAA! OWW!
SMACK!
SMACK!
WHAT D-DID YOU DO TO ME ...?!
Upupupupu!
ba-doooon!
THAT DARN MONOKUMA TURNED ME INTO MONOMI...
I couldn't care less...
um...
Monomi!
HE EVEN TOOK MY MAGIC STICK...HERE I'M YOUR TEACHER, AND I CAN'T PROTECT YOU. I FEEL AWFUL!
sniff
sniff
HEY, BY ANY CHANCE, DO YOU KNOW WHAT THIS TIMER IS FOR?
UH?
MER?

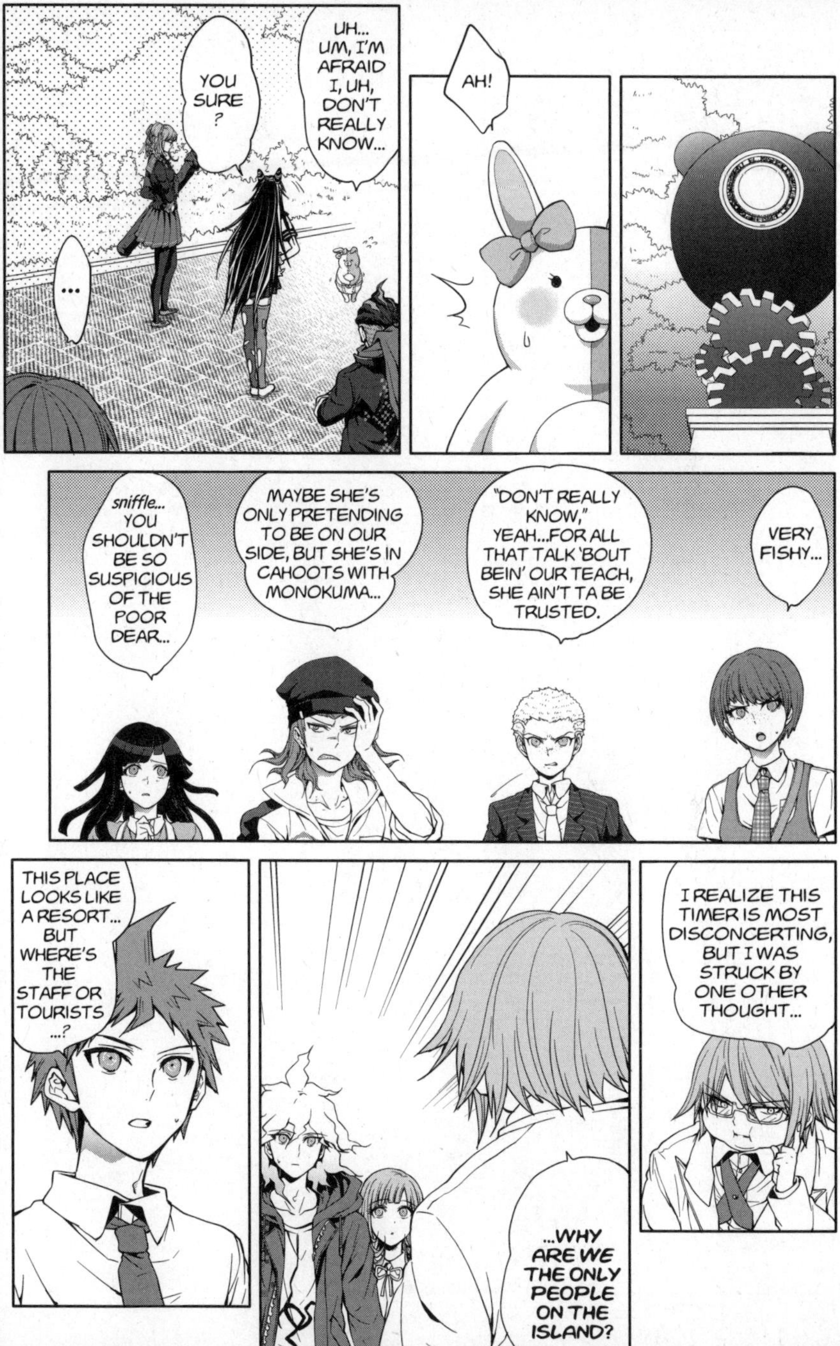
AH!
UH... UM, I'M AFRAID I, UH, DON'T REALLY KNOW...
YOU SURE ?
...
VERY FISHY...
"DON'T REALLY KNOW," YEAH...FOR ALL THAT TALK 'BOUT BEIN' OUR TEACH, SHE AIN'T TA BE TRUSTED.
MAYBE SHE'S ONLY PRETENDING TO BE ON OUR SIDE, BUT SHE'S IN CAHOOTS WITH MONOKUMA...
sniffle... YOU SHOULDN'T BE SO SUSPICIOUS OF THE POOR DEAR...
I REALIZE THIS TIMER IS MOST DISCONCERTING, BUT I WAS STRUCK BY ONE OTHER THOUGHT...
...WHY ARE WE THE ONLY PEOPLE ON THE ISLAND?
THIS PLACE LOOKS LIKE A RESORT... BUT WHERE'S THE STAFF OR TOURISTS ...?

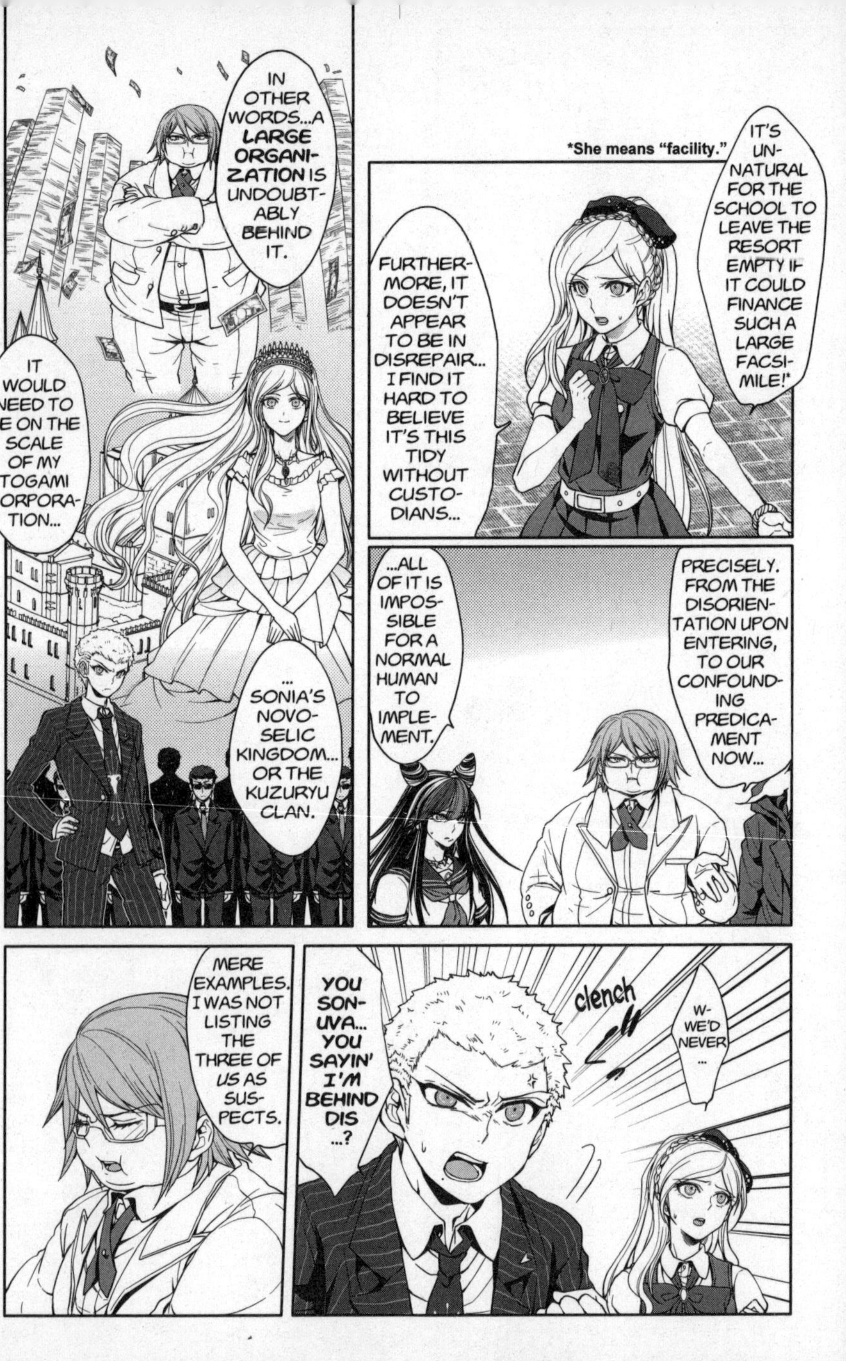
IT'S UNNATURAL FOR THE SCHOOL TO LEAVE THE RESORT EMPTY IF IT COULD FINANCE SUCH A LARGE FACSIMILE!*
*She means "facility."
FURTHERMORE, IT DOESN'T APPEAR TO BE IN DISREPAIR... I FIND IT HARD TO BELIEVE IT'S THIS TIDY WITHOUT CUSTODIANS...
PRECISELY. FROM THE DISORIENTATION UPON ENTERING, TO OUR CONFOUNDING PREDICAMENT NOW...
...ALL OF IT IS IMPOSSIBLE FOR A NORMAL HUMAN TO IMPLEMENT.
IN OTHER WORDS...A **LARGE ORGANIZATION** IS UNDOUBTABLY BEHIND IT.
IT WOULD NEED TO BE ON THE SCALE OF MY TOGAMI CORPORATION...
... SONIA'S NOVOSELIC KINGDOM... OR THE KUZURYU CLAN.
W-WE'D NEVER ...
clench
YOU SONUVA... YOU SAYIN' I'M BEHIND DIS ...?
MERE EXAMPLES. I WAS NOT LISTING THE THREE OF *US* AS SUSPECTS.

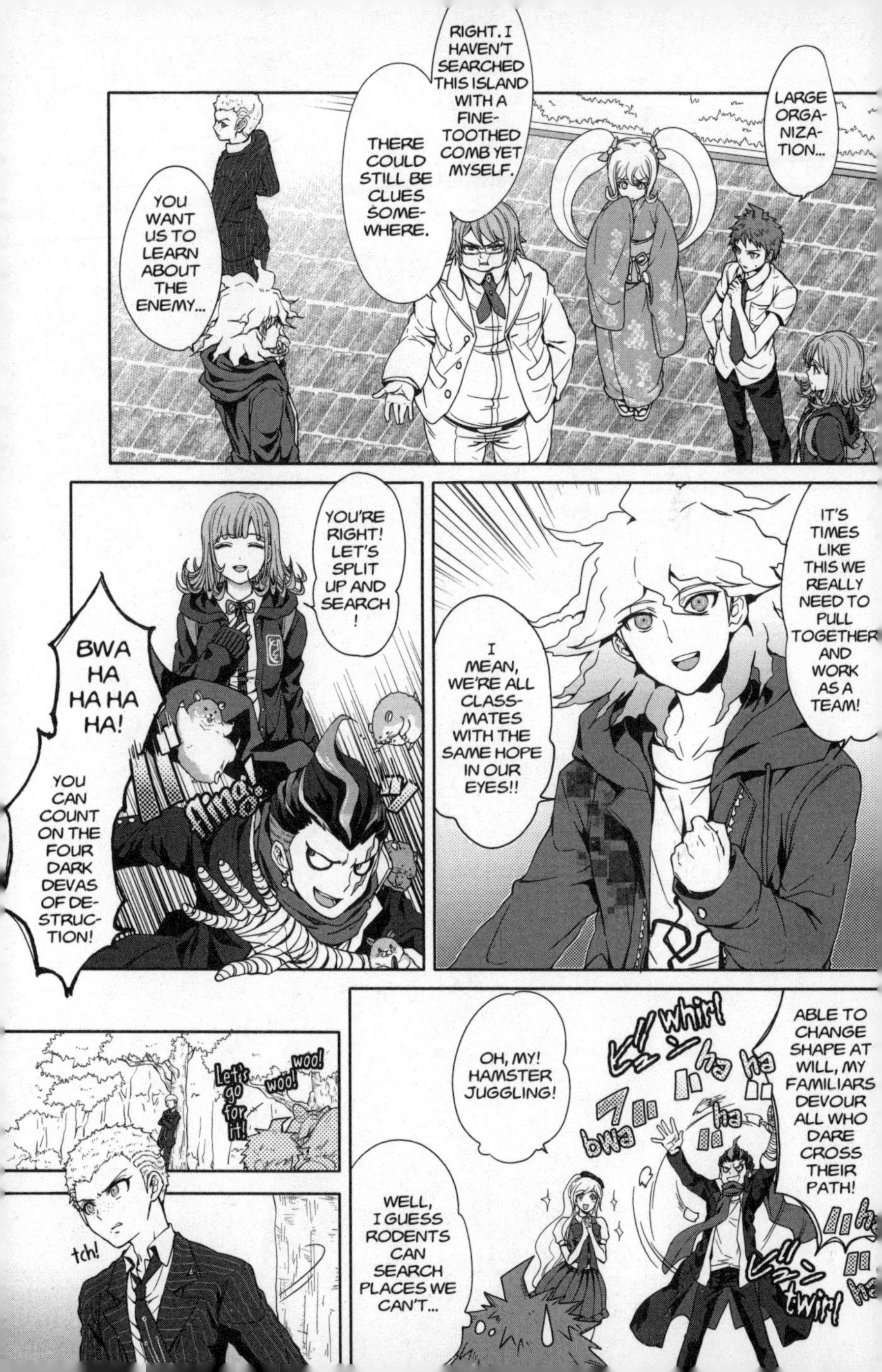
LARGE ORGANIZATION...
RIGHT. I HAVEN'T SEARCHED THIS ISLAND WITH A FINE-TOOTHED COMB YET MYSELF.
THERE COULD STILL BE CLUES SOMEWHERE.
YOU WANT US TO LEARN ABOUT THE ENEMY...
IT'S TIMES LIKE THIS WE REALLY NEED TO PULL TOGETHER AND WORK AS A TEAM!
I MEAN, WE'RE ALL CLASSMATES WITH THE SAME HOPE IN OUR EYES!!
YOU'RE RIGHT! LET'S SPLIT UP AND SEARCH!
BWA HA HA HA HA!
fling!
YOU CAN COUNT ON THE FOUR DARK DEVAS OF DESTRUCTION!
ABLE TO CHANGE SHAPE AT WILL, MY FAMILIARS DEVOUR ALL WHO DARE CROSS THEIR PATH!
whirl
ha ha
bwa ha
OH, MY! HAMSTER JUGGLING!
WELL, I GUESS RODENTS CAN SEARCH PLACES WE CAN'T...
twirl
ha ha
woo! woo!
Let's go for it!
tch!

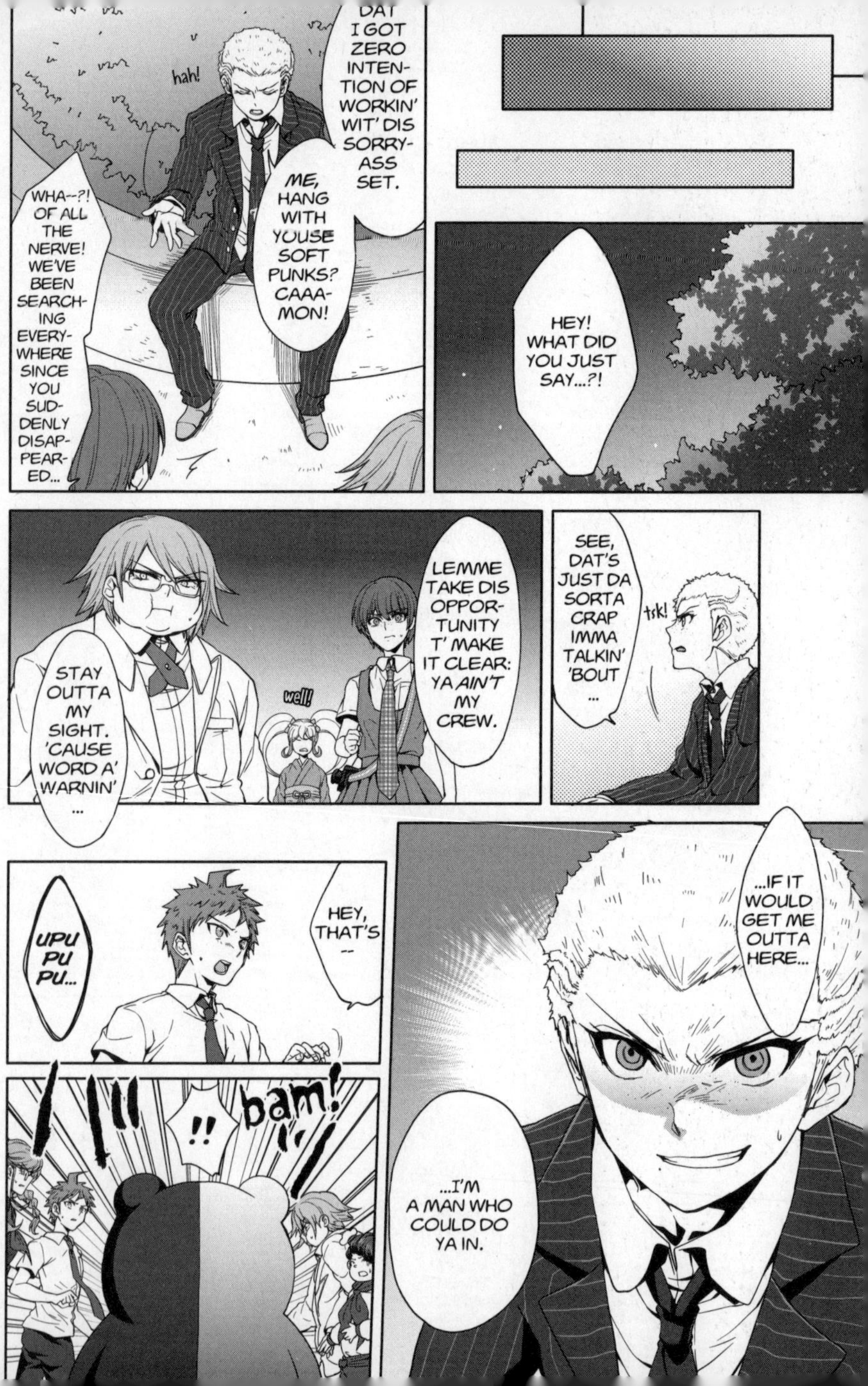
HEY! WHAT DID YOU JUST SAY...?!
DAT I GOT ZERO INTENTION OF WORKIN' WIT' DIS SORRY-ASS SET.
ME, HANG WITH YOUSE SOFT PUNKS? CAAA-MON!
hah!
WHA--?! OF ALL THE NERVE! WE'VE BEEN SEARCHING EVERYWHERE SINCE YOU SUDDENLY DISAPPEARED...
SEE, DAT'S JUST DA SORTA CRAP IMMA TALKIN' 'BOUT...
tsk!
LEMME TAKE DIS OPPORTUNITY T' MAKE IT CLEAR: YA AIN'T MY CREW.
well!
STAY OUTTA MY SIGHT. 'CAUSE WORD A' WARNIN'...
...IF IT WOULD GET ME OUTTA HERE...
...I'M A MAN WHO COULD DO YA IN.
HEY, THAT'S --
UPU PU PU...
bam!
!!

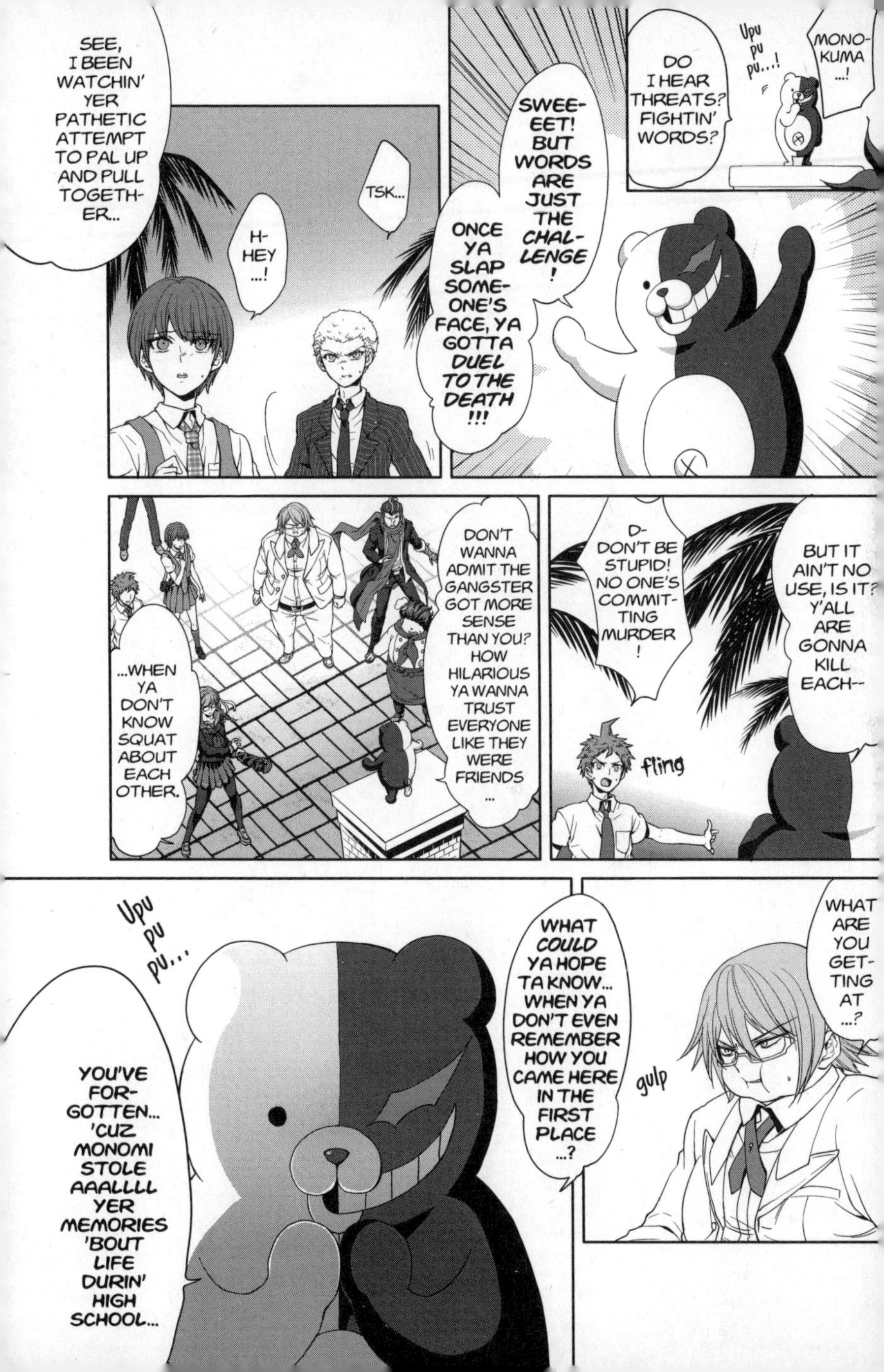
MONO-KUMA ...!
Upu pu pu...!
DO I HEAR THREATS? FIGHTIN' WORDS?
SWEEE-EET! BUT WORDS ARE JUST THE CHAL-LENGE!
ONCE YA SLAP SOME-ONE'S FACE, YA GOTTA DUEL TO THE DEATH!!!
TSK...
H-HEY ...!
SEE, I BEEN WATCHIN' YER PATHETIC ATTEMPT TO PAL UP AND PULL TOGETH-ER...
BUT IT AIN'T NO USE, IS IT? Y'ALL ARE GONNA KILL EACH--
D-DON'T BE STUPID! NO ONE'S COMMIT-TING MURDER!
fling
DON'T WANNA ADMIT THE GANGSTER GOT MORE SENSE THAN YOU? HOW HILARIOUS YA WANNA TRUST EVERYONE LIKE THEY WERE FRIENDS ...
...WHEN YA DON'T KNOW SQUAT ABOUT EACH OTHER.
WHAT ARE YOU GET-TING AT ...?
gulp
WHAT COULD YA HOPE TA KNOW... WHEN YA DON'T EVEN REMEMBER HOW YOU CAME HERE IN THE FIRST PLACE ...?
Upu pu pu...
YOU'VE FOR-GOTTEN... 'CUZ MONOMI STOLE AAALLLL YER MEMORIES 'BOUT LIFE DURIN' HIGH SCHOOL...

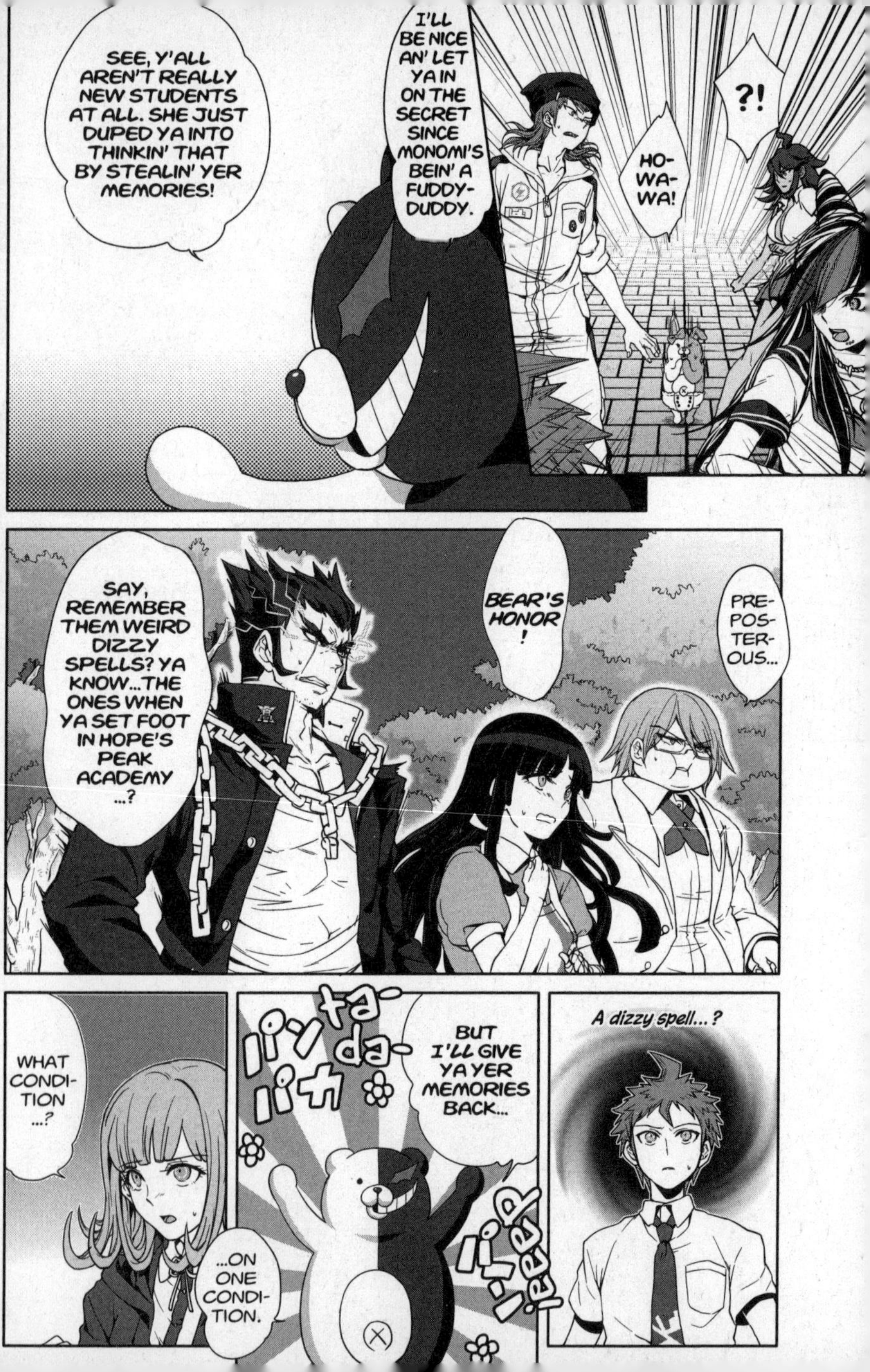
?!
HO-WA-WA!
I'LL BE NICE AN' LET YA IN ON THE SECRET SINCE MONOMI'S BEIN' A FUDDY-DUDDY.
SEE, Y'ALL AREN'T REALLY NEW STUDENTS AT ALL. SHE JUST DUPED YA INTO THINKIN' THAT BY STEALIN' YER MEMORIES!
PRE-POS-TER-OUS...
BEAR'S HONOR!
SAY, REMEMBER THEM WEIRD DIZZY SPELLS? YA KNOW...THE ONES WHEN YA SET FOOT IN HOPE'S PEAK ACADEMY ...?
A dizzy spell...?
BUT I'LL GIVE YA YER MEMORIES BACK...
ta-da-
...ON ONE CONDITION.
WHAT CONDITION ...?

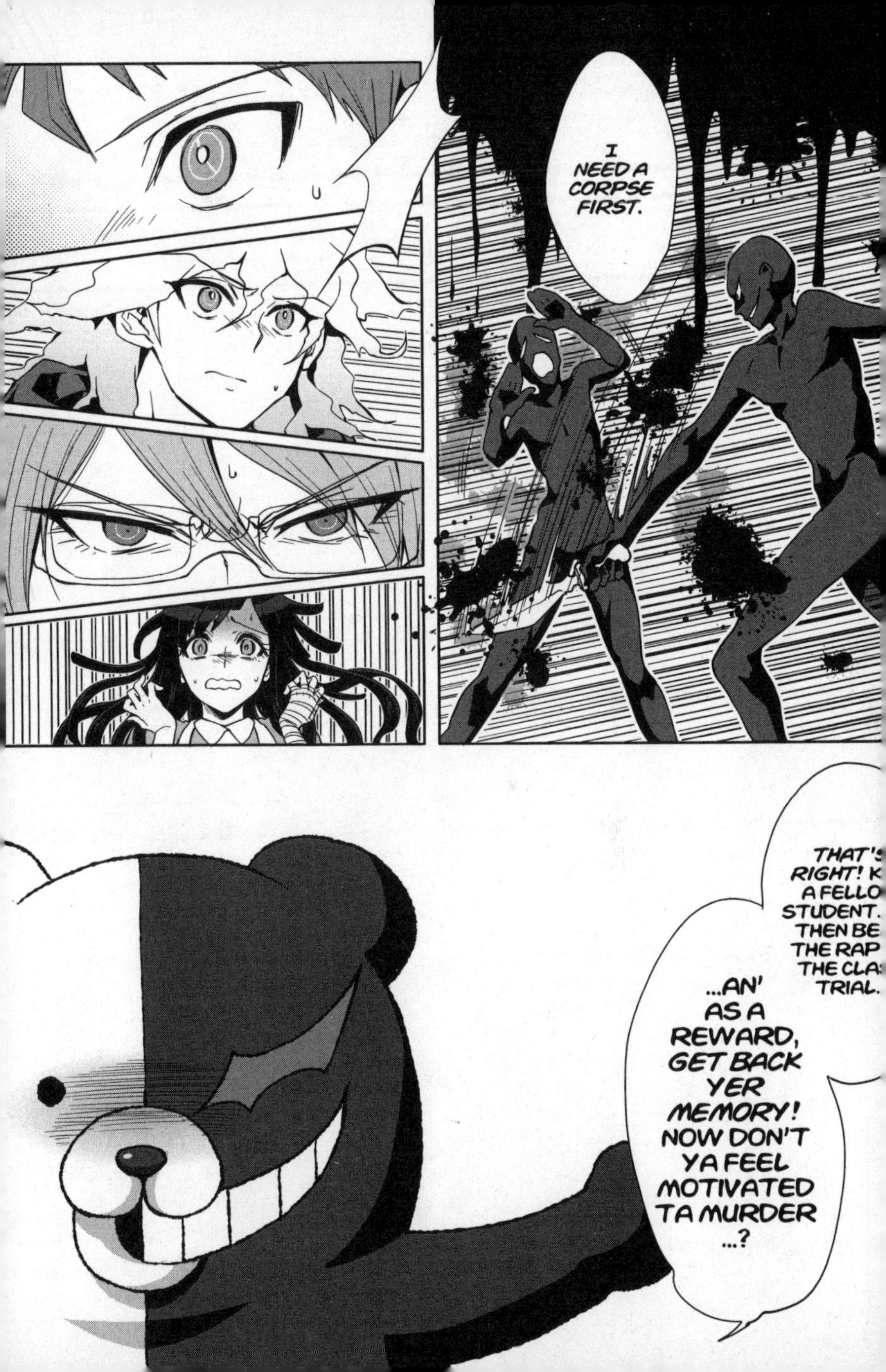
I NEED A CORPSE FIRST.
THAT'S RIGHT! K A FELLO STUDENT. THEN BE THE RAP THE CLA TRIAL.
...AN' AS A REWARD, GET BACK YER MEMORY! NOW DON'T YA FEEL MOTIVATED TA MURDER ...?

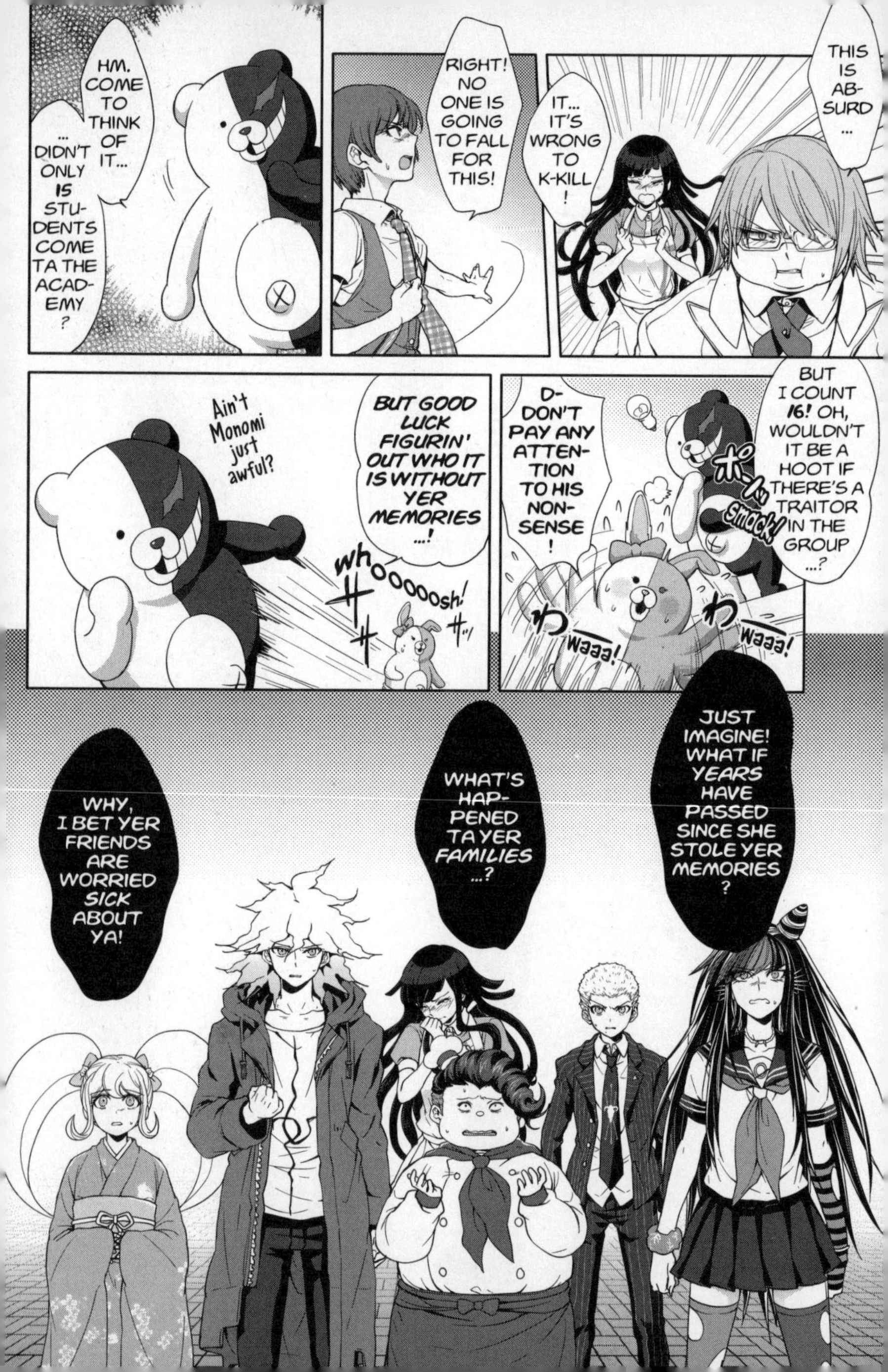
THIS IS ABSURD...
IT... IT'S WRONG TO K-KILL!
RIGHT! NO ONE IS GOING TO FALL FOR THIS!
HM. COME TO THINK OF IT...
...DIDN'T ONLY 15 STUDENTS COME TA THE ACADEMY?
BUT I COUNT 16! OH, WOULDN'T IT BE A HOOT IF THERE'S A TRAITOR IN THE GROUP...?
smack!
D-DON'T PAY ANY ATTENTION TO HIS NONSENSE!
waaa!
waaa!
BUT GOOD LUCK FIGURIN' OUT WHO IT IS WITHOUT YER MEMORIES...!
whoooooosh!
Ain't Monomi just awful?
JUST IMAGINE! WHAT IF YEARS HAVE PASSED SINCE SHE STOLE YER MEMORIES?
WHAT'S HAPPENED TA YER FAMILIES...?
WHY, I BET YER FRIENDS ARE WORRIED SICK ABOUT YA!

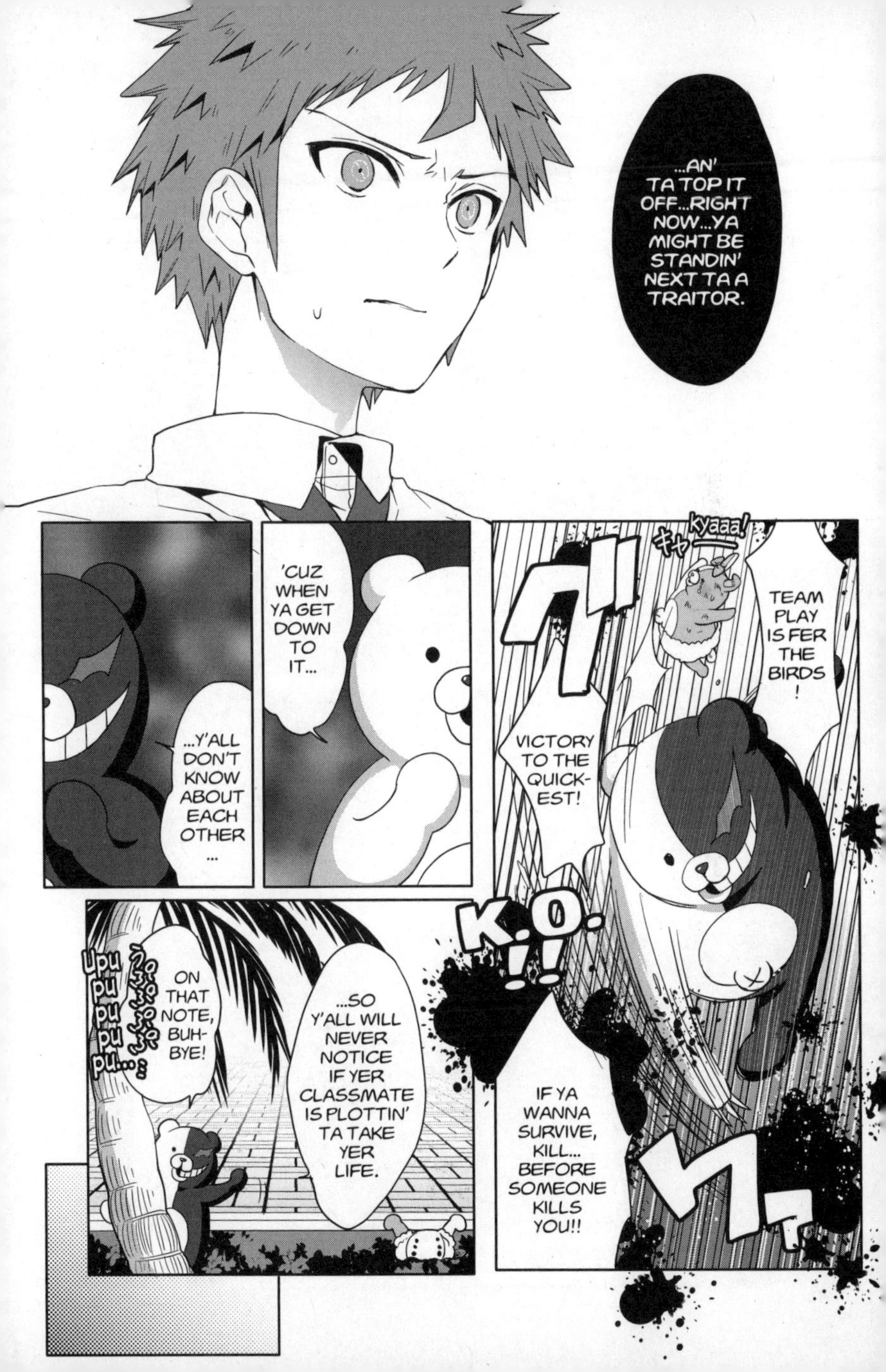

...AN' TA TOP IT OFF...RIGHT NOW...YA MIGHT BE STANDIN' NEXT TA A TRAITOR.
kyaaa!
TEAM PLAY IS FER THE BIRDS!
VICTORY TO THE QUICKEST!
K.O.!!
IF YA WANNA SURVIVE, KILL... BEFORE SOMEONE KILLS YOU!!
'CUZ WHEN YA GET DOWN TO IT...
...Y'ALL DON'T KNOW ABOUT EACH OTHER...
...SO Y'ALL WILL NEVER NOTICE IF YER CLASSMATE IS PLOTTIN' TA TAKE YER LIFE.
ON THAT NOTE, BUH-BYE!
Upu pu pu pu pu...

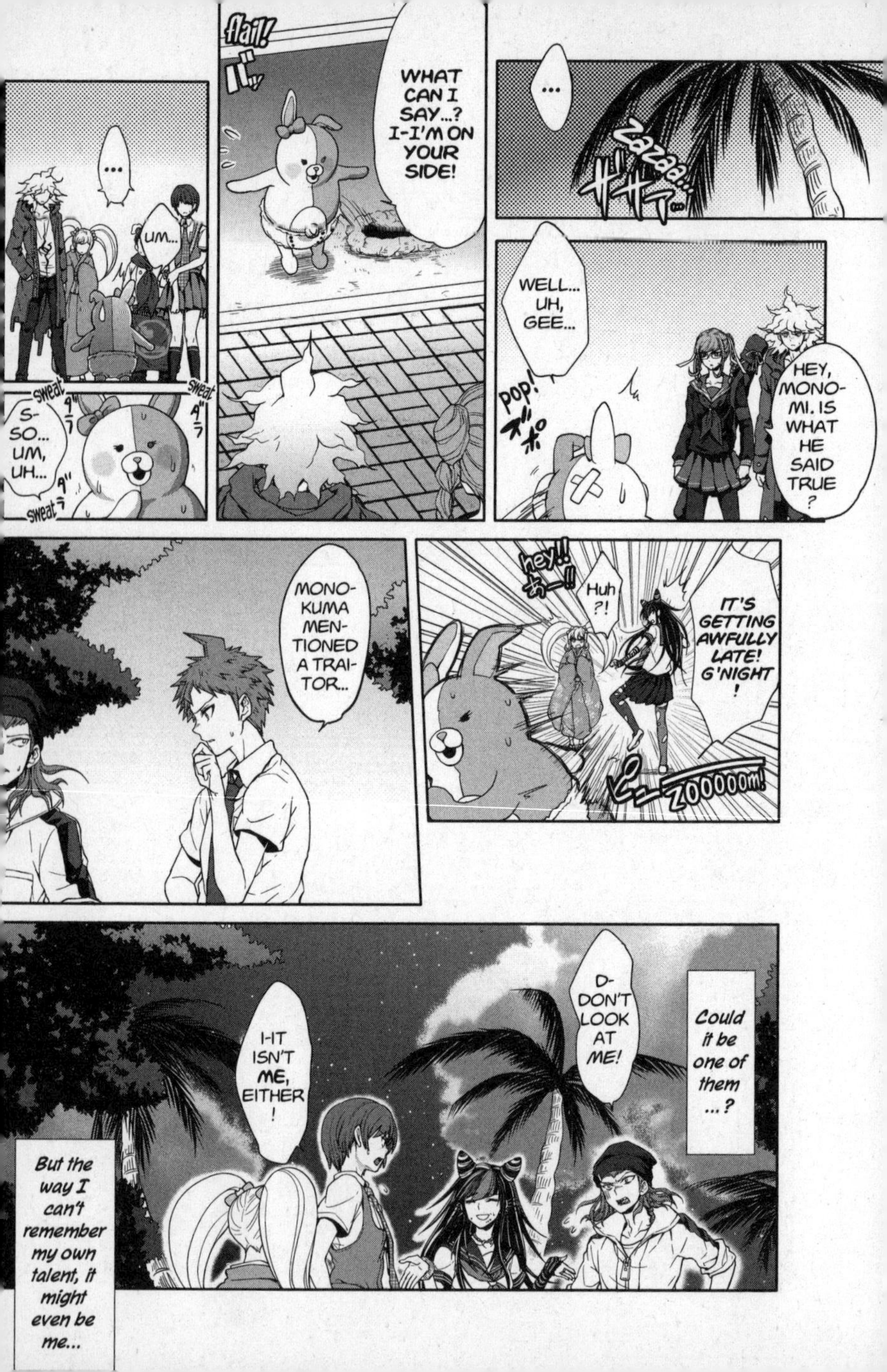
...
zazaa...
ザザァ...
HEY, MONOMI. IS WHAT HE SAID TRUE?
WELL... UH, GEE...
pop!
flail!
WHAT CAN I SAY...? I-I'M ON YOUR SIDE!
...
UM...
sweat
S-SO... UM, UH...
sweat
sweat
IT'S GETTING AWFULLY LATE! G'NIGHT!
Huh?!
hey!!
あー!!
zoooom!
MONOKUMA MENTIONED A TRAITOR...
Could it be one of them...?
D-DON'T LOOK AT ME!
I-IT ISN'T ME, EITHER!
But the way I can't remember my own talent, it might even be me...

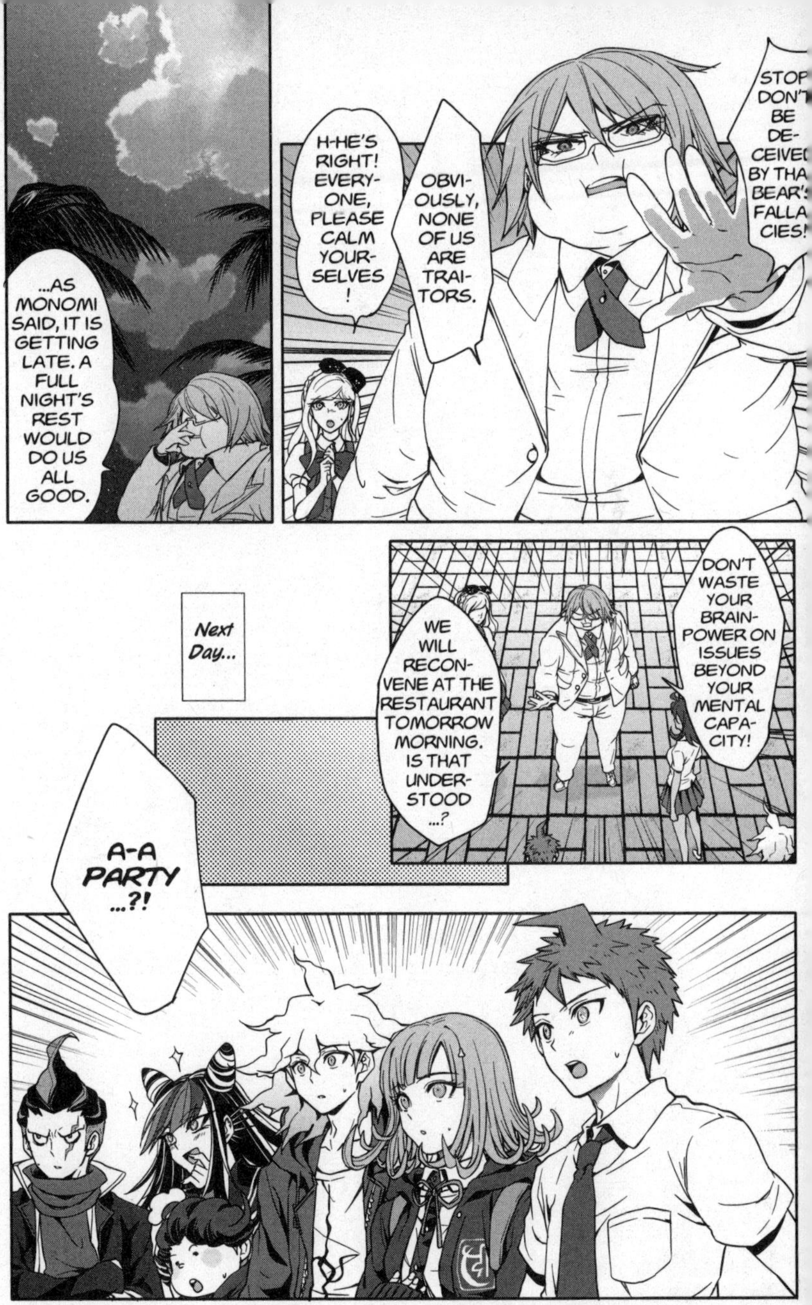
STOP DON'T BE DECEIVE BY THA BEAR'S FALLACIES!
OBVIOUSLY, NONE OF US ARE TRAITORS.
H-HE'S RIGHT! EVERYONE, PLEASE CALM YOURSELVES!
...AS MONOMI SAID, IT IS GETTING LATE. A FULL NIGHT'S REST WOULD DO US ALL GOOD.
DON'T WASTE YOUR BRAINPOWER ON ISSUES BEYOND YOUR MENTAL CAPACITY!
WE WILL RECONVENE AT THE RESTAURANT TOMORROW MORNING. IS THAT UNDERSTOOD...?
Next Day...
A-A PARTY...?!

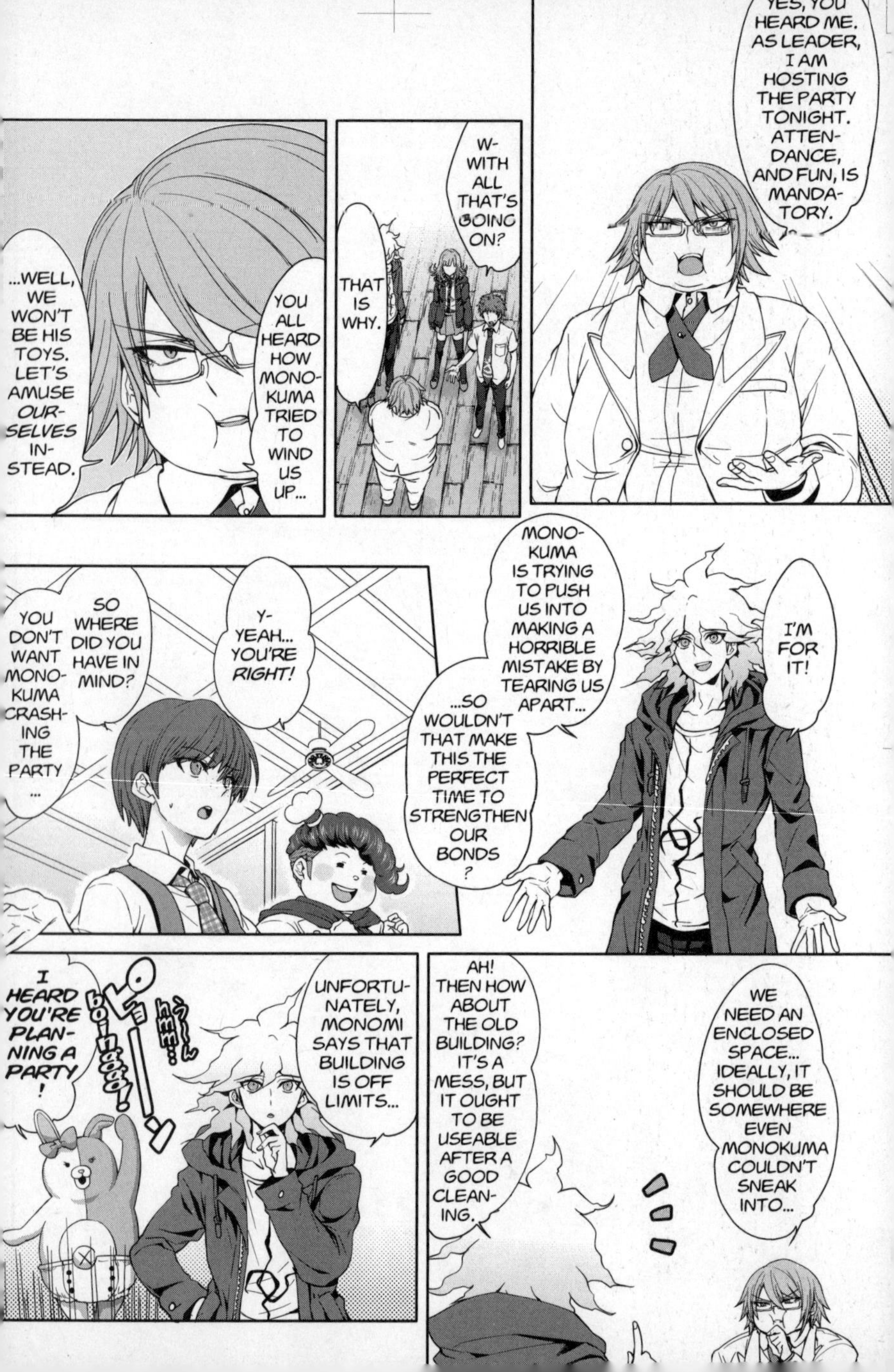
YES, YOU HEARD ME. AS LEADER, I AM HOSTING THE PARTY TONIGHT. ATTENDANCE, AND FUN, IS MANDATORY.
W-WITH ALL THAT'S GOING ON?
THAT IS WHY.
YOU ALL HEARD HOW MONOKUMA TRIED TO WIND US UP...
...WELL, WE WON'T BE HIS TOYS. LET'S AMUSE *OURSELVES* INSTEAD.
I'M FOR IT!
MONOKUMA IS TRYING TO PUSH US INTO MAKING A HORRIBLE MISTAKE BY TEARING US APART...
...SO WOULDN'T THAT MAKE THIS THE PERFECT TIME TO STRENGTHEN OUR BONDS?
Y-YEAH... YOU'RE *RIGHT!*
SO WHERE DID YOU HAVE IN MIND?
YOU DON'T WANT MONOKUMA CRASHING THE PARTY...
WE NEED AN ENCLOSED SPACE... IDEALLY, IT SHOULD BE SOMEWHERE EVEN MONOKUMA COULDN'T SNEAK INTO...
AH! THEN HOW ABOUT THE OLD BUILDING? IT'S A MESS, BUT IT OUGHT TO BE USEABLE AFTER A GOOD CLEANING.
UNFORTUNATELY, MONOMI SAYS THAT BUILDING IS OFF LIMITS...
hmm...
boingggg!
I HEARD YOU'RE PLANNING A PARTY!

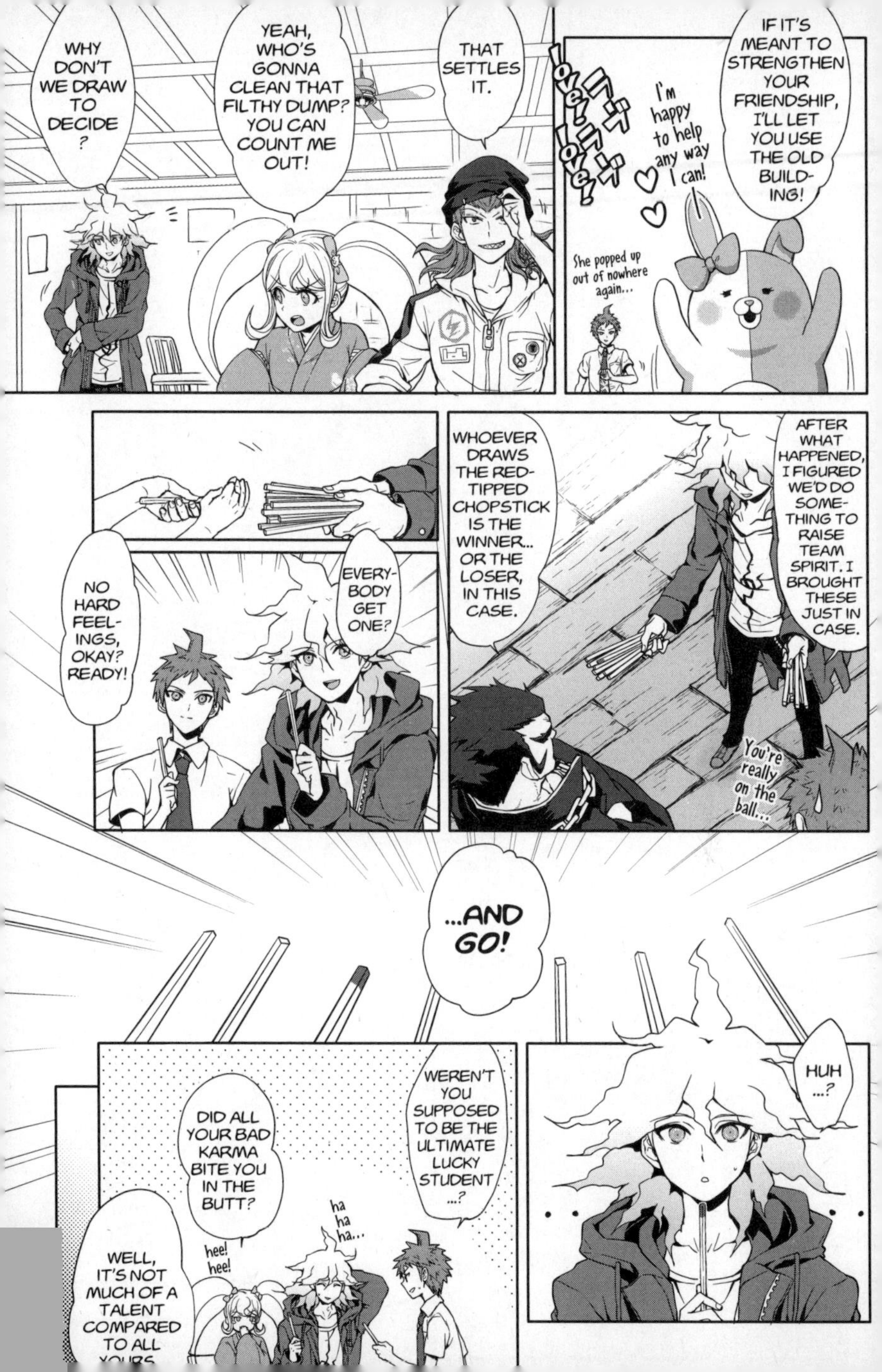
IF IT'S MEANT TO STRENGTHEN YOUR FRIENDSHIP, I'LL LET YOU USE THE OLD BUILDING!
I'm happy to help any way I can!
love! love!
She popped up out of nowhere again...
THAT SETTLES IT.
YEAH, WHO'S GONNA CLEAN THAT FILTHY DUMP? YOU CAN COUNT ME OUT!
WHY DON'T WE DRAW TO DECIDE?
AFTER WHAT HAPPENED, I FIGURED WE'D DO SOMETHING TO RAISE TEAM SPIRIT. I BROUGHT THESE JUST IN CASE.
You're really on the ball...
WHOEVER DRAWS THE RED-TIPPED CHOPSTICK IS THE WINNER... OR THE LOSER, IN THIS CASE.
EVERYBODY GET ONE?
NO HARD FEELINGS, OKAY? READY!
...AND GO!
HUH...?
WEREN'T YOU SUPPOSED TO BE THE ULTIMATE LUCKY STUDENT...?
DID ALL YOUR BAD KARMA BITE YOU IN THE BUTT?
ha ha ha...
hee! hee!
WELL, IT'S NOT MUCH OF A TALENT COMPARED TO ALL

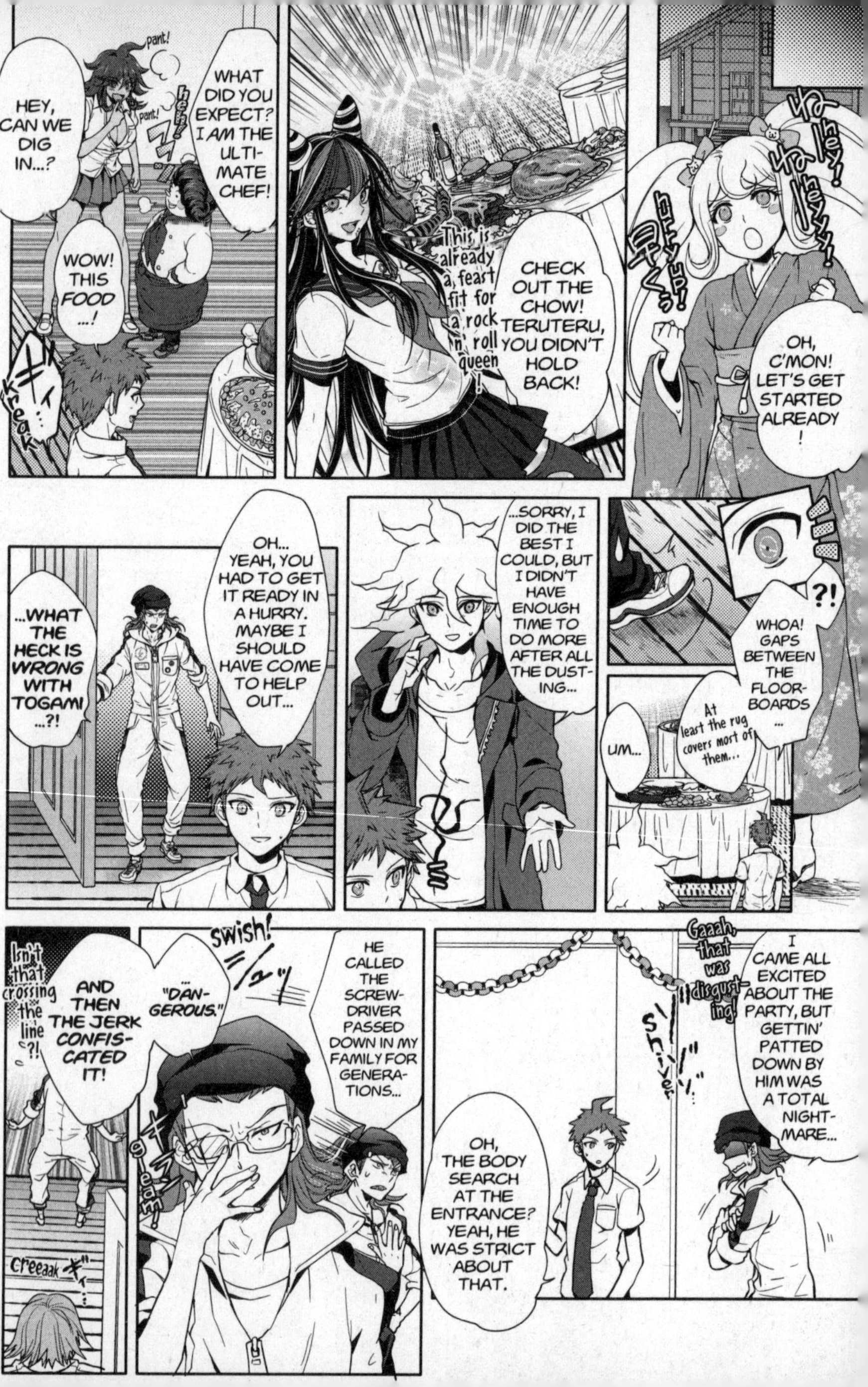
hey!
heyyy!
hurry up!
OH, C'MON! LET'S GET STARTED ALREADY!
CHECK OUT THE CHOW! TERUTERU, YOU DIDN'T HOLD BACK!
This is already a feast fit for a rock n' roll queen!
HEY, CAN WE DIG IN...?
pant!
pant!
heh!
WHAT DID YOU EXPECT? I AM THE ULTIMATE CHEF!
WOW! THIS FOOD...!
kreak
?!
WHOA! GAPS BETWEEN THE FLOORBOARDS...
At least the rug covers most of them...
UM...
...SORRY, I DID THE BEST I COULD, BUT I DIDN'T HAVE ENOUGH TIME TO DO MORE AFTER ALL THE DUSTING...
OH... YEAH, YOU HAD TO GET IT READY IN A HURRY. MAYBE I SHOULD HAVE COME TO HELP OUT...
...WHAT THE HECK IS WRONG WITH TOGAMI...?!
I CAME ALL EXCITED ABOUT THE PARTY, BUT GETTIN' PATTED DOWN BY HIM WAS A TOTAL NIGHTMARE...
Gaaah, that was disgusting!
shiver
OH, THE BODY SEARCH AT THE ENTRANCE? YEAH, HE WAS STRICT ABOUT THAT.
HE CALLED THE SCREWDRIVER PASSED DOWN IN MY FAMILY FOR GENERATIONS...
swish!
... "DANGEROUS."
gleam
AND THEN THE JERK CONFISCATED IT!
Isn't that crossing the line?!
creeaak

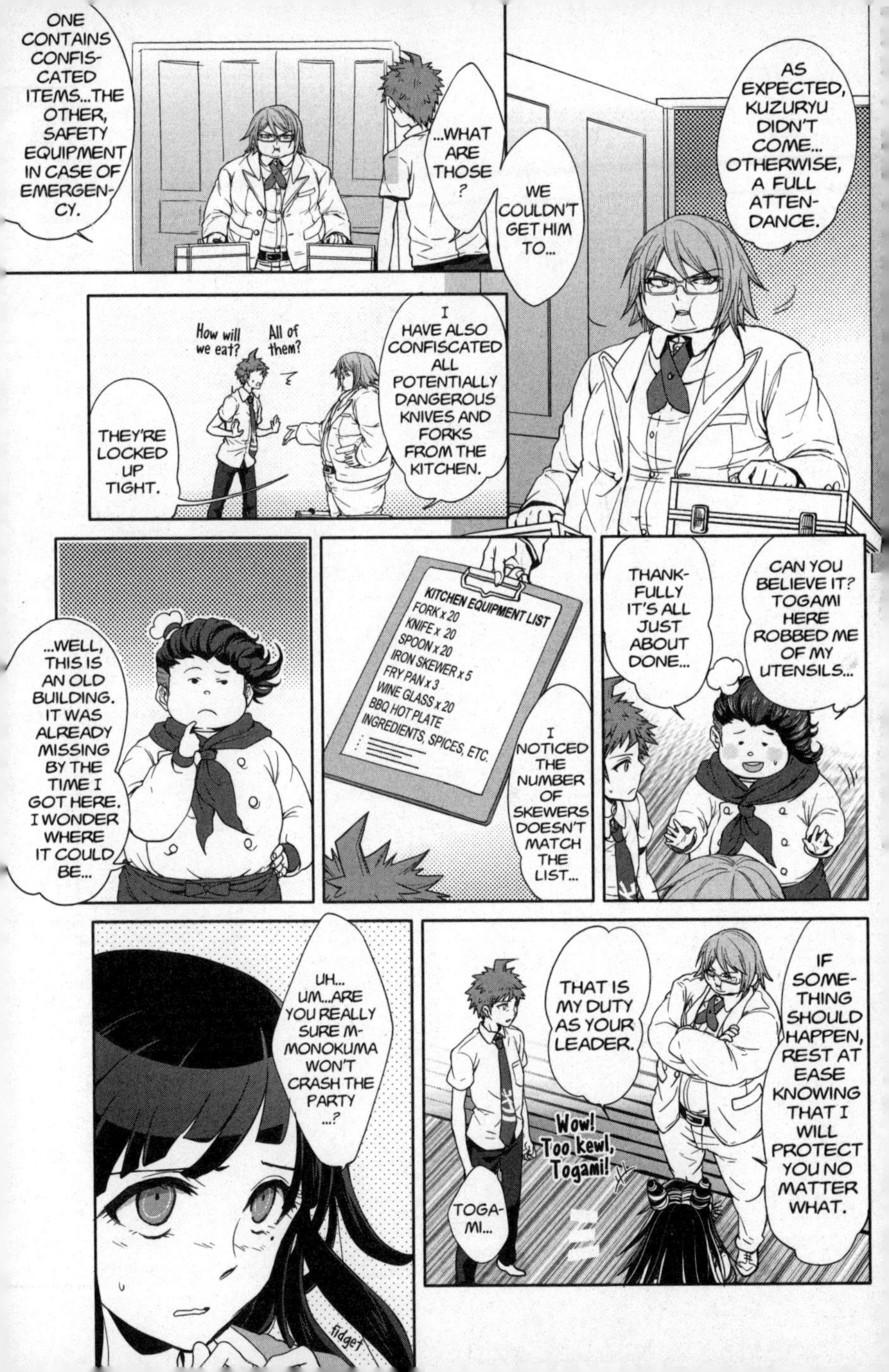

AS EXPECTED, KUZURYU DIDN'T COME... OTHERWISE, A FULL ATTEN-DANCE.
WE COULDN'T GET HIM TO...
...WHAT ARE THOSE?
ONE CONTAINS CONFIS-CATED ITEMS...THE OTHER, SAFETY EQUIPMENT IN CASE OF EMERGEN-CY.
I HAVE ALSO CONFISCATED ALL POTENTIALLY DANGEROUS KNIVES AND FORKS FROM THE KITCHEN.
All of them?
How will we eat?
THEY'RE LOCKED UP TIGHT.
CAN YOU BELIEVE IT? TOGAMI HERE ROBBED ME OF MY UTENSILS...
THANK-FULLY IT'S ALL JUST ABOUT DONE...
KITCHEN EQUIPMENT LIST
FORK x 20
KNIFE x 20
SPOON x 20
IRON SKEWER x 5
FRY PAN x 3
WINE GLASS x 20
BBQ HOT PLATE
INGREDIENTS, SPICES, ETC.
I NOTICED THE NUMBER OF SKEWERS DOESN'T MATCH THE LIST...
...WELL, THIS IS AN OLD BUILDING. IT WAS ALREADY MISSING BY THE TIME I GOT HERE. I WONDER WHERE IT COULD BE...
IF SOME-THING SHOULD HAPPEN, REST AT EASE KNOWING THAT I WILL PROTECT YOU NO MATTER WHAT.
THAT IS MY DUTY AS YOUR LEADER.
Wow! Too kewl, Togami!
TOGA-MI...
UH... UM...ARE YOU REALLY SURE M-MONOKUMA WON'T CRASH THE PARTY ...?
fidget

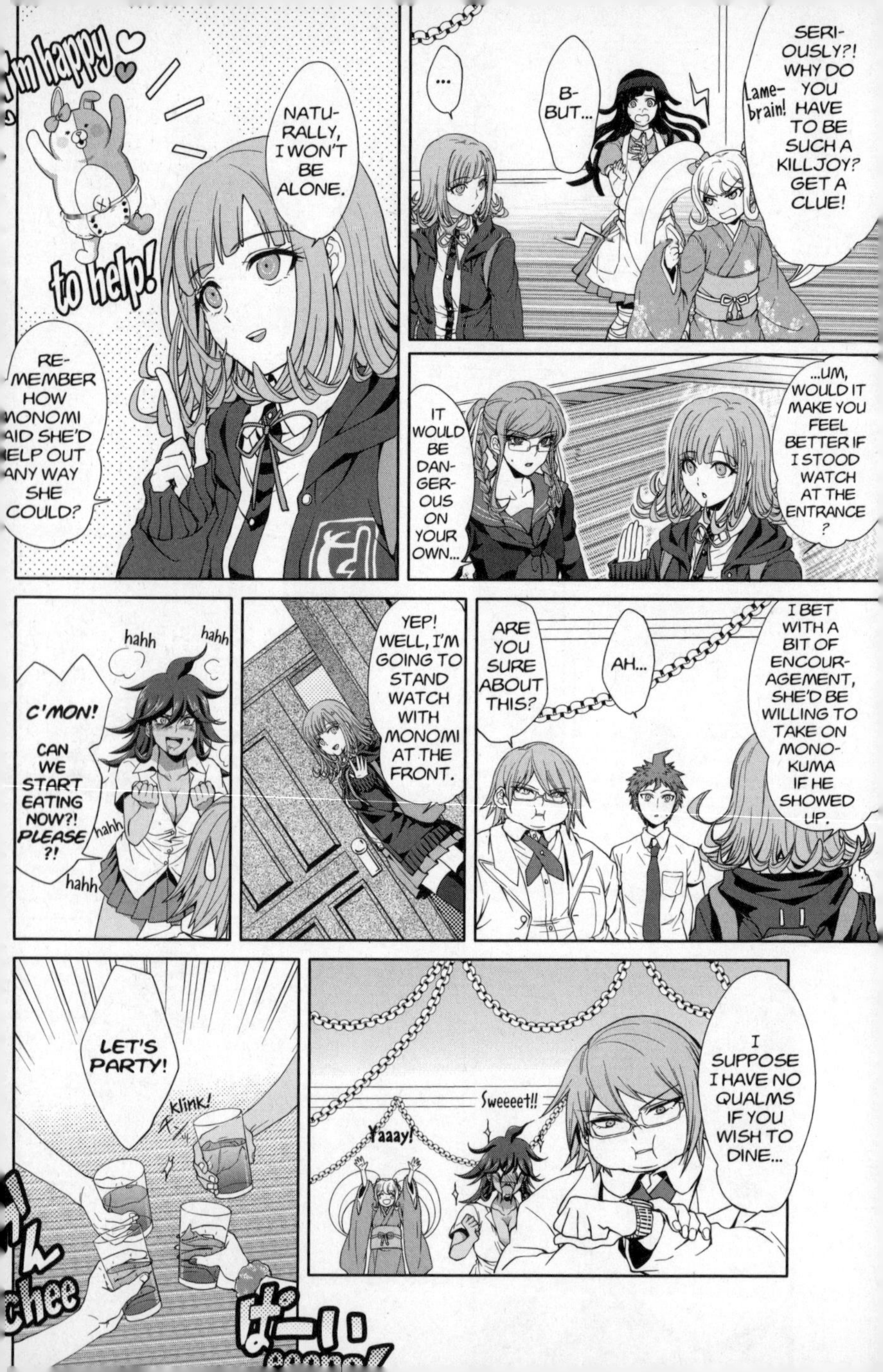
SERI-OUSLY?! WHY DO YOU HAVE TO BE SUCH A KILLJOY? GET A CLUE!
Lame-brain!
B-BUT...
...
...UM, WOULD IT MAKE YOU FEEL BETTER IF I STOOD WATCH AT THE ENTRANCE?
IT WOULD BE DANG-ER-OUS ON YOUR OWN...
NATU-RALLY, I WON'T BE ALONE.
I'm happy to help!
RE-MEMBER HOW MONOMI AID SHE'D ELP OUT ANY WAY SHE COULD?
I BET WITH A BIT OF ENCOUR-AGEMENT, SHE'D BE WILLING TO TAKE ON MONO-KUMA IF HE SHOWED UP.
AH...
ARE YOU SURE ABOUT THIS?
YEP! WELL, I'M GOING TO STAND WATCH WITH MONOMI AT THE FRONT.
hahh
hahh
C'MON! CAN WE START EATING NOW?! PLEASE?!
hahh
hahh
I SUPPOSE I HAVE NO QUALMS IF YOU WISH TO DINE...
Sweeeet!!
Yaaay!
LET'S PARTY!
klink!
chee

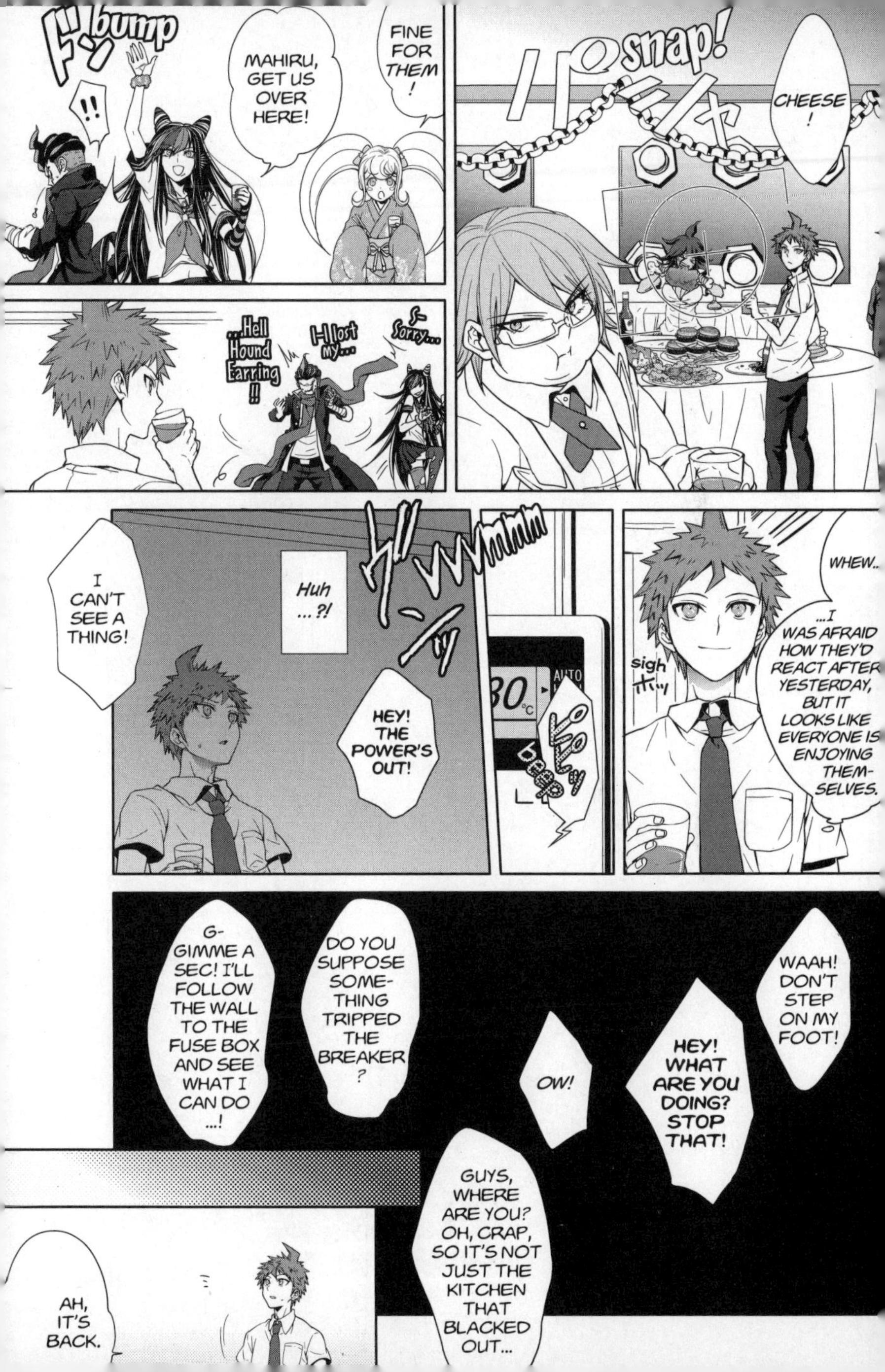
snap!
CHEESE!
FINE FOR THEM!
MAHIRU, GET US OVER HERE!
bump
!!
S-Sorry...
I-I lost my...
...Hell Hound Earring!!
WHEW... ...I WAS AFRAID HOW THEY'D REACT AFTER YESTERDAY, BUT IT LOOKS LIKE EVERYONE IS ENJOYING THEMSELVES.
sigh
beep
Wmmm
Huh ...?!
HEY! THE POWER'S OUT!
I CAN'T SEE A THING!
WAAH! DON'T STEP ON MY FOOT!
HEY! WHAT ARE YOU DOING? STOP THAT!
OW!
DO YOU SUPPOSE SOMETHING TRIPPED THE BREAKER?
G-GIMME A SEC! I'LL FOLLOW THE WALL TO THE FUSE BOX AND SEE WHAT I CAN DO...!
GUYS, WHERE ARE YOU? OH, CRAP, SO IT'S NOT JUST THE KITCHEN THAT BLACKED OUT...
AH, IT'S BACK.

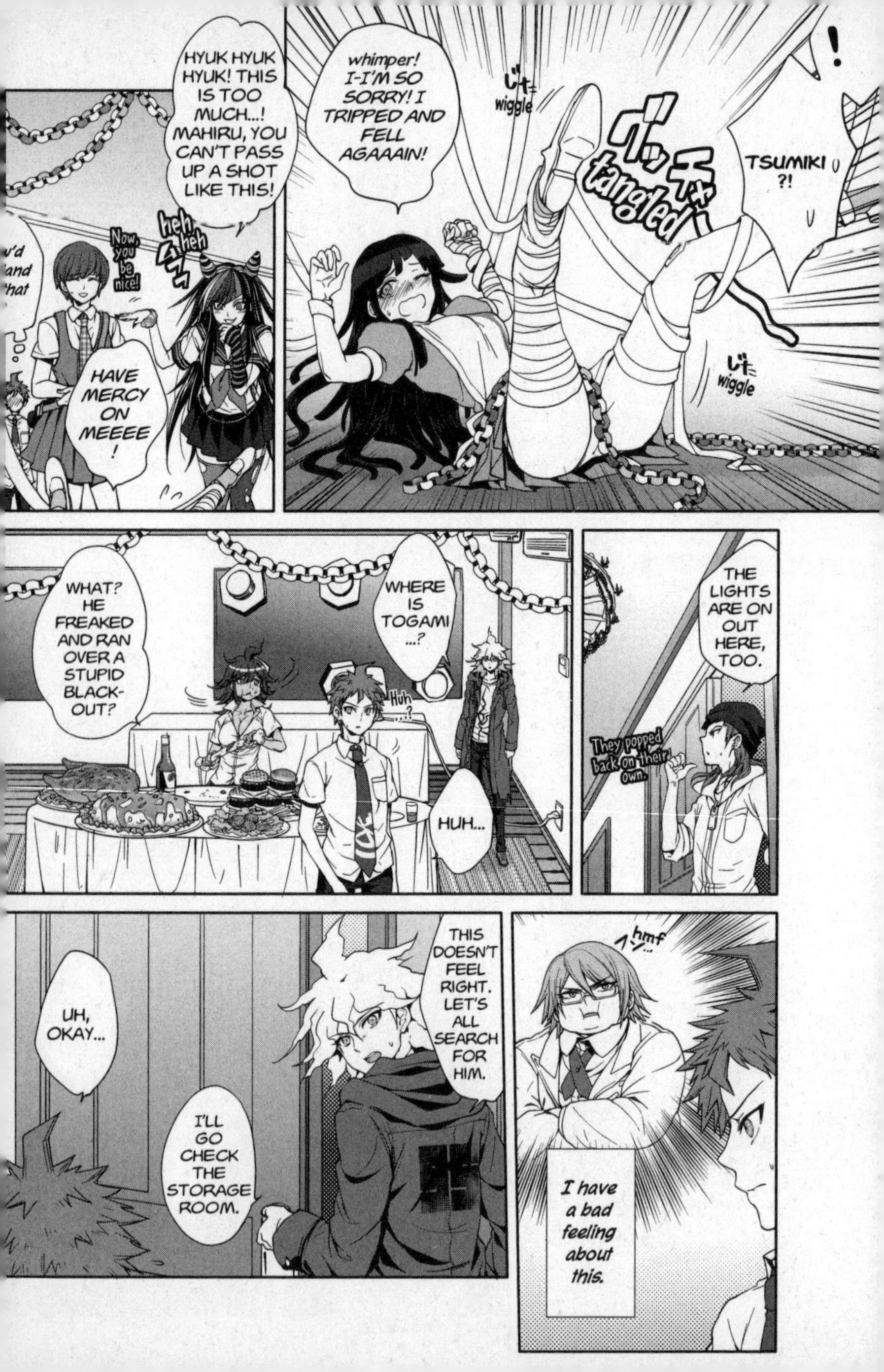
!
TSUMIKI ?!
tangled
wiggle
wiggle
whimper! I-I'M SO SORRY! I TRIPPED AND FELL AGAAAIN!
HYUK HYUK HYUK! THIS IS TOO MUCH...! MAHIRU, YOU CAN'T PASS UP A SHOT LIKE THIS!
heh heh
Now, you be nice!
HAVE MERCY ON MEEEE!
THE LIGHTS ARE ON OUT HERE, TOO.
They popped back on their own.
WHERE IS TOGAMI ...?
Huh ...?
WHAT? HE FREAKED AND RAN OVER A STUPID BLACK-OUT?
HUH...
hmf
I have a bad feeling about this.
THIS DOESN'T FEEL RIGHT. LET'S ALL SEARCH FOR HIM.
UH, OKAY...
I'LL GO CHECK THE STORAGE ROOM.

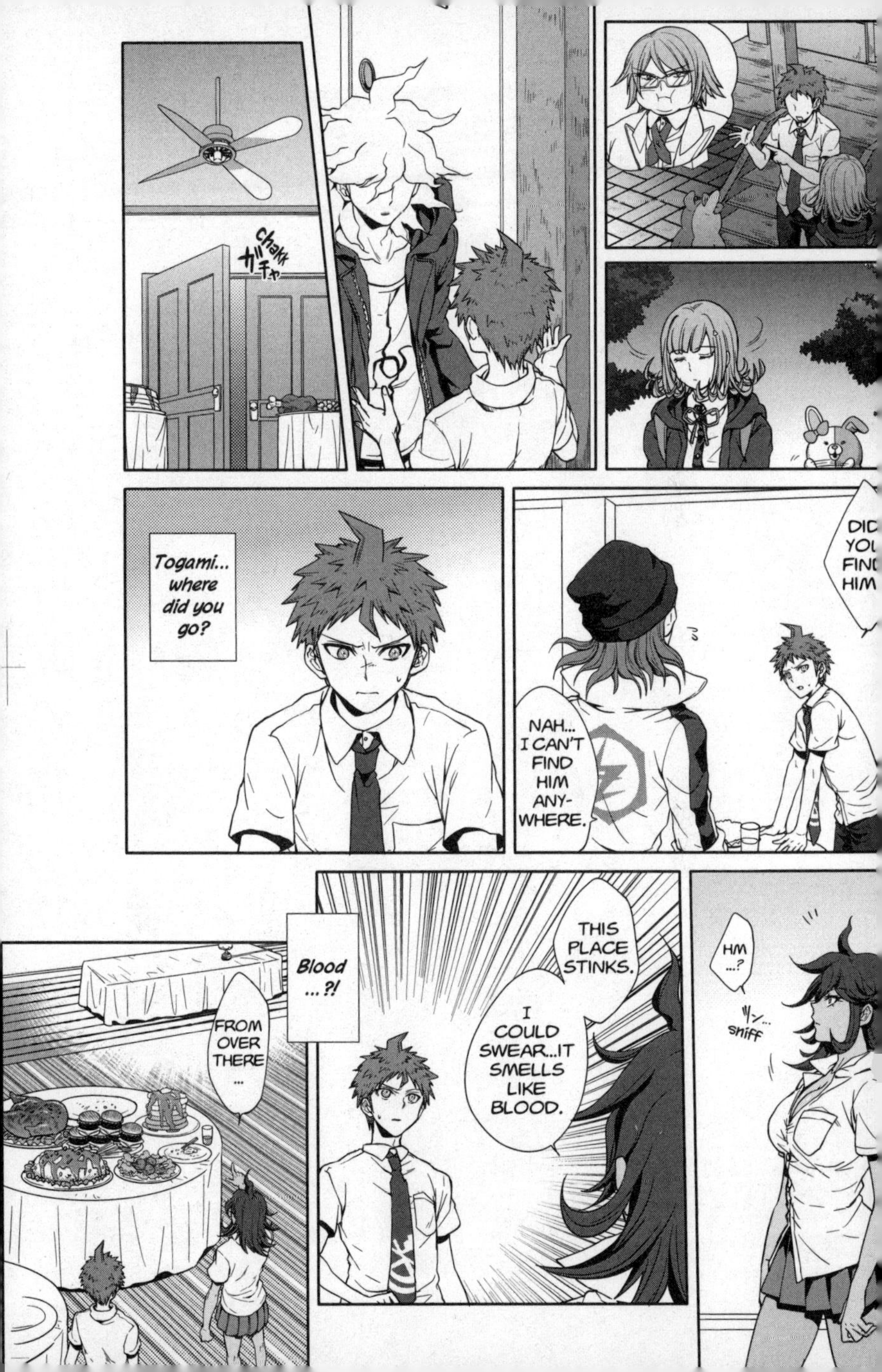
Chakk
ガチャ
DID YOU FIN HIM
NAH... I CAN'T FIND HIM ANY-WHERE.
Togami... where did you go?
HM ...?
ツン...
sniff
THIS PLACE STINKS.
I COULD SWEAR...IT SMELLS LIKE BLOOD.
Blood ...?!
FROM OVER THERE ...

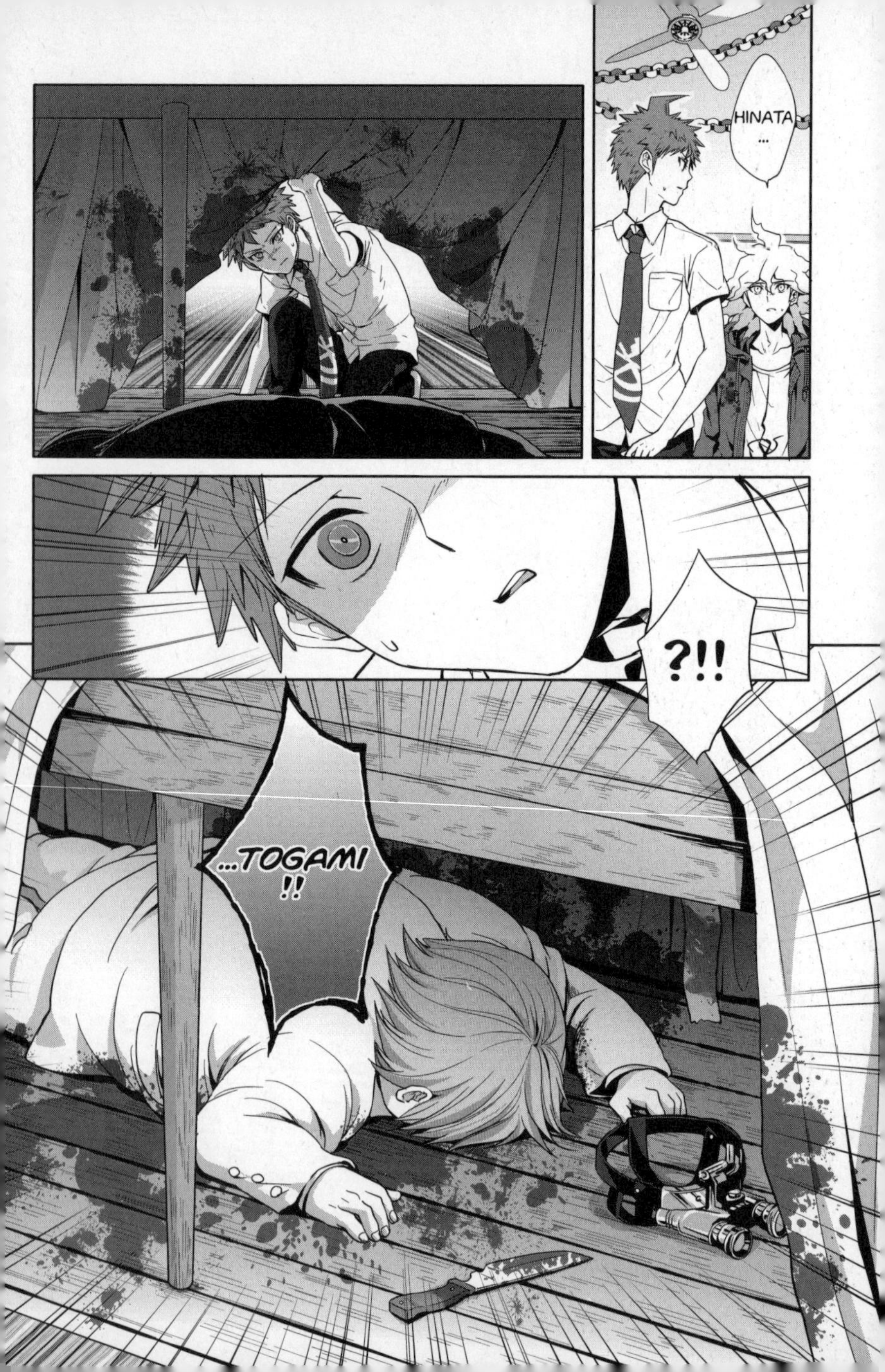
HINATA ...
?!!
...TOGAMI !!

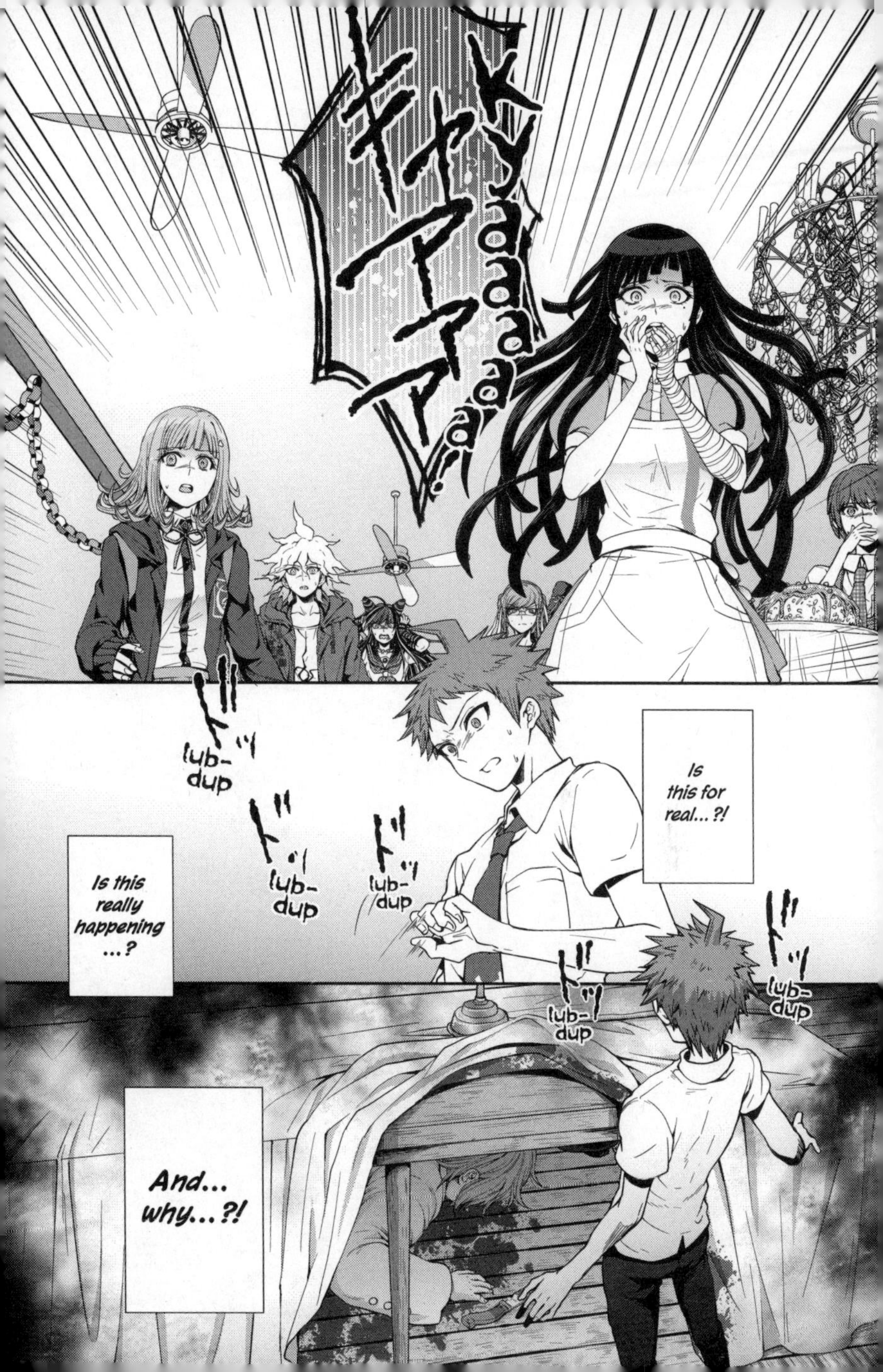
Kyaaaaa!
Is this for real...?!
lub-dup
lub-dup
lub-dup
Is this really happening...?
lub-dup
lub-dup
And... why...?!

CHAPTER 2 [PART ONE]: THE FIRST MURDER

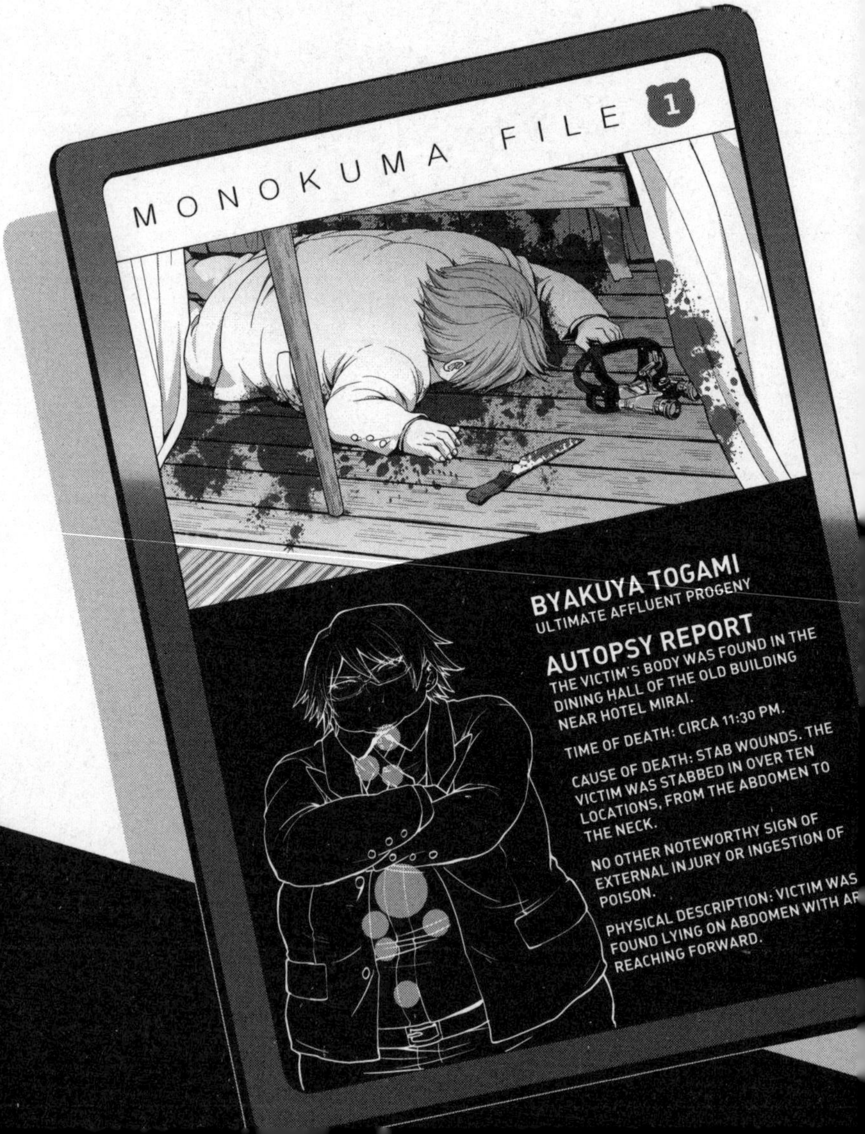
MONOKUMA FILE
1
BYAKUYA TOGAMI
ULTIMATE AFFLUENT PROGENY
AUTOPSY REPORT
THE VICTIM'S BODY WAS FOUND IN THE DINING HALL OF THE OLD BUILDING NEAR HOTEL MIRAI.
TIME OF DEATH: CIRCA 11:30 PM.
CAUSE OF DEATH: STAB WOUNDS. THE VICTIM WAS STABBED IN OVER TEN LOCATIONS, FROM THE ABDOMEN TO THE NECK.
NO OTHER NOTEWORTHY SIGN OF EXTERNAL INJURY OR INGESTION OF POISON.
PHYSICAL DESCRIPTION: VICTIM WAS FOUND LYING ON ABDOMEN WITH AR
REACHING FORWARD.

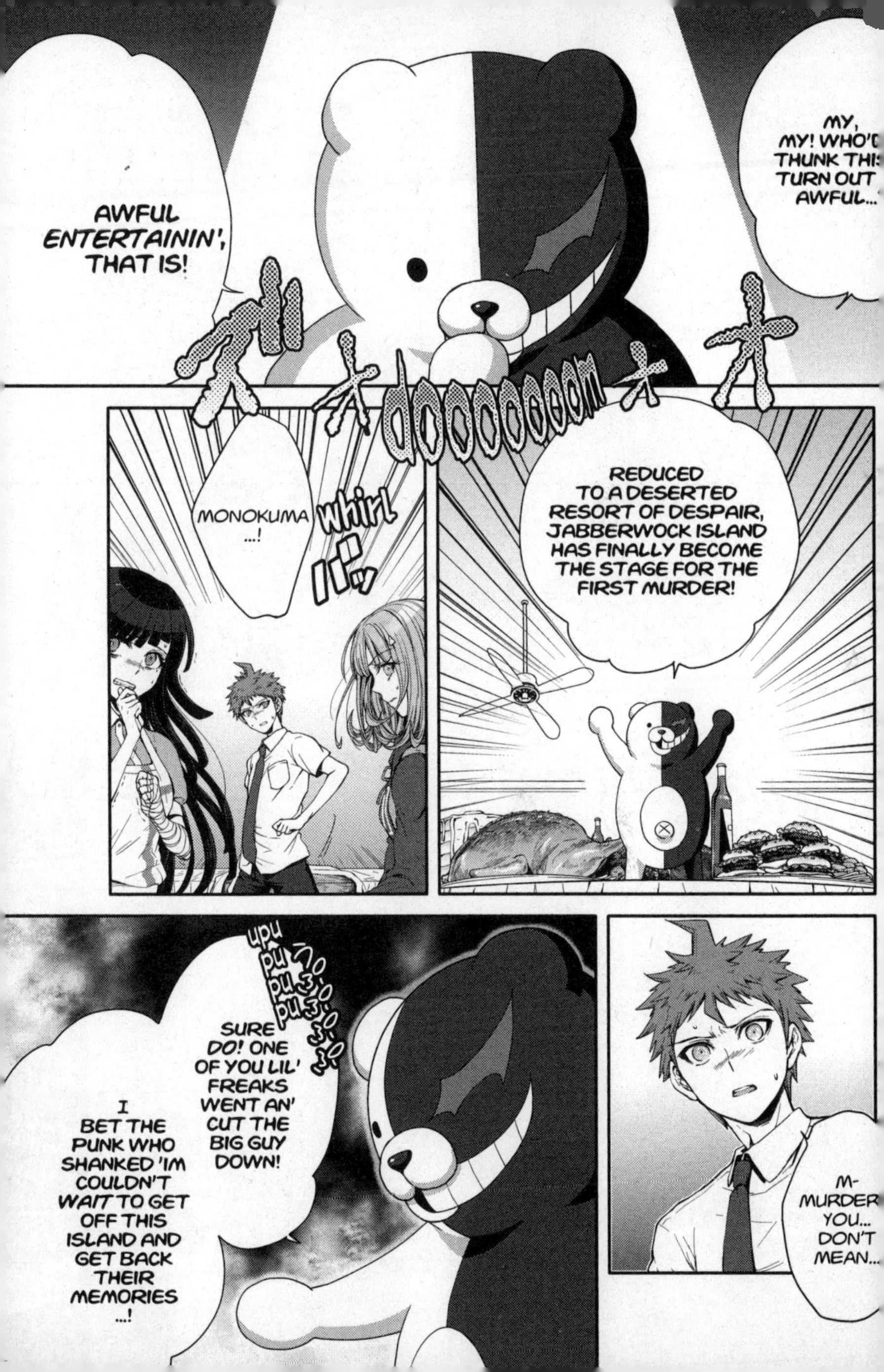
MY, MY! WHO'D THUNK THIS TURN OUT AWFUL...
AWFUL ENTERTAININ', THAT IS!
doooooooom
REDUCED TO A DESERTED RESORT OF DESPAIR, JABBERWOCK ISLAND HAS FINALLY BECOME THE STAGE FOR THE FIRST MURDER!
MONOKUMA ...!
whirl
パッ
M-MURDER YOU... DON'T MEAN...
upu pu pu pu
SURE DO! ONE OF YOU LIL' FREAKS WENT AN' CUT THE BIG GUY DOWN!
I BET THE PUNK WHO SHANKED 'IM COULDN'T WAIT TO GET OFF THIS ISLAND AND GET BACK THEIR MEMORIES ...!

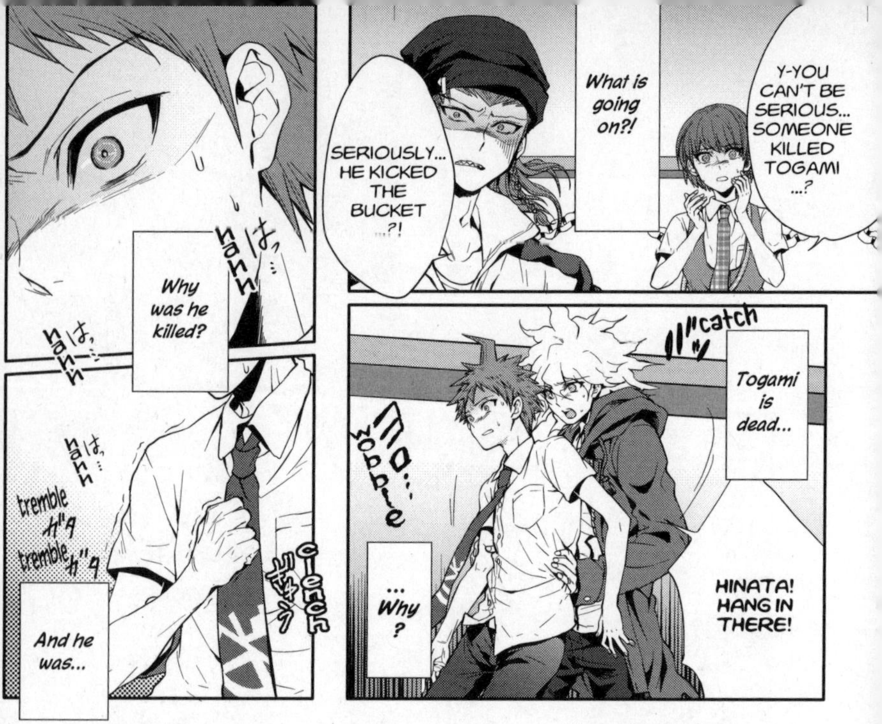
Y-YOU CAN'T BE SERIOUS... SOMEONE KILLED TOGAMI ...?
What is going on?!
SERIOUSLY... HE KICKED THE BUCKET ...?!
hahh
Why was he killed?
hahh
catch
Togami is dead...
HINATA! HANG IN THERE!
wobble
... Why ?
hahh
tremble
tremble
clench
And he was...

...murdered by one of us?

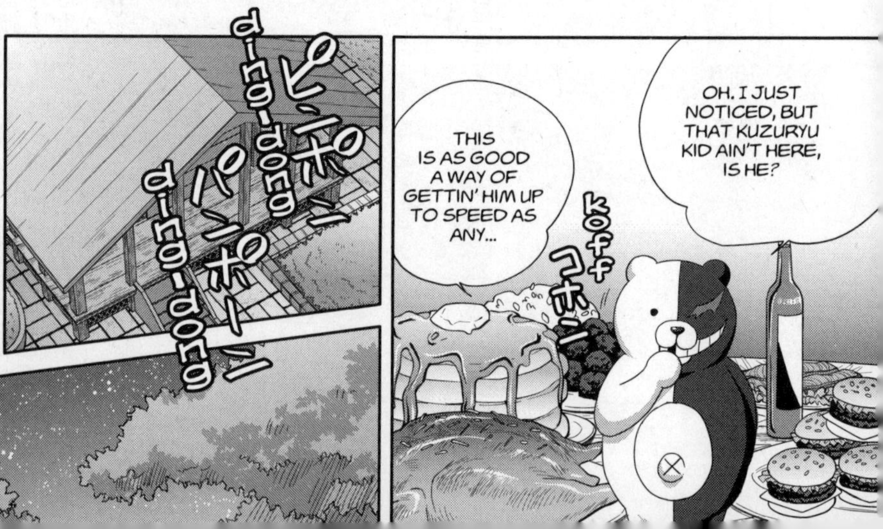
OH. I JUST NOTICED, BUT THAT KUZURYU KID AIN'T HERE, IS HE?
koff
THIS IS AS GOOD A WAY OF GETTIN' HIM UP TO SPEED AS ANY...
ding-dong
ding-dong

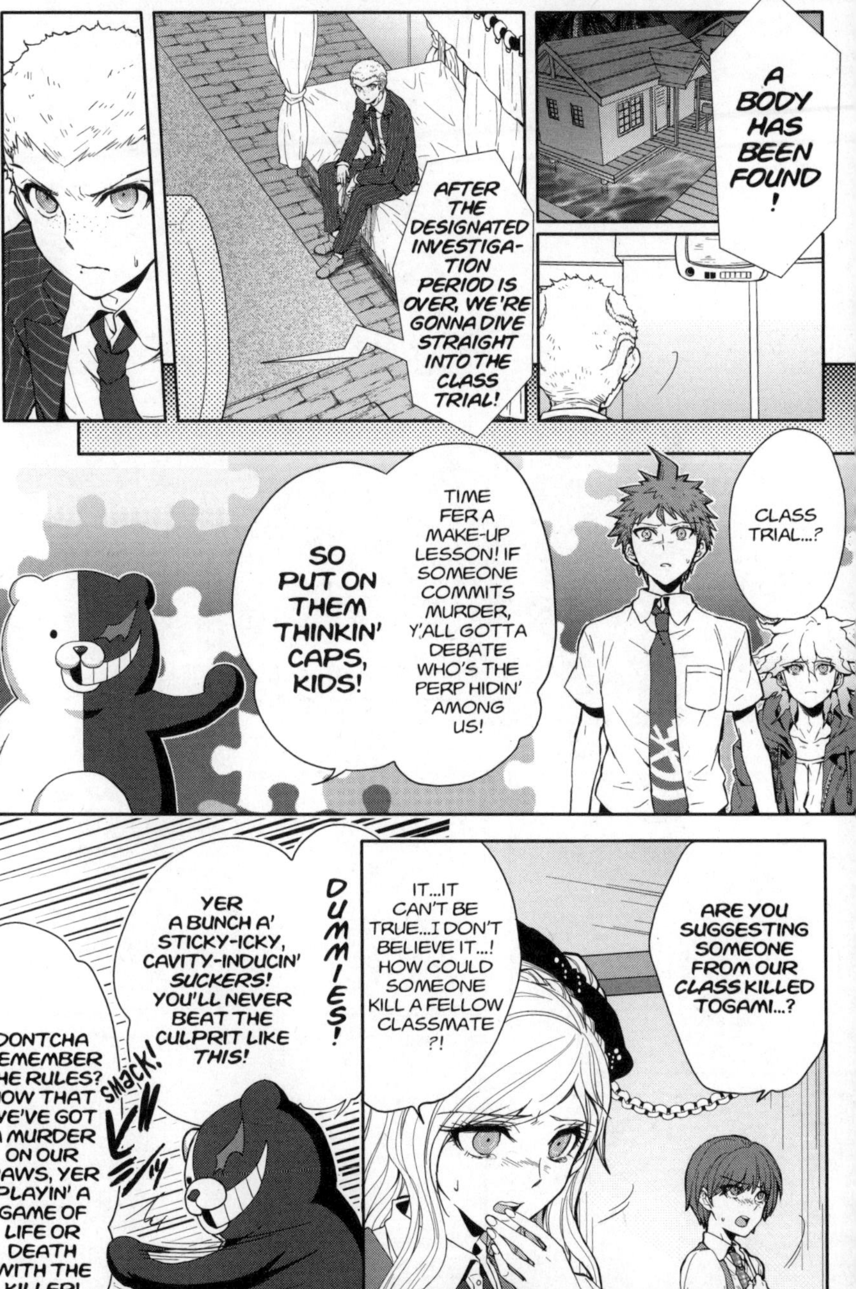
A BODY HAS BEEN FOUND!
AFTER THE DESIGNATED INVESTIGA-TION PERIOD IS OVER, WE'RE GONNA DIVE STRAIGHT INTO THE CLASS TRIAL!
CLASS TRIAL...?
TIME FER A MAKE-UP LESSON! IF SOMEONE COMMITS MURDER, Y'ALL GOTTA DEBATE WHO'S THE PERP HIDIN' AMONG US!
SO PUT ON THEM THINKIN' CAPS, KIDS!
ARE YOU SUGGESTING SOMEONE FROM OUR CLASS KILLED TOGAMI...?
IT...IT CAN'T BE TRUE...I DON'T BELIEVE IT...! HOW COULD SOMEONE KILL A FELLOW CLASSMATE?!
DUMMIES!
YER A BUNCH A' STICKY-ICKY, CAVITY-INDUCIN' SUCKERS! YOU'LL NEVER BEAT THE CULPRIT LIKE THIS!
SMACK!
DONTCHA REMEMBER THE RULES? NOW THAT WE'VE GOT A MURDER ON OUR PAWS, YER PLAYIN' A GAME OF LIFE OR DEATH WITH THE KILLER!

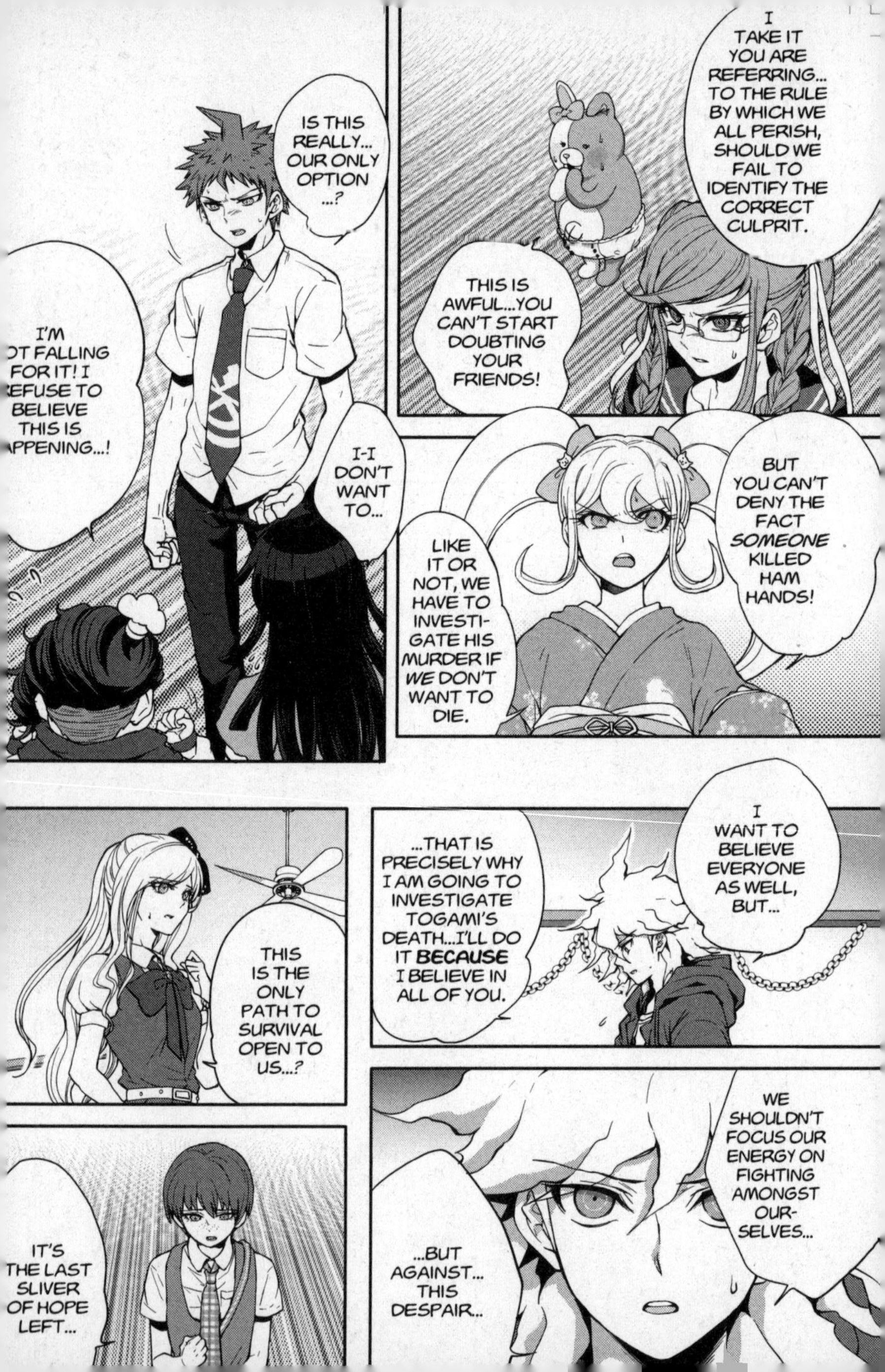
I TAKE IT YOU ARE REFERRING... TO THE RULE BY WHICH WE ALL PERISH, SHOULD WE FAIL TO IDENTIFY THE CORRECT CULPRIT.
THIS IS AWFUL...YOU CAN'T START DOUBTING YOUR FRIENDS!
BUT YOU CAN'T DENY THE FACT *SOMEONE* KILLED HAM HANDS!
LIKE IT OR NOT, WE HAVE TO INVESTI-GATE HIS MURDER IF *WE* DON'T WANT TO DIE.
IS THIS REALLY... OUR ONLY OPTION ...?
I'M OT FALLING FOR IT! I EFUSE TO BELIEVE THIS IS APPENING...!
I-I DON'T WANT TO...
I WANT TO BELIEVE EVERYONE AS WELL, BUT...
...THAT IS PRECISELY WHY I AM GOING TO INVESTIGATE TOGAMI'S DEATH...I'LL DO IT **BECAUSE** I BELIEVE IN ALL OF YOU.
THIS IS THE ONLY PATH TO SURVIVAL OPEN TO US...?
WE SHOULDN'T FOCUS OUR ENERGY ON FIGHTING AMONGST OUR-SELVES...
...BUT AGAINST... THIS DESPAIR...
IT'S THE LAST SLIVER OF HOPE LEFT...

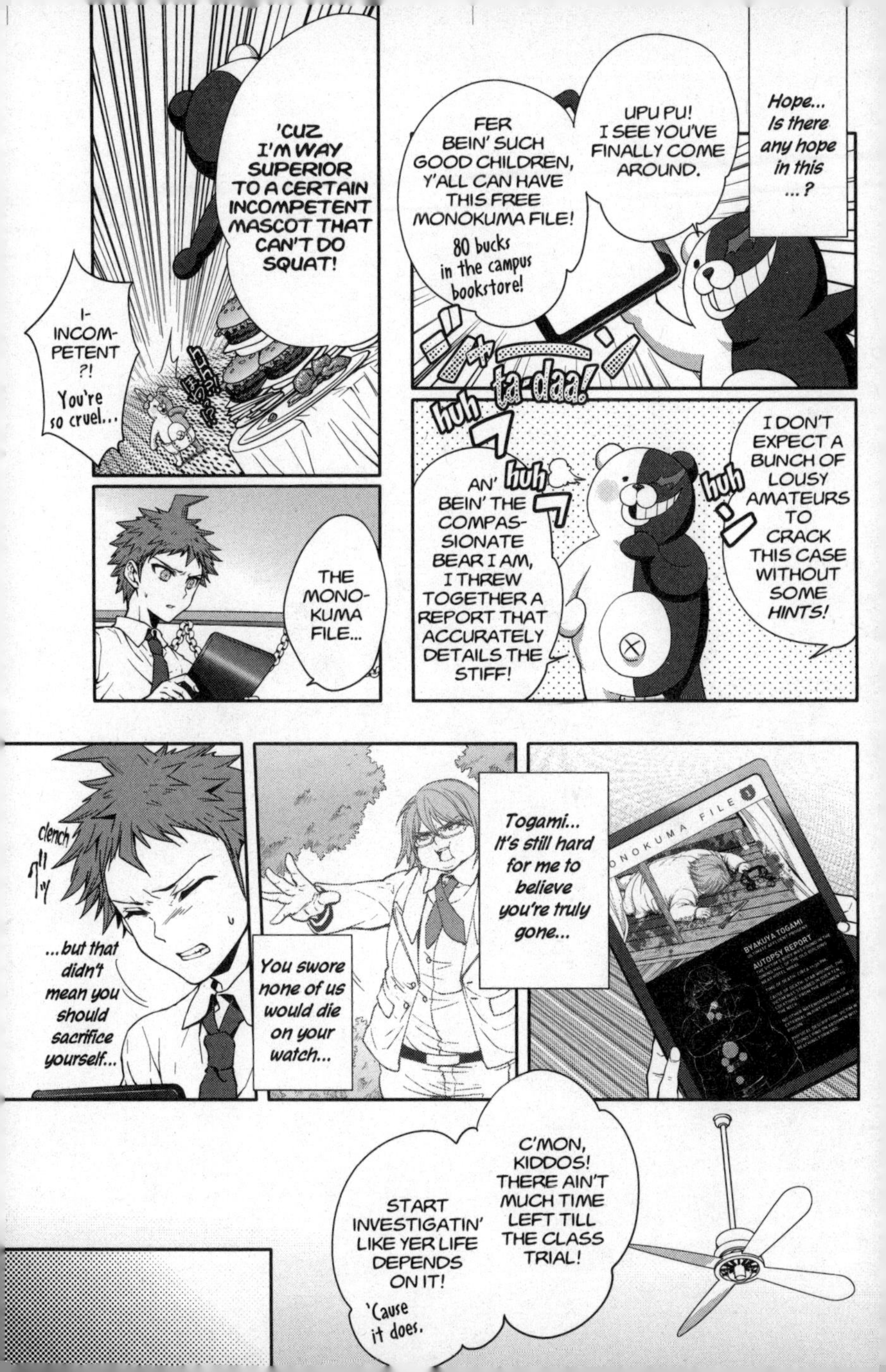
Hope... Is there any hope in this ...?
UPU PU! I SEE YOU'VE FINALLY COME AROUND.
FER BEIN' SUCH GOOD CHILDREN, Y'ALL CAN HAVE THIS FREE MONOKUMA FILE!
80 bucks in the campus bookstore!
ta-daa!
'CUZ I'M WAY SUPERIOR TO A CERTAIN INCOMPETENT MASCOT THAT CAN'T DO SQUAT!
I-INCOMPETENT?!
You're so cruel...
huh
huh
huh
I DON'T EXPECT A BUNCH OF LOUSY AMATEURS TO CRACK THIS CASE WITHOUT SOME HINTS!
AN' BEIN' THE COMPASSIONATE BEAR I AM, I THREW TOGETHER A REPORT THAT ACCURATELY DETAILS THE STIFF!
THE MONOKUMA FILE...
BYAKUYA TOGAMI
AUTOPSY REPORT
Togami... It's still hard for me to believe you're truly gone...
You swore none of us would die on your watch...
clench
...but that didn't mean you should sacrifice yourself...
C'MON, KIDDOS! THERE AIN'T MUCH TIME LEFT TILL THE CLASS TRIAL!
START INVESTIGATIN' LIKE YER LIFE DEPENDS ON IT!
'Cause it does.

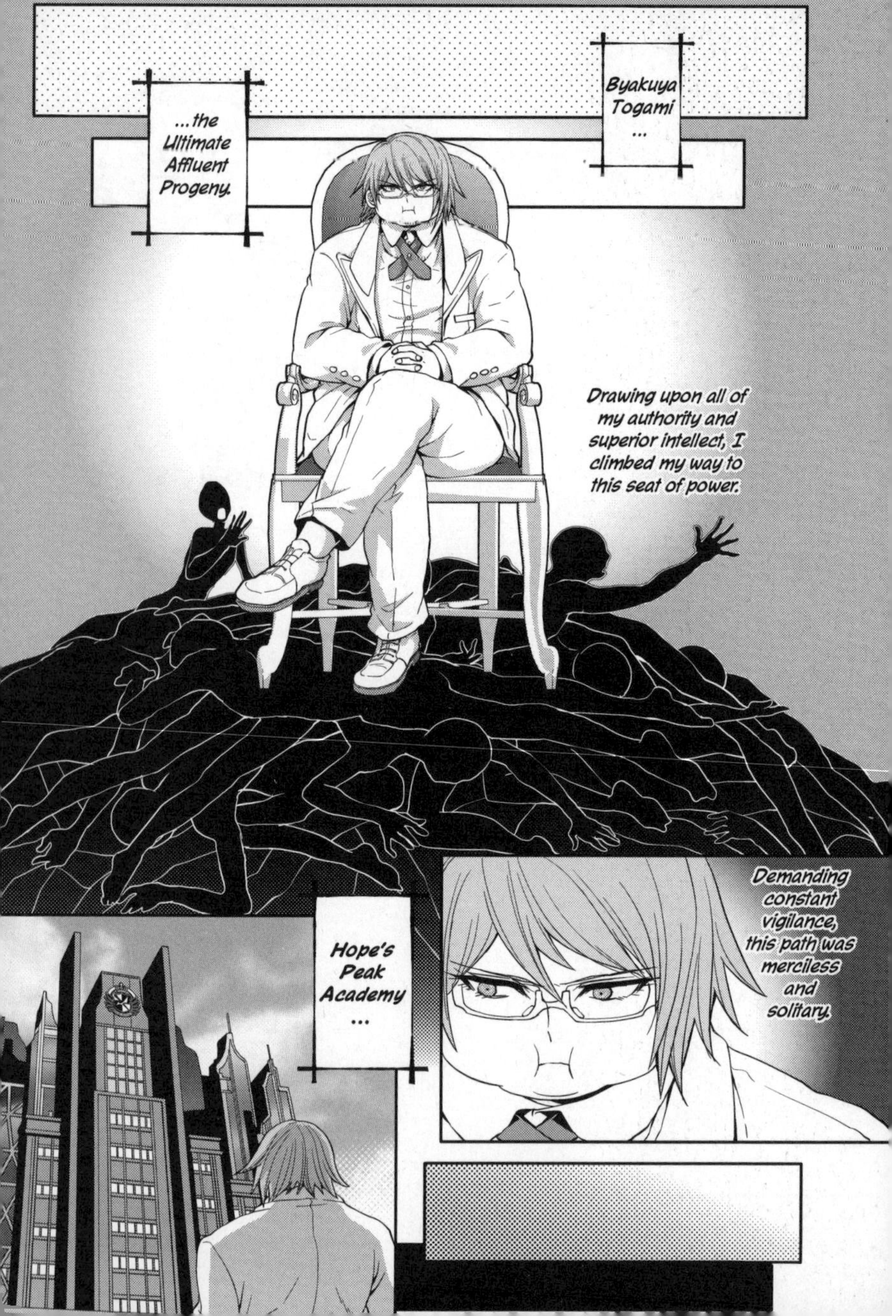
Byakuya Togami ...
...the Ultimate Affluent Progeny.
Drawing upon all of my authority and superior intellect, I climbed my way to this seat of power.
Demanding constant vigilance, this path was merciless and solitary.
Hope's Peak Academy ...

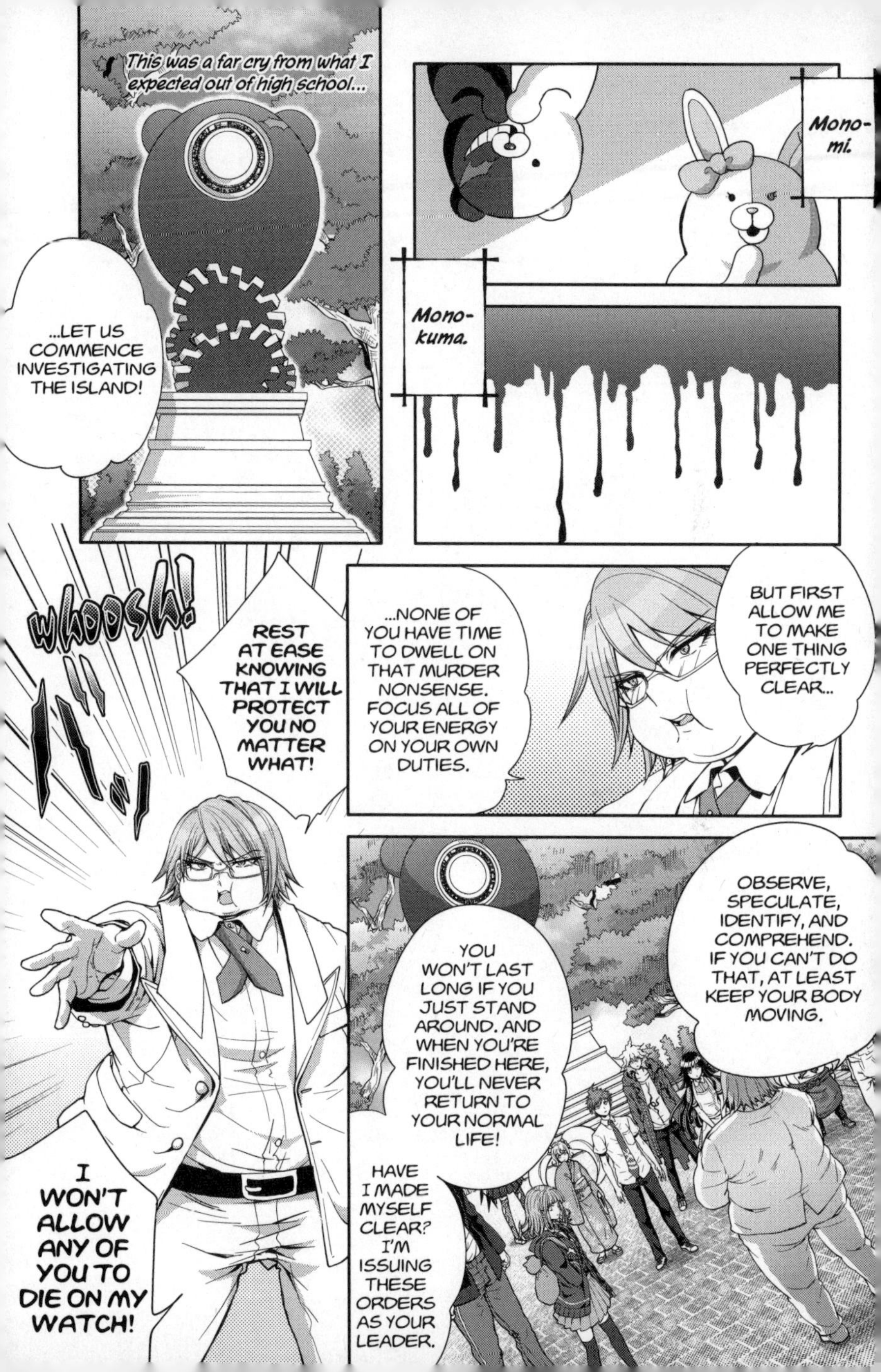
Mono-mi.
Mono-kuma.
This was a far cry from what I expected out of high school...
...LET US COMMENCE INVESTIGATING THE ISLAND!
BUT FIRST ALLOW ME TO MAKE ONE THING PERFECTLY CLEAR...
...NONE OF YOU HAVE TIME TO DWELL ON THAT MURDER NONSENSE. FOCUS ALL OF YOUR ENERGY ON YOUR OWN DUTIES.
OBSERVE, SPECULATE, IDENTIFY, AND COMPREHEND. IF YOU CAN'T DO THAT, AT LEAST KEEP YOUR BODY MOVING.
YOU WON'T LAST LONG IF YOU JUST STAND AROUND. AND WHEN YOU'RE FINISHED HERE, YOU'LL NEVER RETURN TO YOUR NORMAL LIFE!
HAVE I MADE MYSELF CLEAR? I'M ISSUING THESE ORDERS AS YOUR LEADER.
WHOOSH!
バッ
REST AT EASE KNOWING THAT I WILL PROTECT YOU NO MATTER WHAT!
I WON'T ALLOW ANY OF YOU TO DIE ON MY WATCH!

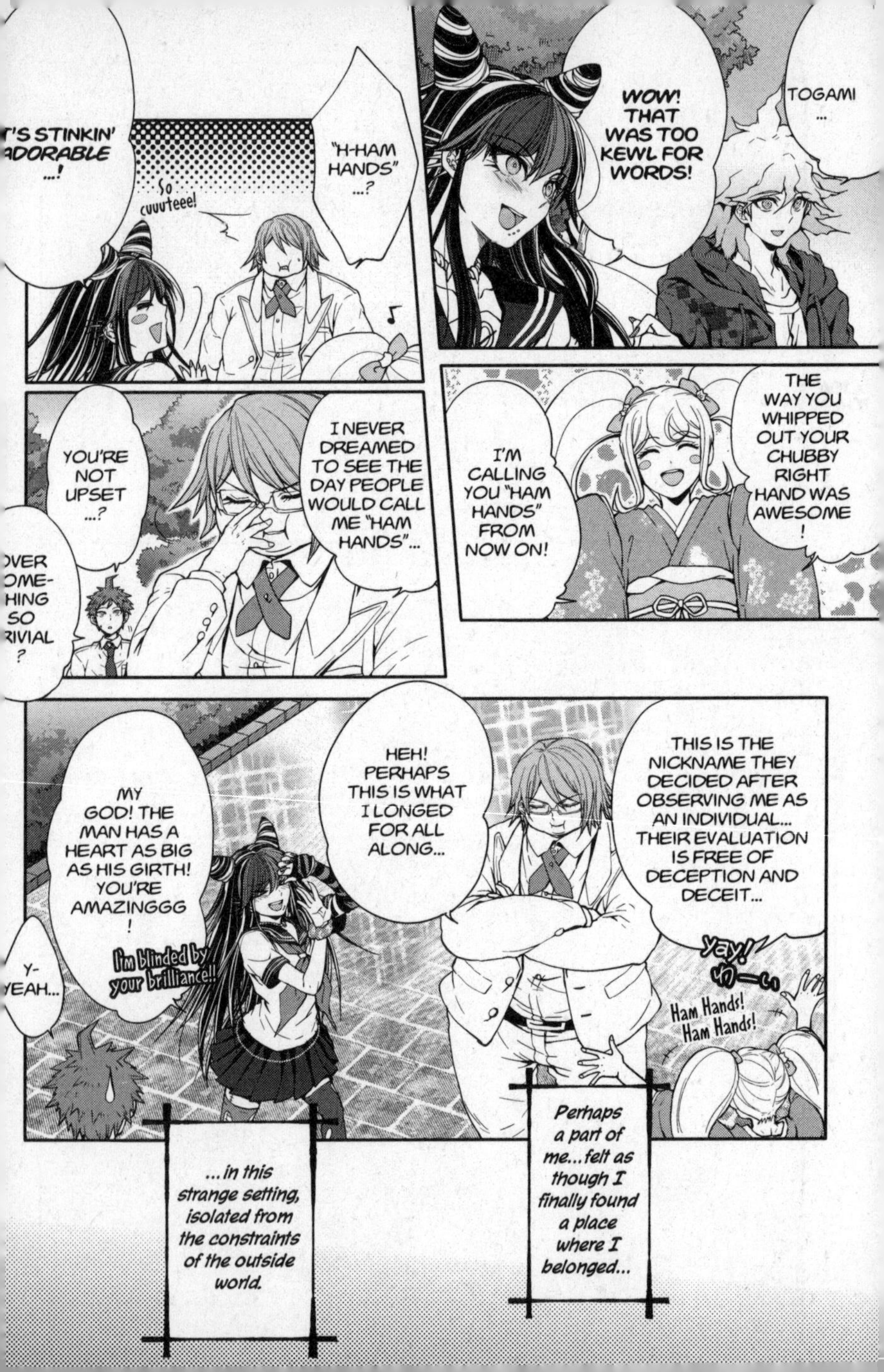
TOGAMI ...
WOW! THAT WAS TOO KEWL FOR WORDS!
"H-HAM HANDS" ...?
T'S STINKIN' ADORABLE ...!
So cuuuteee!
THE WAY YOU WHIPPED OUT YOUR CHUBBY RIGHT HAND WAS AWESOME!
I'M CALLING YOU "HAM HANDS" FROM NOW ON!
I NEVER DREAMED TO SEE THE DAY PEOPLE WOULD CALL ME "HAM HANDS"...
YOU'RE NOT UPSET ...?
VER OME- HING SO RIVIAL ?
THIS IS THE NICKNAME THEY DECIDED AFTER OBSERVING ME AS AN INDIVIDUAL... THEIR EVALUATION IS FREE OF DECEPTION AND DECEIT...
yay! わーい
Ham Hands! Ham Hands!
HEH! PERHAPS THIS IS WHAT I LONGED FOR ALL ALONG...
MY GOD! THE MAN HAS A HEART AS BIG AS HIS GIRTH! YOU'RE AMAZINGGG!
I'm blinded by your brilliance!!
Y-YEAH...
Perhaps a part of me...felt as though I finally found a place where I belonged...
...in this strange setting, isolated from the constraints of the outside world.

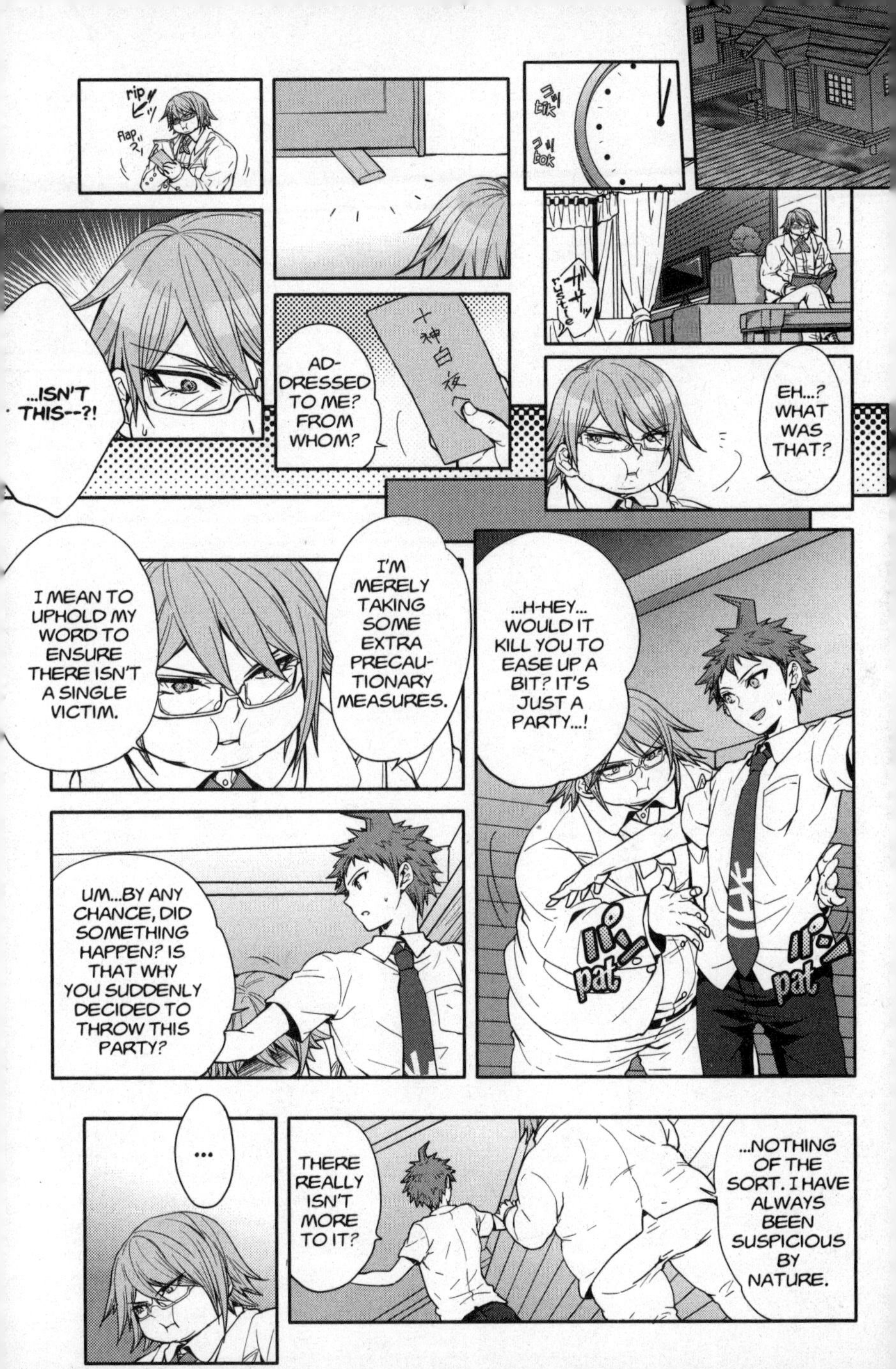
tik
tok
rustle
rip
flap
EH...? WHAT WAS THAT?
AD-DRESSED TO ME? FROM WHOM?
十神白夜
...ISN'T THIS--?!
...H-HEY... WOULD IT KILL YOU TO EASE UP A BIT? IT'S JUST A PARTY...!
pat
pat
I'M MERELY TAKING SOME EXTRA PRECAU-TIONARY MEASURES.
I MEAN TO UPHOLD MY WORD TO ENSURE THERE ISN'T A SINGLE VICTIM.
UM...BY ANY CHANCE, DID SOMETHING HAPPEN? IS THAT WHY YOU SUDDENLY DECIDED TO THROW THIS PARTY?
...NOTHING OF THE SORT. I HAVE ALWAYS BEEN SUSPICIOUS BY NATURE.
THERE REALLY ISN'T MORE TO IT?
...

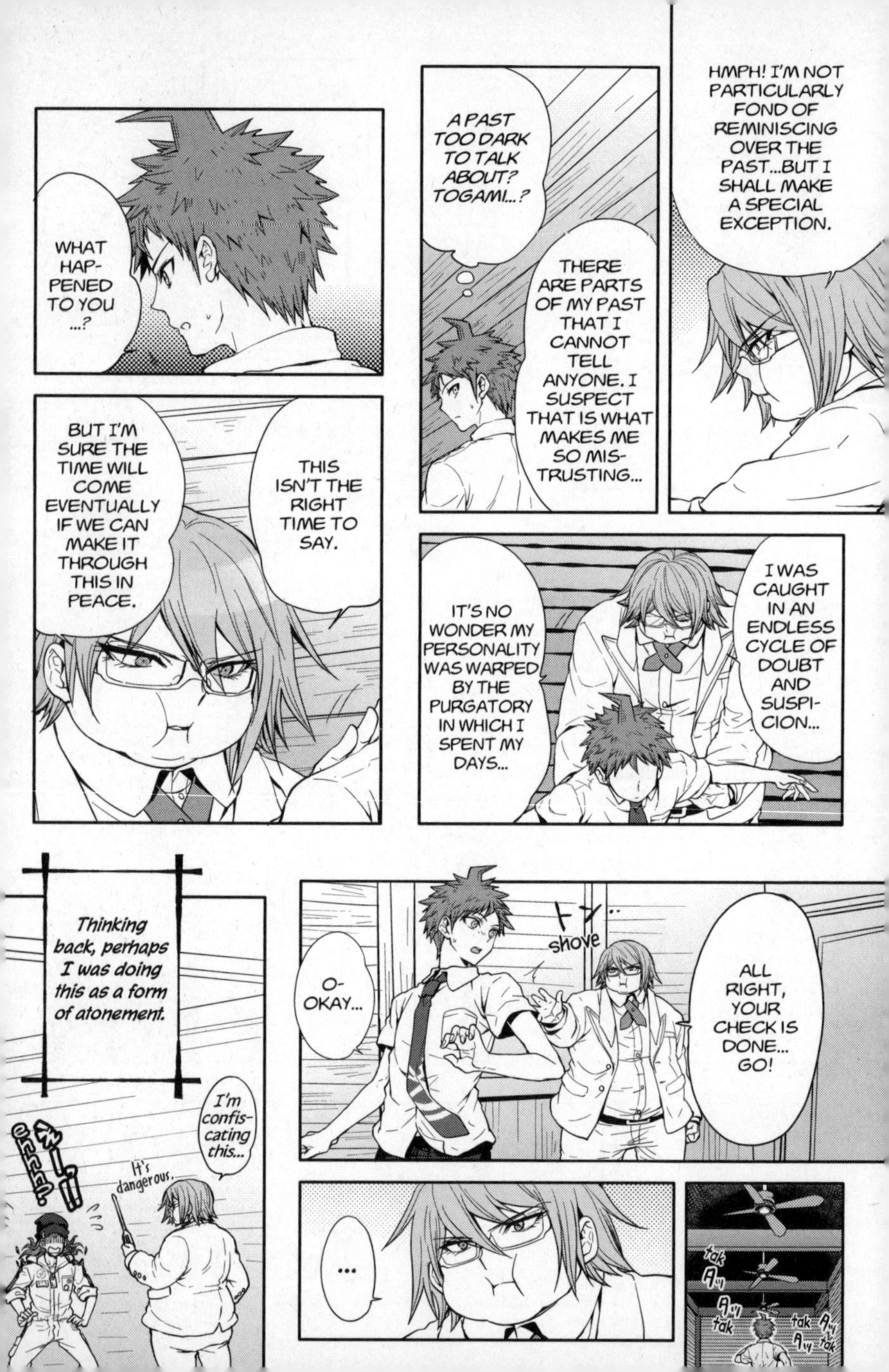
HMPH! I'M NOT PARTICULARLY FOND OF REMINISCING OVER THE PAST...BUT I SHALL MAKE A SPECIAL EXCEPTION.
THERE ARE PARTS OF MY PAST THAT I CANNOT TELL ANYONE. I SUSPECT THAT IS WHAT MAKES ME SO MIS-TRUSTING...
A PAST TOO DARK TO TALK ABOUT? TOGAMI...?
I WAS CAUGHT IN AN ENDLESS CYCLE OF DOUBT AND SUSPI-CION...
IT'S NO WONDER MY PERSONALITY WAS WARPED BY THE PURGATORY IN WHICH I SPENT MY DAYS...
WHAT HAP-PENED TO YOU ...?
THIS ISN'T THE RIGHT TIME TO SAY.
BUT I'M SURE THE TIME WILL COME EVENTUALLY IF WE CAN MAKE IT THROUGH THIS IN PEACE.
ALL RIGHT, YOUR CHECK IS DONE... GO!
shove
O-OKAY...
tak
Ay
tak
Ay
tak
Ay
tak
Ay
...
Thinking back, perhaps I was doing this as a form of atonement.
I'm confis-cating this...
It's dangerous.

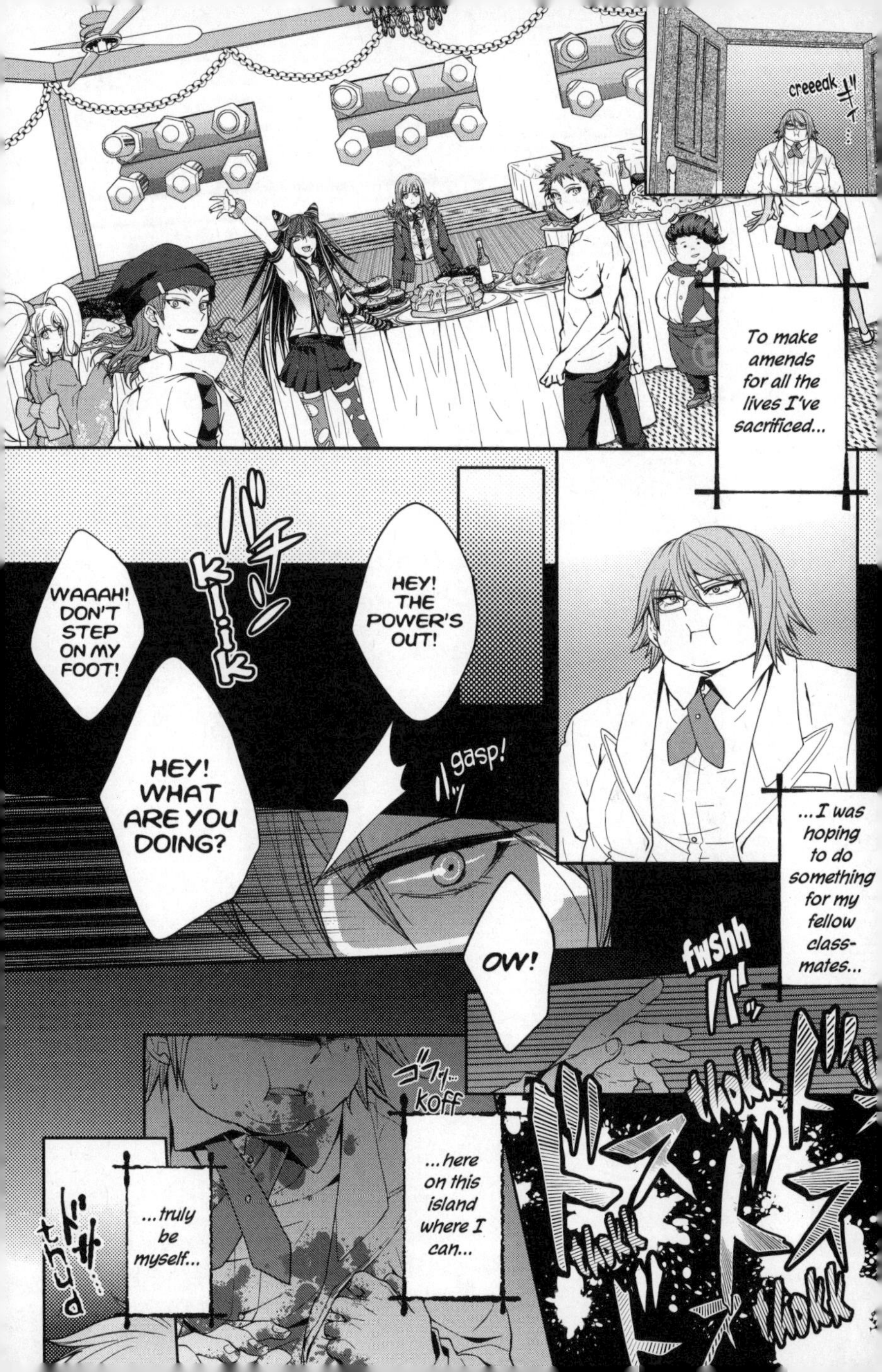

creeeak ギィ…
To make amends for all the lives I've sacrificed...
...I was hoping to do something for my fellow class-mates...
HEY! THE POWER'S OUT!
バチッ Klik
WAAAH! DON'T STEP ON MY FOOT!
HEY! WHAT ARE YOU DOING?
ハッ gasp!
OW!
fwshh バッ
ドス thokk
ドス thokk
ドス thokk
...here on this island where I can...
ゴフッ… koff
...truly be myself...
ドサ… thud

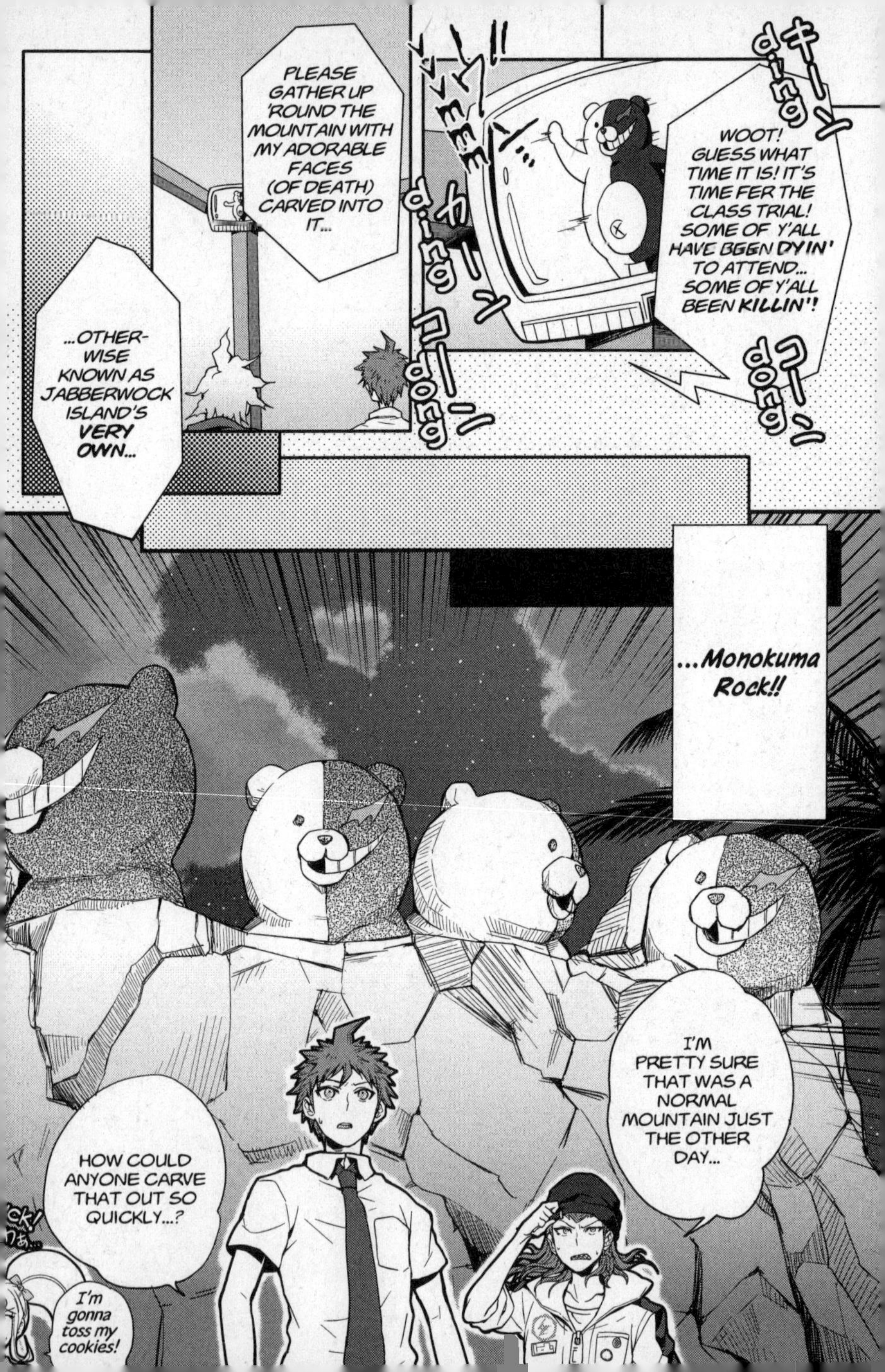
ding
WOOT! GUESS WHAT TIME IT IS! IT'S TIME FER THE CLASS TRIAL! SOME OF Y'ALL HAVE BEEN DYIN' TO ATTEND... SOME OF Y'ALL BEEN KILLIN'!
dong
ding
dong
PLEASE GATHER UP 'ROUND THE MOUNTAIN WITH MY ADORABLE FACES (OF DEATH) CARVED INTO IT...
...OTHERWISE KNOWN AS JABBERWOCK ISLAND'S VERY OWN...
...Monokuma Rock!!
I'M PRETTY SURE THAT WAS A NORMAL MOUNTAIN JUST THE OTHER DAY...
HOW COULD ANYONE CARVE THAT OUT SO QUICKLY...?
I'm gonna toss my cookies!

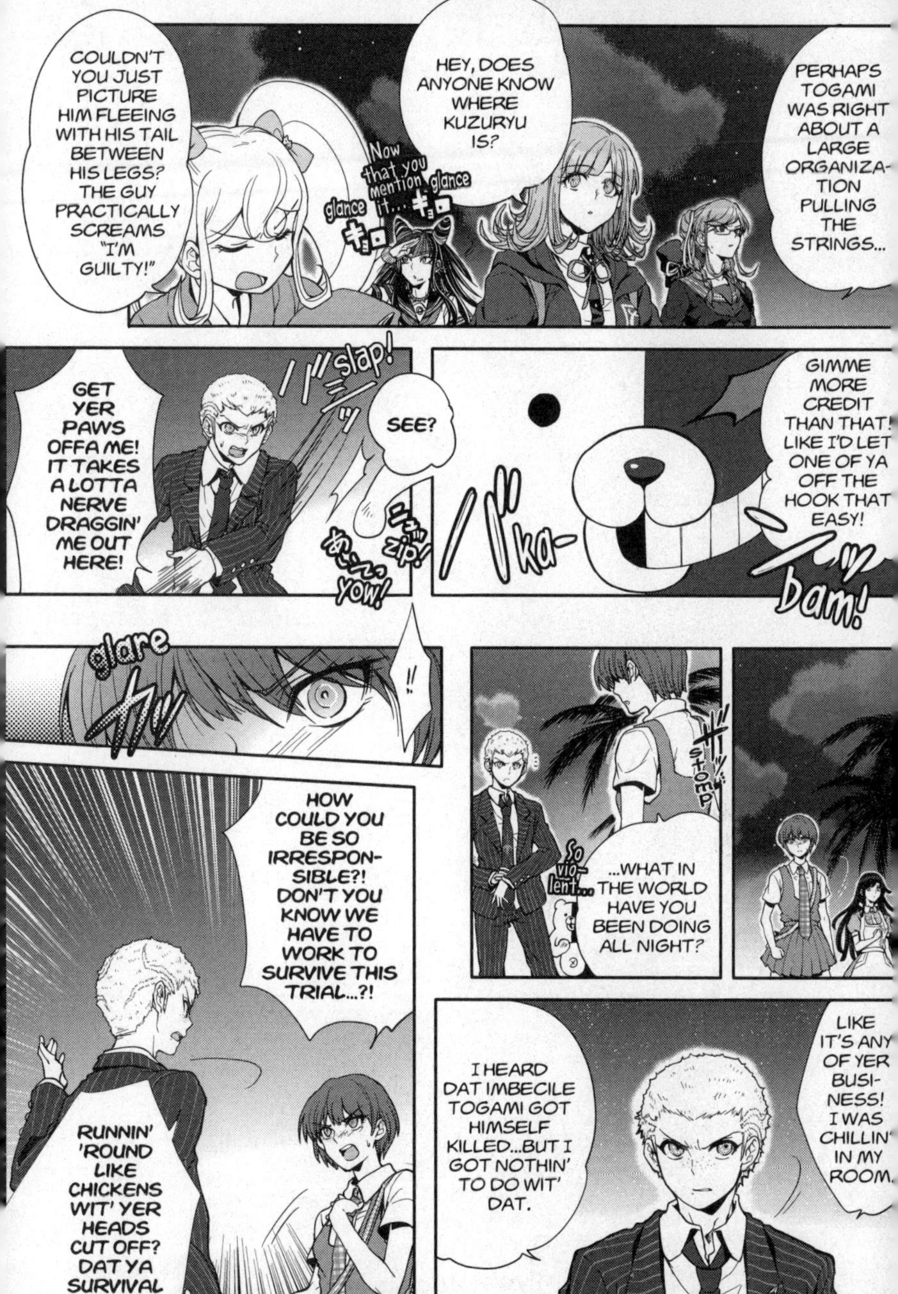
PERHAPS TOGAMI WAS RIGHT ABOUT A LARGE ORGANIZA-TION PULLING THE STRINGS...
HEY, DOES ANYONE KNOW WHERE KUZURYU IS?
glance
Now that you mention it...
glance
COULDN'T YOU JUST PICTURE HIM FLEEING WITH HIS TAIL BETWEEN HIS LEGS? THE GUY PRACTICALLY SCREAMS "I'M GUILTY!"
GIMME MORE CREDIT THAN THAT! LIKE I'D LET ONE OF YA OFF THE HOOK THAT EASY!
ka-
bam!
slap!
SEE?
zip!
yow!
GET YER PAWS OFFA ME! IT TAKES A LOTTA NERVE DRAGGIN' ME OUT HERE!
stomp
...WHAT IN THE WORLD HAVE YOU BEEN DOING ALL NIGHT?
So violent...
glare
!!
LIKE IT'S ANY OF YER BUSI-NESS! I WAS CHILLIN' IN MY ROOM.
I HEARD DAT IMBECILE TOGAMI GOT HIMSELF KILLED...BUT I GOT NOTHIN' TO DO WIT' DAT.
HOW COULD YOU BE SO IRRESPON-SIBLE?! DON'T YOU KNOW WE HAVE TO WORK TO SURVIVE THIS TRIAL...?!
RUNNIN' 'ROUND LIKE CHICKENS WIT' YER HEADS CUT OFF? DAT YA SURVIVAL PLAN?!

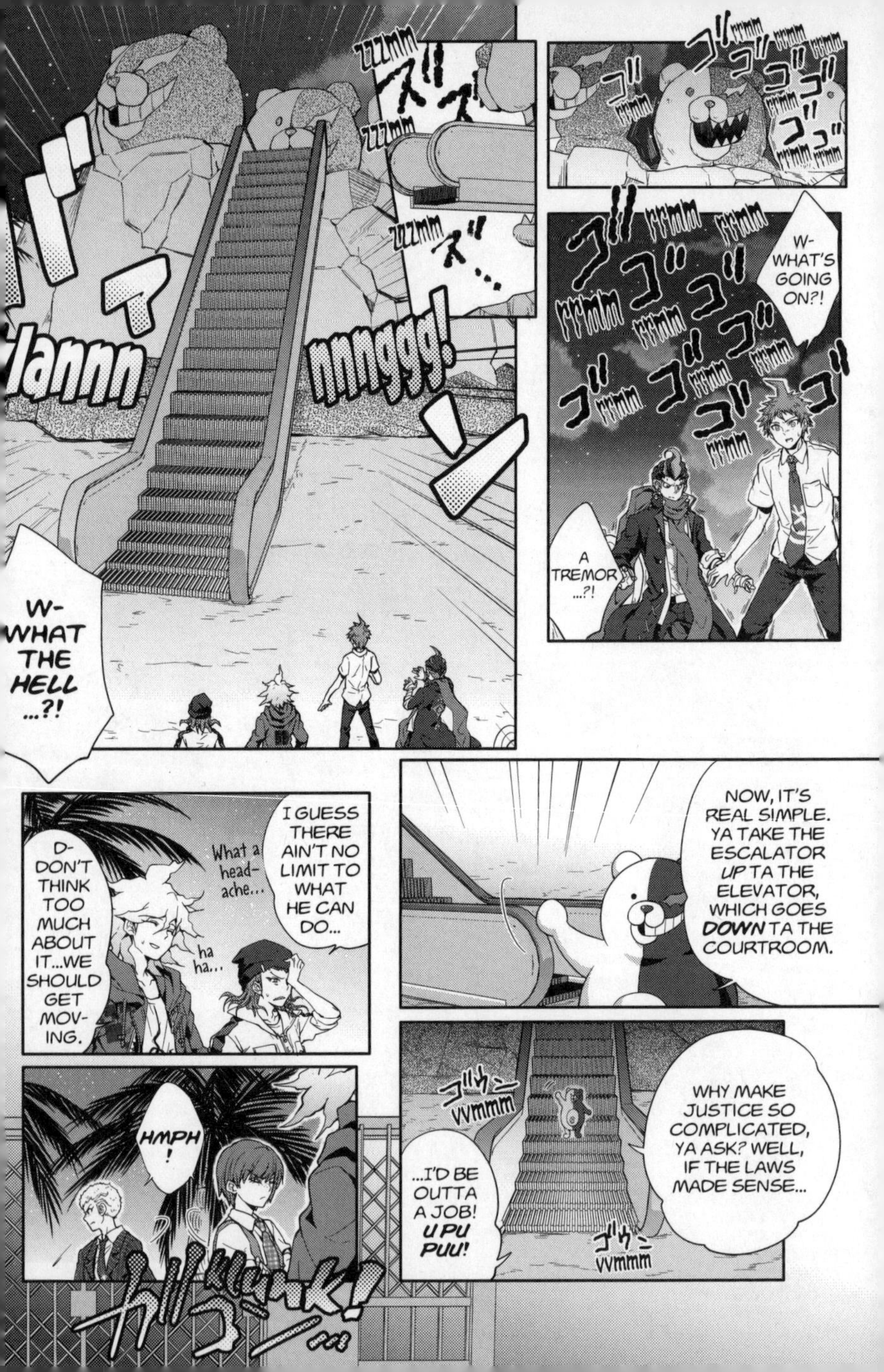

ゴ rrmm ゴゴ rrmm ゴゴ rrmm ゴゴ rrmm
ゴ rrmm ゴ rrmm ゴ rrmm ゴ rrmm ゴ rrmm ゴ rrmm ゴ rrmm ゴ
W-WHAT'S GOING ON?!
A TREMOR ...?!
zzzmm ズ!! ズ!!
zzzmm
zzzmm ズ"...
nnnggg!
ダァ
lannn
W-WHAT THE HELL ...?!
NOW, IT'S REAL SIMPLE. YA TAKE THE ESCALATOR UP TA THE ELEVATOR, WHICH GOES DOWN TA THE COURTROOM.
I GUESS THERE AIN'T NO LIMIT TO WHAT HE CAN DO...
What a headache...
ha ha...
D-DON'T THINK TOO MUCH ABOUT IT...WE SHOULD GET MOVING.
WHY MAKE JUSTICE SO COMPLICATED, YA ASK? WELL, IF THE LAWS MADE SENSE...
ゴウン vvmmm
...I'D BE OUTTA A JOB! UPU PUU!
ゴウン vvmmm
HMPH!
clunk!

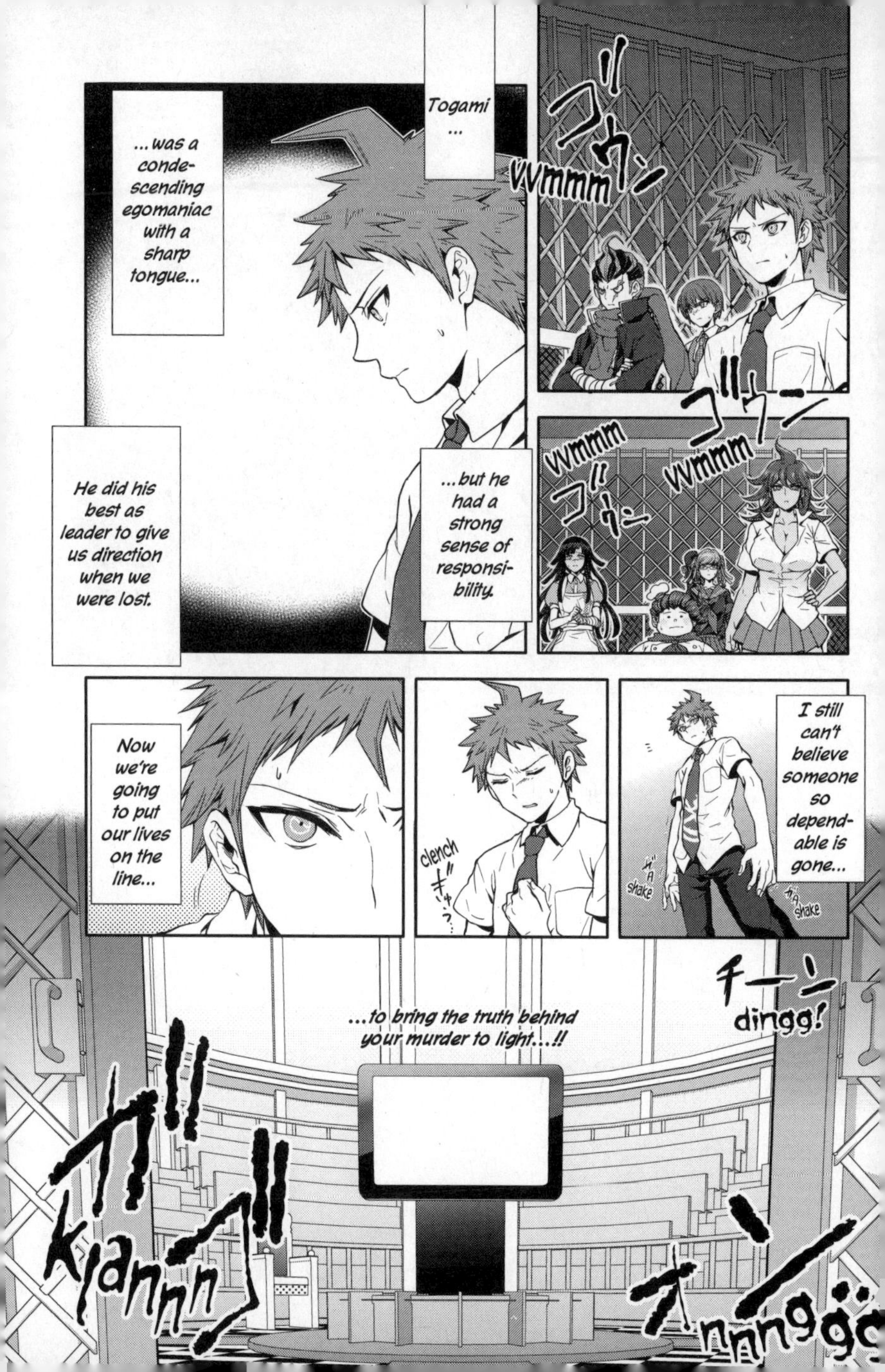
vvmmm
vvmmm
vvmmm
Togami ...
...was a conde-scending egomaniac with a sharp tongue...
...but he had a strong sense of responsi-bility.
He did his best as leader to give us direction when we were lost.
I still can't believe someone so depend-able is gone...
shake
shake
clench
Now we're going to put our lives on the line...
dingg!
...to bring the truth behind your murder to light...!!
kiannn
nnnggg

DANGANRONPA2

CHAPTER 2 [PART TWO]: THE CLASS TRIAL IS NOW IN SESSION

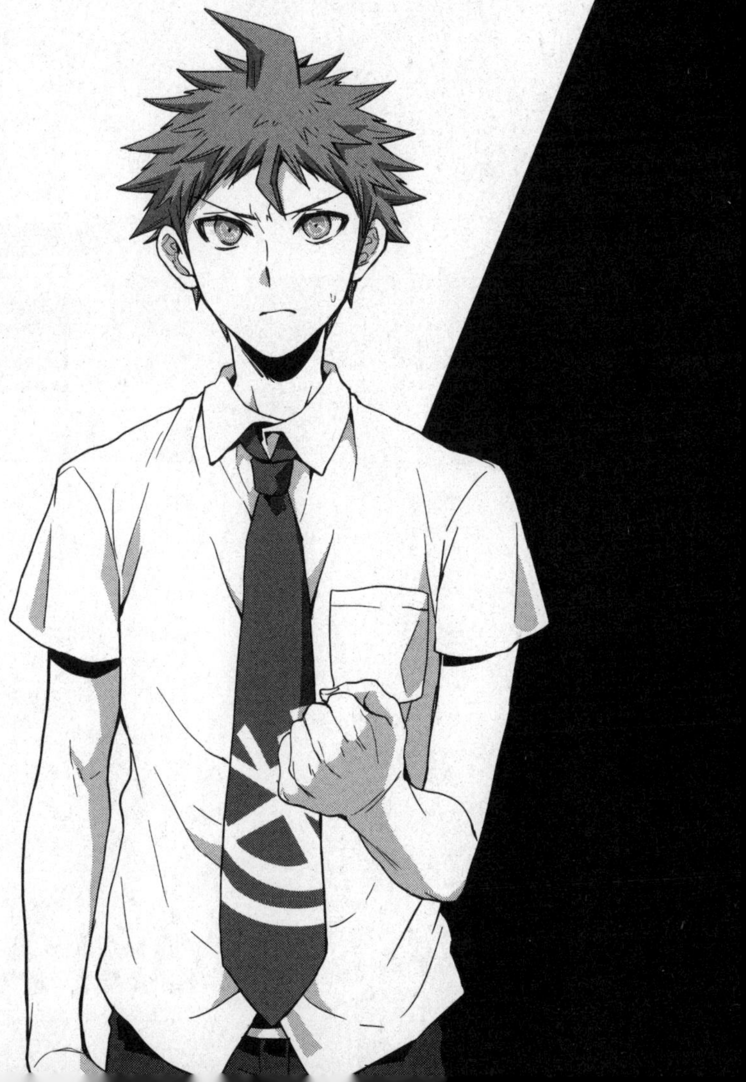

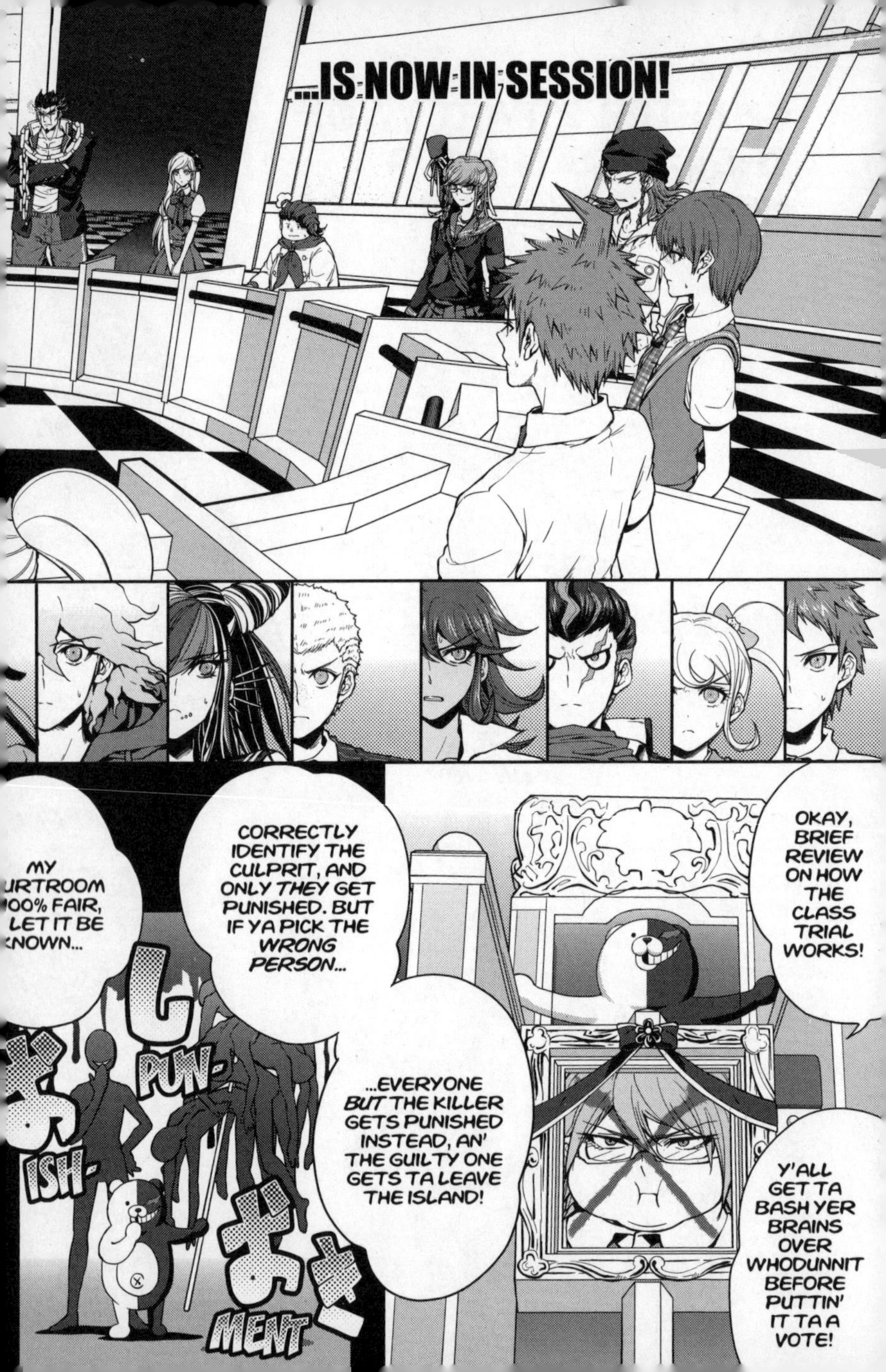
...IS NOW IN SESSION!
OKAY, BRIEF REVIEW ON HOW THE CLASS TRIAL WORKS!
Y'ALL GET TA BASH YER BRAINS OVER WHODUNNIT BEFORE PUTTIN' IT TA A VOTE!
MY URTROOM 00% FAIR, LET IT BE KNOWN...
CORRECTLY IDENTIFY THE CULPRIT, AND ONLY *THEY* GET PUNISHED. BUT IF YA PICK THE *WRONG* PERSON...
...EVERYONE *BUT* THE KILLER GETS PUNISHED INSTEAD, AN' THE GUILTY ONE GETS TA LEAVE THE ISLAND!
PUN- ISH- MENT

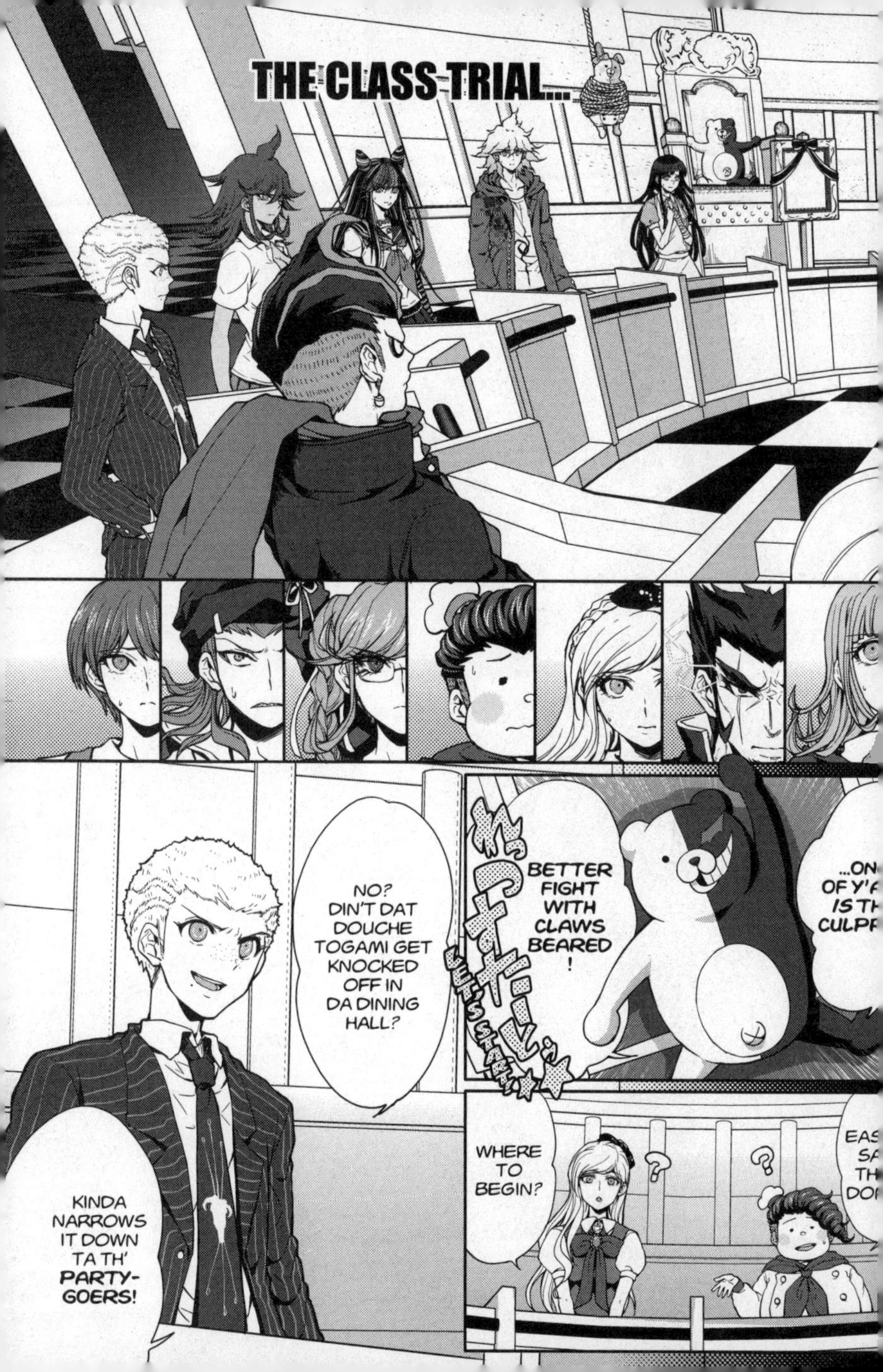
THE CLASS TRIAL...
...ON OF Y'A IS TH CULPR
BETTER FIGHT WITH CLAWS BEARED!
LET'S START!
EAS SA TH DO
WHERE TO BEGIN?
NO? DIN'T DAT DOUCHE TOGAMI GET KNOCKED OFF IN DA DINING HALL?
KINDA NARROWS IT DOWN TA TH' PARTY-GOERS!

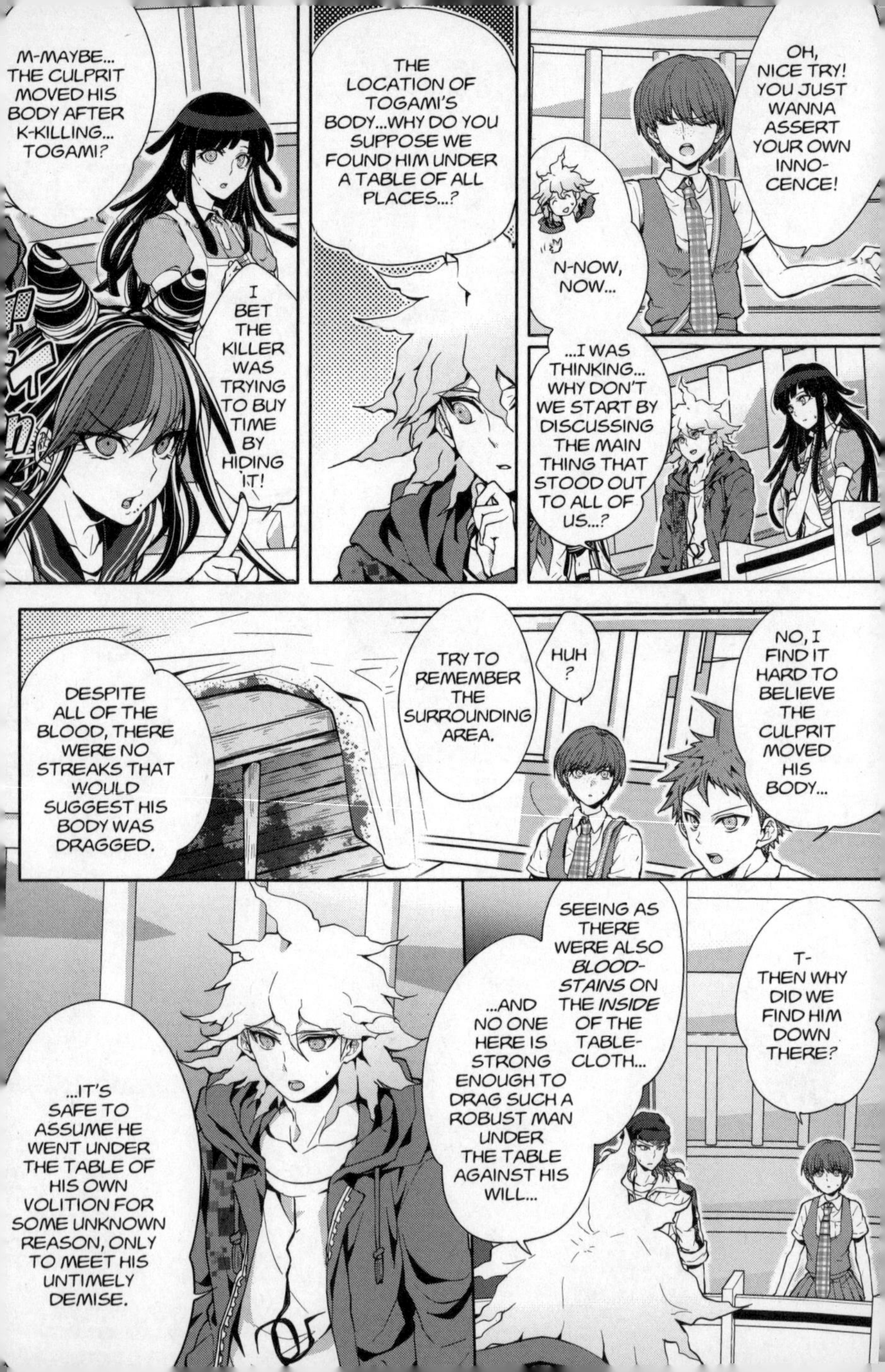

OH, NICE TRY! YOU JUST WANNA ASSERT YOUR OWN INNOCENCE!
N-NOW, NOW...
...I WAS THINKING... WHY DON'T WE START BY DISCUSSING THE MAIN THING THAT STOOD OUT TO ALL OF US...?
THE LOCATION OF TOGAMI'S BODY...WHY DO YOU SUPPOSE WE FOUND HIM UNDER A TABLE OF ALL PLACES...?
M-MAYBE... THE CULPRIT MOVED HIS BODY AFTER K-KILLING... TOGAMI?
I BET THE KILLER WAS TRYING TO BUY TIME BY HIDING IT!
NO, I FIND IT HARD TO BELIEVE THE CULPRIT MOVED HIS BODY...
HUH?
TRY TO REMEMBER THE SURROUNDING AREA.
DESPITE ALL OF THE BLOOD, THERE WERE NO STREAKS THAT WOULD SUGGEST HIS BODY WAS DRAGGED.
T-THEN WHY DID WE FIND HIM DOWN THERE?
SEEING AS THERE WERE ALSO *BLOOD-STAINS* ON THE *INSIDE* OF THE TABLE-CLOTH...
...AND NO ONE HERE IS STRONG ENOUGH TO DRAG SUCH A ROBUST MAN UNDER THE TABLE AGAINST HIS WILL...
...IT'S SAFE TO ASSUME HE WENT UNDER THE TABLE OF HIS OWN VOLITION FOR SOME UNKNOWN REASON, ONLY TO MEET HIS UNTIMELY DEMISE.

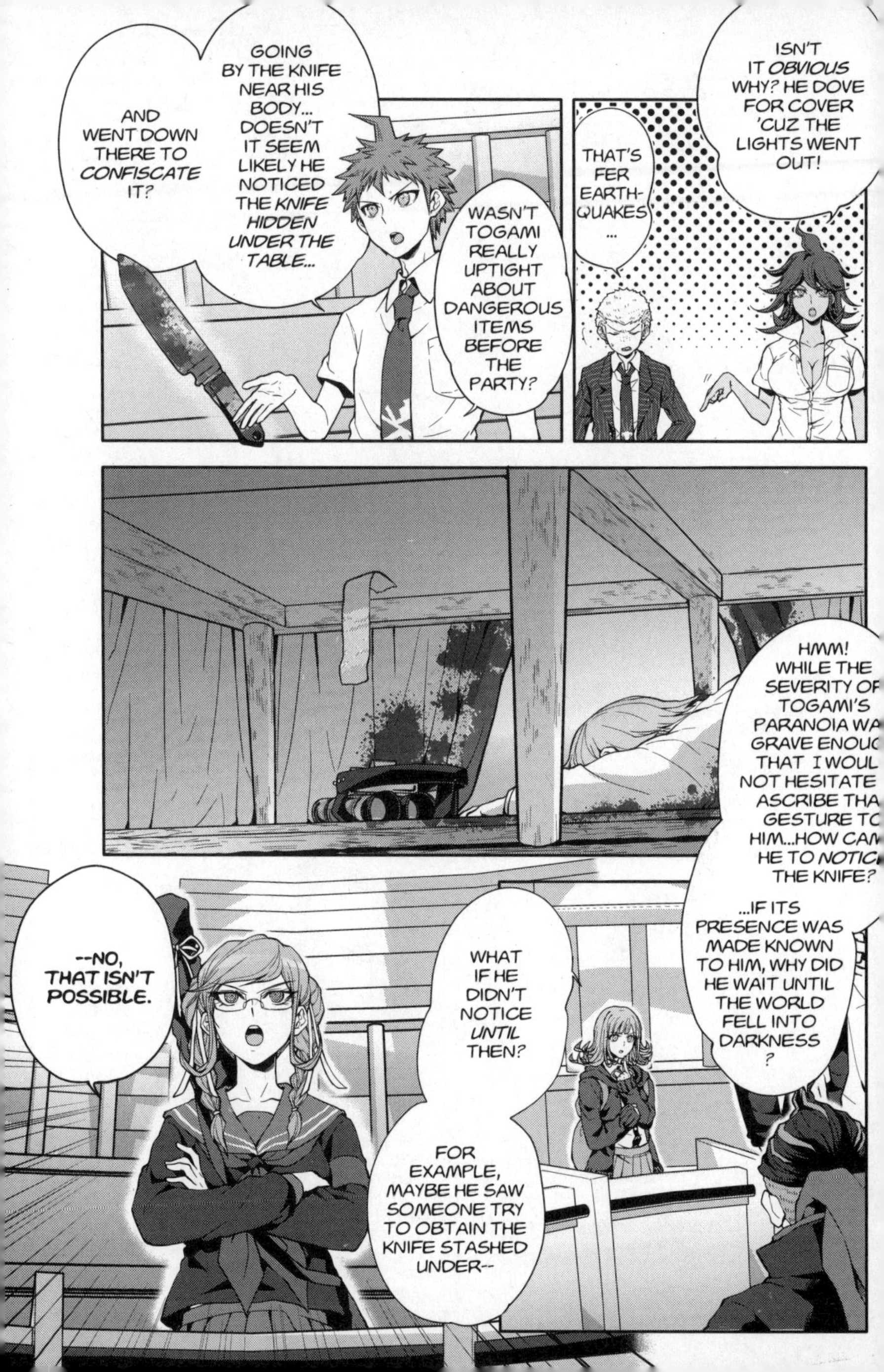
ISN'T IT *OBVIOUS* WHY? HE DOVE FOR COVER 'CUZ THE LIGHTS WENT OUT!
THAT'S FER EARTH-QUAKES...
WASN'T TOGAMI REALLY UPTIGHT ABOUT DANGEROUS ITEMS BEFORE THE PARTY?
GOING BY THE KNIFE NEAR HIS BODY... DOESN'T IT SEEM LIKELY HE NOTICED THE *KNIFE HIDDEN UNDER THE TABLE...*
AND WENT DOWN THERE TO *CONFISCATE* IT?
HMM! WHILE THE SEVERITY OF TOGAMI'S PARANOIA WA GRAVE ENOUG THAT I WOUL NOT HESITATE ASCRIBE THA GESTURE TO HIM...HOW CAM HE TO *NOTIC* THE KNIFE?
...IF ITS PRESENCE WAS MADE KNOWN TO HIM, WHY DID HE WAIT UNTIL THE WORLD FELL INTO DARKNESS?
WHAT IF HE DIDN'T NOTICE *UNTIL* THEN?
FOR EXAMPLE, MAYBE HE SAW SOMEONE TRY TO OBTAIN THE KNIFE STASHED UNDER--
--NO, THAT ISN'T POSSIBLE.

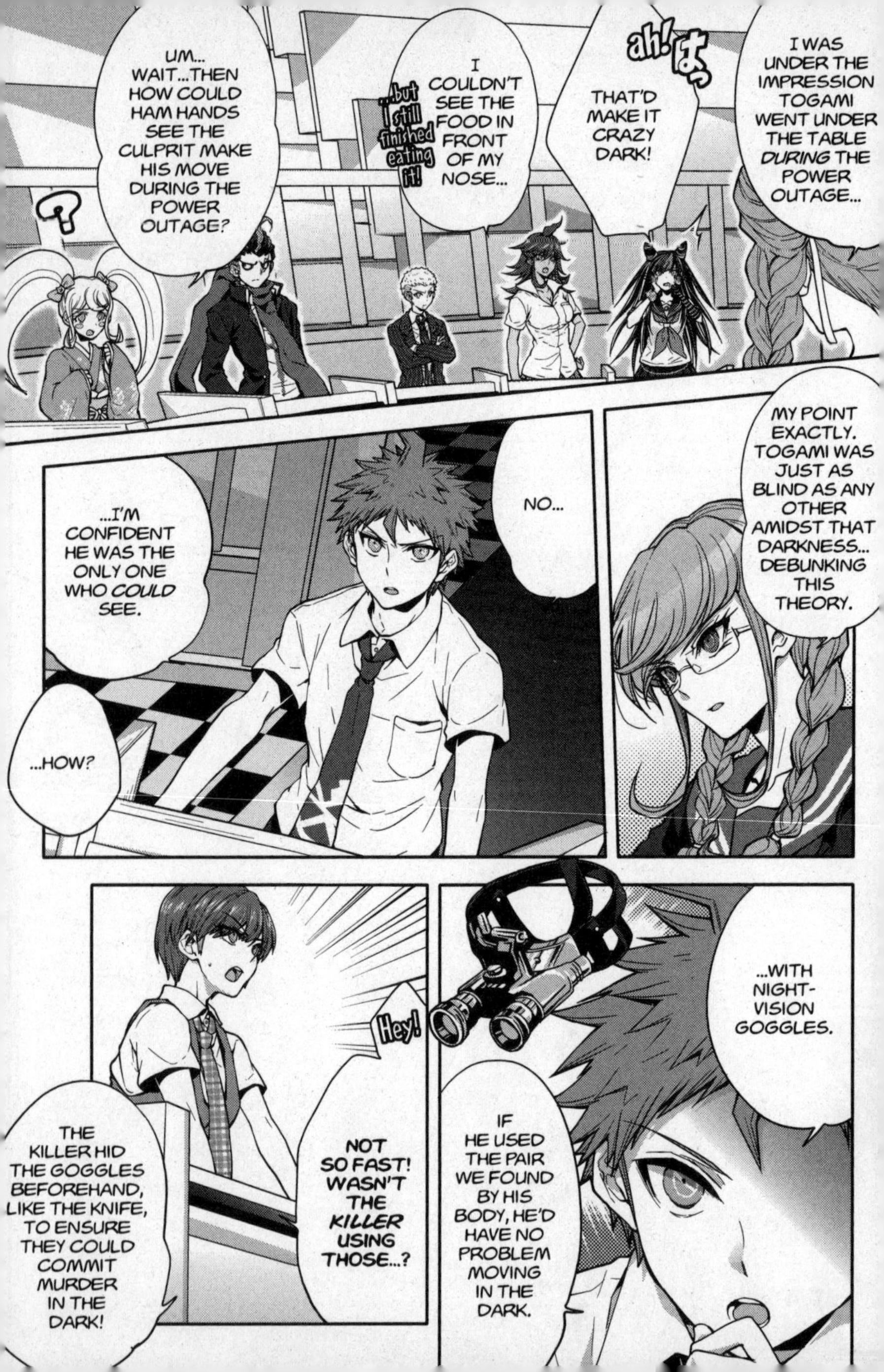
I WAS UNDER THE IMPRESSION TOGAMI WENT UNDER THE TABLE *DURING* THE POWER OUTAGE...
ah! はっ
THAT'D MAKE IT CRAZY DARK!
I COULDN'T SEE THE FOOD IN FRONT OF MY NOSE...
...but I still finished eating it!
UM... WAIT...THEN HOW COULD HAM HANDS SEE THE CULPRIT MAKE HIS MOVE DURING THE POWER OUTAGE?
?
MY POINT EXACTLY. TOGAMI WAS JUST AS BLIND AS ANY OTHER AMIDST THAT DARKNESS... DEBUNKING THIS THEORY.
NO...
...I'M CONFIDENT HE WAS THE ONLY ONE WHO *COULD* SEE.
...HOW?
...WITH NIGHT-VISION GOGGLES.
IF HE USED THE PAIR WE FOUND BY HIS BODY, HE'D HAVE NO PROBLEM MOVING IN THE DARK.
Hey!
NOT SO FAST! WASN'T THE *KILLER* USING THOSE...?
THE KILLER HID THE GOGGLES BEFOREHAND, LIKE THE KNIFE, TO ENSURE THEY COULD COMMIT MURDER IN THE DARK!

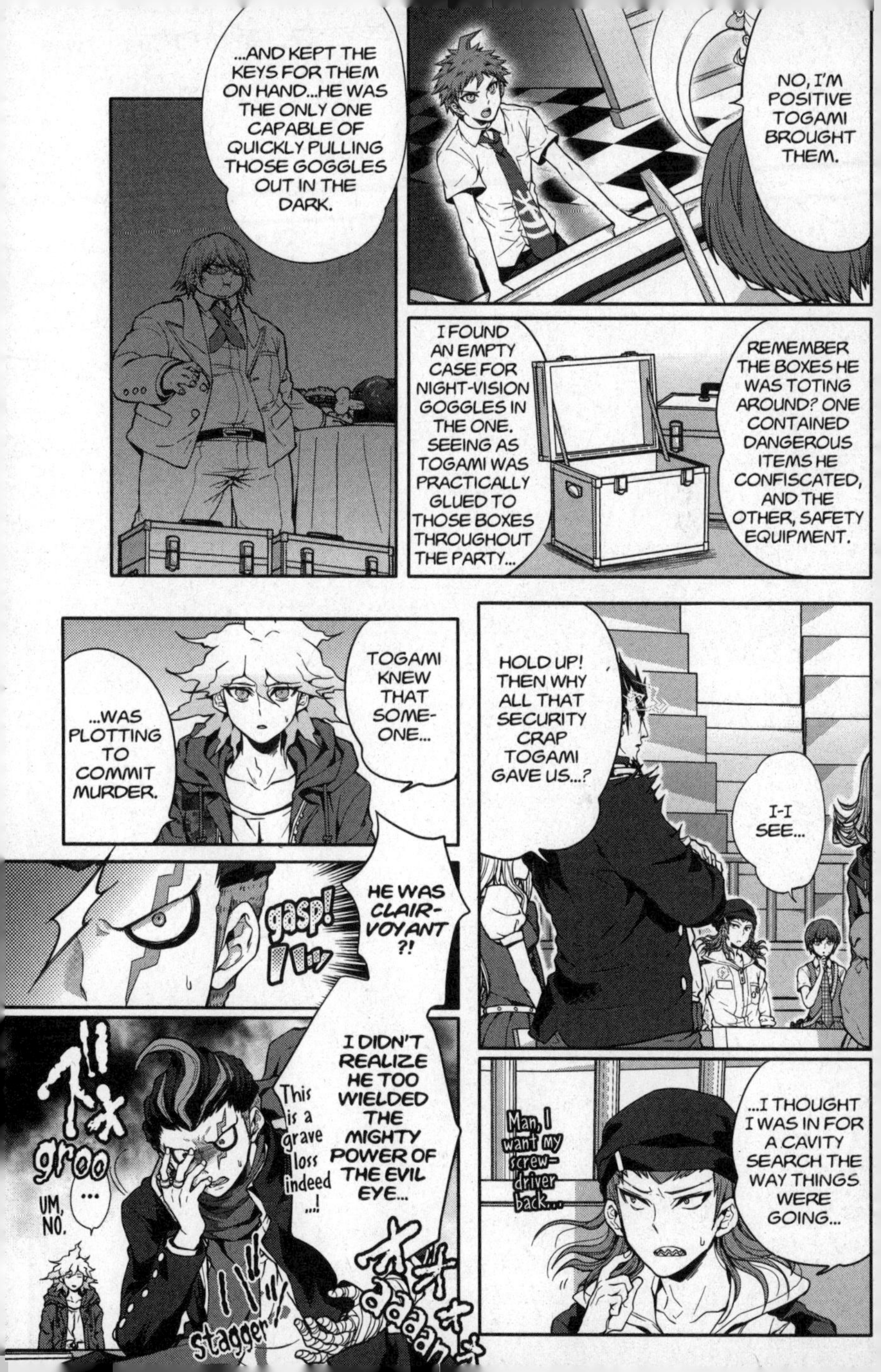

NO, I'M POSITIVE TOGAMI BROUGHT THEM.
REMEMBER THE BOXES HE WAS TOTING AROUND? ONE CONTAINED DANGEROUS ITEMS HE CONFISCATED, AND THE OTHER, SAFETY EQUIPMENT.
I FOUND AN EMPTY CASE FOR NIGHT-VISION GOGGLES IN THE ONE. SEEING AS TOGAMI WAS PRACTICALLY GLUED TO THOSE BOXES THROUGHOUT THE PARTY...
...AND KEPT THE KEYS FOR THEM ON HAND...HE WAS THE ONLY ONE CAPABLE OF QUICKLY PULLING THOSE GOGGLES OUT IN THE DARK.
HOLD UP! THEN WHY ALL THAT SECURITY CRAP TOGAMI GAVE US...?
I-I SEE...
TOGAMI KNEW THAT SOME-ONE...
...WAS PLOTTING TO COMMIT MURDER.
HE WAS CLAIR-VOYANT?!
gasp!
...I THOUGHT I WAS IN FOR A CAVITY SEARCH THE WAY THINGS WERE GOING...
Man, I want my screw-driver back...
I DIDN'T REALIZE HE TOO WIELDED THE MIGHTY POWER OF THE EVIL EYE...
This is a grave loss indeed...!
groo...
UM, NO.
stagger
dodan

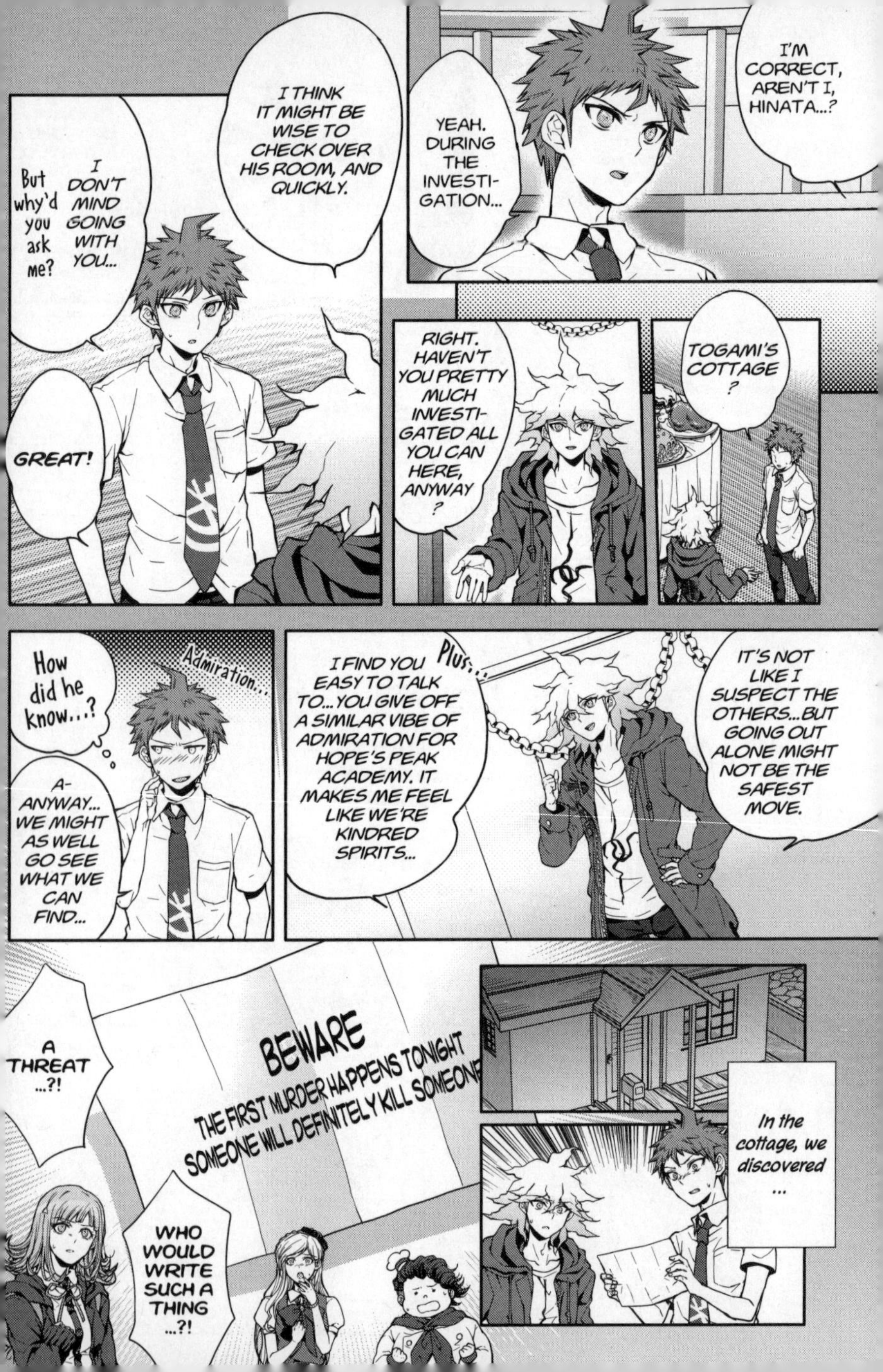
I'M CORRECT, AREN'T I, HINATA...?
YEAH. DURING THE INVESTIGATION...
TOGAMI'S COTTAGE ?
RIGHT. HAVEN'T YOU PRETTY MUCH INVESTIGATED ALL YOU CAN HERE, ANYWAY ?
I THINK IT MIGHT BE WISE TO CHECK OVER HIS ROOM, AND QUICKLY.
I DON'T MIND GOING WITH YOU...
But why'd you ask me?
GREAT!
IT'S NOT LIKE I SUSPECT THE OTHERS...BUT GOING OUT ALONE MIGHT NOT BE THE SAFEST MOVE.
Plus...
I FIND YOU EASY TO TALK TO...YOU GIVE OFF A SIMILAR VIBE OF ADMIRATION FOR HOPE'S PEAK ACADEMY. IT MAKES ME FEEL LIKE WE'RE KINDRED SPIRITS...
Admiration...
How did he know...?
A-ANYWAY... WE MIGHT AS WELL GO SEE WHAT WE CAN FIND...
In the cottage, we discovered ...
BEWARE
THE FIRST MURDER HAPPENS TONIGHT
SOMEONE WILL DEFINITELY KILL SOMEONE
A THREAT ...?!
WHO WOULD WRITE SUCH A THING ...?!

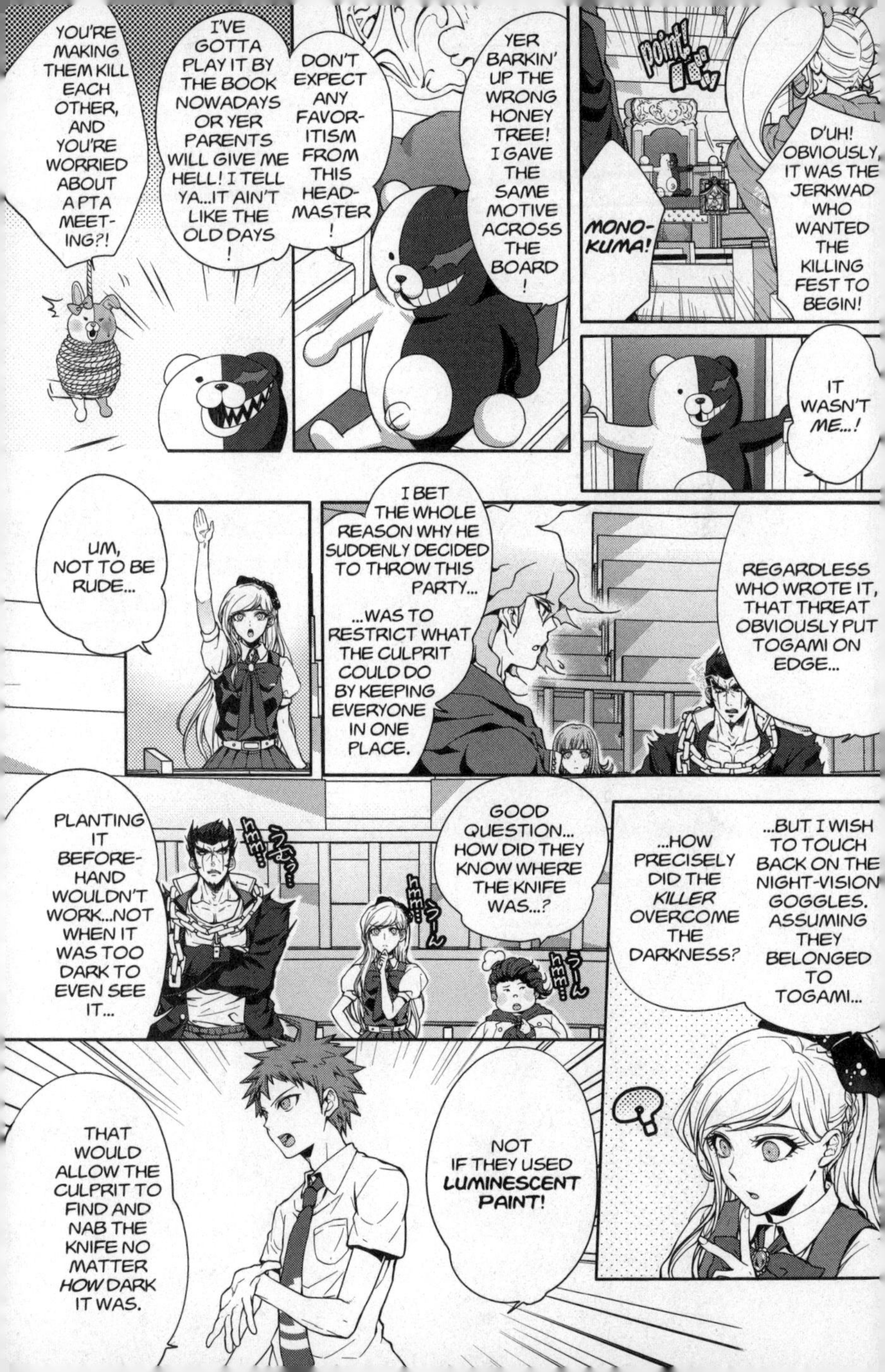

point!
D'UH! OBVIOUSLY, IT WAS THE JERKWAD WHO WANTED THE KILLING FEST TO BEGIN!
MONOKUMA!
IT WASN'T *ME*...!
YER BARKIN' UP THE WRONG HONEY TREE! I GAVE THE SAME MOTIVE ACROSS THE BOARD!
DON'T EXPECT ANY FAVORITISM FROM THIS HEADMASTER!
I'VE GOTTA PLAY IT BY THE BOOK NOWADAYS OR YER PARENTS WILL GIVE ME HELL! I TELL YA...IT AIN'T LIKE THE OLD DAYS!
YOU'RE MAKING THEM KILL EACH OTHER, AND YOU'RE WORRIED ABOUT A PTA MEETING?!
REGARDLESS WHO WROTE IT, THAT THREAT OBVIOUSLY PUT TOGAMI ON EDGE...
I BET THE WHOLE REASON WHY HE SUDDENLY DECIDED TO THROW THIS PARTY...
...WAS TO RESTRICT WHAT THE CULPRIT COULD DO BY KEEPING EVERYONE IN ONE PLACE.
UM, NOT TO BE RUDE...
...BUT I WISH TO TOUCH BACK ON THE NIGHT-VISION GOGGLES. ASSUMING THEY BELONGED TO TOGAMI...
...HOW PRECISELY DID THE *KILLER* OVERCOME THE DARKNESS?
hmm...
hmm...
GOOD QUESTION... HOW DID THEY KNOW WHERE THE KNIFE WAS...?
hmm...
PLANTING IT BEFOREHAND WOULDN'T WORK...NOT WHEN IT WAS TOO DARK TO EVEN SEE IT...
?
NOT IF THEY USED **LUMINESCENT PAINT**!
THAT WOULD ALLOW THE CULPRIT TO FIND AND NAB THE KNIFE NO MATTER *HOW* DARK IT WAS.

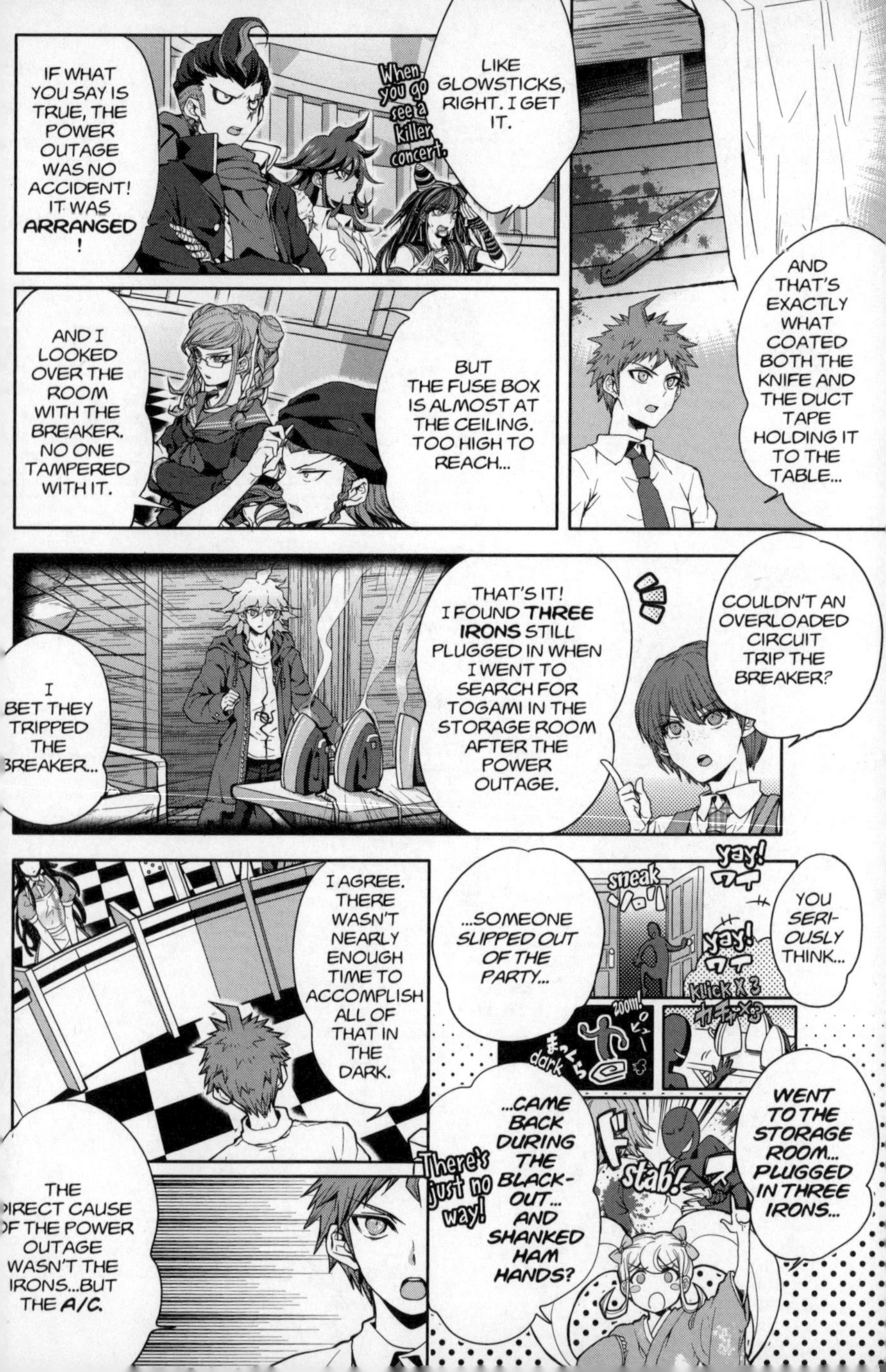
AND THAT'S EXACTLY WHAT COATED BOTH THE KNIFE AND THE DUCT TAPE HOLDING IT TO THE TABLE...
LIKE GLOWSTICKS, RIGHT. I GET IT.
When you go see a killer concert.
IF WHAT YOU SAY IS TRUE, THE POWER OUTAGE WAS NO ACCIDENT! IT WAS **ARRANGED**!
BUT THE FUSE BOX IS ALMOST AT THE CEILING. TOO HIGH TO REACH...
AND I LOOKED OVER THE ROOM WITH THE BREAKER. NO ONE TAMPERED WITH IT.
COULDN'T AN OVERLOADED CIRCUIT TRIP THE BREAKER?
THAT'S IT! I FOUND **THREE IRONS** STILL PLUGGED IN WHEN I WENT TO SEARCH FOR TOGAMI IN THE STORAGE ROOM AFTER THE POWER OUTAGE.
I BET THEY TRIPPED THE REAKER...
YOU SERI-OUSLY THINK...
yay! ワイ
yay! ワイ
sneak ノロ
...SOMEONE SLIPPED OUT OF THE PARTY...
klick X 3 カチャ×3
zoom! ピュー
まっくら dark
WENT TO THE STORAGE ROOM... PLUGGED IN THREE IRONS...
stab! ドス
...CAME BACK DURING THE BLACK-OUT... AND SHANKED HAM HANDS?
There's just no way!
I AGREE. THERE WASN'T NEARLY ENOUGH TIME TO ACCOMPLISH ALL OF THAT IN THE DARK.
THE IRECT CAUSE F THE POWER OUTAGE WASN'T THE IRONS...BUT THE *A/C*.

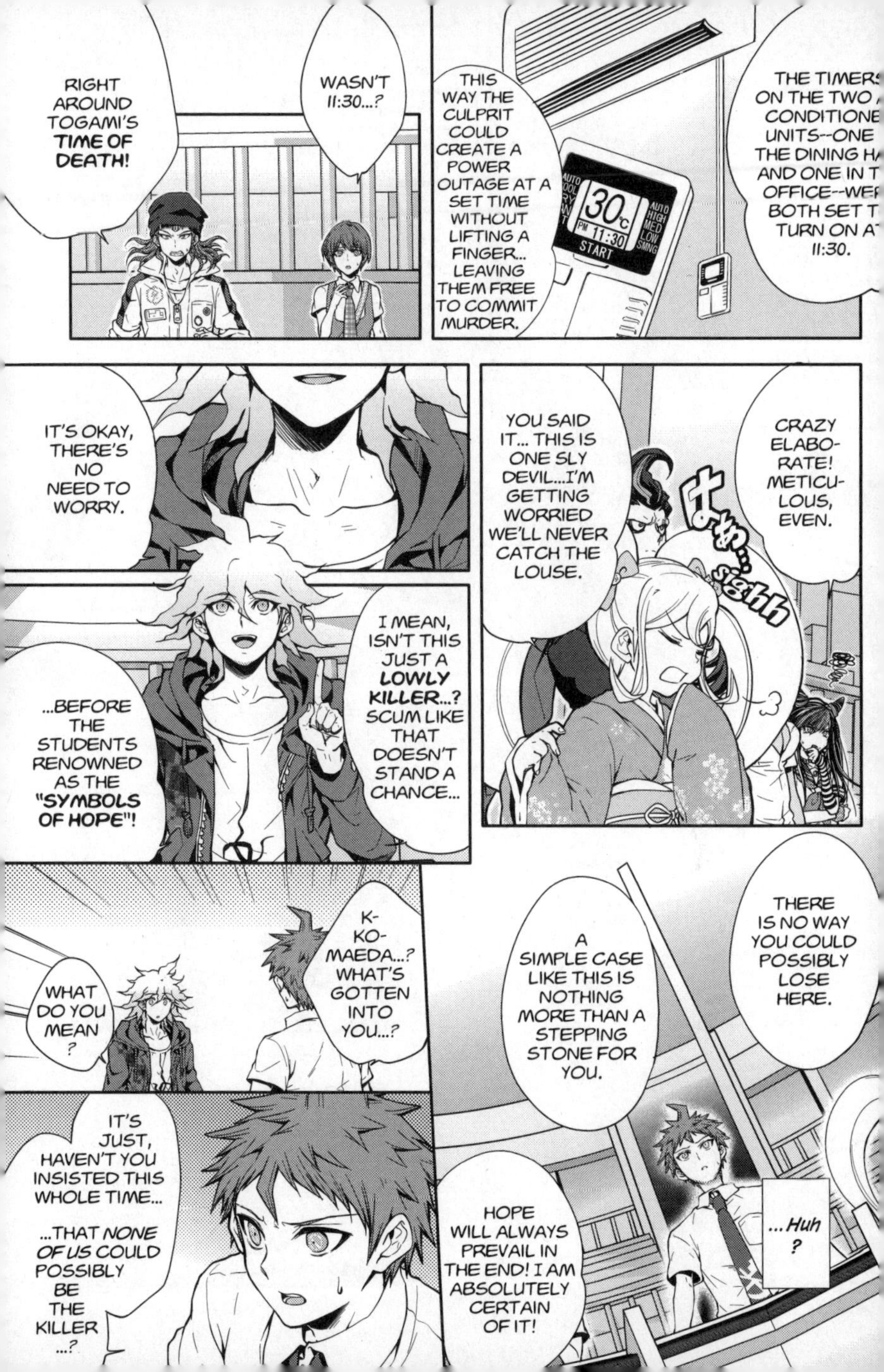
THE TIMERS ON THE TWO A CONDITIONE UNITS--ONE THE DINING HA AND ONE IN T OFFICE--WER BOTH SET T TURN ON AT 11:30.
30°C
PM 11:30
START
AUTO HIGH MED LOW SMNG
THIS WAY THE CULPRIT COULD CREATE A POWER OUTAGE AT A SET TIME WITHOUT LIFTING A FINGER... LEAVING THEM FREE TO COMMIT MURDER.
WASN'T 11:30...?
RIGHT AROUND TOGAMI'S **TIME OF DEATH**!
CRAZY ELABO-RATE! METICU-LOUS, EVEN.
はぁ… sighh
YOU SAID IT... THIS IS ONE SLY DEVIL...I'M GETTING WORRIED WE'LL NEVER CATCH THE LOUSE.
IT'S OKAY, THERE'S NO NEED TO WORRY.
I MEAN, ISN'T THIS JUST A **LOWLY KILLER**...? SCUM LIKE THAT DOESN'T STAND A CHANCE...
...BEFORE THE STUDENTS RENOWNED AS THE **"SYMBOLS OF HOPE"**!
THERE IS NO WAY YOU COULD POSSIBLY LOSE HERE.
A SIMPLE CASE LIKE THIS IS NOTHING MORE THAN A STEPPING STONE FOR YOU.
HOPE WILL ALWAYS PREVAIL IN THE END! I AM ABSOLUTELY CERTAIN OF IT!
...Huh?
K-KO-MAEDA...? WHAT'S GOTTEN INTO YOU...?
WHAT DO YOU MEAN?
IT'S JUST, HAVEN'T YOU INSISTED THIS WHOLE TIME...
...THAT *NONE OF US* COULD POSSIBLY BE THE KILLER...?

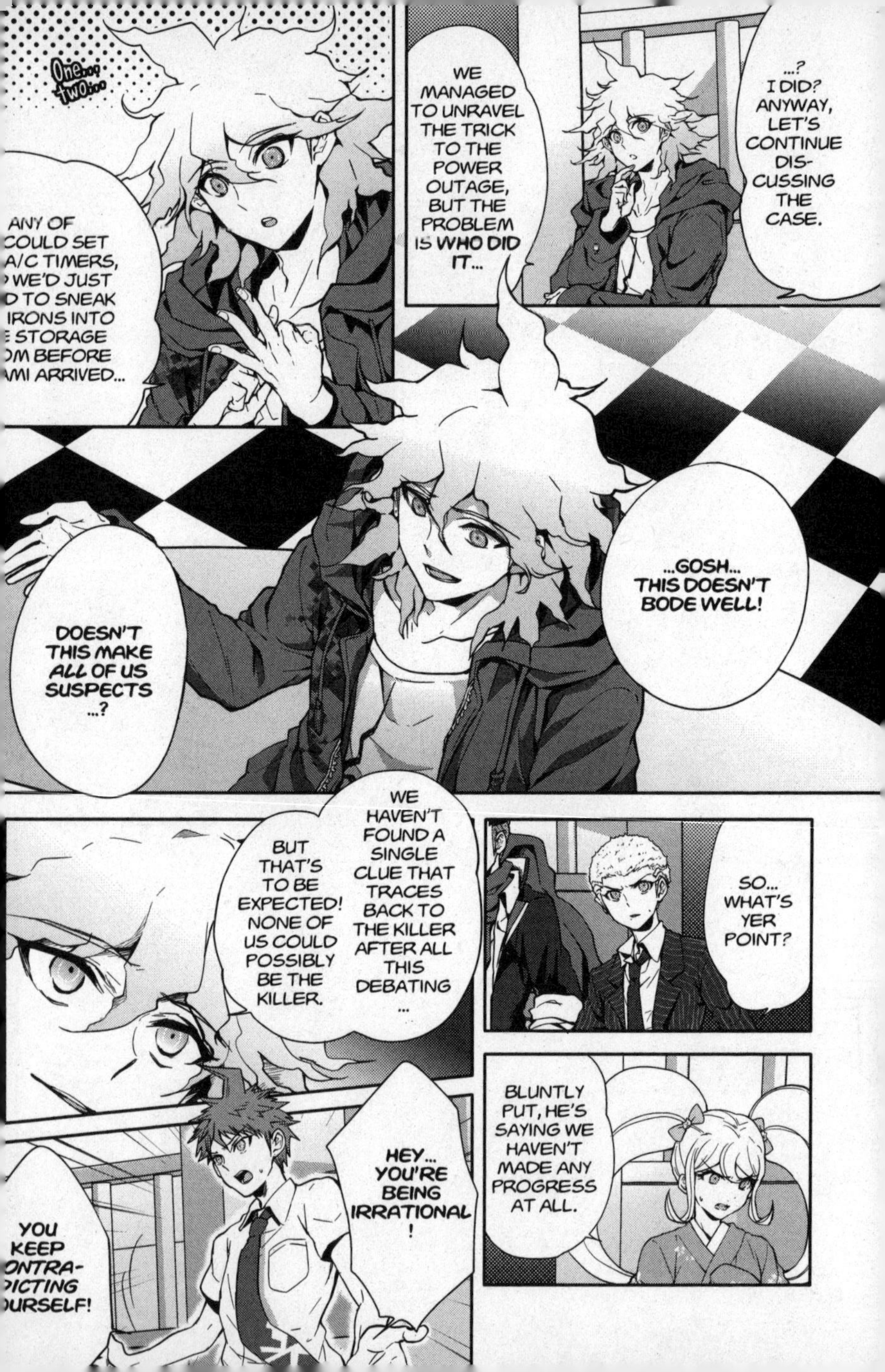

One… two…
ANY OF COULD SET A/C TIMERS, WE'D JUST D TO SNEAK IRONS INTO E STORAGE OM BEFORE AMI ARRIVED…
WE MANAGED TO UNRAVEL THE TRICK TO THE POWER OUTAGE, BUT THE PROBLEM IS **WHO DID IT**…
…? I DID? ANYWAY, LET'S CONTINUE DIS-CUSSING THE CASE.
DOESN'T THIS MAKE ***ALL*** OF US SUSPECTS …?
…GOSH… THIS DOESN'T BODE WELL!
WE HAVEN'T FOUND A SINGLE CLUE THAT TRACES BACK TO THE KILLER AFTER ALL THIS DEBATING …
BUT THAT'S TO BE EXPECTED! NONE OF US COULD POSSIBLY BE THE KILLER.
SO… WHAT'S YER POINT?
BLUNTLY PUT, HE'S SAYING WE HAVEN'T MADE ANY PROGRESS AT ALL.
HEY… YOU'RE BEING IRRATIONAL !
YOU KEEP ONTRA-DICTING OURSELF!

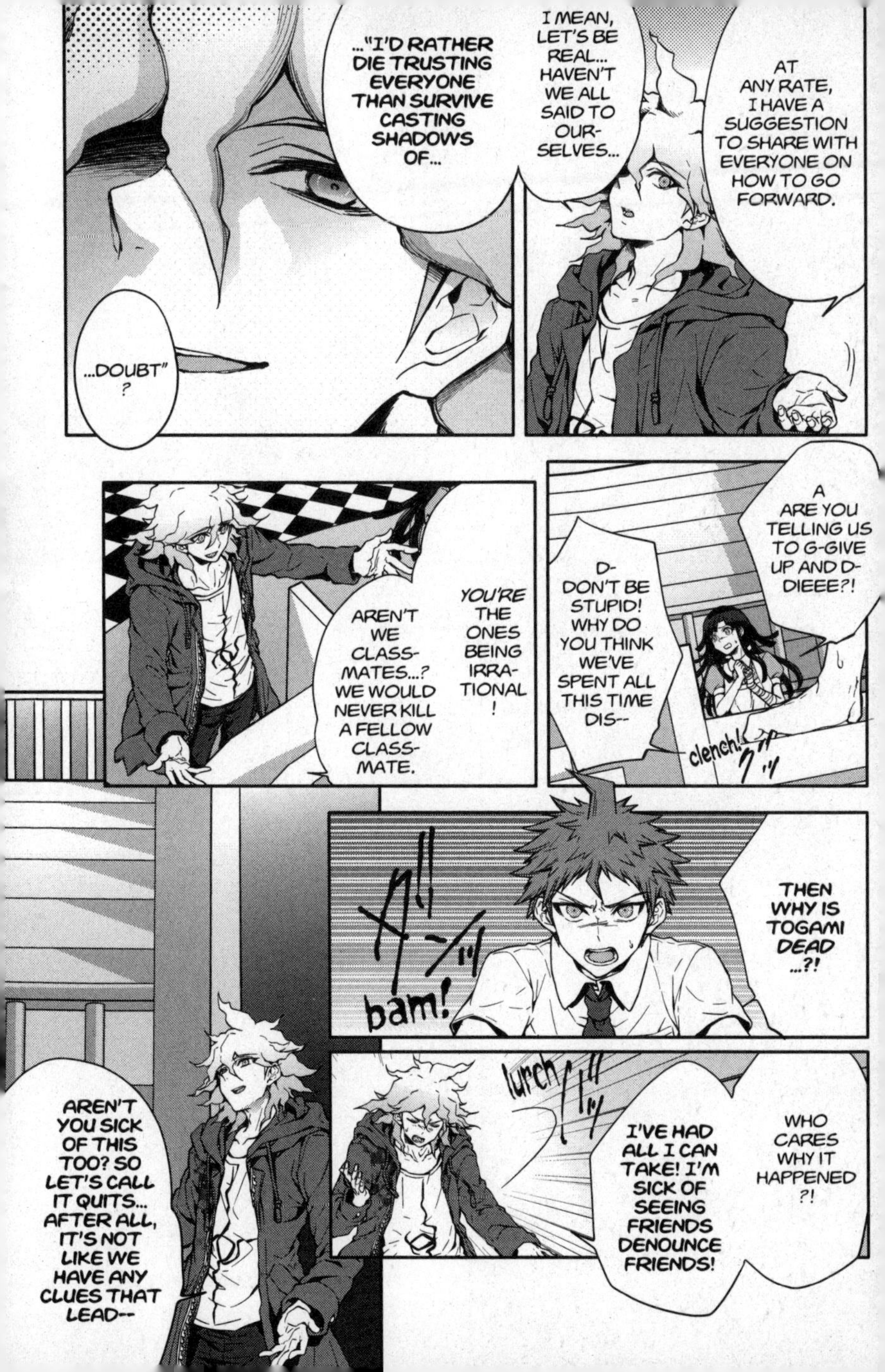
AT ANY RATE, I HAVE A SUGGESTION TO SHARE WITH EVERYONE ON HOW TO GO FORWARD.
I MEAN, LET'S BE REAL... HAVEN'T WE ALL SAID TO OURSELVES...
..."I'D RATHER DIE TRUSTING EVERYONE THAN SURVIVE CASTING SHADOWS OF...
...DOUBT"?
A ARE YOU TELLING US TO G-GIVE UP AND D-DIEEE?!
D-DON'T BE STUPID! WHY DO YOU THINK WE'VE SPENT ALL THIS TIME DIS--
clench!
YOU'RE THE ONES BEING IRRATIONAL!
AREN'T WE CLASSMATES...? WE WOULD NEVER KILL A FELLOW CLASSMATE.
THEN WHY IS TOGAMI DEAD...?!
bam!
WHO CARES WHY IT HAPPENED?!
I'VE HAD ALL I CAN TAKE! I'M SICK OF SEEING FRIENDS DENOUNCE FRIENDS!
lurch
AREN'T YOU SICK OF THIS TOO? SO LET'S CALL IT QUITS... AFTER ALL, IT'S NOT LIKE WE HAVE ANY CLUES THAT LEAD--

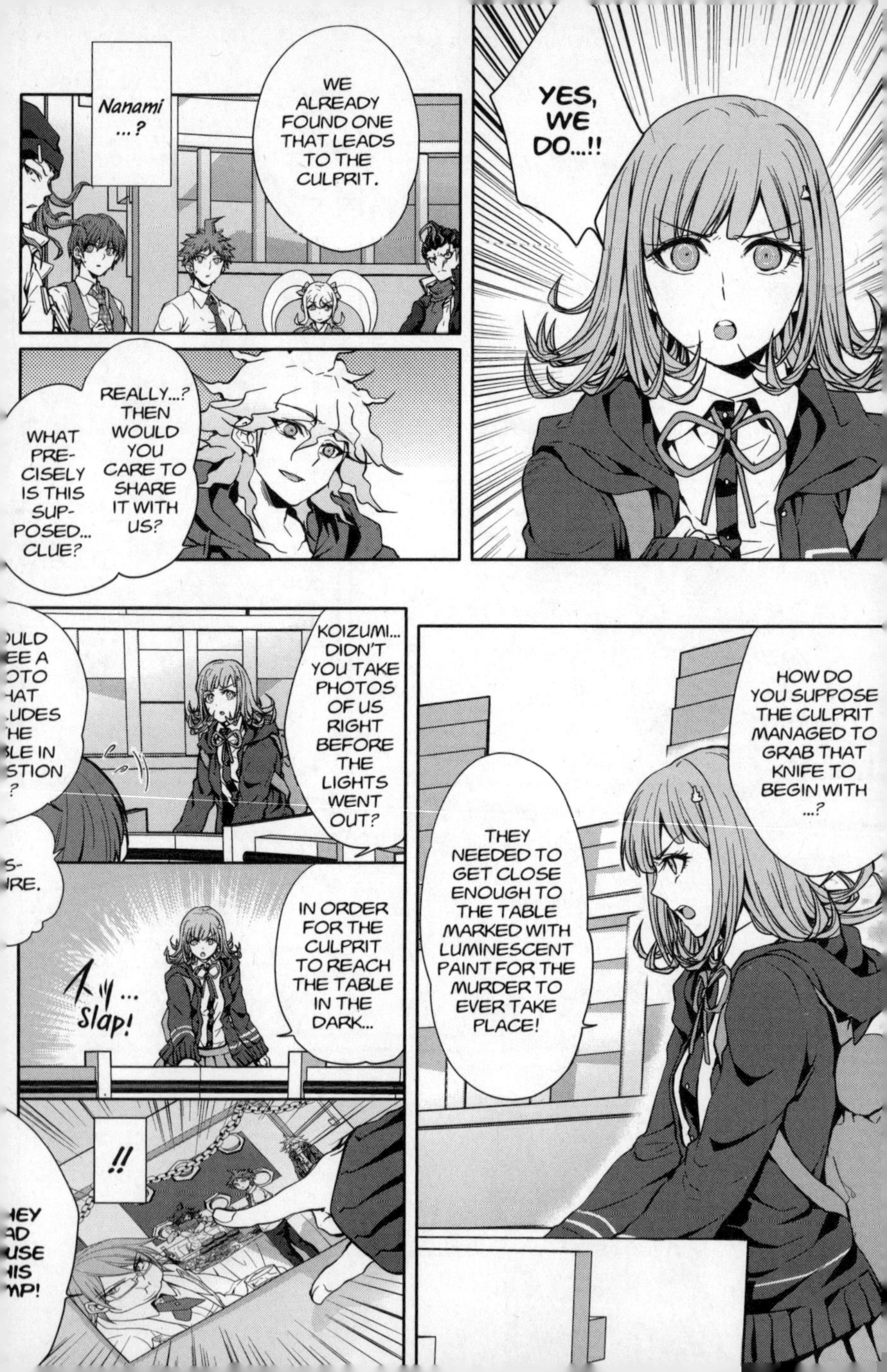
YES, WE DO...!!
Nanami ...?
WE ALREADY FOUND ONE THAT LEADS TO THE CULPRIT.
REALLY...? THEN WOULD YOU CARE TO SHARE IT WITH US?
WHAT PRECISELY IS THIS SUPPOSED... CLUE?
HOW DO YOU SUPPOSE THE CULPRIT MANAGED TO GRAB THAT KNIFE TO BEGIN WITH ...?
THEY NEEDED TO GET CLOSE ENOUGH TO THE TABLE MARKED WITH LUMINESCENT PAINT FOR THE MURDER TO EVER TAKE PLACE!
KOIZUMI... DIDN'T YOU TAKE PHOTOS OF US RIGHT BEFORE THE LIGHTS WENT OUT?
IN ORDER FOR THE CULPRIT TO REACH THE TABLE IN THE DARK...
スッ... slap!
!!

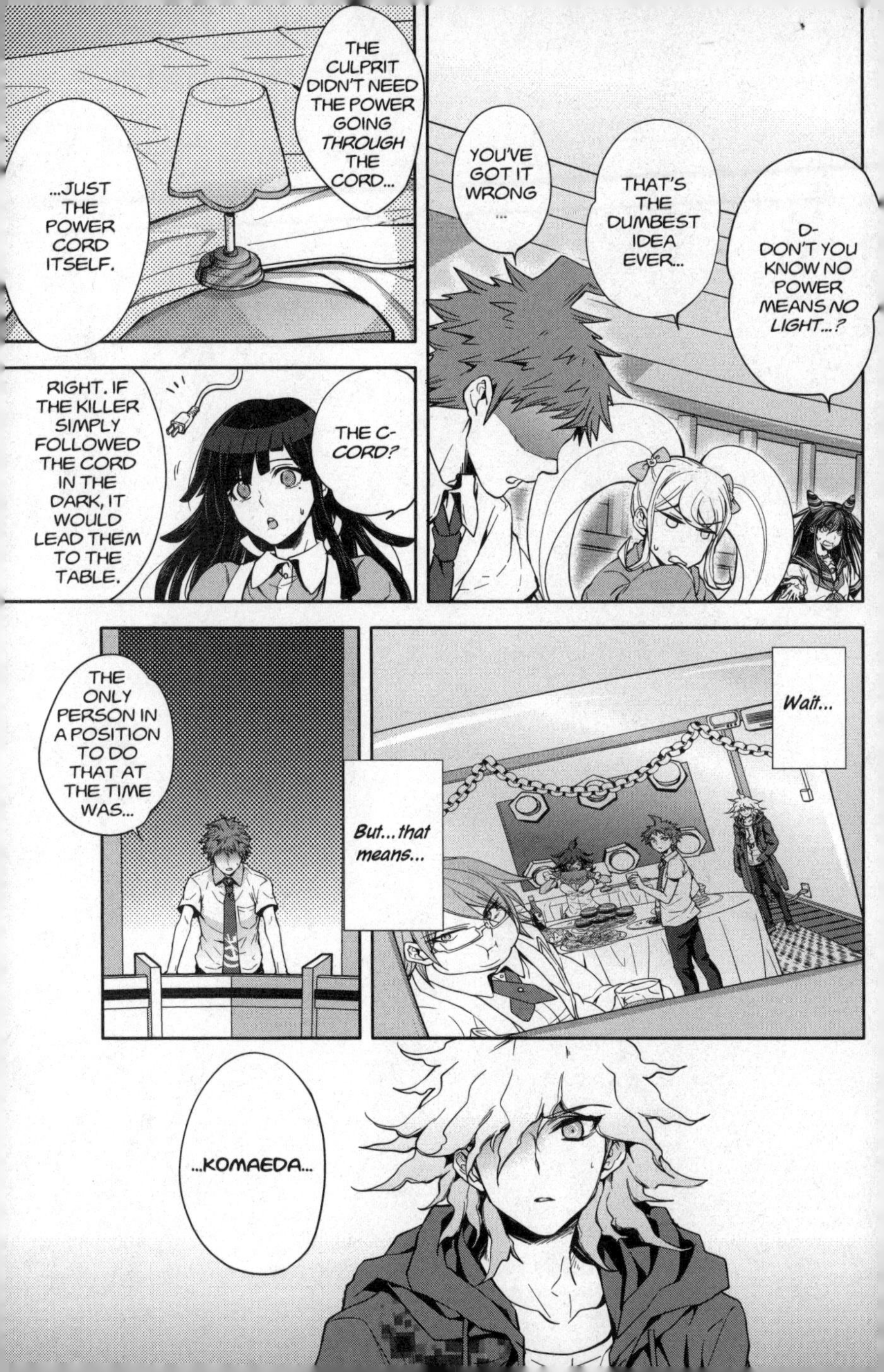
D- DON'T YOU KNOW NO POWER MEANS NO LIGHT...?
THAT'S THE DUMBEST IDEA EVER...
YOU'VE GOT IT WRONG ...
THE CULPRIT DIDN'T NEED THE POWER GOING *THROUGH* THE CORD...
...JUST THE POWER CORD ITSELF.
THE C-CORD?
RIGHT. IF THE KILLER SIMPLY FOLLOWED THE CORD IN THE DARK, IT WOULD LEAD THEM TO THE TABLE.
Wait...
But...that means...
THE ONLY PERSON IN A POSITION TO DO THAT AT THE TIME WAS...
...KOMAEDA...

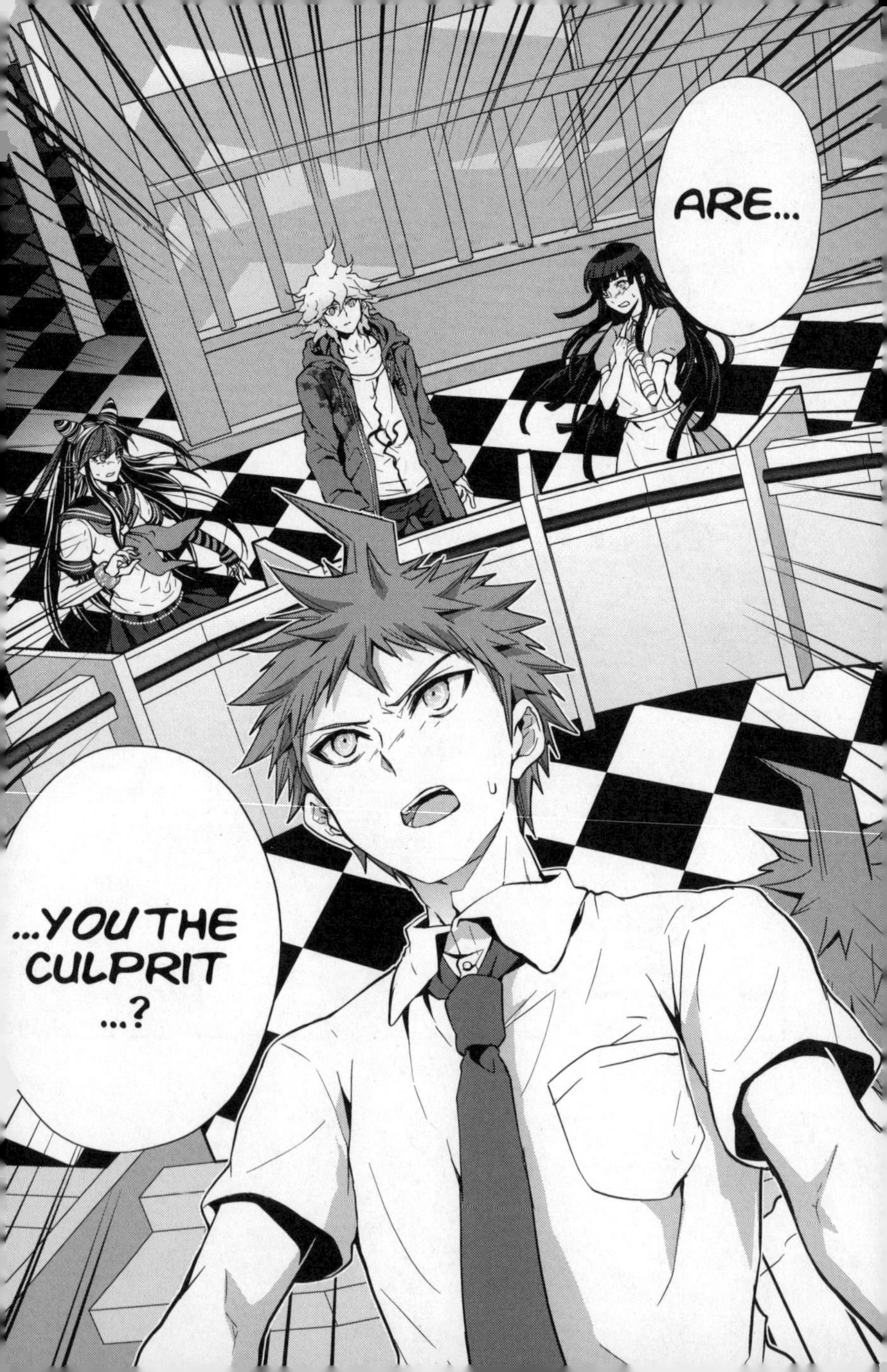
ARE...
...YOU THE CULPRIT ...?

DANGAN
RONPA 2
GOODBYE
DESPAIR

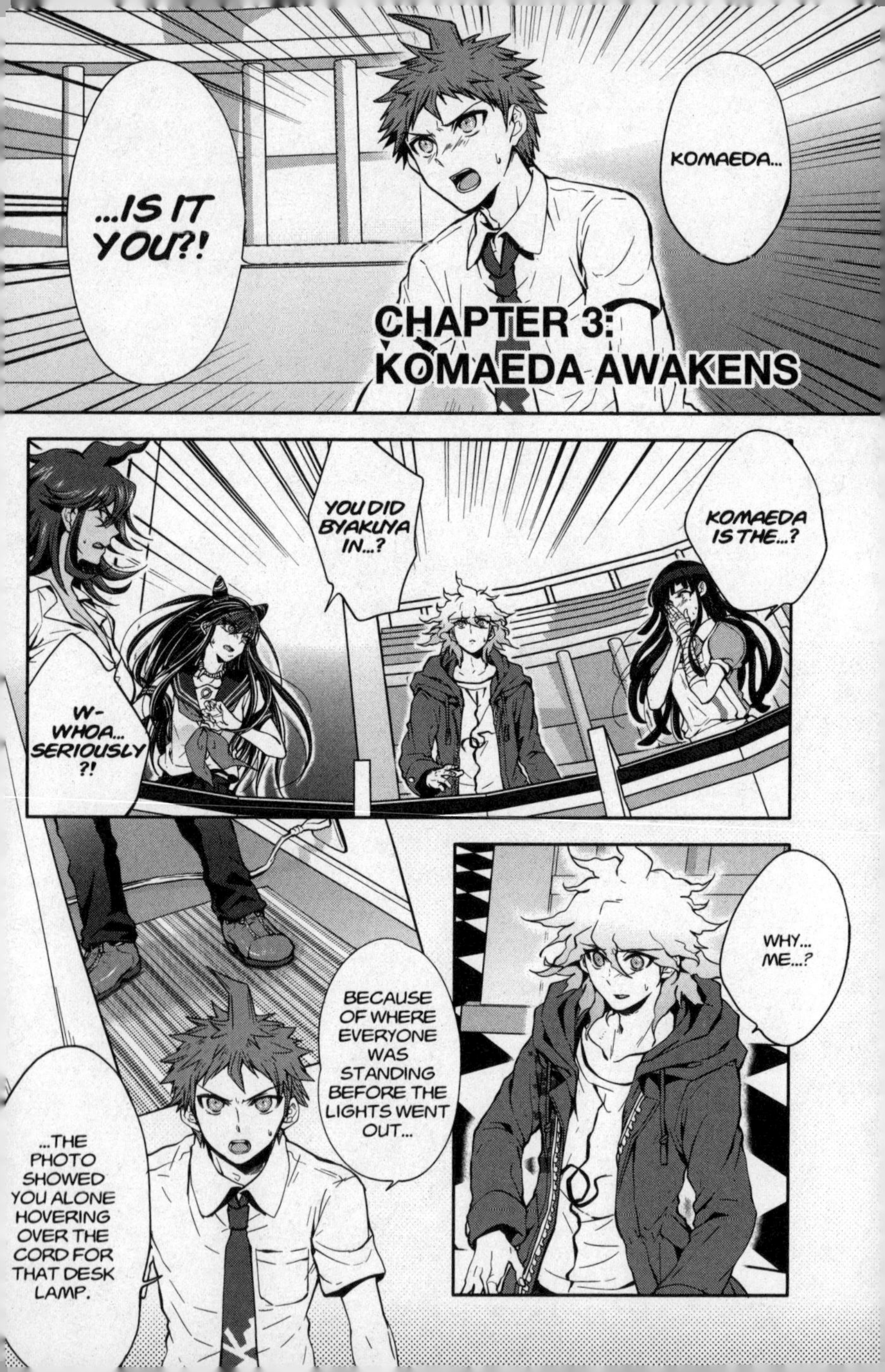
KOMAEDA...
...IS IT YOU?!
CHAPTER 3: KOMAEDA AWAKENS
KOMAEDA IS THE...?
YOU DID BYAKUYA IN...?
W-WHOA... SERIOUSLY?!
WHY... ME...?
BECAUSE OF WHERE EVERYONE WAS STANDING BEFORE THE LIGHTS WENT OUT...
...THE PHOTO SHOWED YOU ALONE HOVERING OVER THE CORD FOR THAT DESK LAMP.

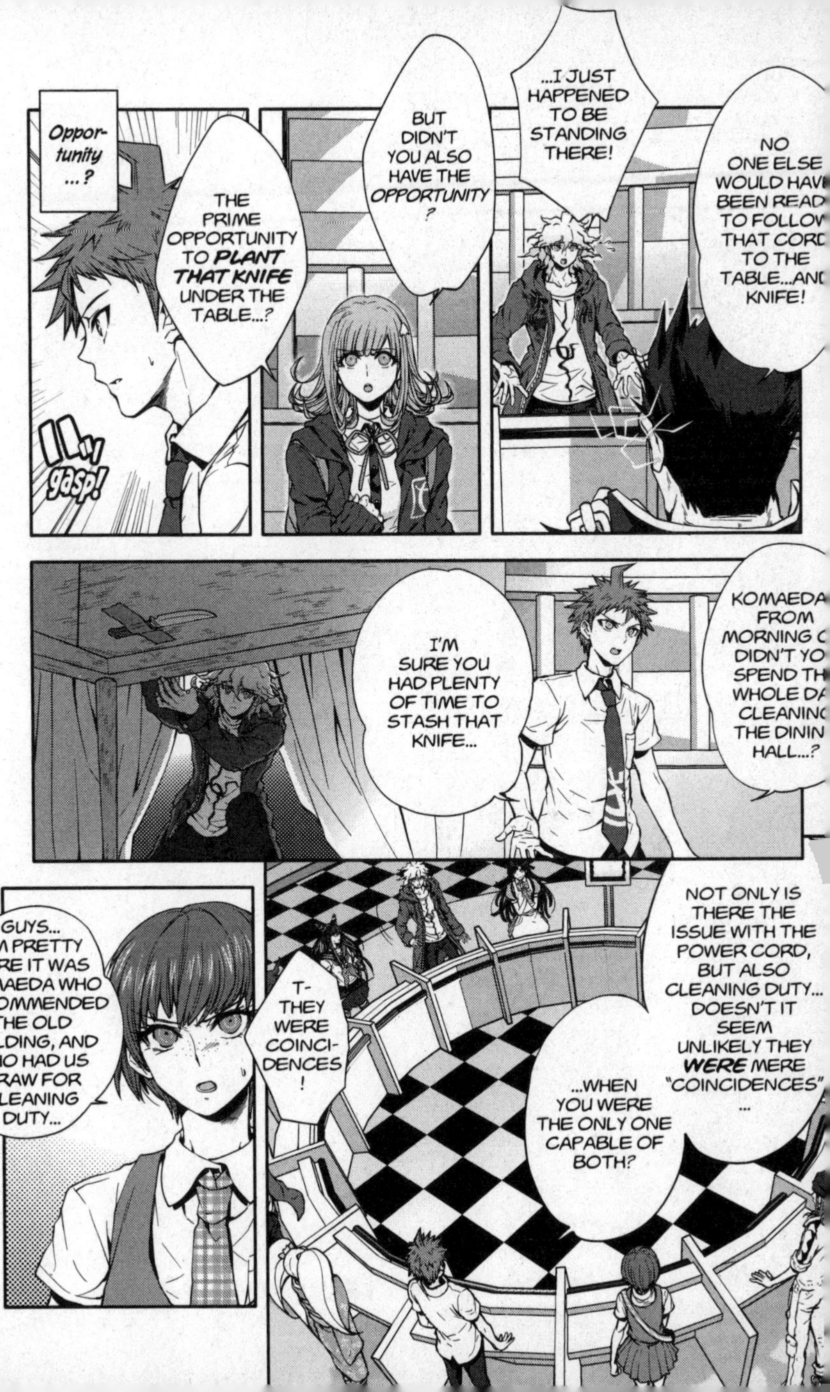
NO ONE ELSE WOULD HAV BEEN READ TO FOLLOW THAT CORD TO THE TABLE...AN KNIFE!
...I JUST HAPPENED TO BE STANDING THERE!
BUT DIDN'T YOU ALSO HAVE THE *OPPORTUNITY* ?
THE PRIME OPPORTUNITY TO ***PLANT THAT KNIFE*** UNDER THE TABLE...?
Opportunity ...?
gasp!
KOMAEDA FROM MORNING C DIDN'T YO SPEND TH WHOLE DA CLEANIN THE DININ HALL...?
I'M SURE YOU HAD PLENTY OF TIME TO STASH THAT KNIFE...
NOT ONLY IS THERE THE ISSUE WITH THE POWER CORD, BUT ALSO CLEANING DUTY... DOESN'T IT SEEM UNLIKELY THEY ***WERE*** MERE "COINCIDENCES" ...
...WHEN YOU WERE THE ONLY ONE CAPABLE OF BOTH?
T- THEY WERE COINCIDENCES !
GUYS... I'M PRETTY SURE IT WAS KOMAEDA WHO RECOMMENDED THE OLD BUILDING, AND WHO HAD US DRAW FOR CLEANING DUTY...

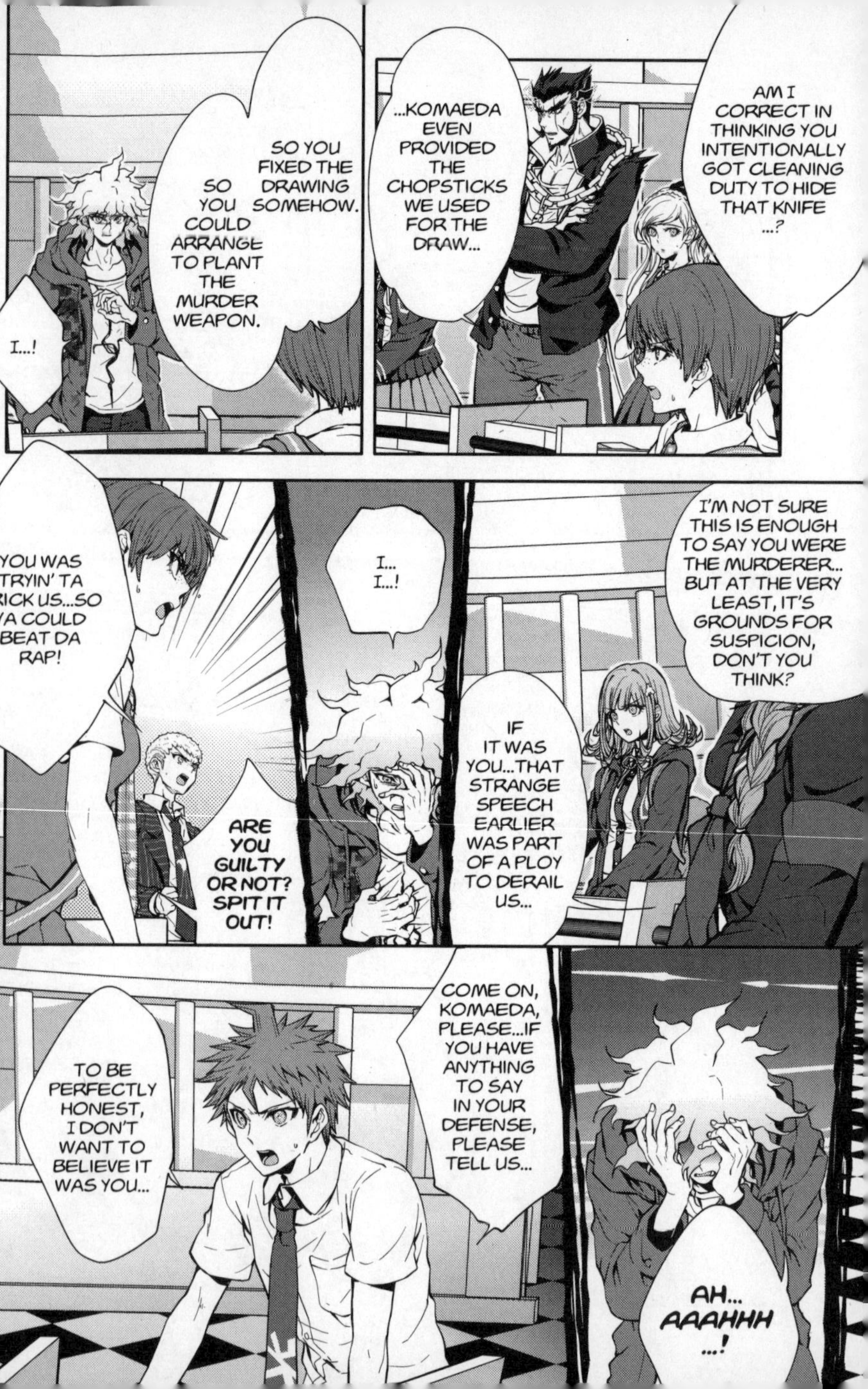
AM I CORRECT IN THINKING YOU INTENTIONALLY GOT CLEANING DUTY TO HIDE THAT KNIFE ...?
...KOMAEDA EVEN PROVIDED THE CHOPSTICKS WE USED FOR THE DRAW...
SO YOU FIXED THE DRAWING SOMEHOW.
SO YOU COULD ARRANGE TO PLANT THE MURDER WEAPON.
I...!
I'M NOT SURE THIS IS ENOUGH TO SAY YOU WERE THE MURDERER... BUT AT THE VERY LEAST, IT'S GROUNDS FOR SUSPICION, DON'T YOU THINK?
IF IT WAS YOU...THAT STRANGE SPEECH EARLIER WAS PART OF A PLOY TO DERAIL US...
I... I...!
YOU WAS TRYIN' TA TRICK US...SO YA COULD BEAT DA RAP!
ARE YOU GUILTY OR NOT? SPIT IT OUT!
AH... AAAHHH ...!
COME ON, KOMAEDA, PLEASE...IF YOU HAVE ANYTHING TO SAY IN YOUR DEFENSE, PLEASE TELL US...
TO BE PERFECTLY HONEST, I DON'T WANT TO BELIEVE IT WAS YOU...

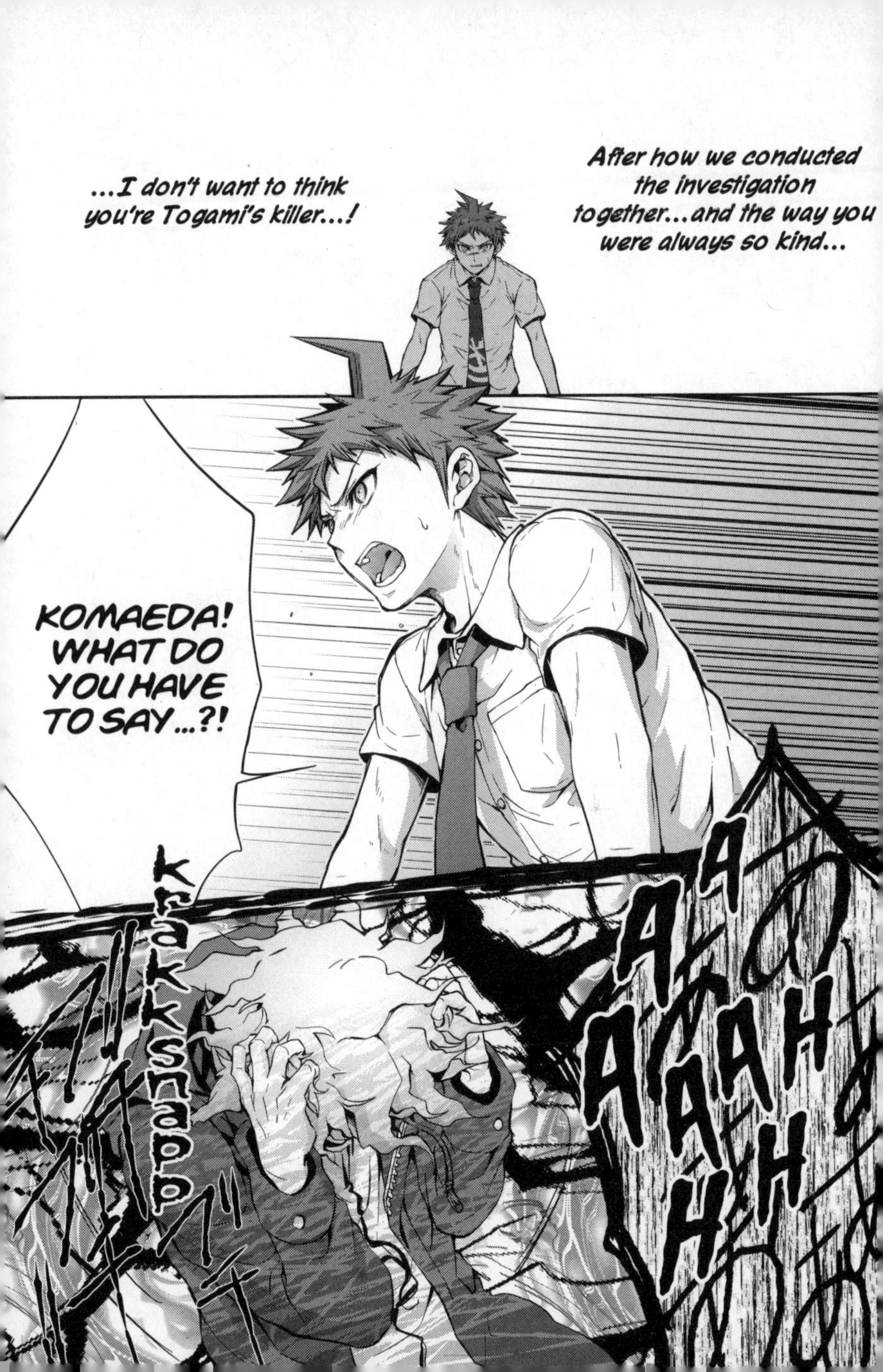
After how we conducted the investigation together...and the way you were always so kind...
...I don't want to think you're Togami's killer...!
KOMAEDA! WHAT DO YOU HAVE TO SAY...?!
AAAAAAAH
krakksnapp

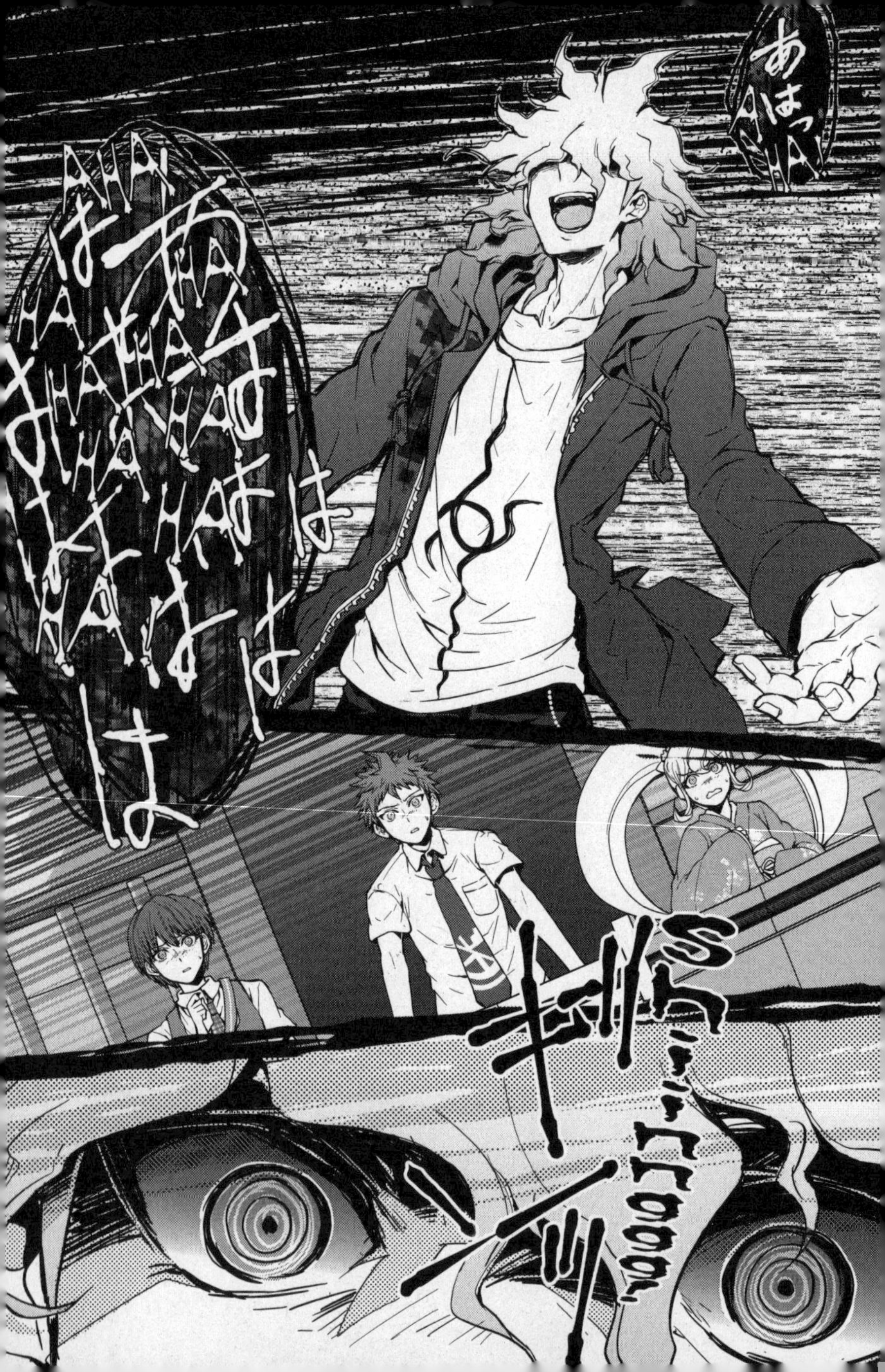
あはっ
AHA!
あはははははは
AHA! HA HA HA HA HA HA HA HA HA HA

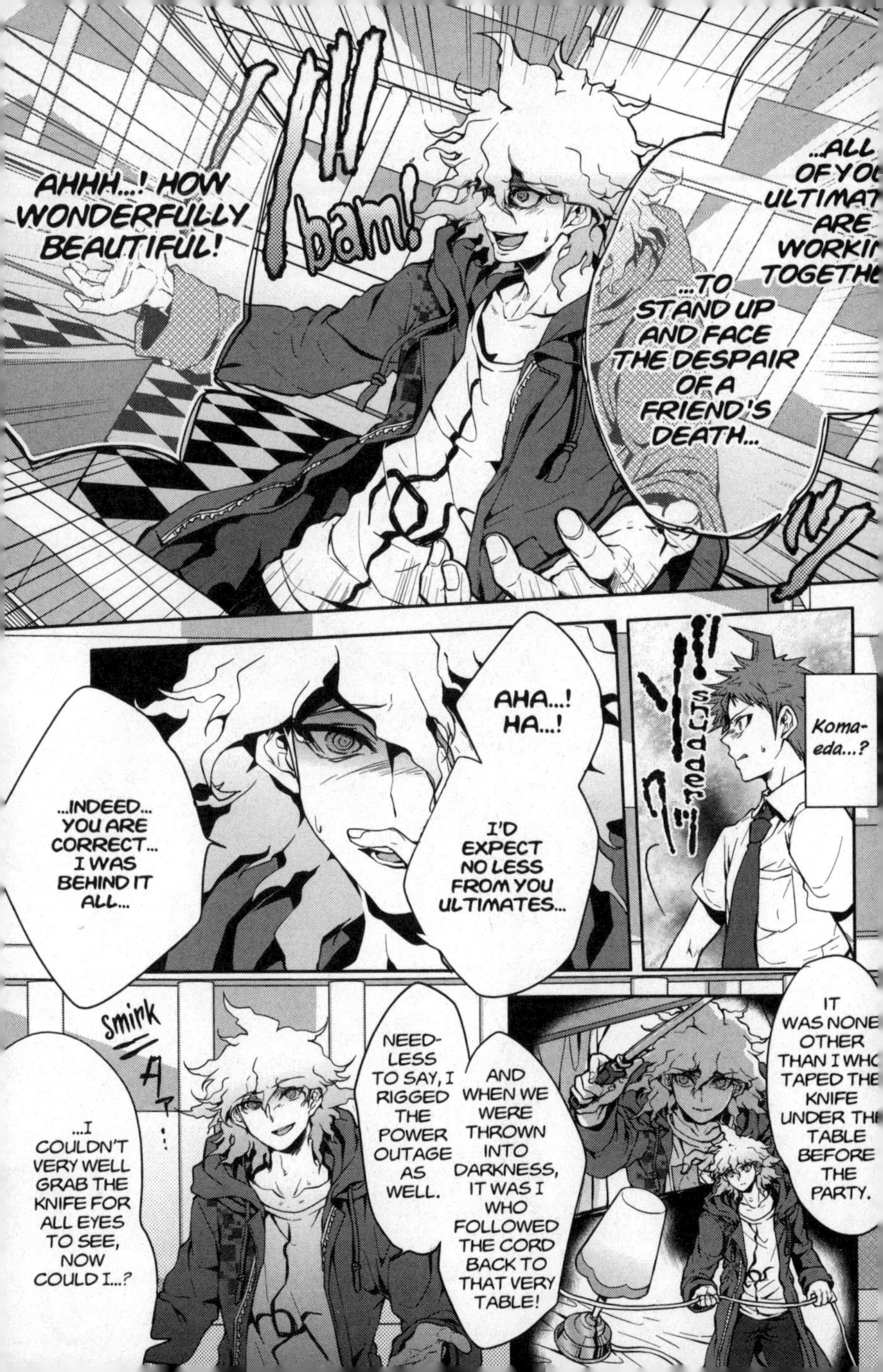

...ALL OF YOU ULTIMAT ARE WORKIN TOGETHE
...TO STAND UP AND FACE THE DESPAIR OF A FRIEND'S DEATH...
bam!
AHHH...! HOW WONDERFULLY BEAUTIFUL!
Koma-eda...?
shudder
AHA...! HA...!
I'D EXPECT NO LESS FROM YOU ULTIMATES...
...INDEED... YOU ARE CORRECT... I WAS BEHIND IT ALL...
IT WAS NONE OTHER THAN I WHO TAPED THE KNIFE UNDER TH TABLE BEFORE THE PARTY.
NEED-LESS TO SAY, I RIGGED THE POWER OUTAGE AS WELL.
AND WHEN WE WERE THROWN INTO DARKNESS, IT WAS I WHO FOLLOWED THE CORD BACK TO THAT VERY TABLE!
smirk
...I COULDN'T VERY WELL GRAB THE KNIFE FOR ALL EYES TO SEE, NOW COULD I...?

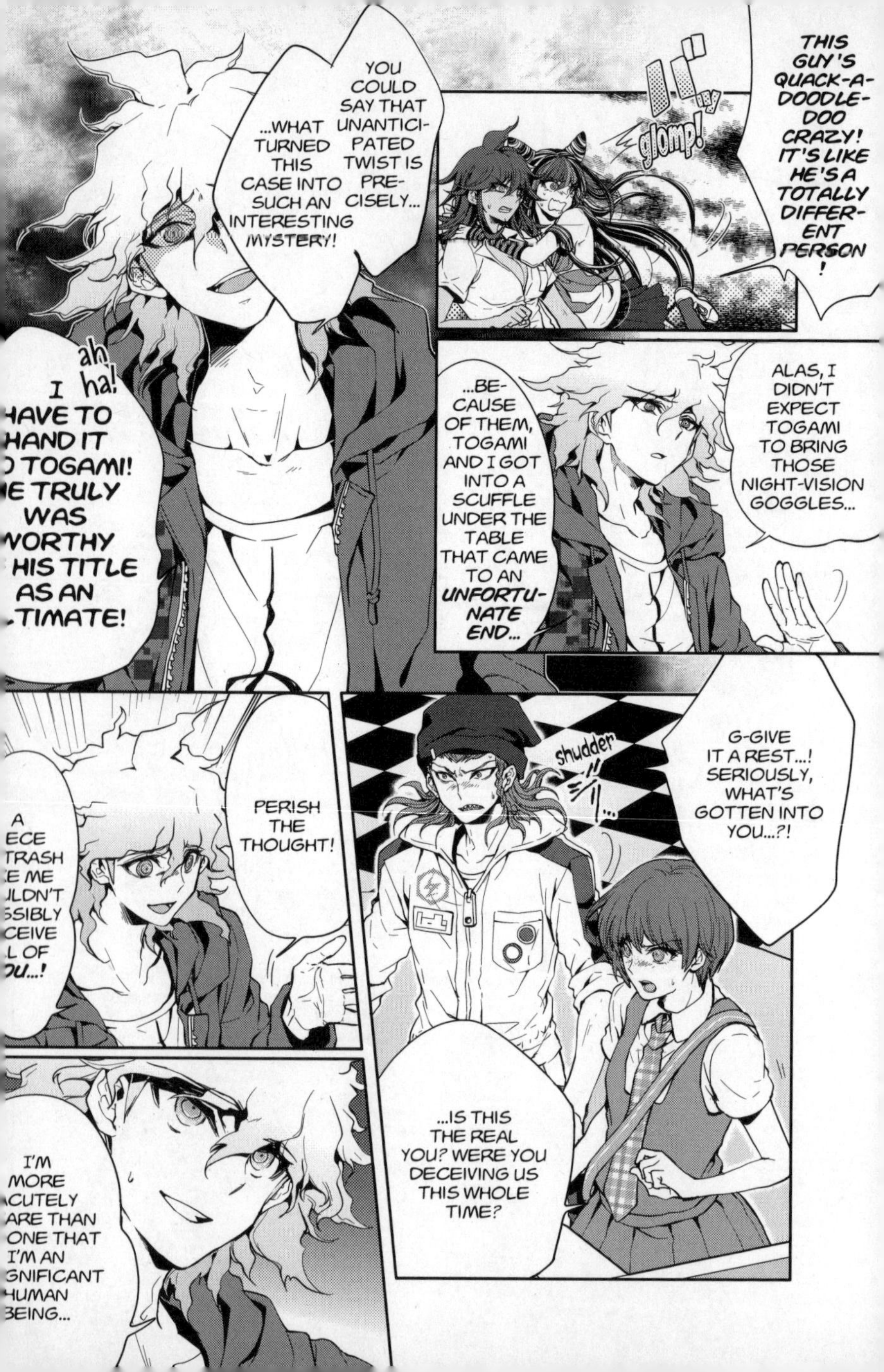
glomp!
THIS GUY'S QUACK-A-DOODLE-DOO CRAZY! IT'S LIKE HE'S A TOTALLY DIFFER-ENT PERSON!
ALAS, I DIDN'T EXPECT TOGAMI TO BRING THOSE NIGHT-VISION GOGGLES...
...BE-CAUSE OF THEM, TOGAMI AND I GOT INTO A SCUFFLE UNDER THE TABLE THAT CAME TO AN *UNFORTU-NATE* END...
YOU COULD SAY THAT UNANTICI-PATED TWIST IS PRE-CISELY...
...WHAT TURNED THIS CASE INTO SUCH AN INTERESTING MYSTERY!
ah ha!
I HAVE TO HAND IT O TOGAMI! E TRULY WAS ORTHY HIS TITLE AS AN TIMATE!
G-GIVE IT A REST...! SERIOUSLY, WHAT'S GOTTEN INTO YOU...?!
shudder
...IS THIS THE REAL YOU? WERE YOU DECEIVING US THIS WHOLE TIME?
PERISH THE THOUGHT!
A ECE TRASH E ME ULDN'T SSIBLY CEIVE L OF OU...!
I'M MORE CUTELY ARE THAN ONE THAT I'M AN GNIFICANT HUMAN BEING...

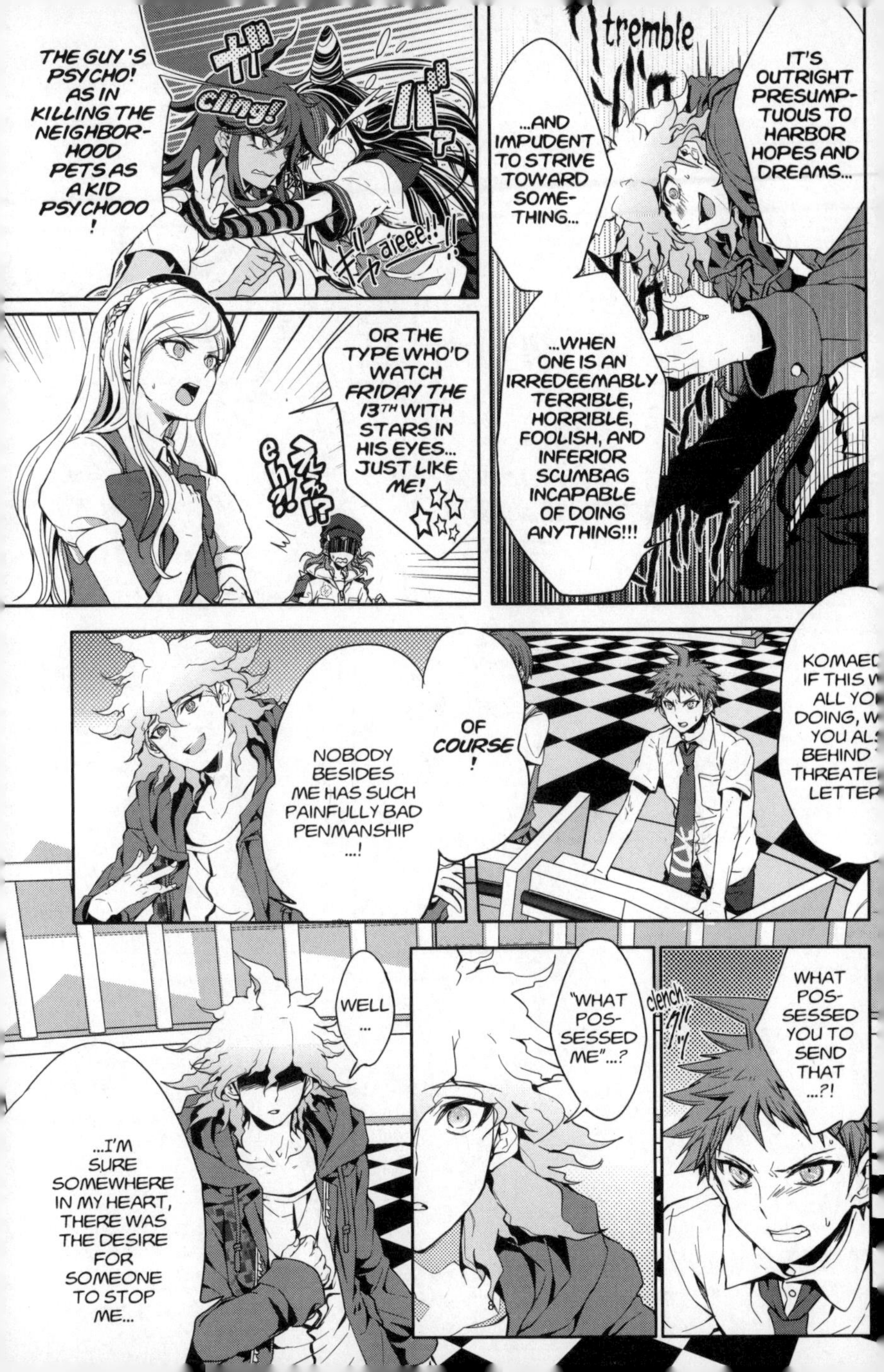
tremble
IT'S OUTRIGHT PRESUMPTUOUS TO HARBOR HOPES AND DREAMS...
...AND IMPUDENT TO STRIVE TOWARD SOMETHING...
...WHEN ONE IS AN IRREDEEMABLY TERRIBLE, HORRIBLE, FOOLISH, AND INFERIOR SCUMBAG INCAPABLE OF DOING ANYTHING!!!
THE GUY'S PSYCHO! AS IN KILLING THE NEIGHBORHOOD PETS AS A KID PSYCHOOO!
cling!
aieee!!
OR THE TYPE WHO'D WATCH FRIDAY THE 13TH WITH STARS IN HIS EYES... JUST LIKE ME!
eh?!
KOMAED
IF THIS W
ALL YO
DOING, W
YOU ALS
BEHIND
THREATE
LETTER
OF COURSE!
NOBODY BESIDES ME HAS SUCH PAINFULLY BAD PENMANSHIP ...!
WHAT POSSESSED YOU TO SEND THAT ...?!
clench
"WHAT POSSESSED ME"...?
WELL ...
...I'M SURE SOMEWHERE IN MY HEART, THERE WAS THE DESIRE FOR SOMEONE TO STOP ME...

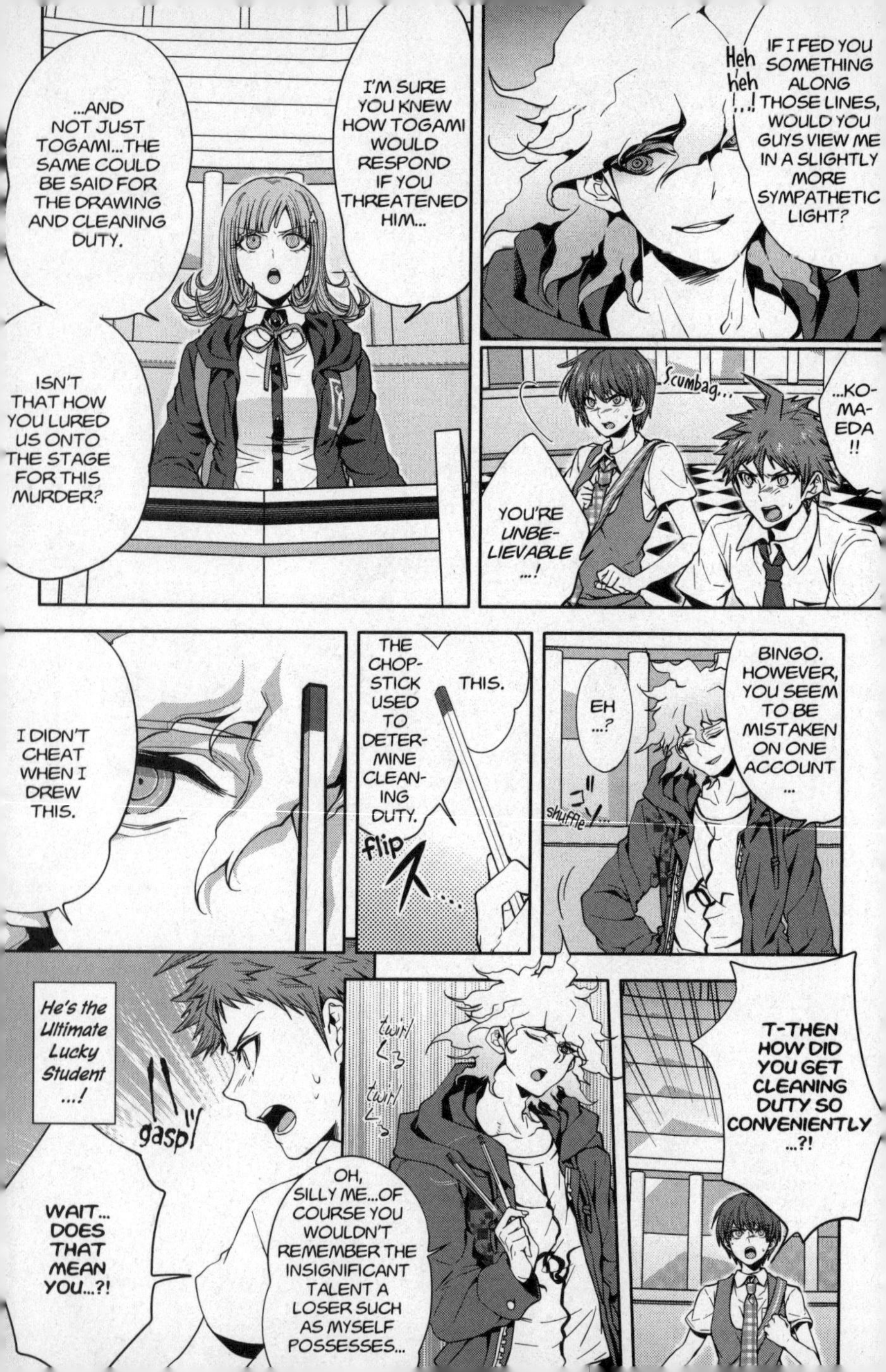
IF I FED YOU SOMETHING ALONG THOSE LINES, WOULD YOU GUYS VIEW ME IN A SLIGHTLY MORE SYMPATHETIC LIGHT?
Heh heh ...!
...KO-MA-EDA !!
Scumbag...
YOU'RE UNBE-LIEVABLE ...!
I'M SURE YOU KNEW HOW TOGAMI WOULD RESPOND IF YOU THREATENED HIM...
...AND NOT JUST TOGAMI...THE SAME COULD BE SAID FOR THE DRAWING AND CLEANING DUTY.
ISN'T THAT HOW YOU LURED US ONTO THE STAGE FOR THIS MURDER?
BINGO. HOWEVER, YOU SEEM TO BE MISTAKEN ON ONE ACCOUNT ...
EH ...?
shuffle...
THIS.
THE CHOP-STICK USED TO DETER-MINE CLEAN-ING DUTY.
flip
I DIDN'T CHEAT WHEN I DREW THIS.
T-THEN HOW DID YOU GET CLEANING DUTY SO CONVENIENTLY ...?!
twirl
twirl
OH, SILLY ME...OF COURSE YOU WOULDN'T REMEMBER THE INSIGNIFICANT TALENT A LOSER SUCH AS MYSELF POSSESSES...
He's the Ultimate Lucky Student ...!
gasp!
WAIT... DOES THAT MEAN YOU...?!

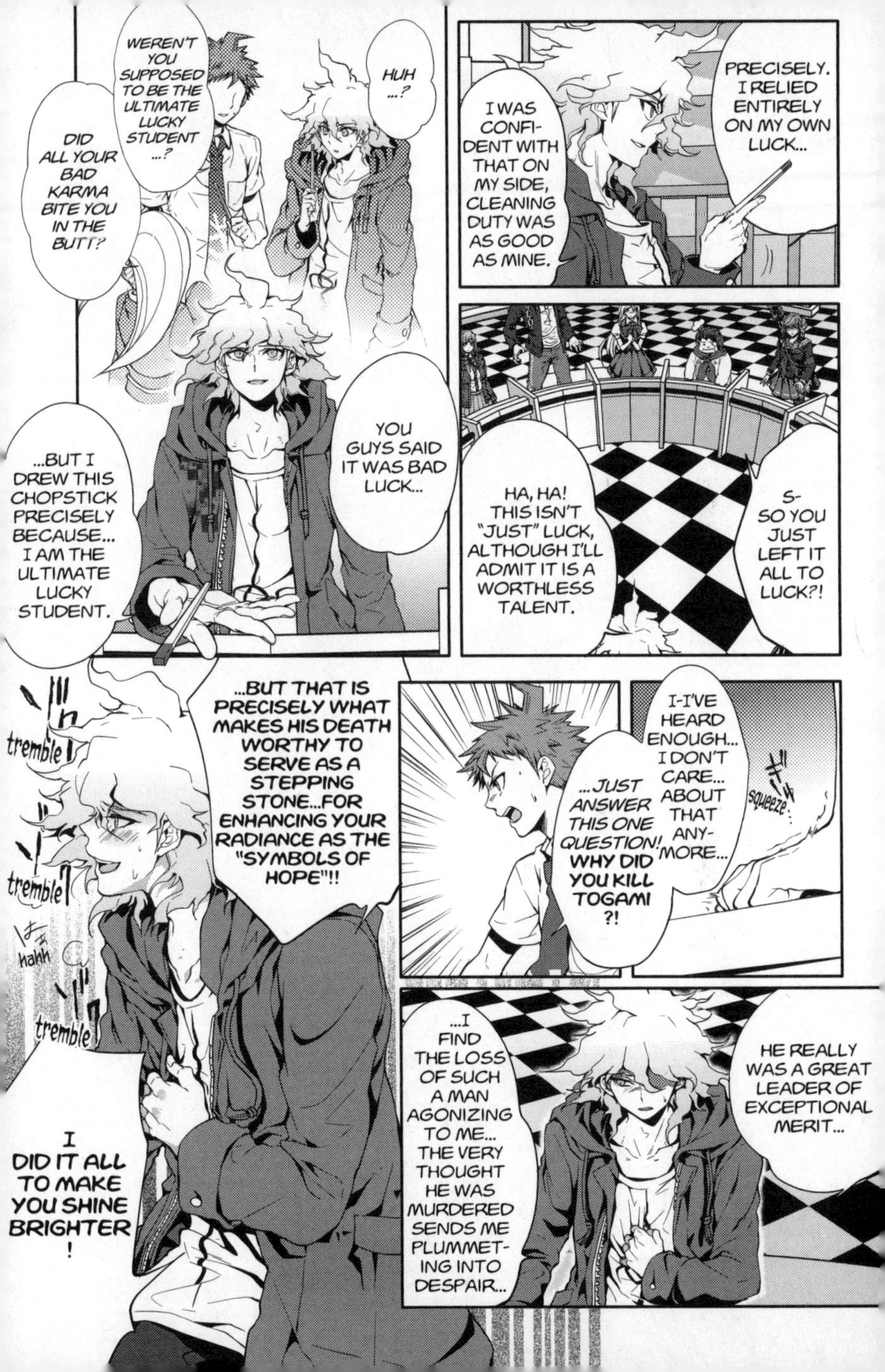
PRECISELY. I RELIED ENTIRELY ON MY OWN LUCK...
I WAS CONFIDENT WITH THAT ON MY SIDE, CLEANING DUTY WAS AS GOOD AS MINE.
S-SO YOU JUST LEFT IT ALL TO LUCK?!
HA, HA! THIS ISN'T "JUST" LUCK, ALTHOUGH I'LL ADMIT IT IS A WORTHLESS TALENT.
HUH ...?
WEREN'T YOU SUPPOSED TO BE THE ULTIMATE LUCKY STUDENT ...?
DID ALL YOUR BAD KARMA BITE YOU IN THE BUTT?
YOU GUYS SAID IT WAS BAD LUCK...
...BUT I DREW THIS CHOPSTICK PRECISELY BECAUSE... I AM THE ULTIMATE LUCKY STUDENT.
squeeze
I-I'VE HEARD ENOUGH... I DON'T CARE... ABOUT THAT ANYMORE...
...JUST ANSWER THIS ONE QUESTION! WHY DID YOU KILL TOGAMI ?!
HE REALLY WAS A GREAT LEADER OF EXCEPTIONAL MERIT...
...I FIND THE LOSS OF SUCH A MAN AGONIZING TO ME... THE VERY THOUGHT HE WAS MURDERED SENDS ME PLUMMETING INTO DESPAIR...
...BUT THAT IS PRECISELY WHAT MAKES HIS DEATH WORTHY TO SERVE AS A STEPPING STONE...FOR ENHANCING YOUR RADIANCE AS THE "SYMBOLS OF HOPE"!!
tremble
tremble
hahh
tremble
I DID IT ALL TO MAKE YOU SHINE BRIGHTER !

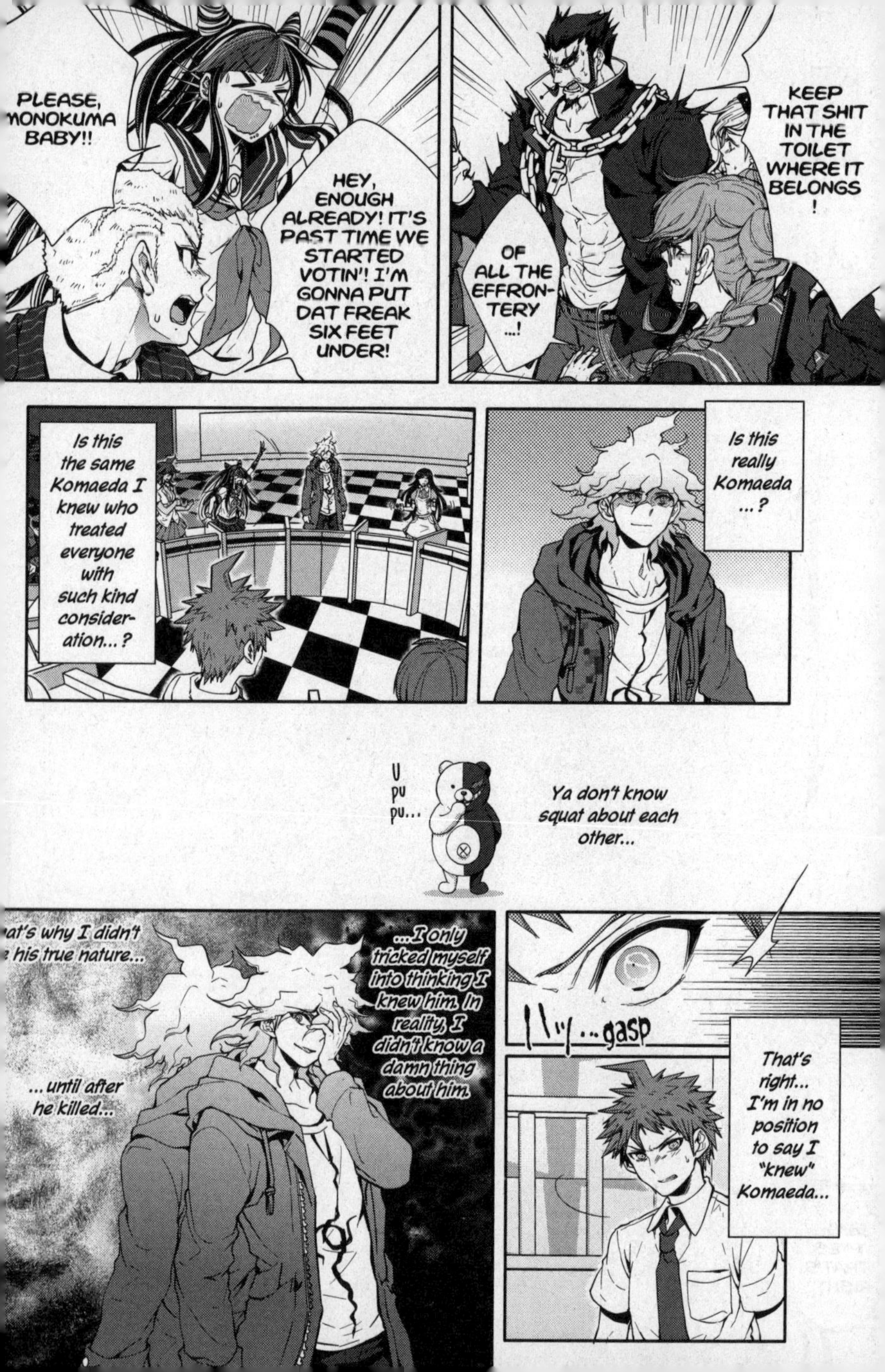
KEEP THAT SHIT IN THE TOILET WHERE IT BELONGS!
OF ALL THE EFFRONTERY...!
HEY, ENOUGH ALREADY! IT'S PAST TIME WE STARTED VOTIN'! I'M GONNA PUT DAT FREAK SIX FEET UNDER!
PLEASE, MONOKUMA BABY!!
Is this really Komaeda...?
Is this the same Komaeda I knew who treated everyone with such kind consider-ation...?
Ya don't know squat about each other...
U pu pu...
...gasp
That's right... I'm in no position to say I "knew" Komaeda...
...I only tricked myself into thinking I knew him. In reality, I didn't know a damn thing about him.
at's why I didn't
his true nature...
...until after he killed...

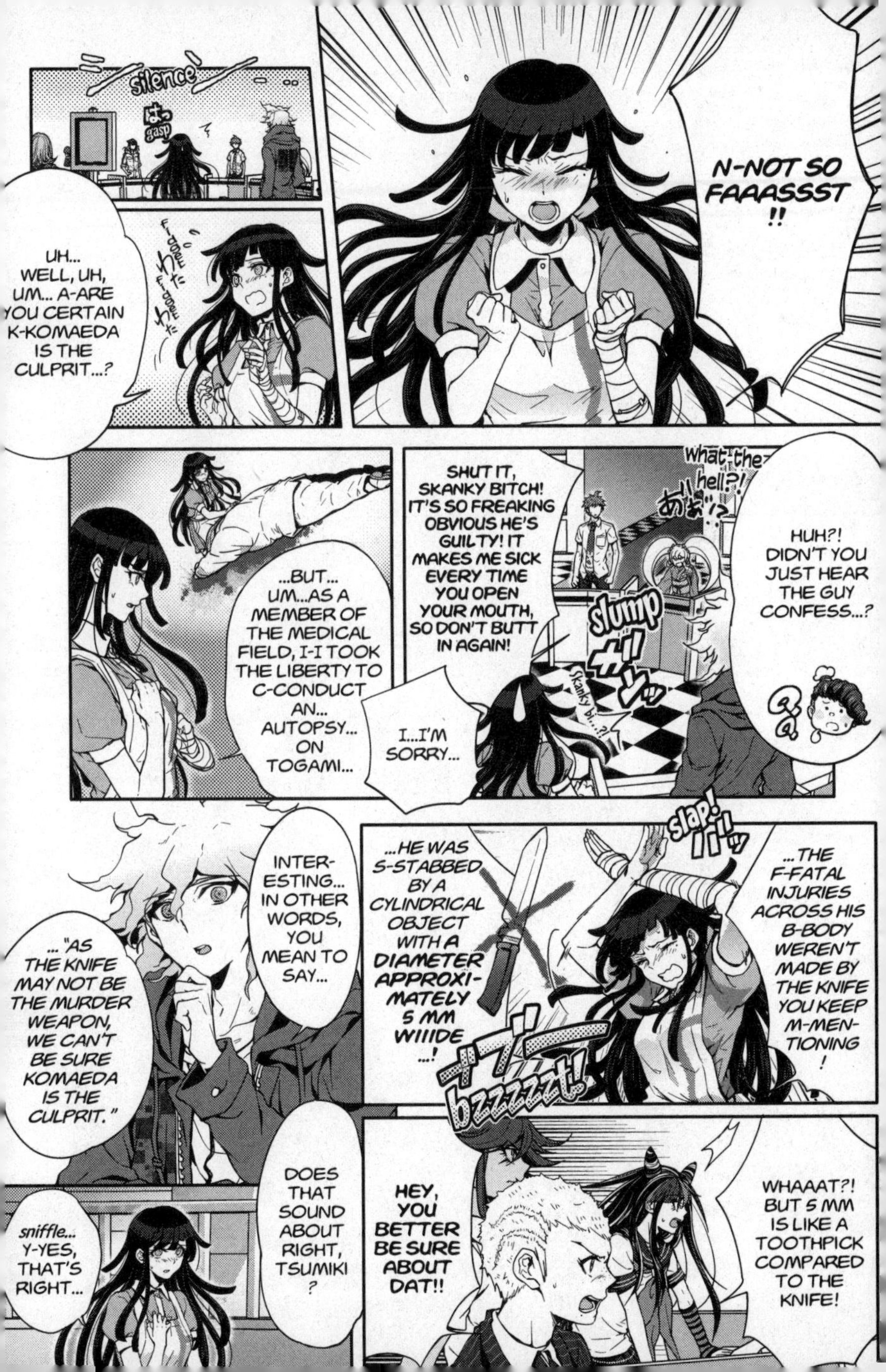
N-NOT SO FAAASSST!!
silence
はっ
gasp
UH... WELL, UH, UM... A-ARE YOU CERTAIN K-KOMAEDA IS THE CULPRIT...?
fidget
fidget
HUH?! DIDN'T YOU JUST HEAR THE GUY CONFESS...?
what the hell?!
SHUT IT, SKANKY BITCH! IT'S SO FREAKING OBVIOUS HE'S GUILTY! IT MAKES ME SICK EVERY TIME YOU OPEN YOUR MOUTH, SO DON'T BUTT IN AGAIN!
slump
Skanky bi...?!
I...I'M SORRY...
...BUT... UM...AS A MEMBER OF THE MEDICAL FIELD, I-I TOOK THE LIBERTY TO C-CONDUCT AN... AUTOPSY... ON TOGAMI...
...THE F-FATAL INJURIES ACROSS HIS B-BODY WEREN'T MADE BY THE KNIFE YOU KEEP M-MEN-TIONING!
slap!
...HE WAS S-STABBED BY A CYLINDRICAL OBJECT WITH A DIAMETER APPROXI-MATELY 5 MM WIIIDE...!
bzzzzzzt!
INTER-ESTING... IN OTHER WORDS, YOU MEAN TO SAY...
..."AS THE KNIFE MAY NOT BE THE MURDER WEAPON, WE CAN'T BE SURE KOMAEDA IS THE CULPRIT."
WHAAAT?! BUT 5 MM IS LIKE A TOOTHPICK COMPARED TO THE KNIFE!
HEY, YOU BETTER BE SURE ABOUT DAT!!
DOES THAT SOUND ABOUT RIGHT, TSUMIKI?
sniffle... Y-YES, THAT'S RIGHT...

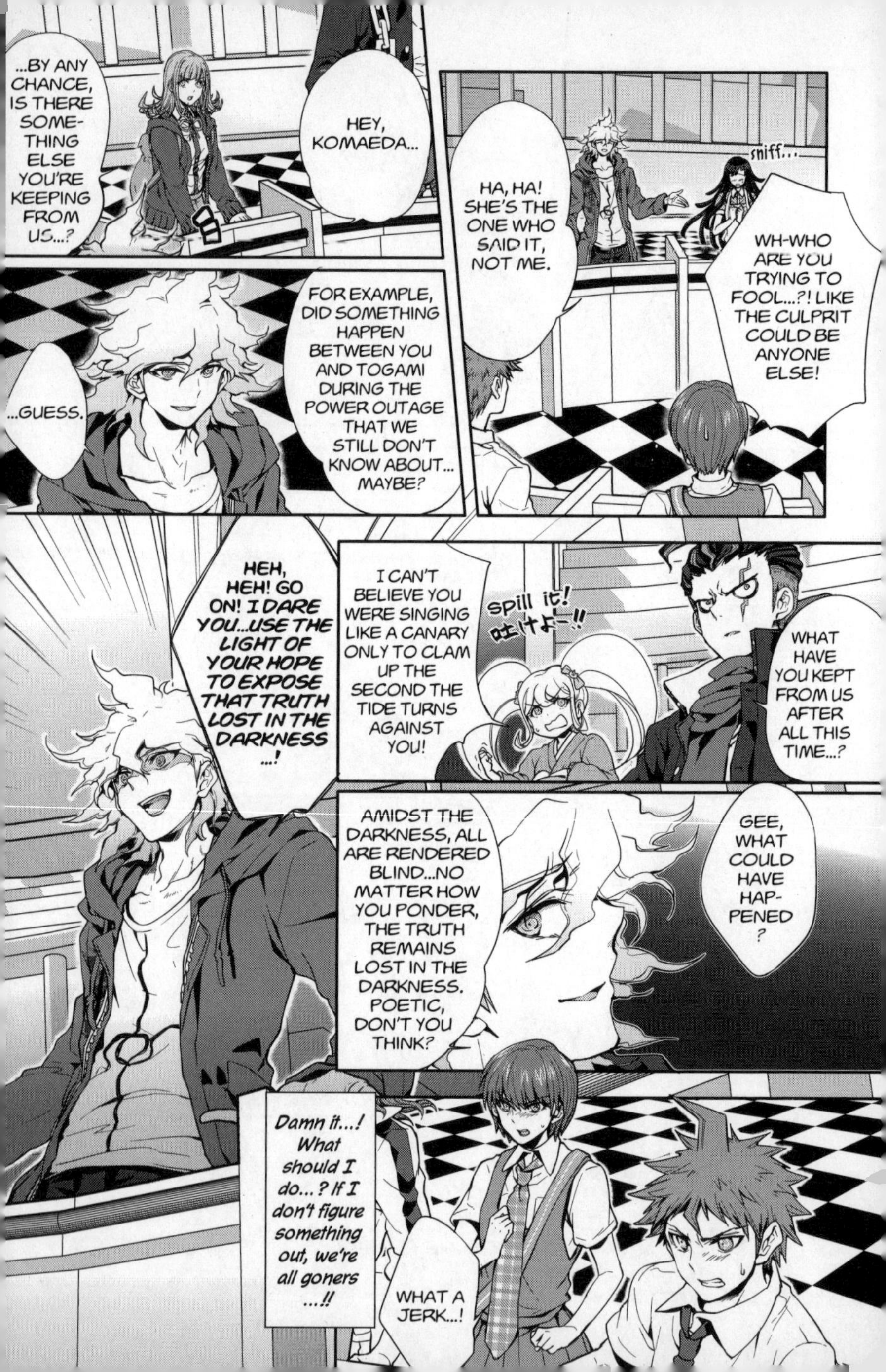
HA, HA! SHE'S THE ONE WHO SAID IT, NOT ME.
sniff...
WH-WHO ARE YOU TRYING TO FOOL...?! LIKE THE CULPRIT COULD BE ANYONE ELSE!
HEY, KOMAEDA...
...BY ANY CHANCE, IS THERE SOME-THING ELSE YOU'RE KEEPING FROM US...?
FOR EXAMPLE, DID SOMETHING HAPPEN BETWEEN YOU AND TOGAMI DURING THE POWER OUTAGE THAT WE STILL DON'T KNOW ABOUT... MAYBE?
...GUESS.
WHAT HAVE YOU KEPT FROM US AFTER ALL THIS TIME...?
spill it! 吐けよー!!
I CAN'T BELIEVE YOU WERE SINGING LIKE A CANARY ONLY TO CLAM UP THE SECOND THE TIDE TURNS AGAINST YOU!
GEE, WHAT COULD HAVE HAP-PENED?
AMIDST THE DARKNESS, ALL ARE RENDERED BLIND...NO MATTER HOW YOU PONDER, THE TRUTH REMAINS LOST IN THE DARKNESS. POETIC, DON'T YOU THINK?
WHAT A JERK...!
Damn it...! What should I do...? If I don't figure something out, we're all goners ...!!
HEH, HEH! GO ON! I DARE YOU...USE THE LIGHT OF YOUR HOPE TO EXPOSE THAT TRUTH LOST IN THE DARKNESS ...!

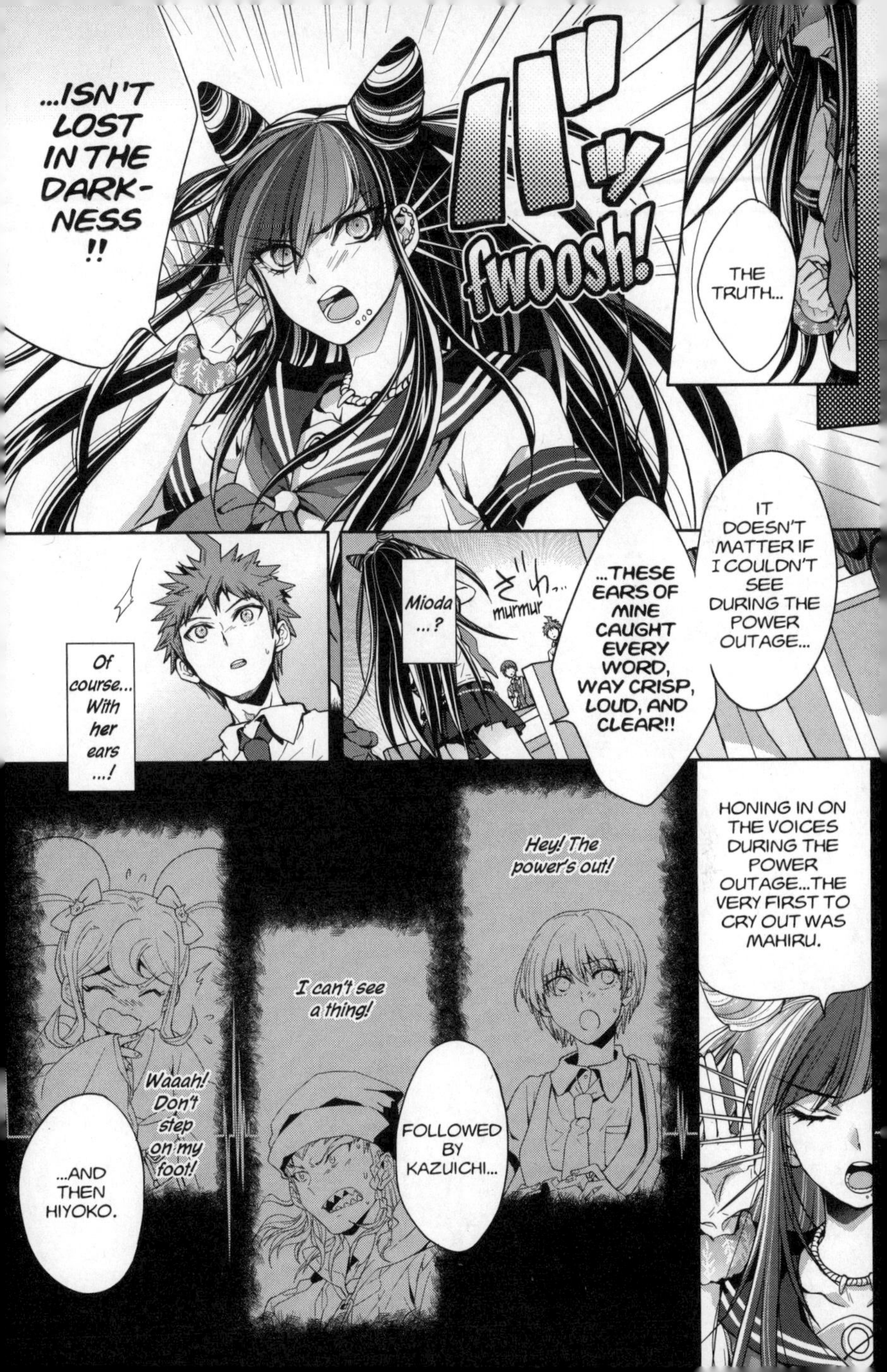
THE TRUTH...
...ISN'T LOST IN THE DARKNESS!!
バッ
fwoosh!
IT DOESN'T MATTER IF I COULDN'T SEE DURING THE POWER OUTAGE...
...THESE EARS OF MINE CAUGHT EVERY WORD, WAY CRISP, LOUD, AND CLEAR!!
ざわ...
murmur
Mioda ...?
Of course... With her ears ...!
HONING IN ON THE VOICES DURING THE POWER OUTAGE...THE VERY FIRST TO CRY OUT WAS MAHIRU.
Hey! The power's out!
FOLLOWED BY KAZUICHI...
I can't see a thing!
Waaah! Don't step on my foot!
...AND THEN HIYOKO.

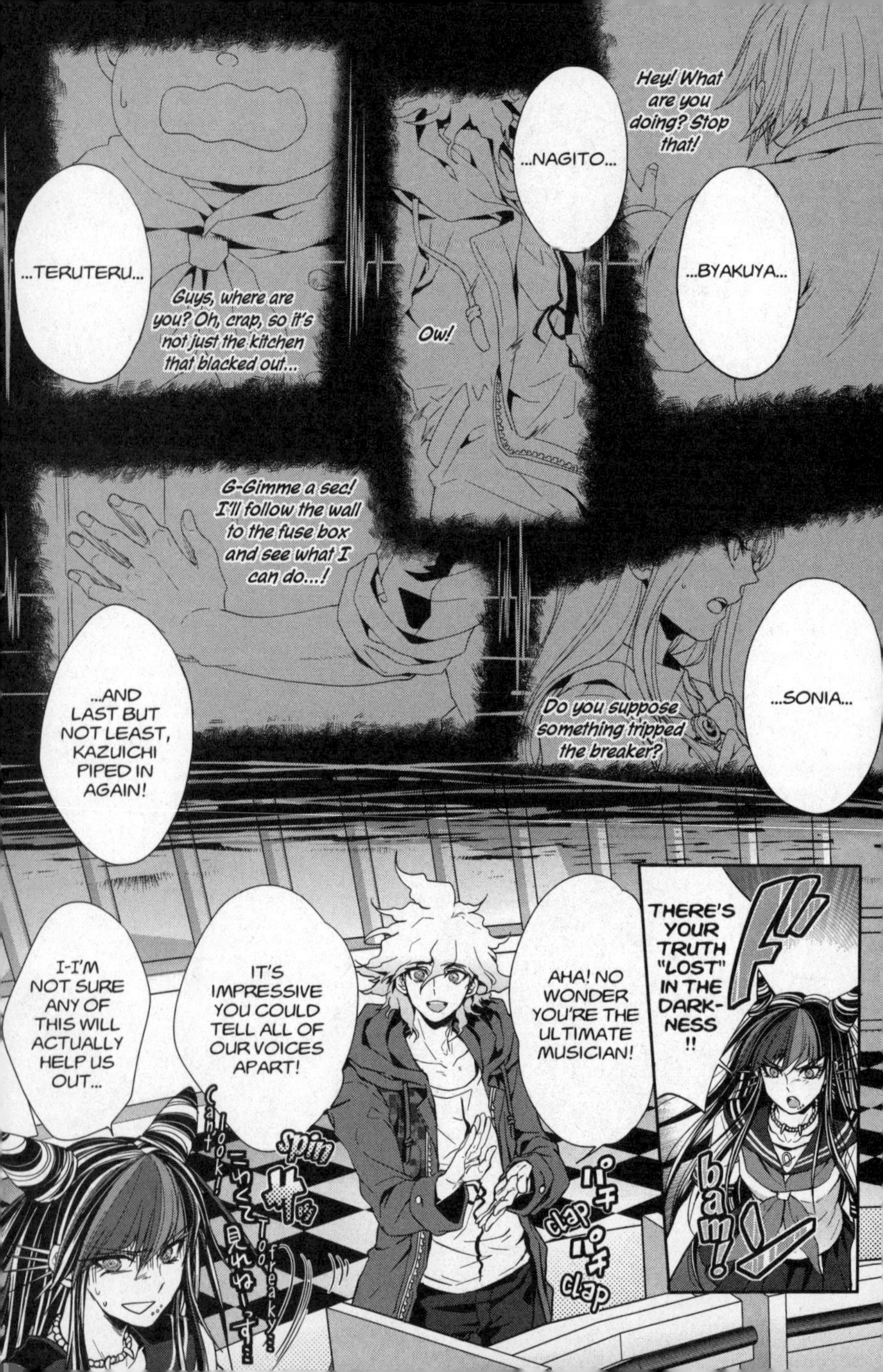
Hey! What are you doing? Stop that!
...BYAKUYA...
...NAGITO...
Ow!
...TERUTERU...
Guys, where are you? Oh, crap, so it's not just the kitchen that blacked out...
...SONIA...
Do you suppose something tripped the breaker?
G-Gimme a sec! I'll follow the wall to the fuse box and see what I can do...!
...AND LAST BUT NOT LEAST, KAZUICHI PIPED IN AGAIN!
THERE'S YOUR TRUTH "LOST" IN THE DARK-NESS !!
bam!
AHA! NO WONDER YOU'RE THE ULTIMATE MUSICIAN!
パチ clap
パチ clap
IT'S IMPRESSIVE YOU COULD TELL ALL OF OUR VOICES APART!
spin
I-I'M NOT SURE ANY OF THIS WILL ACTUALLY HELP US OUT...
Can't look! Too freaky...
こわくて見れねーっす

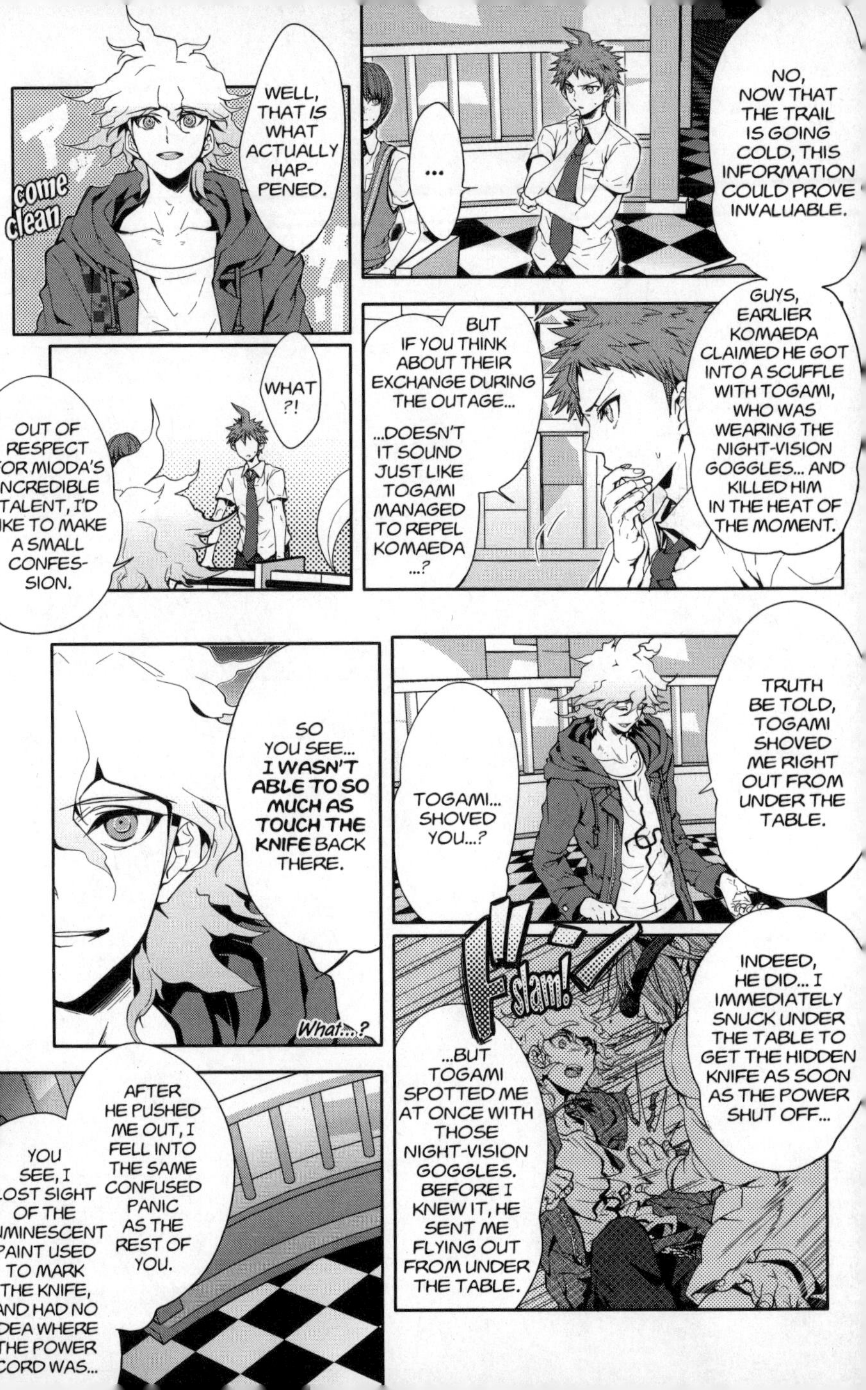
NO, NOW THAT THE TRAIL IS GOING COLD, THIS INFORMATION COULD PROVE INVALUABLE.
...
WELL, THAT IS WHAT ACTUALLY HAP-PENED.
come clean
GUYS, EARLIER KOMAEDA CLAIMED HE GOT INTO A SCUFFLE WITH TOGAMI, WHO WAS WEARING THE NIGHT-VISION GOGGLES... AND KILLED HIM IN THE HEAT OF THE MOMENT.
BUT IF YOU THINK ABOUT THEIR EXCHANGE DURING THE OUTAGE...
...DOESN'T IT SOUND JUST LIKE TOGAMI MANAGED TO REPEL KOMAEDA ...?
WHAT ?!
OUT OF RESPECT FOR MIODA'S INCREDIBLE TALENT, I'D LIKE TO MAKE A SMALL CONFES-SION.
TRUTH BE TOLD, TOGAMI SHOVED ME RIGHT OUT FROM UNDER THE TABLE.
TOGAMI... SHOVED YOU...?
INDEED, HE DID... I IMMEDIATELY SNUCK UNDER THE TABLE TO GET THE HIDDEN KNIFE AS SOON AS THE POWER SHUT OFF...
slam!
...BUT TOGAMI SPOTTED ME AT ONCE WITH THOSE NIGHT-VISION GOGGLES. BEFORE I KNEW IT, HE SENT ME FLYING OUT FROM UNDER THE TABLE.
SO YOU SEE... I WASN'T ABLE TO SO MUCH AS TOUCH THE KNIFE BACK THERE.
What...?
AFTER HE PUSHED ME OUT, I FELL INTO THE SAME CONFUSED PANIC AS THE REST OF YOU.
YOU SEE, I LOST SIGHT OF THE LUMINESCENT PAINT USED TO MARK THE KNIFE, AND HAD NO IDEA WHERE THE POWER CORD WAS...

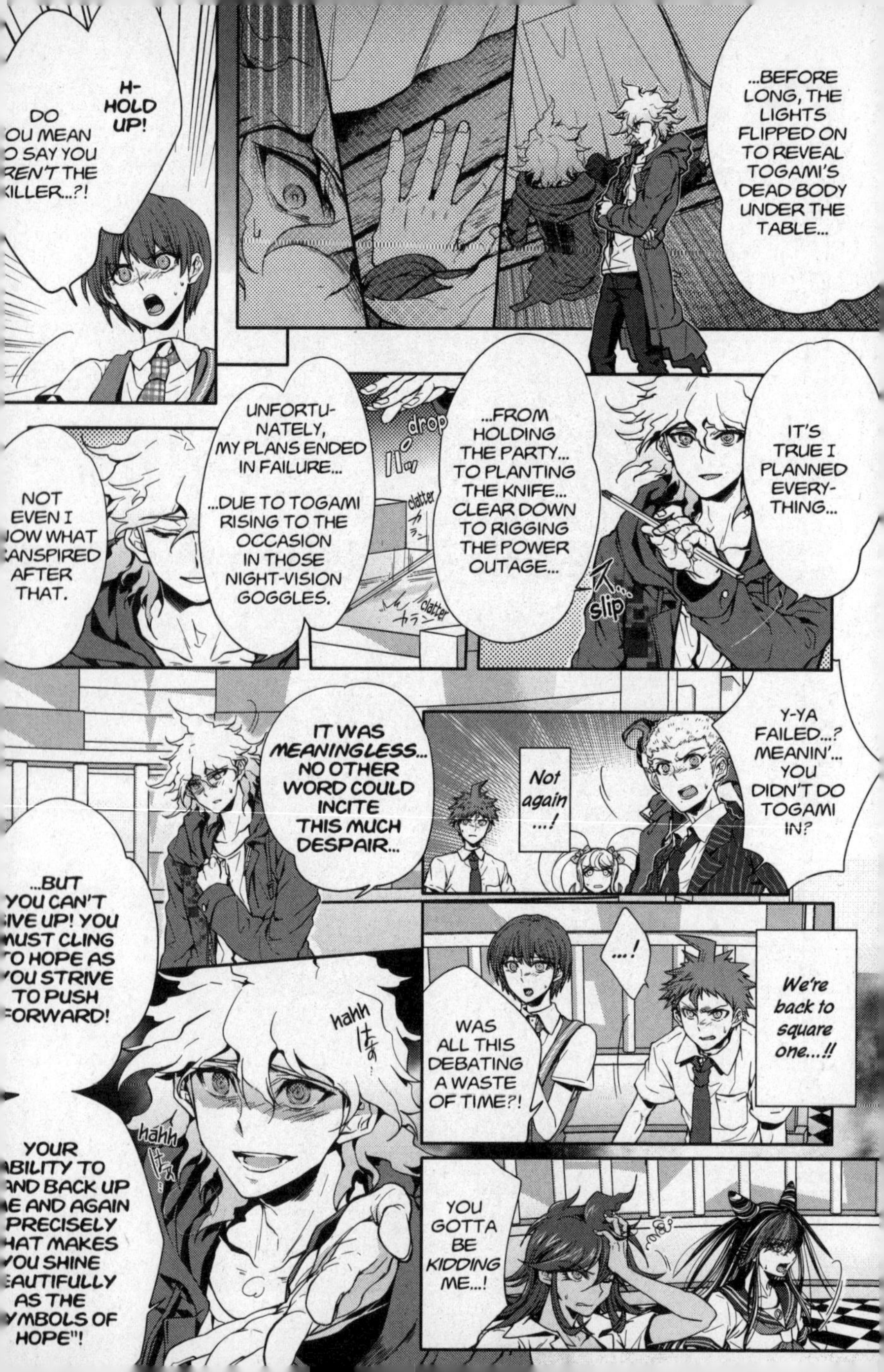
...BEFORE LONG, THE LIGHTS FLIPPED ON TO REVEAL TOGAMI'S DEAD BODY UNDER THE TABLE...
H- HOLD UP!
DO OU MEAN O SAY YOU REN'T THE ILLER...?!
IT'S TRUE I PLANNED EVERY- THING...
slip
...FROM HOLDING THE PARTY... TO PLANTING THE KNIFE... CLEAR DOWN TO RIGGING THE POWER OUTAGE...
drop
clatter
clatter
UNFORTU- NATELY, MY PLANS ENDED IN FAILURE...
...DUE TO TOGAMI RISING TO THE OCCASION IN THOSE NIGHT-VISION GOGGLES.
NOT EVEN I NOW WHAT ANSPIRED AFTER THAT.
Y-YA FAILED...? MEANIN'... YOU DIDN'T DO TOGAMI IN?
Not again...!
IT WAS MEANINGLESS... NO OTHER WORD COULD INCITE THIS MUCH DESPAIR...
We're back to square one...!!
...!
WAS ALL THIS DEBATING A WASTE OF TIME?!
YOU GOTTA BE KIDDING ME...!
...BUT YOU CAN'T IVE UP! YOU MUST CLING TO HOPE AS OU STRIVE TO PUSH ORWARD!
hahh
hahh
YOUR BILITY TO AND BACK UP E AND AGAIN PRECISELY HAT MAKES YOU SHINE EAUTIFULLY AS THE YMBOLS OF HOPE"!

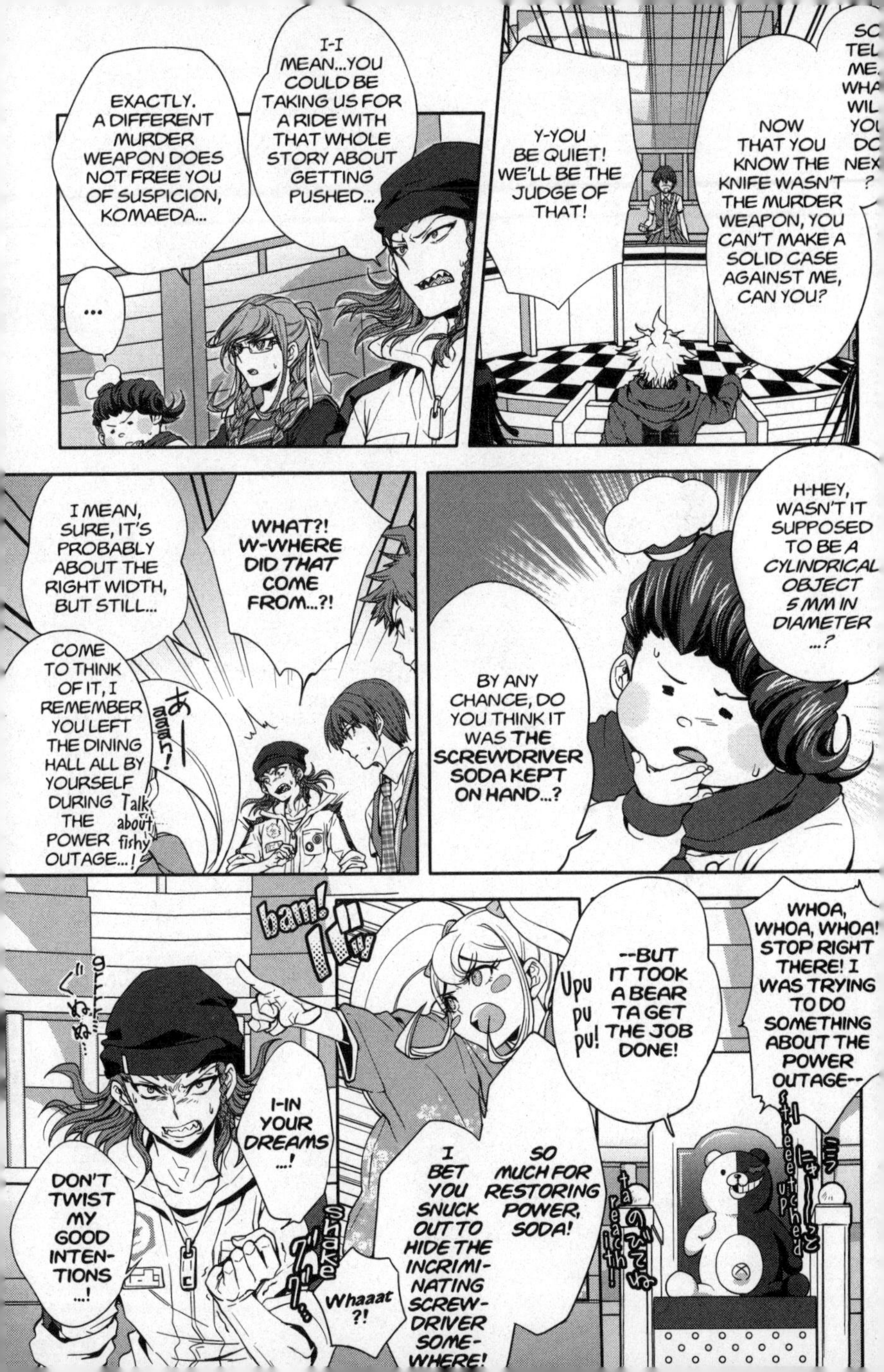
SO
TEL
ME.
WHA
WIL
YOU
DO
NEX
?
NOW THAT YOU KNOW THE KNIFE WASN'T THE MURDER WEAPON, YOU CAN'T MAKE A SOLID CASE AGAINST ME, CAN YOU?
Y-YOU BE QUIET! WE'LL BE THE JUDGE OF THAT!
I-I MEAN...YOU COULD BE TAKING US FOR A RIDE WITH THAT WHOLE STORY ABOUT GETTING PUSHED...
EXACTLY. A DIFFERENT MURDER WEAPON DOES NOT FREE YOU OF SUSPICION, KOMAEDA...
...
H-HEY, WASN'T IT SUPPOSED TO BE A CYLINDRICAL OBJECT 5 MM IN DIAMETER...?
BY ANY CHANCE, DO YOU THINK IT WAS THE SCREWDRIVER SODA KEPT ON HAND...?
WHAT?! W-WHERE DID THAT COME FROM...?!
I MEAN, SURE, IT'S PROBABLY ABOUT THE RIGHT WIDTH, BUT STILL...
あー aaah!
COME TO THINK OF IT, I REMEMBER YOU LEFT THE DINING HALL ALL BY YOURSELF DURING THE POWER OUTAGE...!
Talk about fishy
WHOA, WHOA, WHOA! STOP RIGHT THERE! I WAS TRYING TO DO SOMETHING ABOUT THE POWER OUTAGE--
streeetched up
ta reach it
--BUT IT TOOK A BEAR TA GET THE JOB DONE!
Upu pu pu!
bam!
SO MUCH FOR RESTORING POWER, SODA!
I BET YOU SNUCK OUT TO HIDE THE INCRIMINATING SCREW-DRIVER SOME-WHERE!
I-IN YOUR DREAMS...!
Whaaat?!
shake
DON'T TWIST MY GOOD INTEN-TIONS...!
grrr

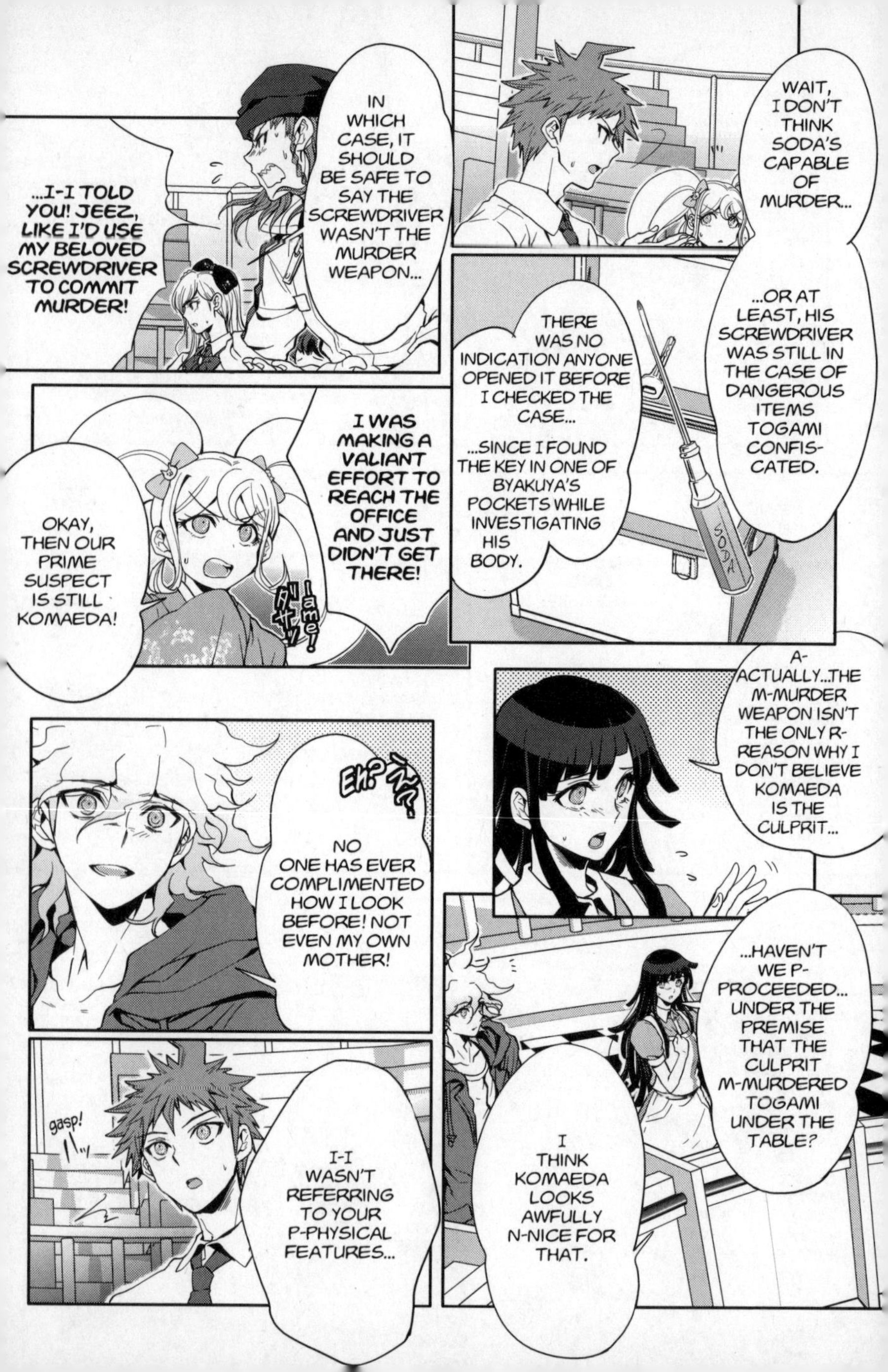
WAIT, I DON'T THINK SODA'S CAPABLE OF MURDER...
...OR AT LEAST, HIS SCREWDRIVER WAS STILL IN THE CASE OF DANGEROUS ITEMS TOGAMI CONFIS-CATED.
THERE WAS NO INDICATION ANYONE OPENED IT BEFORE I CHECKED THE CASE...
...SINCE I FOUND THE KEY IN ONE OF BYAKUYA'S POCKETS WHILE INVESTIGATING HIS BODY.
SODA
IN WHICH CASE, IT SHOULD BE SAFE TO SAY THE SCREWDRIVER WASN'T THE MURDER WEAPON...
...I-I TOLD YOU! JEEZ, LIKE I'D USE MY BELOVED SCREWDRIVER TO COMMIT MURDER!
I WAS MAKING A VALIANT EFFORT TO REACH THE OFFICE AND JUST DIDN'T GET THERE!
lame! ダサッ
OKAY, THEN OUR PRIME SUSPECT IS STILL KOMAEDA!
A-ACTUALLY...THE M-MURDER WEAPON ISN'T THE ONLY R-REASON WHY I DON'T BELIEVE KOMAEDA IS THE CULPRIT...
...HAVEN'T WE P-PROCEEDED... UNDER THE PREMISE THAT THE CULPRIT M-MURDERED TOGAMI UNDER THE TABLE?
I THINK KOMAEDA LOOKS AWFULLY N-NICE FOR THAT.
Eh? えっ
NO ONE HAS EVER COMPLIMENTED HOW I LOOK BEFORE! NOT EVEN MY OWN MOTHER!
gasp!
I-I WASN'T REFERRING TO YOUR P-PHYSICAL FEATURES...

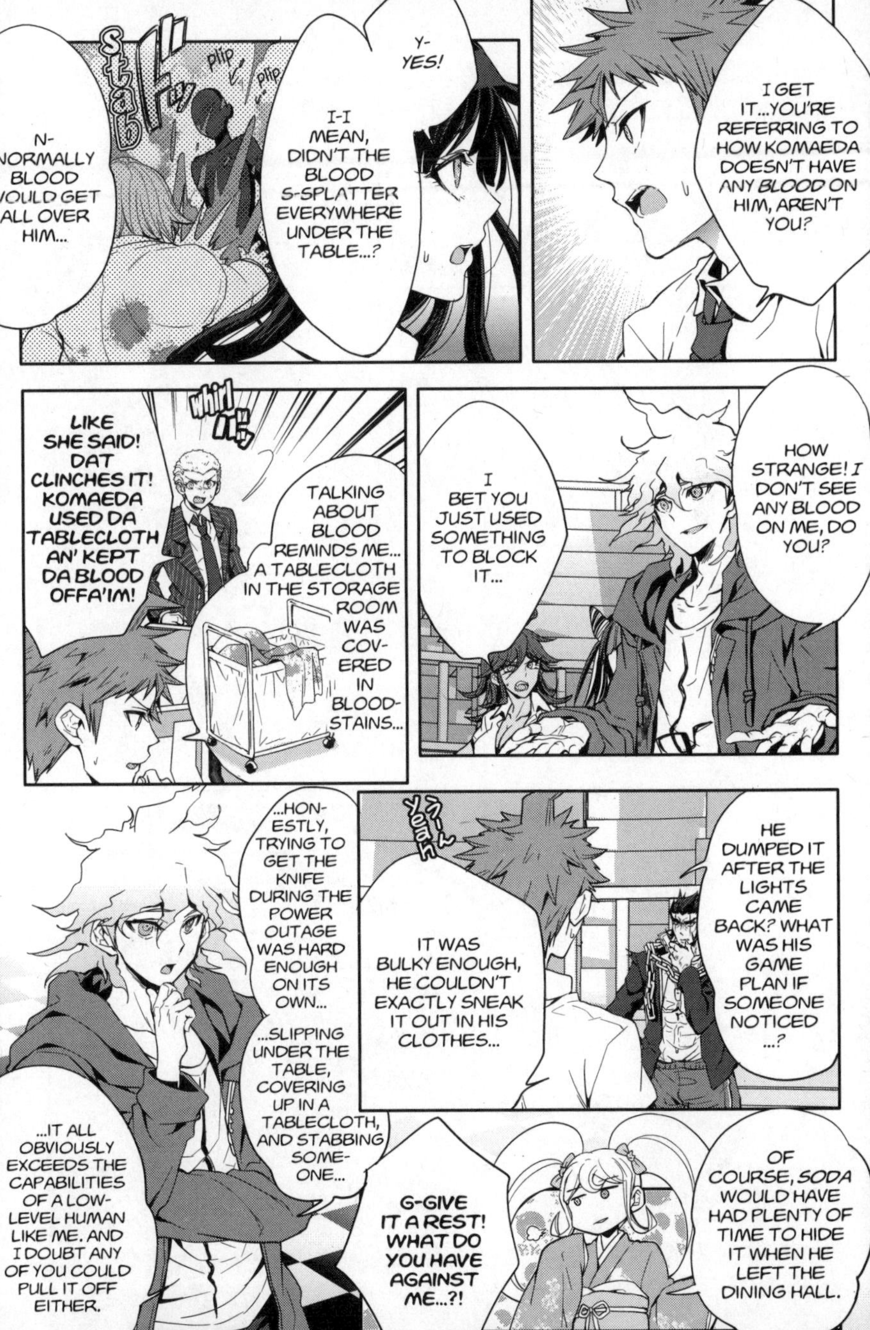

I GET IT...YOU'RE REFERRING TO HOW KOMAEDA DOESN'T HAVE ANY *BLOOD* ON HIM, AREN'T YOU?
Y- YES!
I-I MEAN, DIDN'T THE BLOOD S-SPLATTER EVERYWHERE UNDER THE TABLE...?
plip
plip
stab
N- NORMALLY BLOOD WOULD GET ALL OVER HIM...
HOW STRANGE! *I* DON'T SEE ANY BLOOD ON ME, DO YOU?
I BET YOU JUST USED SOMETHING TO BLOCK IT...
TALKING ABOUT BLOOD REMINDS ME... A TABLECLOTH IN THE STORAGE ROOM WAS COV-ERED IN BLOOD-STAINS...
whirl
LIKE SHE SAID! DAT CLINCHES IT! KOMAEDA USED DA TABLECLOTH AN' KEPT DA BLOOD OFFA'IM!
HE DUMPED IT AFTER THE LIGHTS CAME BACK? WHAT WAS HIS GAME PLAN IF SOMEONE NOTICED ...?
Yeah
IT WAS BULKY ENOUGH, HE COULDN'T EXACTLY SNEAK IT OUT IN HIS CLOTHES...
OF COURSE, *SODA* WOULD HAVE HAD PLENTY OF TIME TO HIDE IT WHEN HE LEFT THE DINING HALL.
G-GIVE IT A REST! WHAT DO YOU HAVE AGAINST ME...?!
...HON-ESTLY, TRYING TO GET THE KNIFE DURING THE POWER OUTAGE WAS HARD ENOUGH ON ITS OWN...
...SLIPPING UNDER THE TABLE, COVERING UP IN A TABLECLOTH, AND STABBING SOME-ONE...
...IT ALL OBVIOUSLY EXCEEDS THE CAPABILITIES OF A LOW-LEVEL HUMAN LIKE ME. AND I DOUBT ANY OF YOU COULD PULL IT OFF EITHER.

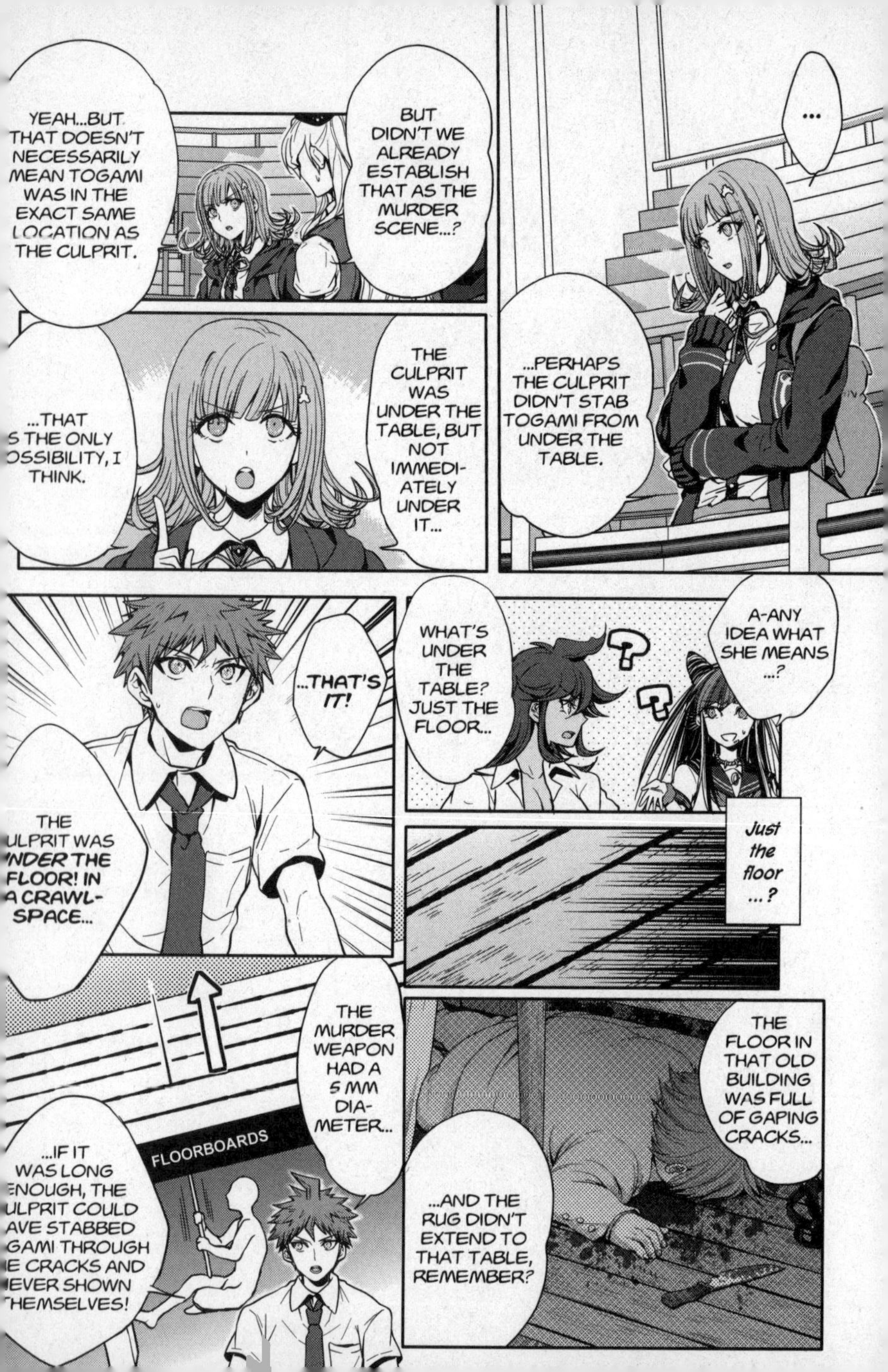
...
...PERHAPS THE CULPRIT DIDN'T STAB TOGAMI FROM UNDER THE TABLE.
BUT DIDN'T WE ALREADY ESTABLISH THAT AS THE MURDER SCENE...?
YEAH...BUT THAT DOESN'T NECESSARILY MEAN TOGAMI WAS IN THE EXACT SAME LOCATION AS THE CULPRIT.
THE CULPRIT WAS UNDER THE TABLE, BUT NOT IMMEDI-ATELY UNDER IT...
...THAT S THE ONLY OSSIBILITY, I THINK.
A-ANY IDEA WHAT SHE MEANS ...?
WHAT'S UNDER THE TABLE? JUST THE FLOOR...
Just the floor ...?
...THAT'S IT!
THE ULPRIT WAS NDER THE FLOOR! IN A CRAWL-SPACE...
THE FLOOR IN THAT OLD BUILDING WAS FULL OF GAPING CRACKS...
...AND THE RUG DIDN'T EXTEND TO THAT TABLE, REMEMBER?
THE MURDER WEAPON HAD A 5 MM DIA-METER...
FLOORBOARDS
...IF IT WAS LONG ENOUGH, THE ULPRIT COULD AVE STABBED GAMI THROUGH E CRACKS AND EVER SHOWN THEMSELVES!

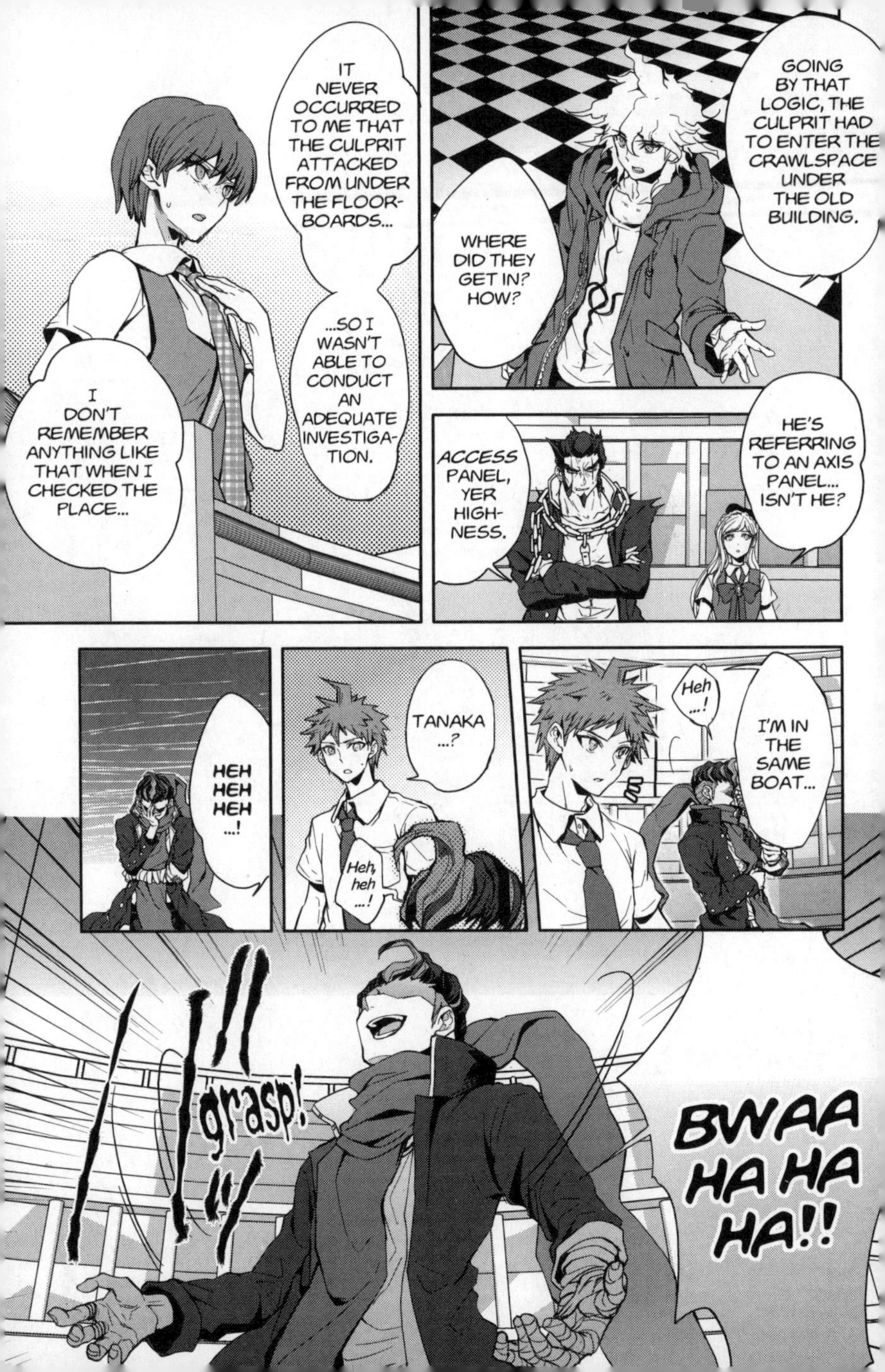
GOING BY THAT LOGIC, THE CULPRIT HAD TO ENTER THE CRAWLSPACE UNDER THE OLD BUILDING.
WHERE DID THEY GET IN? HOW?
HE'S REFERRING TO AN AXIS PANEL... ISN'T HE?
ACCESS PANEL, YER HIGHNESS.
IT NEVER OCCURRED TO ME THAT THE CULPRIT ATTACKED FROM UNDER THE FLOOR-BOARDS...
...SO I WASN'T ABLE TO CONDUCT AN ADEQUATE INVESTIGA-TION.
I DON'T REMEMBER ANYTHING LIKE THAT WHEN I CHECKED THE PLACE...
I'M IN THE SAME BOAT...
Heh ...!
TANAKA ...?
Heh, heh ...!
HEH HEH HEH ...!
BWAA HA HA HA!!
grasp!!

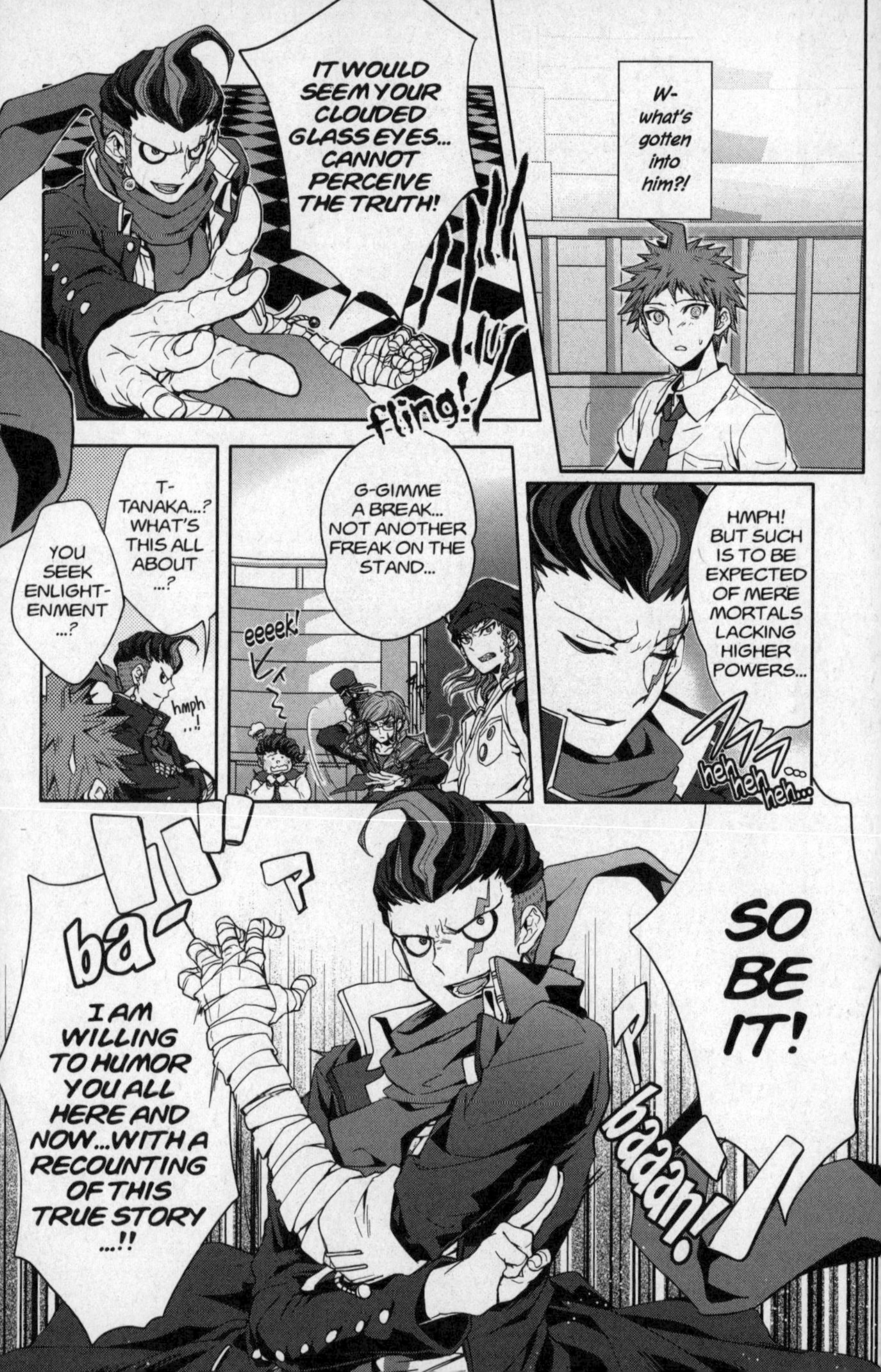
W- what's gotten into him?!
IT WOULD SEEM YOUR CLOUDED GLASS EYES... CANNOT PERCEIVE THE TRUTH!
fling!
HMPH! BUT SUCH IS TO BE EXPECTED OF MERE MORTALS LACKING HIGHER POWERS...
heh heh heh...
G-GIMME A BREAK... NOT ANOTHER FREAK ON THE STAND...
eeeek!
T- TANAKA...? WHAT'S THIS ALL ABOUT ...?
YOU SEEK ENLIGHT- ENMENT ...?
hmph ...!
SO BE IT!
ba-
I AM WILLING TO HUMOR YOU ALL HERE AND NOW...WITH A RECOUNTING OF THIS TRUE STORY ...!!
baaan!

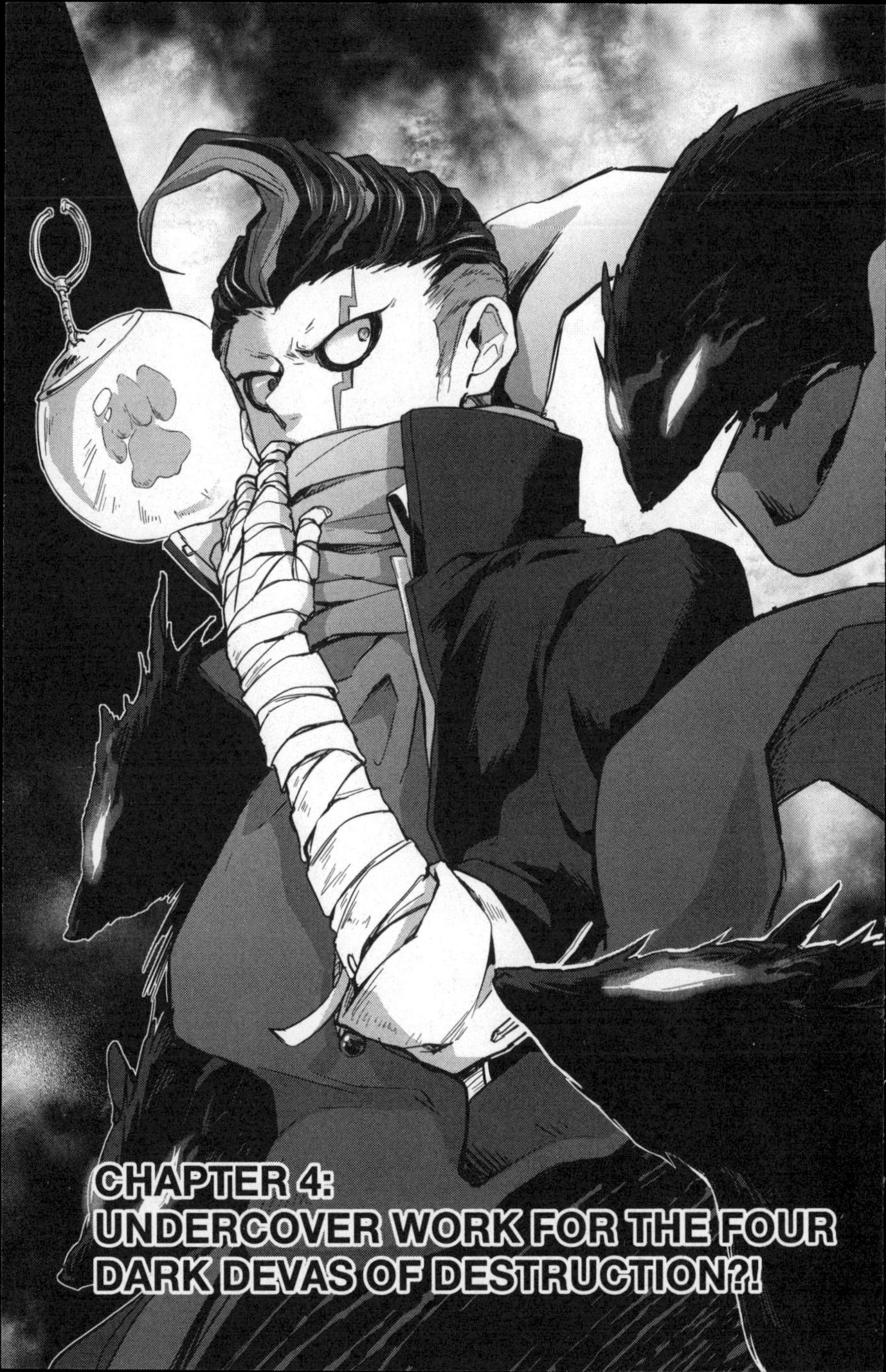
CHAPTER 4:
UNDERCOVER WORK FOR THE FOUR DARK DEVAS OF DESTRUCTION?!

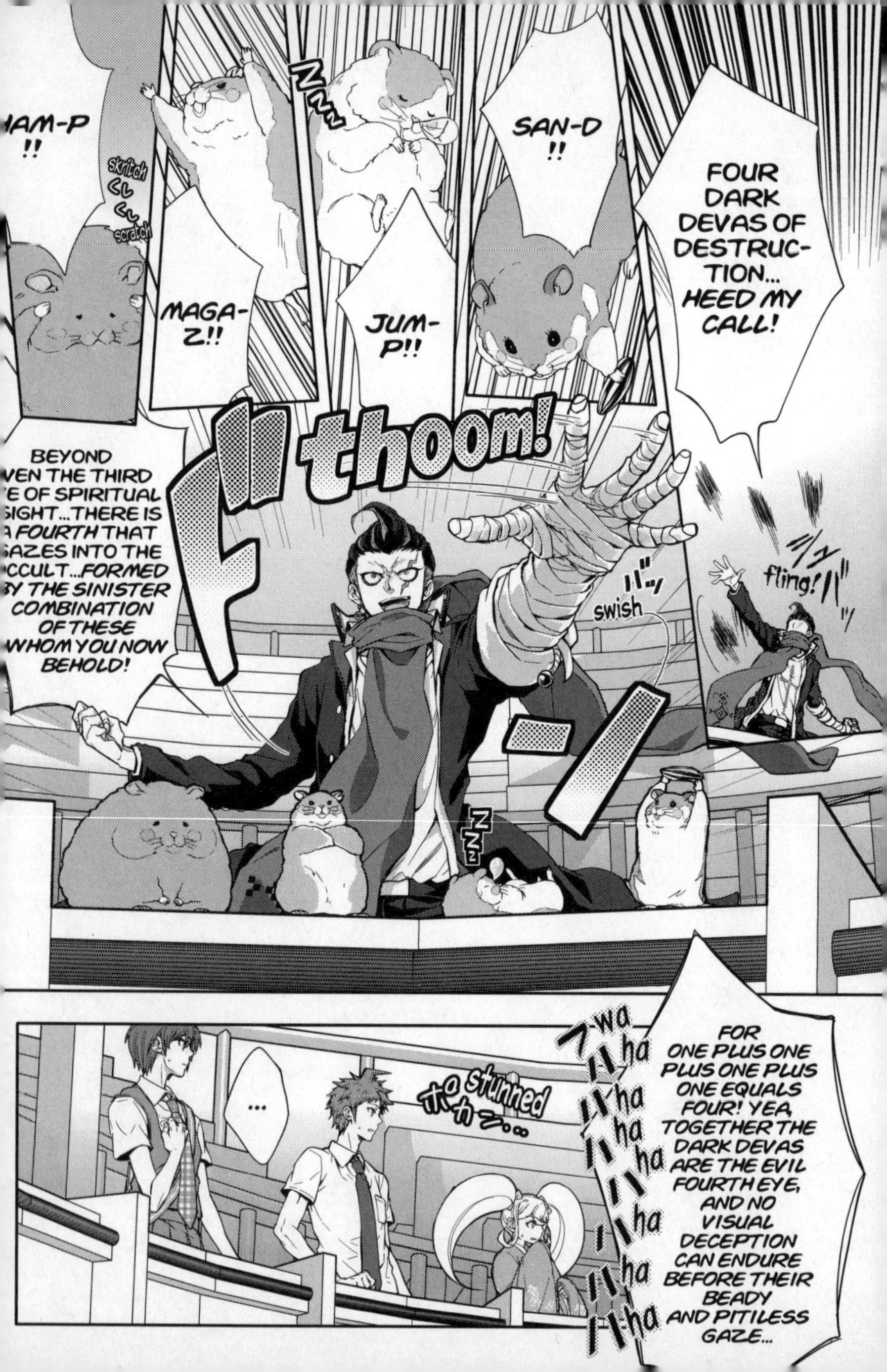
FOUR DARK DEVAS OF DESTRUCTION... HEED MY CALL!
SAN-D!!
JUM-P!!
MAGA-Z!!
AM-P!!
skritch scratch
fling!
thoom!
swish
BEYOND VEN THE THIRD E OF SPIRITUAL SIGHT...THERE IS A FOURTH THAT AZES INTO THE CCULT...FORMED Y THE SINISTER COMBINATION OF THESE WHOM YOU NOW BEHOLD!
FOR ONE PLUS ONE PLUS ONE PLUS ONE EQUALS FOUR! YEA, TOGETHER THE DARK DEVAS ARE THE EVIL FOURTH EYE, AND NO VISUAL DECEPTION CAN ENDURE BEFORE THEIR BEADY AND PITILESS GAZE...
wa ha ha ha ha ha ha ha ha
stunned
...

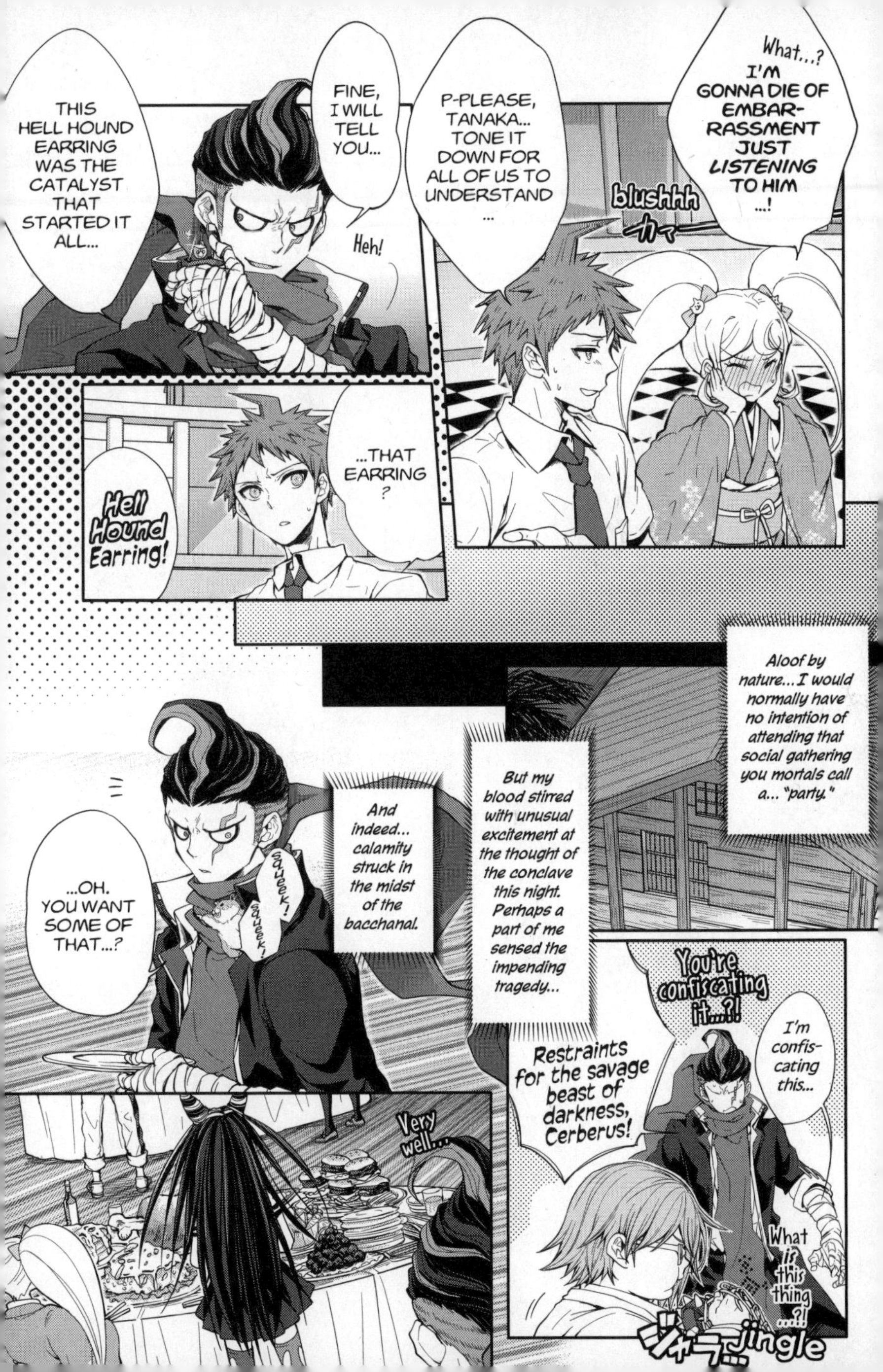
What...? I'M GONNA DIE OF EMBAR-RASSMENT JUST LISTENING TO HIM...!
P-PLEASE, TANAKA... TONE IT DOWN FOR ALL OF US TO UNDERSTAND...
blushhh カァ
FINE, I WILL TELL YOU...
Heh!
THIS HELL HOUND EARRING WAS THE CATALYST THAT STARTED IT ALL...
...THAT EARRING?
Hell Hound Earring!
Aloof by nature... I would normally have no intention of attending that social gathering you mortals call a... "party."
But my blood stirred with unusual excitement at the thought of the conclave this night. Perhaps a part of me sensed the impending tragedy...
And indeed... calamity struck in the midst of the bacchanal.
squeek! squeek!
...OH. YOU WANT SOME OF THAT...?
You're confiscating it...?!
I'm confis-cating this...
Restraints for the savage beast of darkness, Cerberus!
What is this thing...?!
ジャラ jingle
Very well...

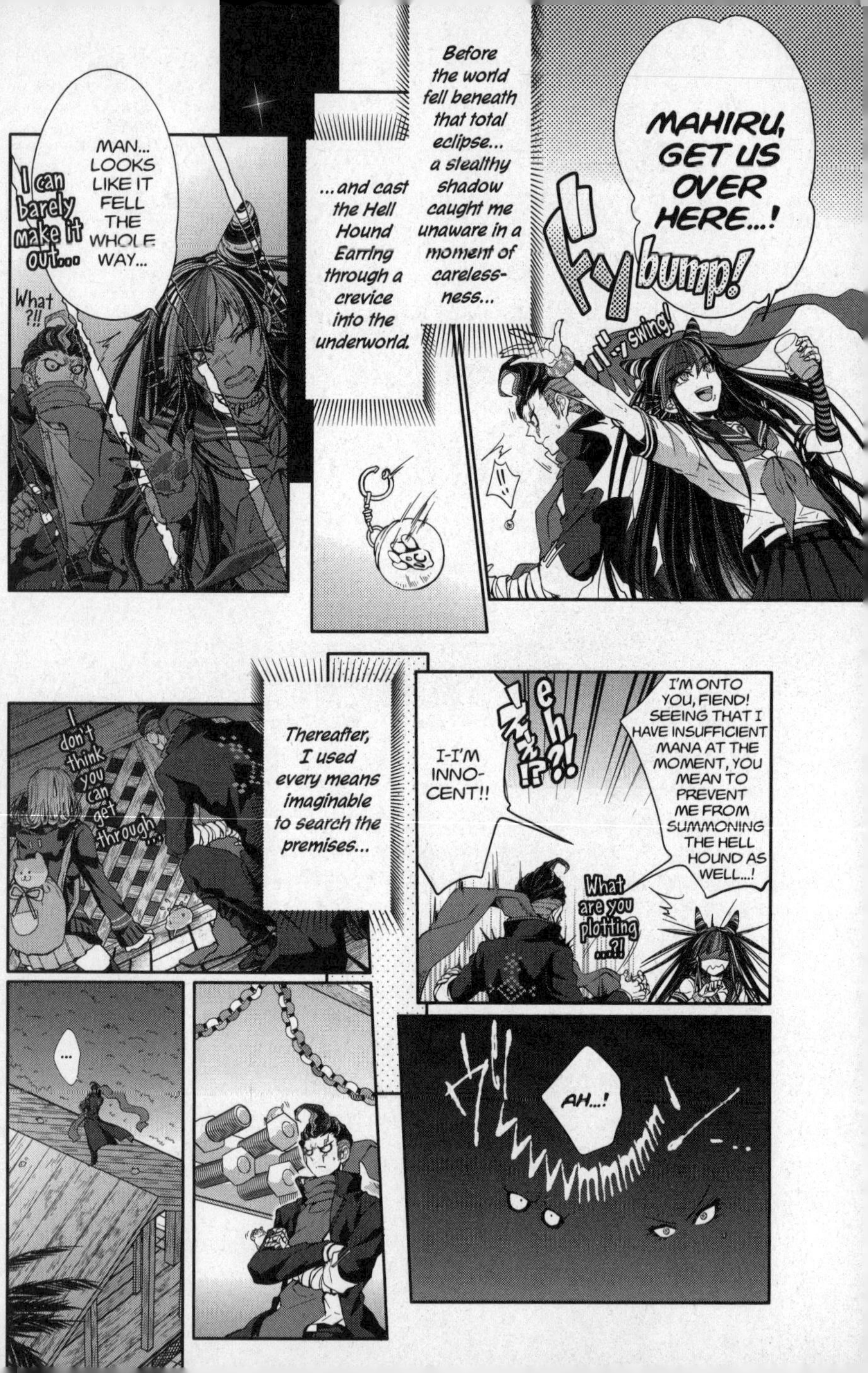
MAHIRU, GET US OVER HERE...!
bump!
swing!
!!
Before the world fell beneath that total eclipse... a stealthy shadow caught me unaware in a moment of careless-ness...
...and cast the Hell Hound Earring through a crevice into the underworld.
MAN... LOOKS LIKE IT FELL THE WHOLE WAY...
I can barely make it out...
What ?!!
eh?!
I'M ONTO YOU, FIEND! SEEING THAT I HAVE INSUFFICIENT MANA AT THE MOMENT, YOU MEAN TO PREVENT ME FROM SUMMONING THE HELL HOUND AS WELL...!
I-I'M INNO-CENT!!
What are you plotting...?!
Thereafter, I used every means imaginable to search the premises...
I don't think you can get through...
AH...!
vvvvvmmmmm
...

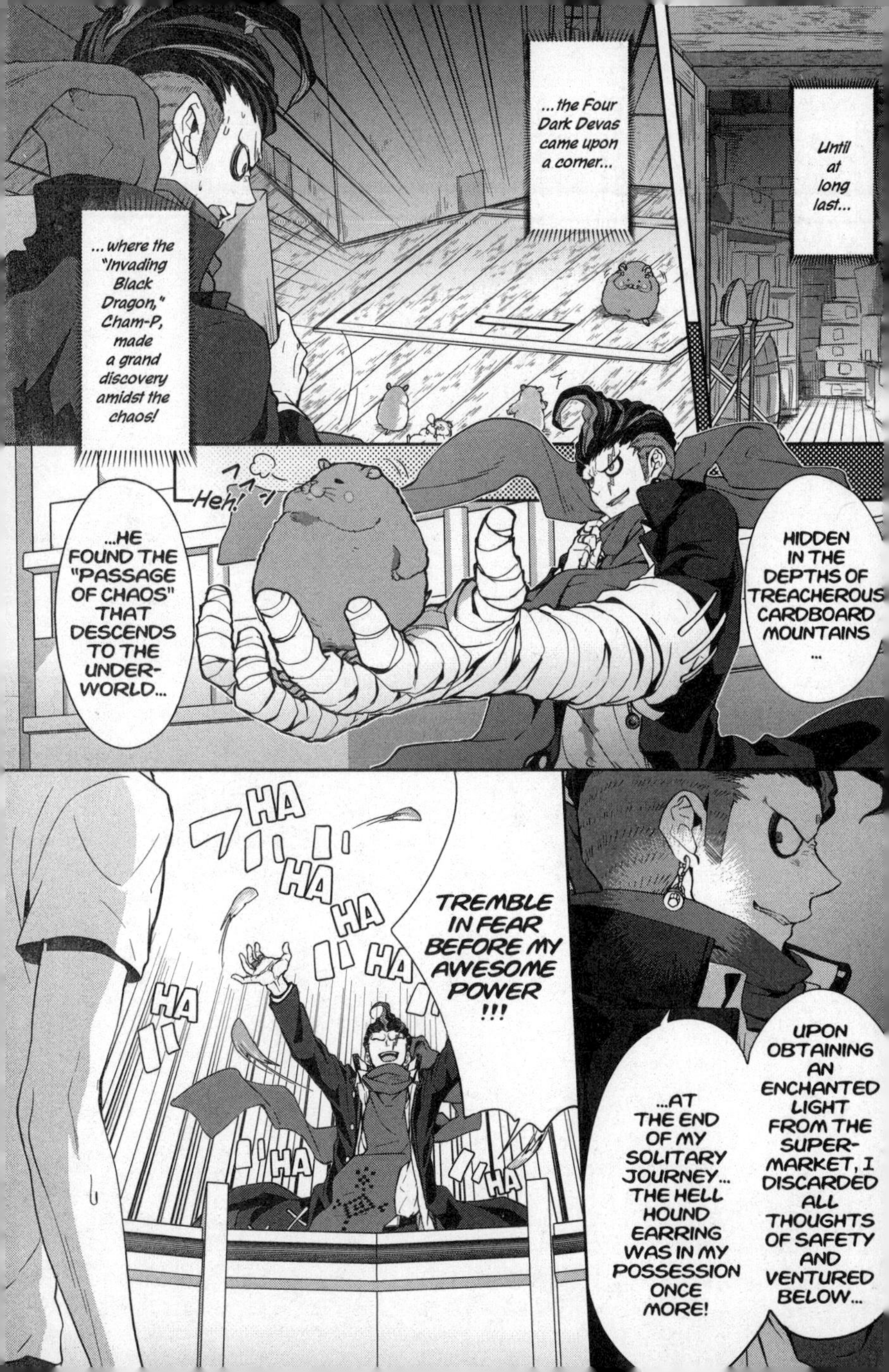
Until at long last...
...the Four Dark Devas came upon a corner...
...where the "Invading Black Dragon," Cham-P, made a grand discovery amidst the chaos!
HIDDEN IN THE DEPTHS OF TREACHEROUS CARDBOARD MOUNTAINS ...
Heh!
...HE FOUND THE "PASSAGE OF CHAOS" THAT DESCENDS TO THE UNDER-WORLD...
UPON OBTAINING AN ENCHANTED LIGHT FROM THE SUPER-MARKET, I DISCARDED ALL THOUGHTS OF SAFETY AND VENTURED BELOW...
...AT THE END OF MY SOLITARY JOURNEY... THE HELL HOUND EARRING WAS IN MY POSSESSION ONCE MORE!
TREMBLE IN FEAR BEFORE MY AWESOME POWER !!!
HA HA HA HA HA HA HA

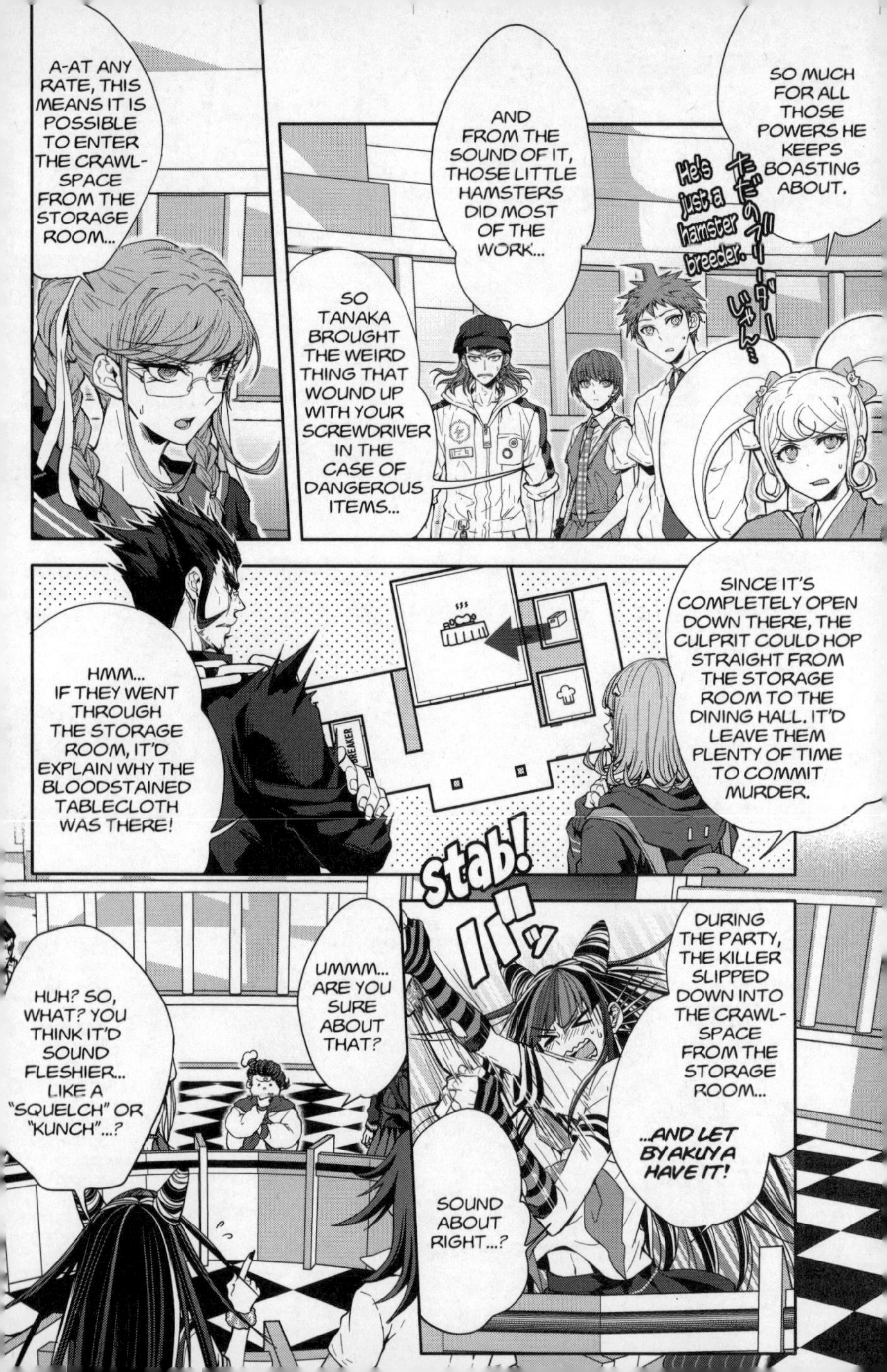
SO MUCH FOR ALL THOSE POWERS HE KEEPS BOASTING ABOUT.
He's just a hamster breeder.
ただのブリーダーじゃん…
AND FROM THE SOUND OF IT, THOSE LITTLE HAMSTERS DID MOST OF THE WORK...
SO TANAKA BROUGHT THE WEIRD THING THAT WOUND UP WITH YOUR SCREWDRIVER IN THE CASE OF DANGEROUS ITEMS...
A-AT ANY RATE, THIS MEANS IT IS POSSIBLE TO ENTER THE CRAWL-SPACE FROM THE STORAGE ROOM...
SINCE IT'S COMPLETELY OPEN DOWN THERE, THE CULPRIT COULD HOP STRAIGHT FROM THE STORAGE ROOM TO THE DINING HALL. IT'D LEAVE THEM PLENTY OF TIME TO COMMIT MURDER.
BREAKER
HMM... IF THEY WENT THROUGH THE STORAGE ROOM, IT'D EXPLAIN WHY THE BLOODSTAINED TABLECLOTH WAS THERE!
stab!
バッ
DURING THE PARTY, THE KILLER SLIPPED DOWN INTO THE CRAWL-SPACE FROM THE STORAGE ROOM...
...AND LET BYAKUYA HAVE IT!
SOUND ABOUT RIGHT...?
UMMM... ARE YOU SURE ABOUT THAT?
HUH? SO, WHAT? YOU THINK IT'D SOUND FLESHIER... LIKE A "SQUELCH" OR "KUNCH"...?

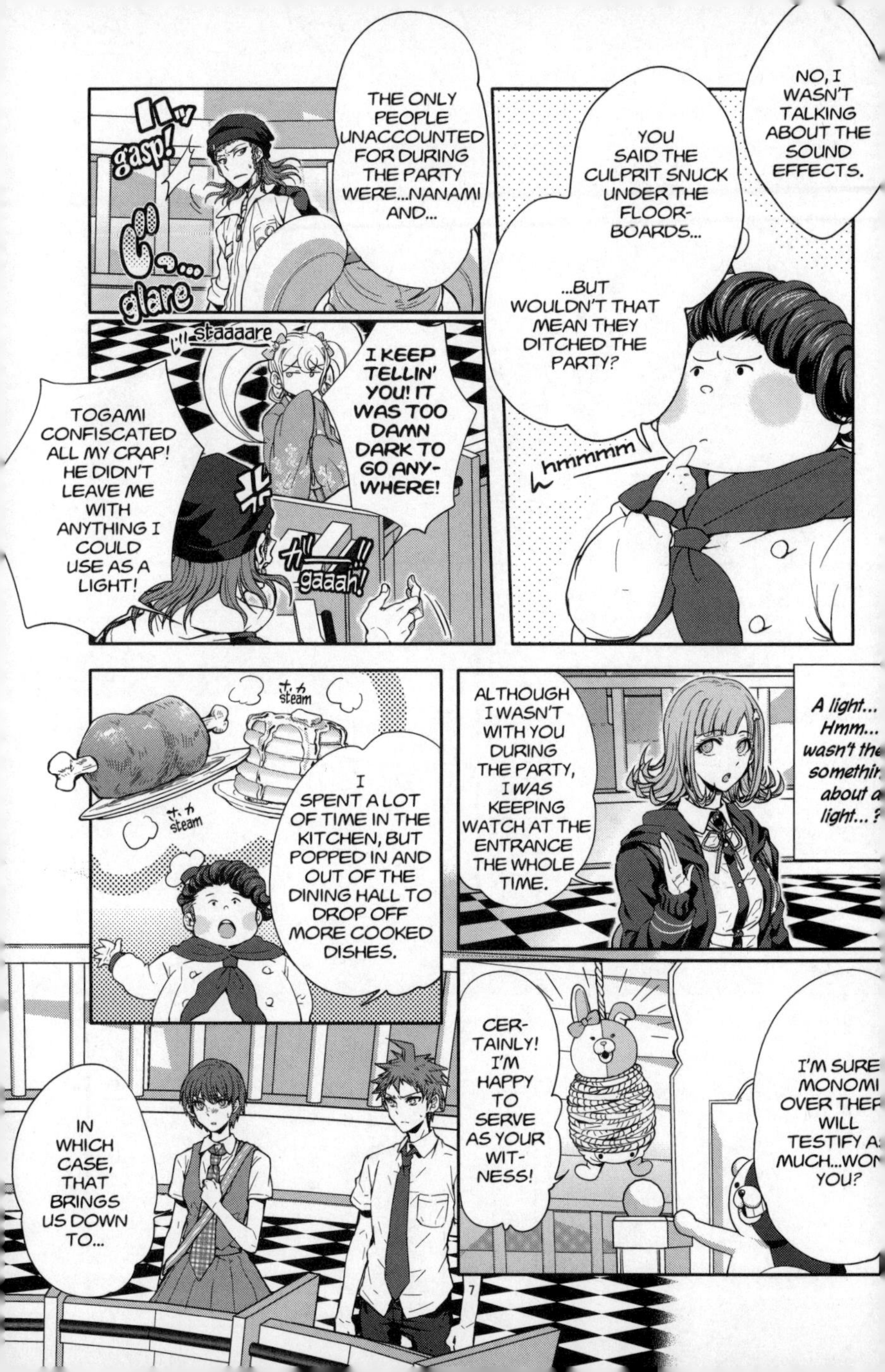
NO, I WASN'T TALKING ABOUT THE SOUND EFFECTS.
YOU SAID THE CULPRIT SNUCK UNDER THE FLOOR-BOARDS...
...BUT WOULDN'T THAT MEAN THEY DITCHED THE PARTY?
hmmmmm
THE ONLY PEOPLE UNACCOUNTED FOR DURING THE PARTY WERE...NANAMI AND...
gasp!
glare
staaaare
I KEEP TELLIN' YOU! IT WAS TOO DAMN DARK TO GO ANY-WHERE!
TOGAMI CONFISCATED ALL MY CRAP! HE DIDN'T LEAVE ME WITH ANYTHING I COULD USE AS A LIGHT!
gaaah!
A light... Hmm... wasn't the somethi about a light...?
ALTHOUGH I WASN'T WITH YOU DURING THE PARTY, I WAS KEEPING WATCH AT THE ENTRANCE THE WHOLE TIME.
steam
steam
I SPENT A LOT OF TIME IN THE KITCHEN, BUT POPPED IN AND OUT OF THE DINING HALL TO DROP OFF MORE COOKED DISHES.
I'M SURE MONOMI OVER THER WILL TESTIFY A MUCH...WON YOU?
CER-TAINLY! I'M HAPPY TO SERVE AS YOUR WIT-NESS!
IN WHICH CASE, THAT BRINGS US DOWN TO...

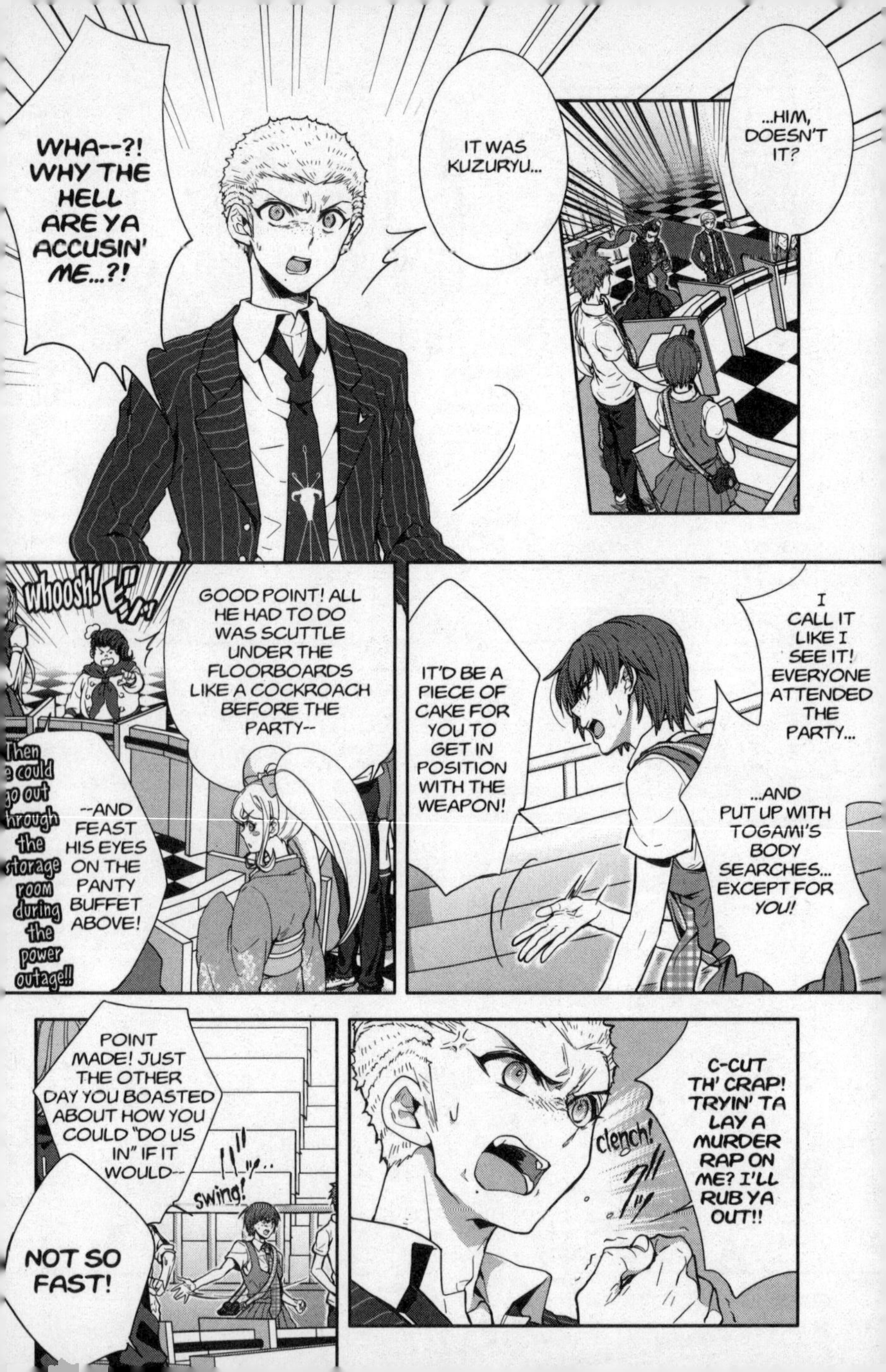
IT WAS KUZURYU...
...HIM, DOESN'T IT?
WHA--?! WHY THE HELL ARE YA ACCUSIN' ME...?!
I CALL IT LIKE I SEE IT! EVERYONE ATTENDED THE PARTY...
...AND PUT UP WITH TOGAMI'S BODY SEARCHES... EXCEPT FOR *YOU!*
IT'D BE A PIECE OF CAKE FOR YOU TO GET IN POSITION WITH THE WEAPON!
whoosh!
GOOD POINT! ALL HE HAD TO DO WAS SCUTTLE UNDER THE FLOORBOARDS LIKE A COCKROACH BEFORE THE PARTY--
--AND FEAST HIS EYES ON THE PANTY BUFFET ABOVE!
Then e could go out hrough the storage room during the power outage!!
clench!
C-CUT TH' CRAP! TRYIN' TA LAY A MURDER RAP ON ME? I'LL RUB YA OUT!!
POINT MADE! JUST THE OTHER DAY YOU BOASTED ABOUT HOW YOU COULD "DO US IN" IF IT WOULD--
swing!
NOT SO FAST!

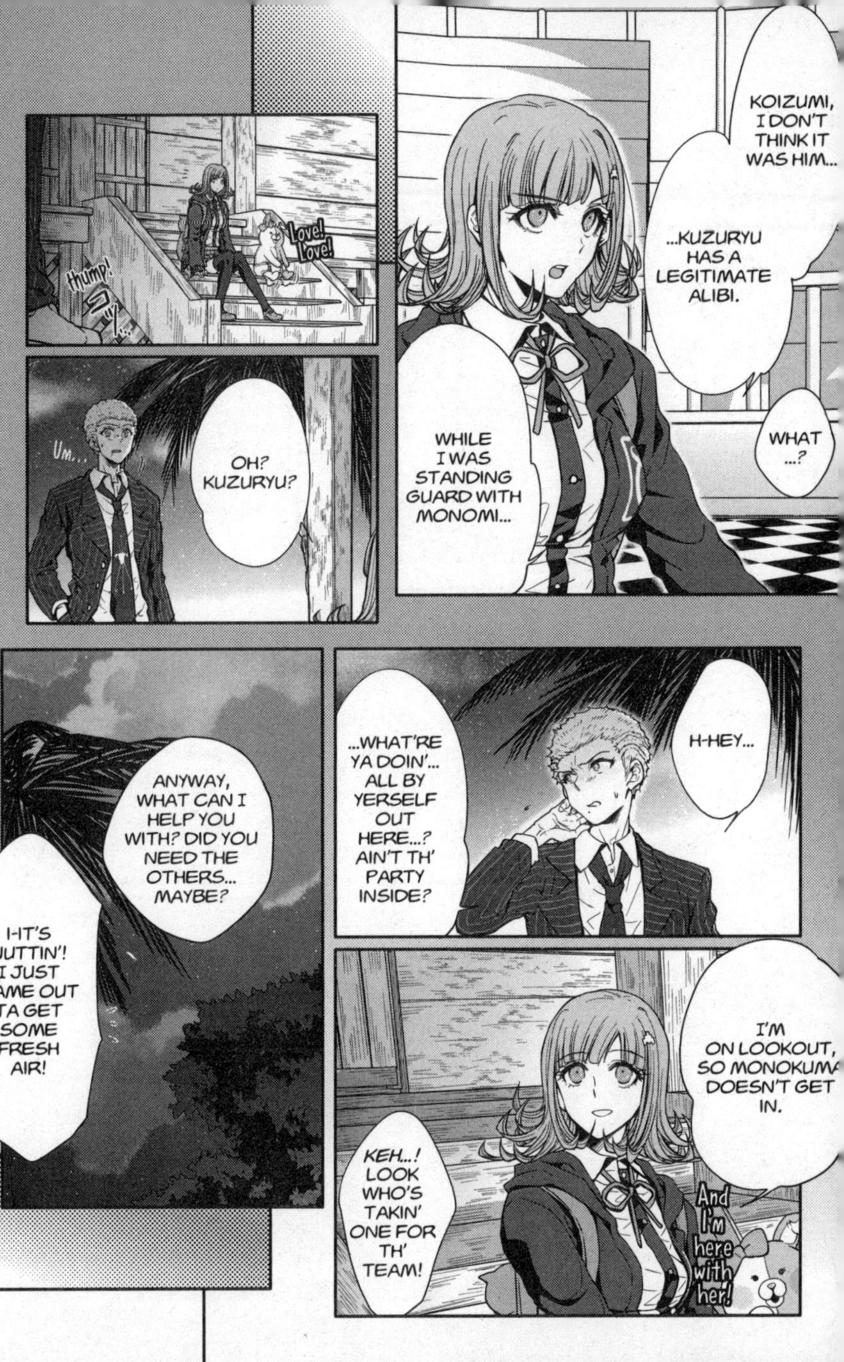

KOIZUMI, I DON'T THINK IT WAS HIM...
...KUZURYU HAS A LEGITIMATE ALIBI.
WHAT ...?
WHILE I WAS STANDING GUARD WITH MONOMI...
Love! Love!
thump!
OH? KUZURYU?
Um...
H-HEY...
...WHAT'RE YA DOIN'... ALL BY YERSELF OUT HERE...? AIN'T TH' PARTY INSIDE?
I'M ON LOOKOUT, SO MONOKUMA DOESN'T GET IN.
And I'm here with her!
KEH...! LOOK WHO'S TAKIN' ONE FOR TH' TEAM!
ANYWAY, WHAT CAN I HELP YOU WITH? DID YOU NEED THE OTHERS... MAYBE?
I-IT'S NUTTIN'! I JUST CAME OUT TA GET SOME FRESH AIR!

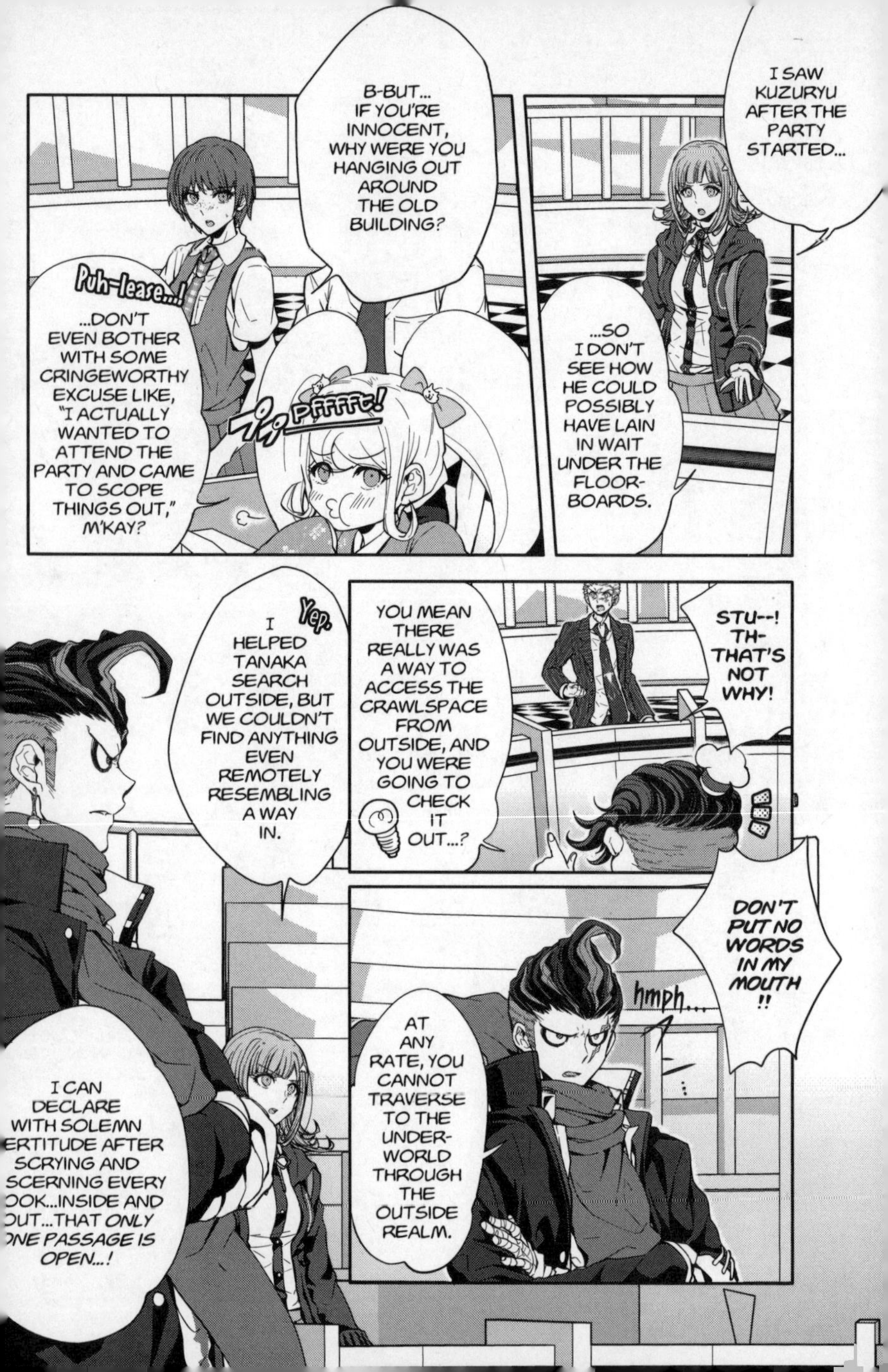

I SAW KUZURYU AFTER THE PARTY STARTED...
...SO I DON'T SEE HOW HE COULD POSSIBLY HAVE LAIN IN WAIT UNDER THE FLOOR-BOARDS.
B-BUT... IF YOU'RE INNOCENT, WHY WERE YOU HANGING OUT AROUND THE OLD BUILDING?
Puh-lease...!
...DON'T EVEN BOTHER WITH SOME CRINGEWORTHY EXCUSE LIKE, "I ACTUALLY WANTED TO ATTEND THE PARTY AND CAME TO SCOPE THINGS OUT," M'KAY?
STU--! TH-THAT'S NOT WHY!
YOU MEAN THERE REALLY WAS A WAY TO ACCESS THE CRAWLSPACE FROM OUTSIDE, AND YOU WERE GOING TO CHECK IT OUT...?
Yep.
I HELPED TANAKA SEARCH OUTSIDE, BUT WE COULDN'T FIND ANYTHING EVEN REMOTELY RESEMBLING A WAY IN.
DON'T PUT NO WORDS IN MY MOUTH!!
hmph...
AT ANY RATE, YOU CANNOT TRAVERSE TO THE UNDER-WORLD THROUGH THE OUTSIDE REALM.
I CAN DECLARE WITH SOLEMN ERTITUDE AFTER SCRYING AND SCERNING EVERY OOK...INSIDE AND OUT...THAT ONLY ONE PASSAGE IS OPEN...!

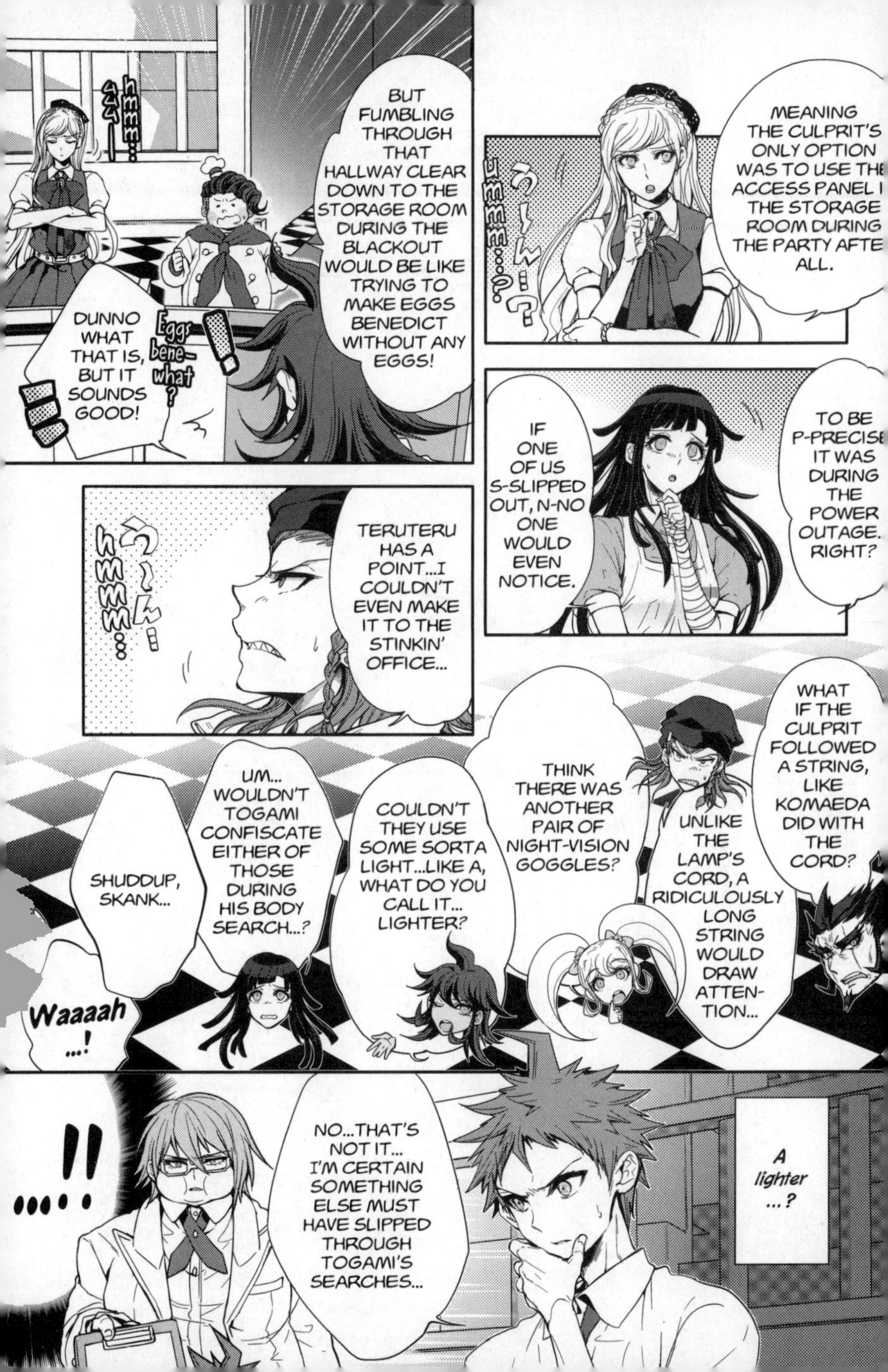
MEANING THE CULPRIT'S ONLY OPTION WAS TO USE THE ACCESS PANEL I THE STORAGE ROOM DURING THE PARTY AFTE ALL.
うーん!?
ummmm...?
BUT FUMBLING THROUGH THAT HALLWAY CLEAR DOWN TO THE STORAGE ROOM DURING THE BLACKOUT WOULD BE LIKE TRYING TO MAKE EGGS BENEDICT WITHOUT ANY EGGS!
ムムム
hmmm...
!
Eggs bene-what?
DUNNO WHAT THAT IS, BUT IT SOUNDS GOOD!
TO BE P-PRECISE IT WAS DURING THE POWER OUTAGE. RIGHT?
IF ONE OF US S-SLIPPED OUT, N-NO ONE WOULD EVEN NOTICE.
TERUTERU HAS A POINT...I COULDN'T EVEN MAKE IT TO THE STINKIN' OFFICE...
うーん!
hmmm...
WHAT IF THE CULPRIT FOLLOWED A STRING, LIKE KOMAEDA DID WITH THE CORD?
UNLIKE THE LAMP'S CORD, A RIDICULOUSLY LONG STRING WOULD DRAW ATTEN-TION...
THINK THERE WAS ANOTHER PAIR OF NIGHT-VISION GOGGLES?
COULDN'T THEY USE SOME SORTA LIGHT...LIKE A, WHAT DO YOU CALL IT... LIGHTER?
UM... WOULDN'T TOGAMI CONFISCATE EITHER OF THOSE DURING HIS BODY SEARCH...?
SHUDDUP, SKANK...
Waaaah...!
A lighter...?
NO...THAT'S NOT IT... I'M CERTAIN SOMETHING ELSE MUST HAVE SLIPPED THROUGH TOGAMI'S SEARCHES...
...!!

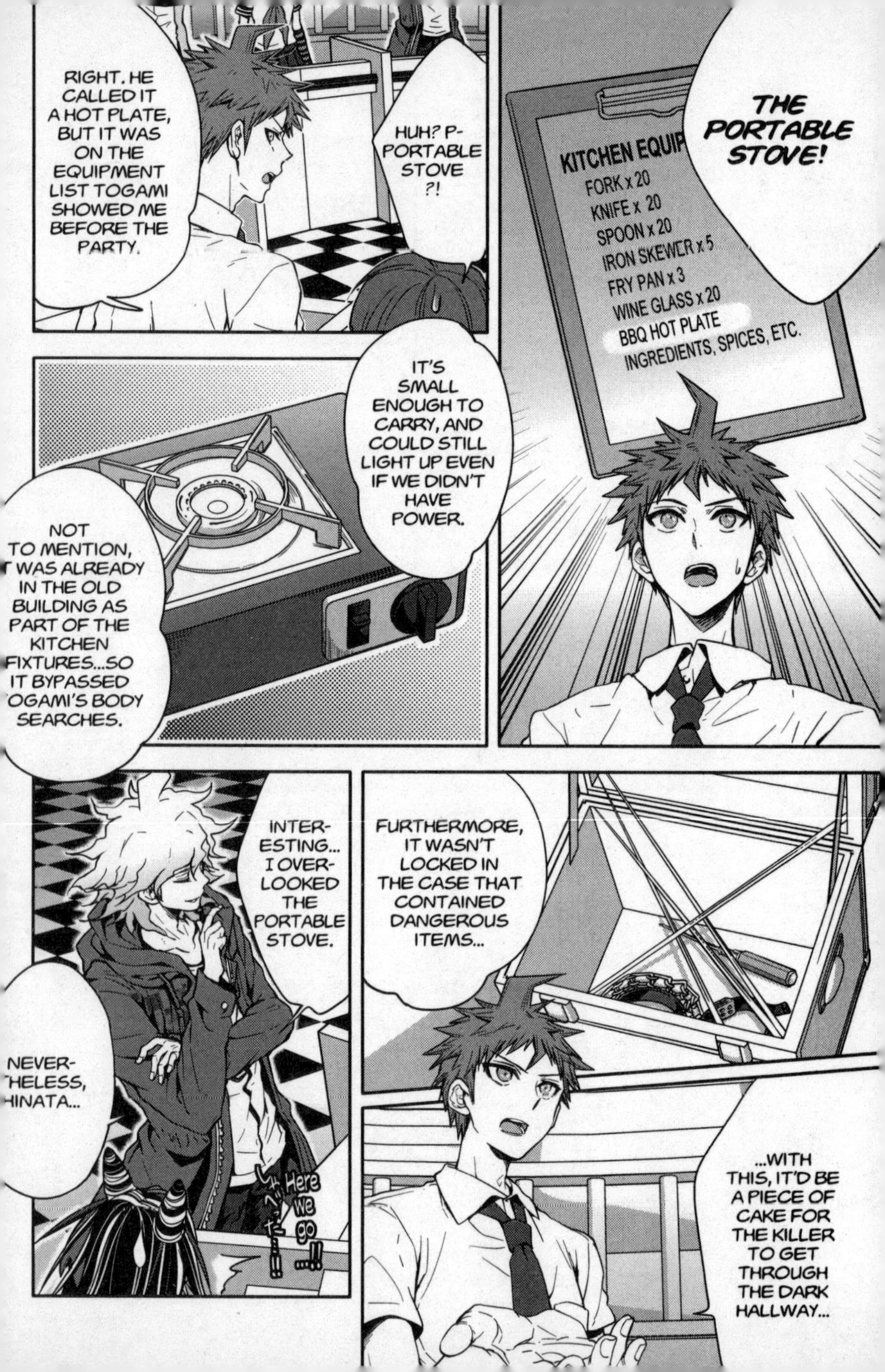
THE PORTABLE STOVE!
KITCHEN EQUIP
FORK x 20
KNIFE x 20
SPOON x 20
IRON SKEWER x 5
FRY PAN x 3
WINE GLASS x 20
BBQ HOT PLATE
INGREDIENTS, SPICES, ETC.
HUH? P-PORTABLE STOVE ?!
RIGHT. HE CALLED IT A HOT PLATE, BUT IT WAS ON THE EQUIPMENT LIST TOGAMI SHOWED ME BEFORE THE PARTY.
IT'S SMALL ENOUGH TO CARRY, AND COULD STILL LIGHT UP EVEN IF WE DIDN'T HAVE POWER.
NOT TO MENTION, T WAS ALREADY IN THE OLD BUILDING AS PART OF THE KITCHEN FIXTURES...SO IT BYPASSED OGAMI'S BODY SEARCHES.
FURTHERMORE, IT WASN'T LOCKED IN THE CASE THAT CONTAINED DANGEROUS ITEMS...
...WITH THIS, IT'D BE A PIECE OF CAKE FOR THE KILLER TO GET THROUGH THE DARK HALLWAY...
INTER-ESTING... I OVER-LOOKED THE PORTABLE STOVE.
NEVER-THELESS, HINATA...
Here we go...!!

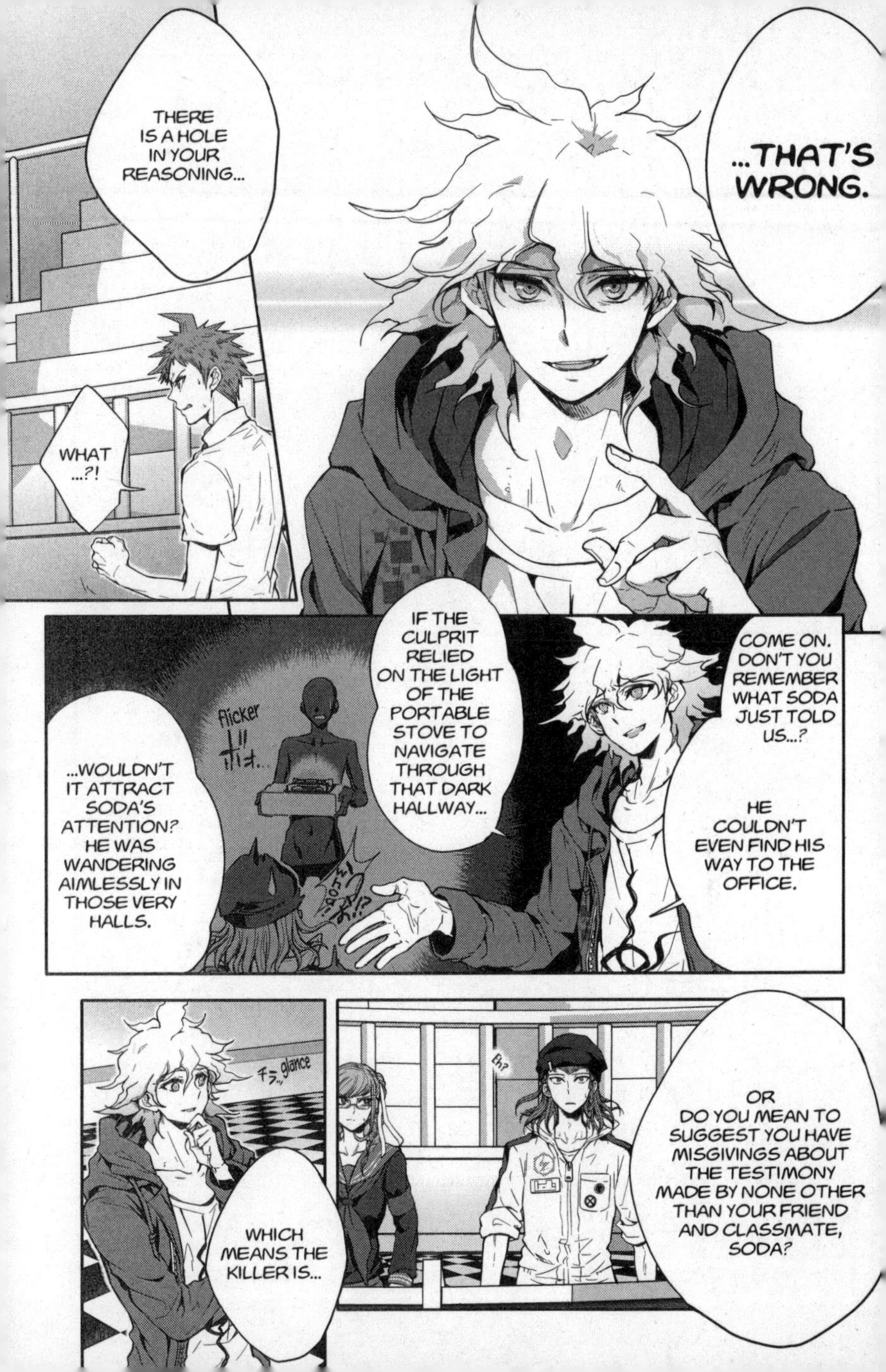
...THAT'S WRONG.
THERE IS A HOLE IN YOUR REASONING...
WHAT ...?!
COME ON. DON'T YOU REMEMBER WHAT SODA JUST TOLD US...?
HE COULDN'T EVEN FIND HIS WAY TO THE OFFICE.
IF THE CULPRIT RELIED ON THE LIGHT OF THE PORTABLE STOVE TO NAVIGATE THROUGH THAT DARK HALLWAY...
flicker
...WOULDN'T IT ATTRACT SODA'S ATTENTION? HE WAS WANDERING AIMLESSLY IN THOSE VERY HALLS.
OR DO YOU MEAN TO SUGGEST YOU HAVE MISGIVINGS ABOUT THE TESTIMONY MADE BY NONE OTHER THAN YOUR FRIEND AND CLASSMATE, SODA?
Eh?
glance
WHICH MEANS THE KILLER IS...

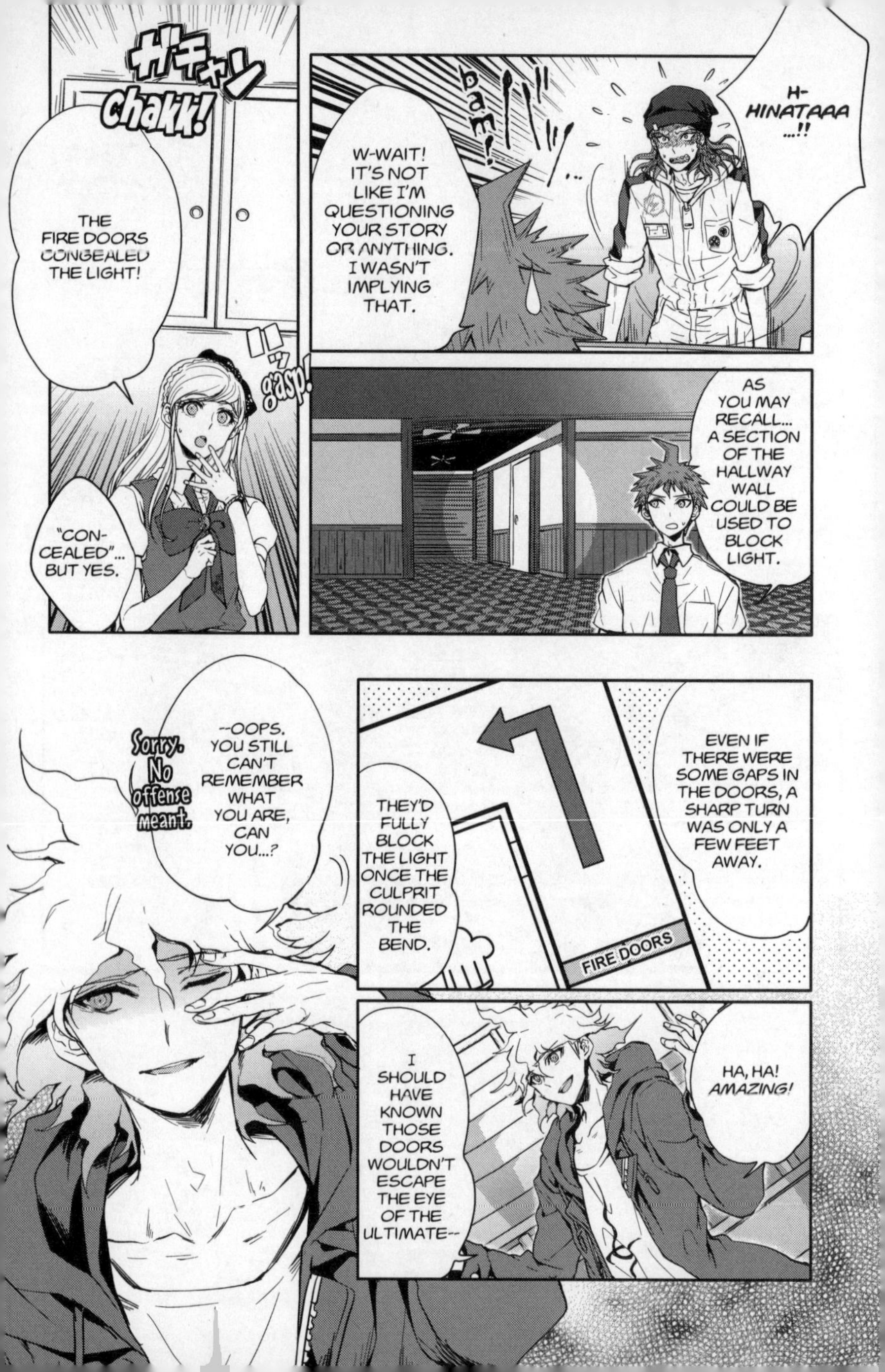
H-HINATAAA ...!!
bam!
W-WAIT! IT'S NOT LIKE I'M QUESTIONING YOUR STORY OR ANYTHING. I WASN'T IMPLYING THAT.
AS YOU MAY RECALL... A SECTION OF THE HALLWAY WALL COULD BE USED TO BLOCK LIGHT.
ガチャン
chakk!
THE FIRE DOORS CONGEALED THE LIGHT!
gasp!
"CON-CEALED"... BUT YES.
EVEN IF THERE WERE SOME GAPS IN THE DOORS, A SHARP TURN WAS ONLY A FEW FEET AWAY.
THEY'D FULLY BLOCK THE LIGHT ONCE THE CULPRIT ROUNDED THE BEND.
FIRE DOORS
HA, HA! AMAZING!
I SHOULD HAVE KNOWN THOSE DOORS WOULDN'T ESCAPE THE EYE OF THE ULTIMATE--
--OOPS. YOU STILL CAN'T REMEMBER WHAT YOU ARE, CAN YOU...?
Sorry. No offense meant.

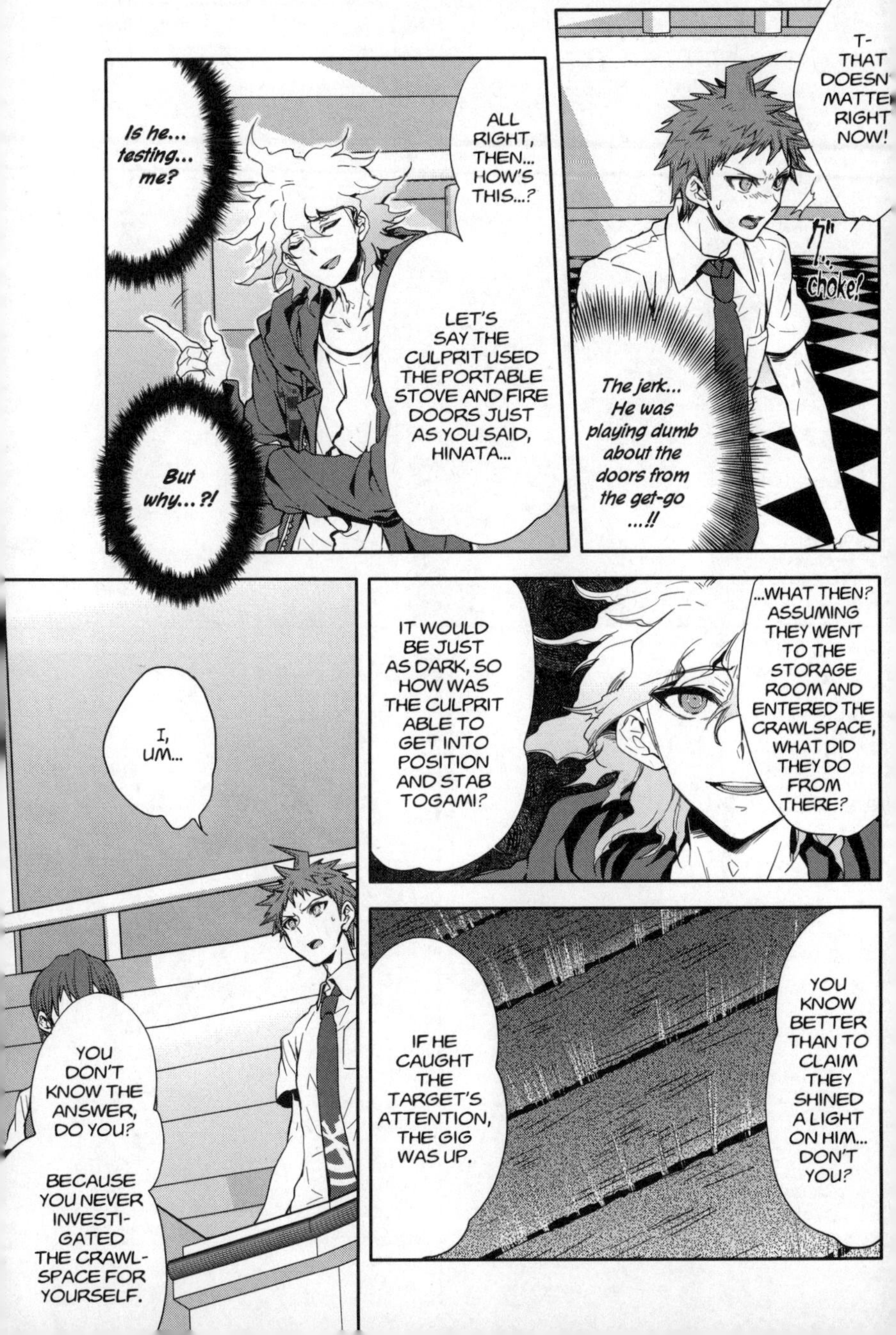

T- THAT DOESN MATTE RIGHT NOW!
ガ''
choke!
The jerk... He was playing dumb about the doors from the get-go ...!!
ALL RIGHT, THEN... HOW'S THIS...?
Is he... testing... me?
LET'S SAY THE CULPRIT USED THE PORTABLE STOVE AND FIRE DOORS JUST AS YOU SAID, HINATA...
But why...?!
...WHAT THEN? ASSUMING THEY WENT TO THE STORAGE ROOM AND ENTERED THE CRAWLSPACE, WHAT DID THEY DO FROM THERE?
IT WOULD BE JUST AS DARK, SO HOW WAS THE CULPRIT ABLE TO GET INTO POSITION AND STAB TOGAMI?
YOU KNOW BETTER THAN TO CLAIM THEY SHINED A LIGHT ON HIM... DON'T YOU?
IF HE CAUGHT THE TARGET'S ATTENTION, THE GIG WAS UP.
I, UM...
YOU DON'T KNOW THE ANSWER, DO YOU?
BECAUSE YOU NEVER INVESTI- GATED THE CRAWL- SPACE FOR YOURSELF.

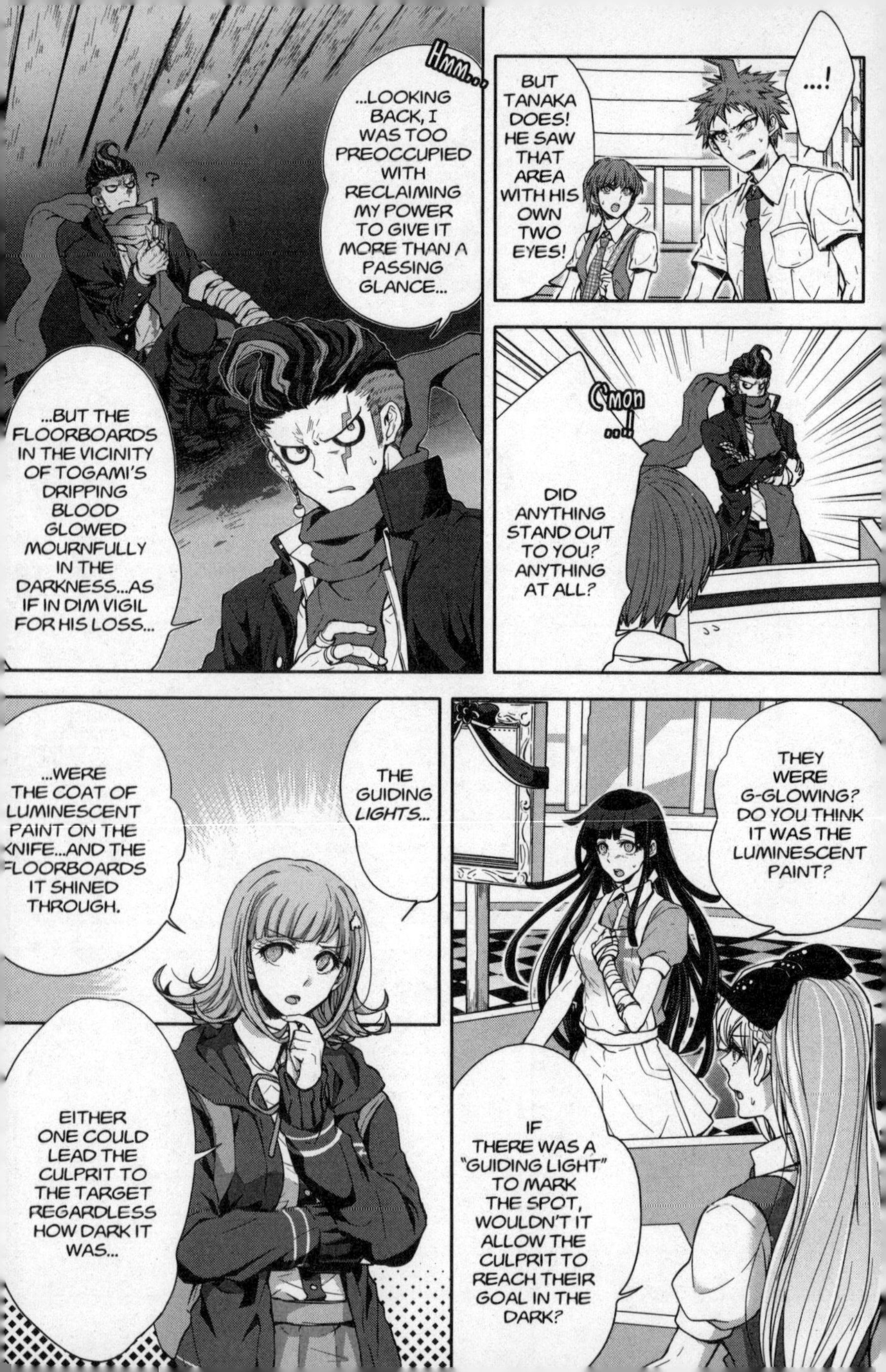
...!
BUT TANAKA DOES! HE SAW THAT AREA WITH HIS OWN TWO EYES!
C'mon...!
DID ANYTHING STAND OUT TO YOU? ANYTHING AT ALL?
HMM...
...LOOKING BACK, I WAS TOO PREOCCUPIED WITH RECLAIMING MY POWER TO GIVE IT MORE THAN A PASSING GLANCE...
...BUT THE FLOORBOARDS IN THE VICINITY OF TOGAMI'S DRIPPING BLOOD GLOWED MOURNFULLY IN THE DARKNESS...AS IF IN DIM VIGIL FOR HIS LOSS...
THEY WERE G-GLOWING? DO YOU THINK IT WAS THE LUMINESCENT PAINT?
IF THERE WAS A "GUIDING LIGHT" TO MARK THE SPOT, WOULDN'T IT ALLOW THE CULPRIT TO REACH THEIR GOAL IN THE DARK?
THE GUIDING *LIGHTS*...
...WERE THE COAT OF LUMINESCENT PAINT ON THE KNIFE...AND THE FLOORBOARDS IT SHINED THROUGH.
EITHER ONE COULD LEAD THE CULPRIT TO THE TARGET REGARDLESS HOW DARK IT WAS...

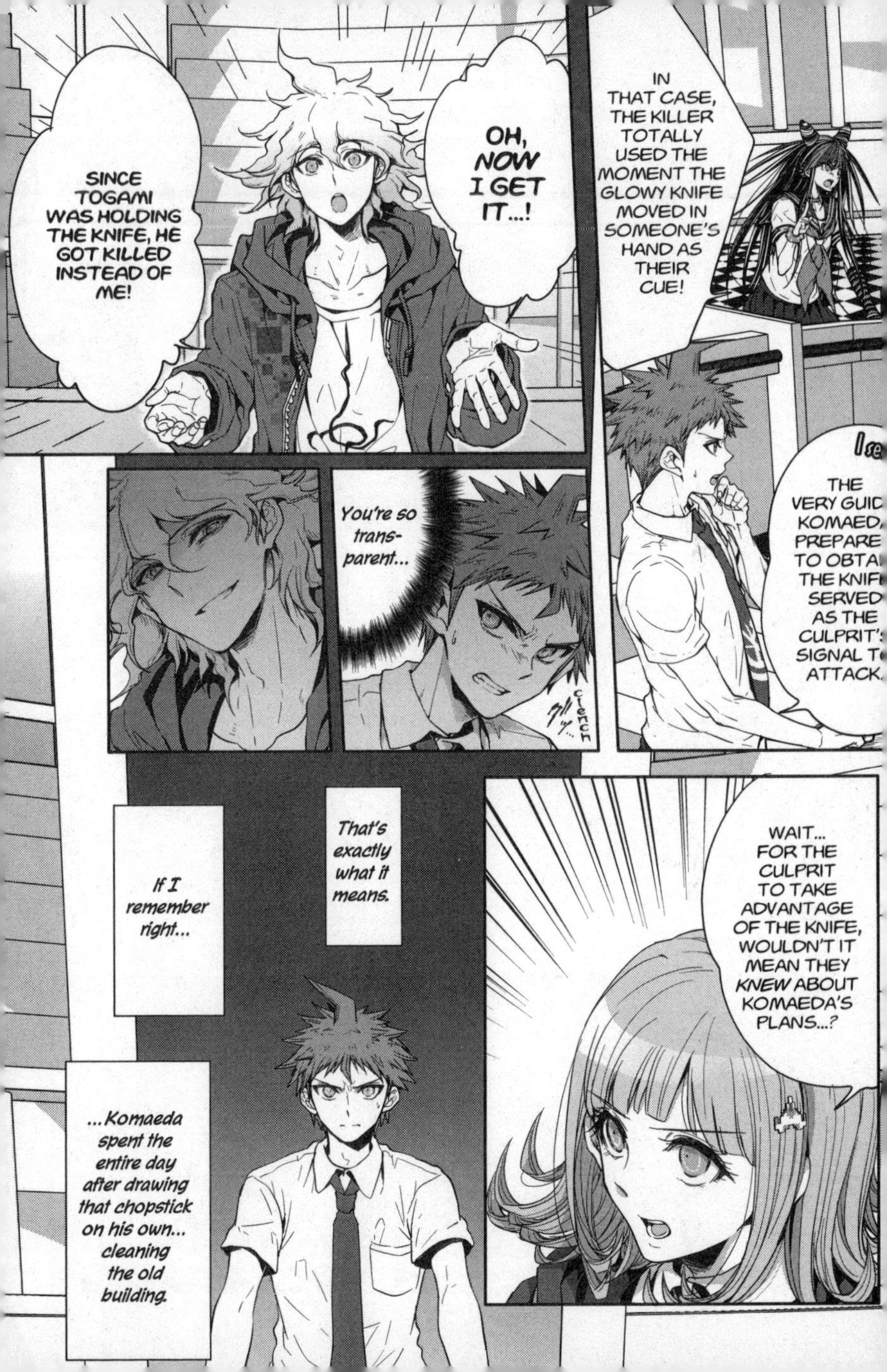
IN THAT CASE, THE KILLER TOTALLY USED THE MOMENT THE GLOWY KNIFE MOVED IN SOMEONE'S HAND AS THEIR CUE!
OH, *NOW* I GET IT...!
SINCE TOGAMI WAS HOLDING THE KNIFE, HE GOT KILLED INSTEAD OF ME!
I se
THE VERY GUID KOMAED PREPARE TO OBTA THE KNIF SERVED AS THE CULPRIT' SIGNAL T ATTACK.
You're so trans-parent...
clench
WAIT... FOR THE CULPRIT TO TAKE ADVANTAGE OF THE KNIFE, WOULDN'T IT MEAN THEY *KNEW* ABOUT KOMAEDA'S PLANS...?
That's exactly what it means.
If I remember right...
...Komaeda spent the entire day after drawing that chopstick on his own... cleaning the old building.

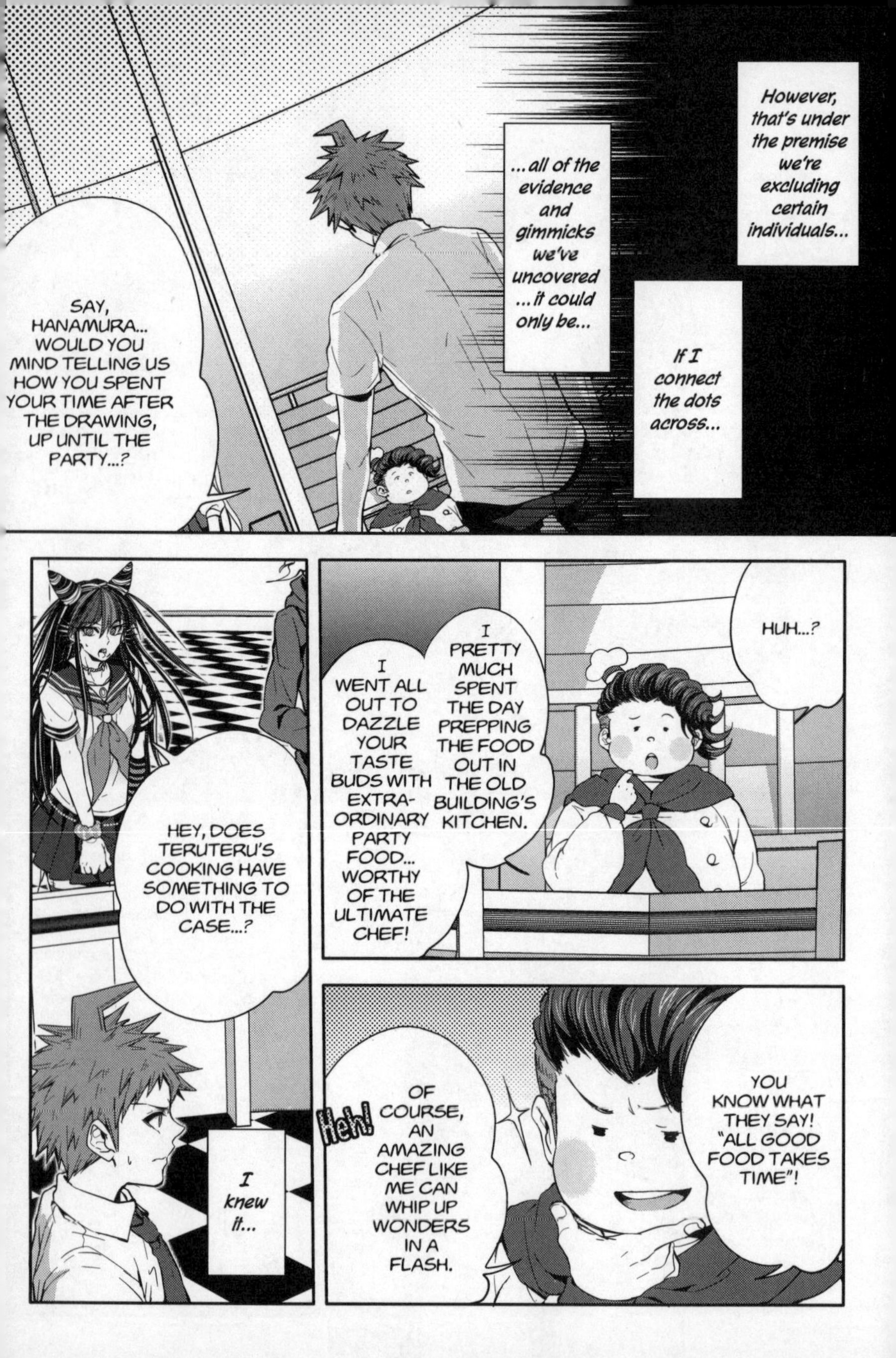
However, that's under the premise we're excluding certain individuals...
If I connect the dots across...
...all of the evidence and gimmicks we've uncovered ...it could only be...
SAY, HANAMURA... WOULD YOU MIND TELLING US HOW YOU SPENT YOUR TIME AFTER THE DRAWING, UP UNTIL THE PARTY...?
HUH...?
I PRETTY MUCH SPENT THE DAY PREPPING THE FOOD OUT IN THE OLD BUILDING'S KITCHEN.
I WENT ALL OUT TO DAZZLE YOUR TASTE BUDS WITH EXTRA-ORDINARY PARTY FOOD... WORTHY OF THE ULTIMATE CHEF!
YOU KNOW WHAT THEY SAY! "ALL GOOD FOOD TAKES TIME"!
OF COURSE, AN AMAZING CHEF LIKE ME CAN WHIP UP WONDERS IN A FLASH.
Heh!
HEY, DOES TERUTERU'S COOKING HAVE SOMETHING TO DO WITH THE CASE...?
I knew it...

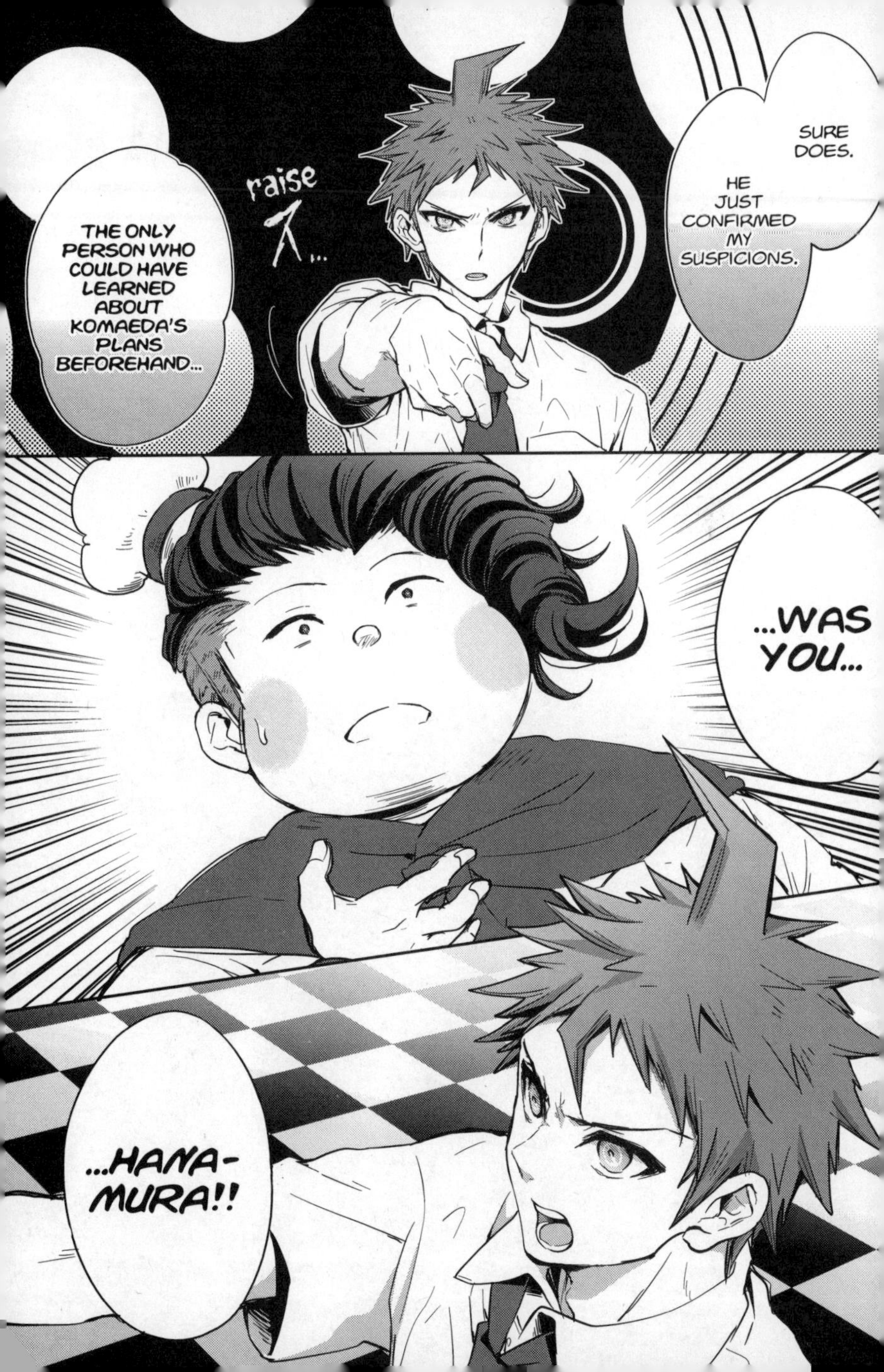
SURE DOES.
HE JUST CONFIRMED MY SUSPICIONS.
raise
THE ONLY PERSON WHO COULD HAVE LEARNED ABOUT KOMAEDA'S PLANS BEFOREHAND...
...WAS YOU...
...HANA-MURA!!

DR2

CHAPTER 5: TRUE CULPRIT

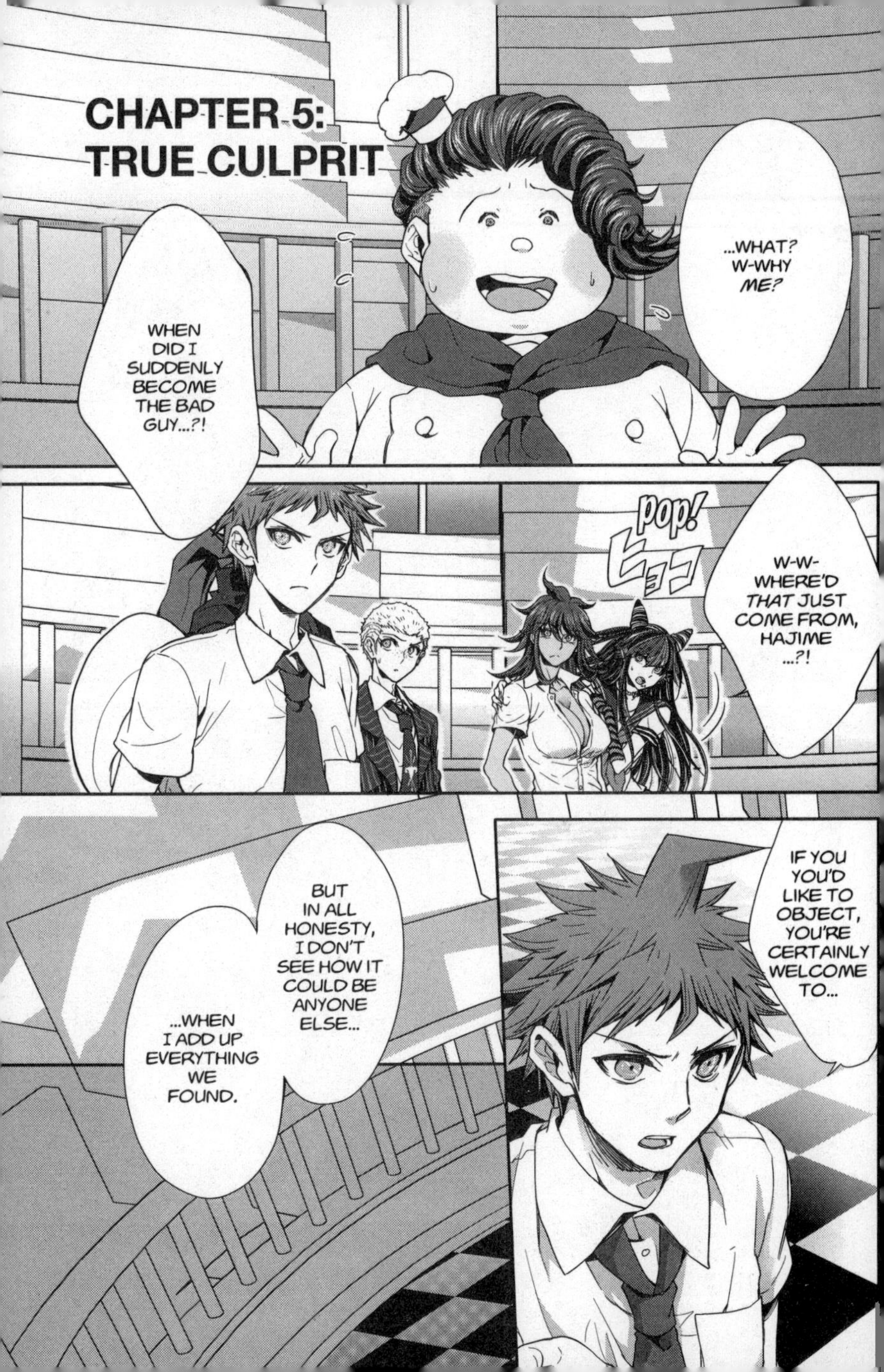
...WHAT? W-WHY *ME?*
WHEN DID I SUDDENLY BECOME THE BAD GUY...?!
pop!
ヒョコ
W-W-WHERE'D *THAT* JUST COME FROM, HAJIME ...?!
IF YOU YOU'D LIKE TO OBJECT, YOU'RE CERTAINLY WELCOME TO...
BUT IN ALL HONESTY, I DON'T SEE HOW IT COULD BE ANYONE ELSE...
...WHEN I ADD UP EVERYTHING WE FOUND.

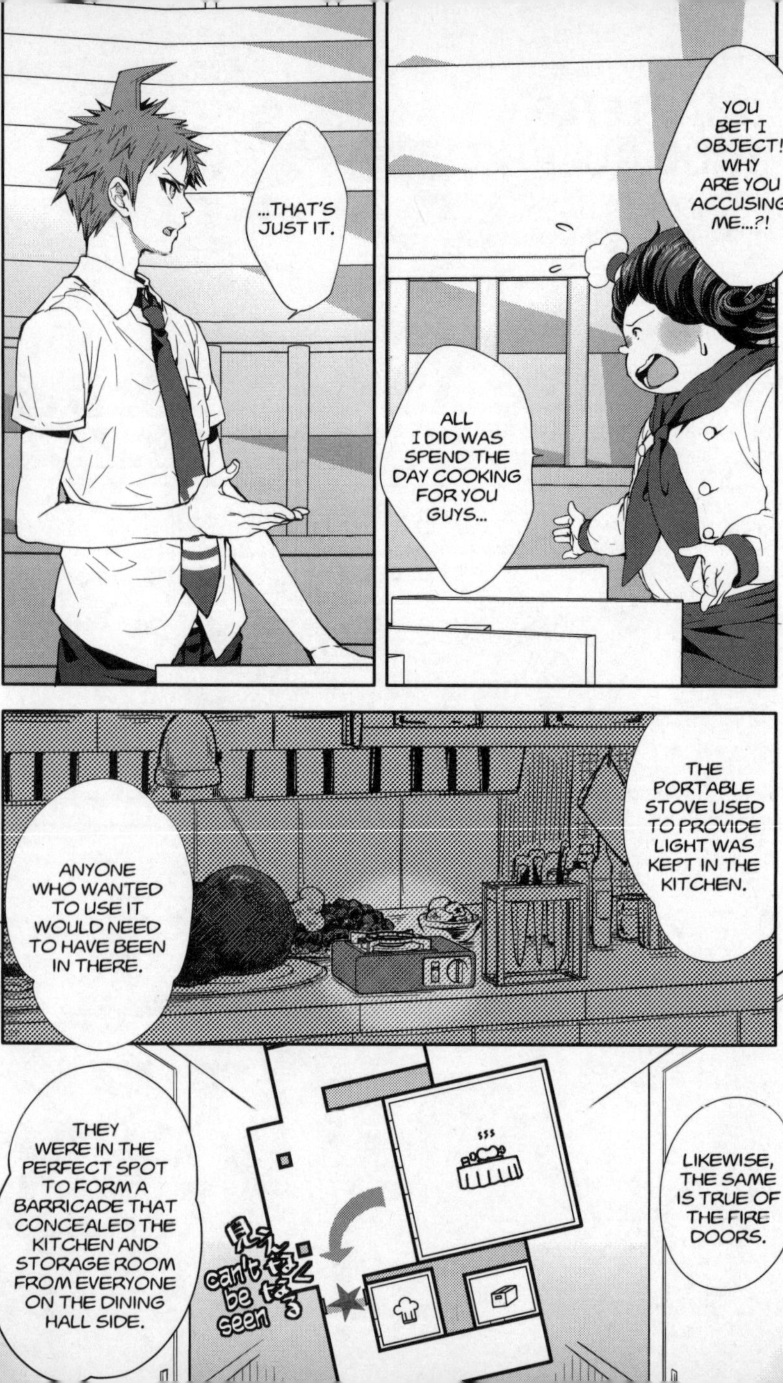
YOU BET I OBJECT! WHY ARE YOU ACCUSING ME...?!
ALL I DID WAS SPEND THE DAY COOKING FOR YOU GUYS...
...THAT'S JUST IT.
THE PORTABLE STOVE USED TO PROVIDE LIGHT WAS KEPT IN THE KITCHEN.
ANYONE WHO WANTED TO USE IT WOULD NEED TO HAVE BEEN IN THERE.
LIKEWISE, THE SAME IS TRUE OF THE FIRE DOORS.
THEY WERE IN THE PERFECT SPOT TO FORM A BARRICADE THAT CONCEALED THE KITCHEN AND STORAGE ROOM FROM EVERYONE ON THE DINING HALL SIDE.
見えなくなる
can't be seen

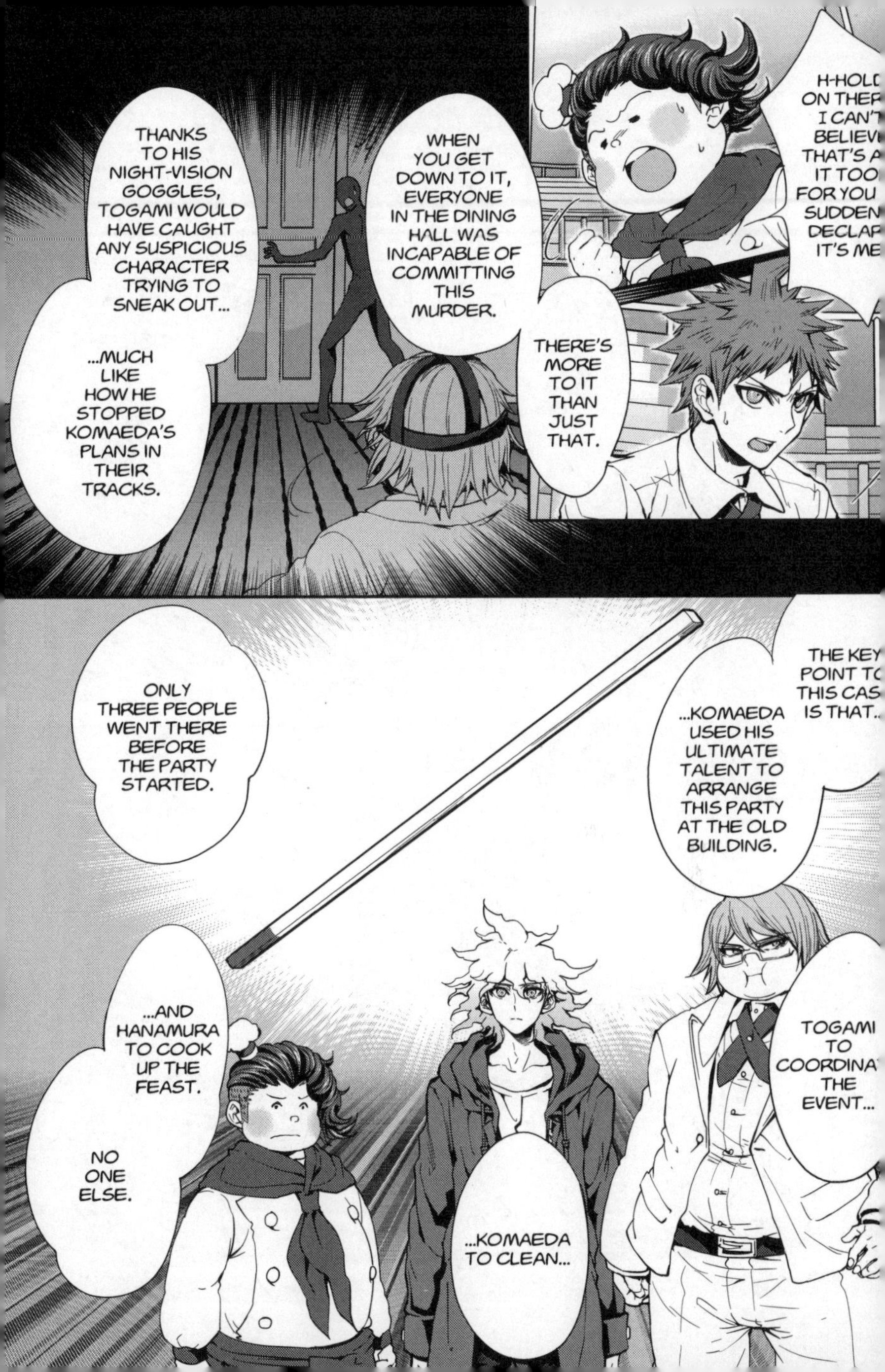
THANKS TO HIS NIGHT-VISION GOGGLES, TOGAMI WOULD HAVE CAUGHT ANY SUSPICIOUS CHARACTER TRYING TO SNEAK OUT...
...MUCH LIKE HOW HE STOPPED KOMAEDA'S PLANS IN THEIR TRACKS.
WHEN YOU GET DOWN TO IT, EVERYONE IN THE DINING HALL WAS INCAPABLE OF COMMITTING THIS MURDER.
H-HOLD ON THER I CAN'T BELIEV THAT'S A IT TOO FOR YOU SUDDEN DECLAR IT'S ME
THERE'S MORE TO IT THAN JUST THAT.
THE KEY POINT TC THIS CAS IS THAT...
...KOMAEDA USED HIS ULTIMATE TALENT TO ARRANGE THIS PARTY AT THE OLD BUILDING.
ONLY THREE PEOPLE WENT THERE BEFORE THE PARTY STARTED.
TOGAMI TO COORDINA THE EVENT...
...KOMAEDA TO CLEAN...
...AND HANAMURA TO COOK UP THE FEAST.
NO ONE ELSE.

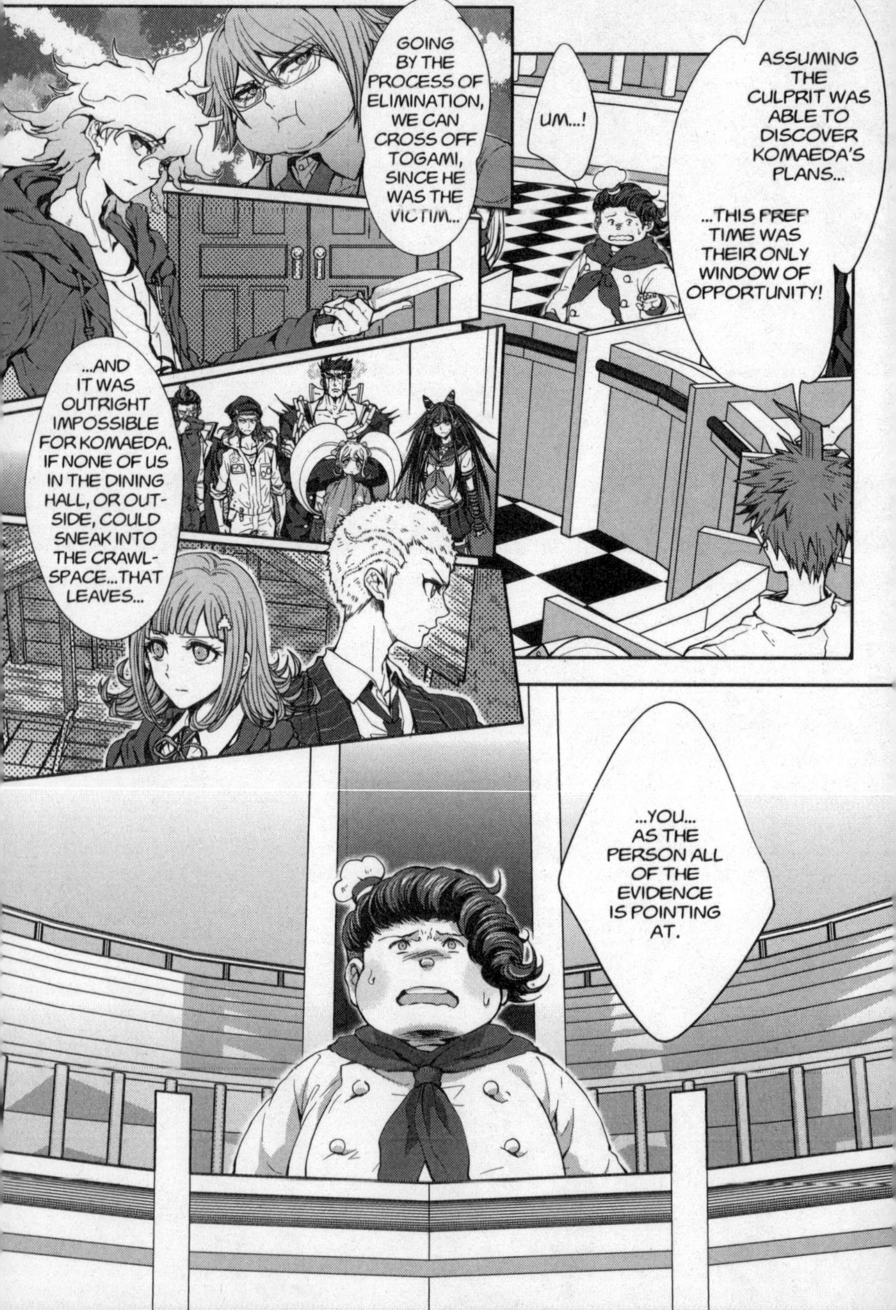
ASSUMING THE CULPRIT WAS ABLE TO DISCOVER KOMAEDA'S PLANS...
...THIS FREE TIME WAS THEIR ONLY WINDOW OF OPPORTUNITY!
UM...!
GOING BY THE PROCESS OF ELIMINATION, WE CAN CROSS OFF TOGAMI, SINCE HE WAS THE VICTIM...
...AND IT WAS OUTRIGHT IMPOSSIBLE FOR KOMAEDA. IF NONE OF US IN THE DINING HALL, OR OUTSIDE, COULD SNEAK INTO THE CRAWLSPACE...THAT LEAVES...
...YOU... AS THE PERSON ALL OF THE EVIDENCE IS POINTING AT.

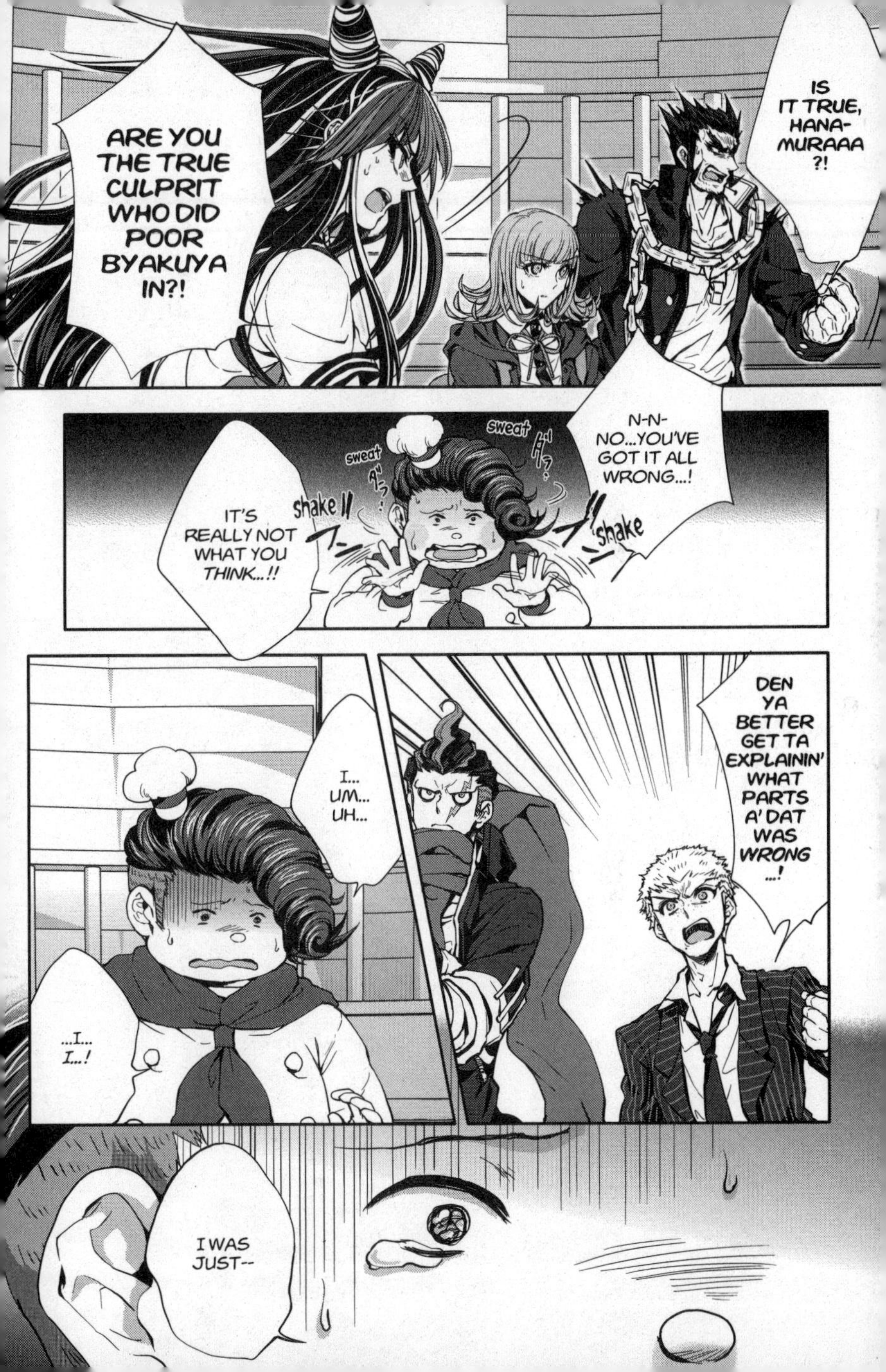
IS IT TRUE, HANA-MURAAA?!
ARE YOU THE TRUE CULPRIT WHO DID POOR BYAKUYA IN?!
N-N-NO...YOU'VE GOT IT ALL WRONG...!
sweat
shake
sweat
shake
IT'S REALLY NOT WHAT YOU THINK...!!
DEN YA BETTER GET TA EXPLAININ' WHAT PARTS A' DAT WAS WRONG...!
I... UM... UH...
...I... I...!
I WAS JUST--

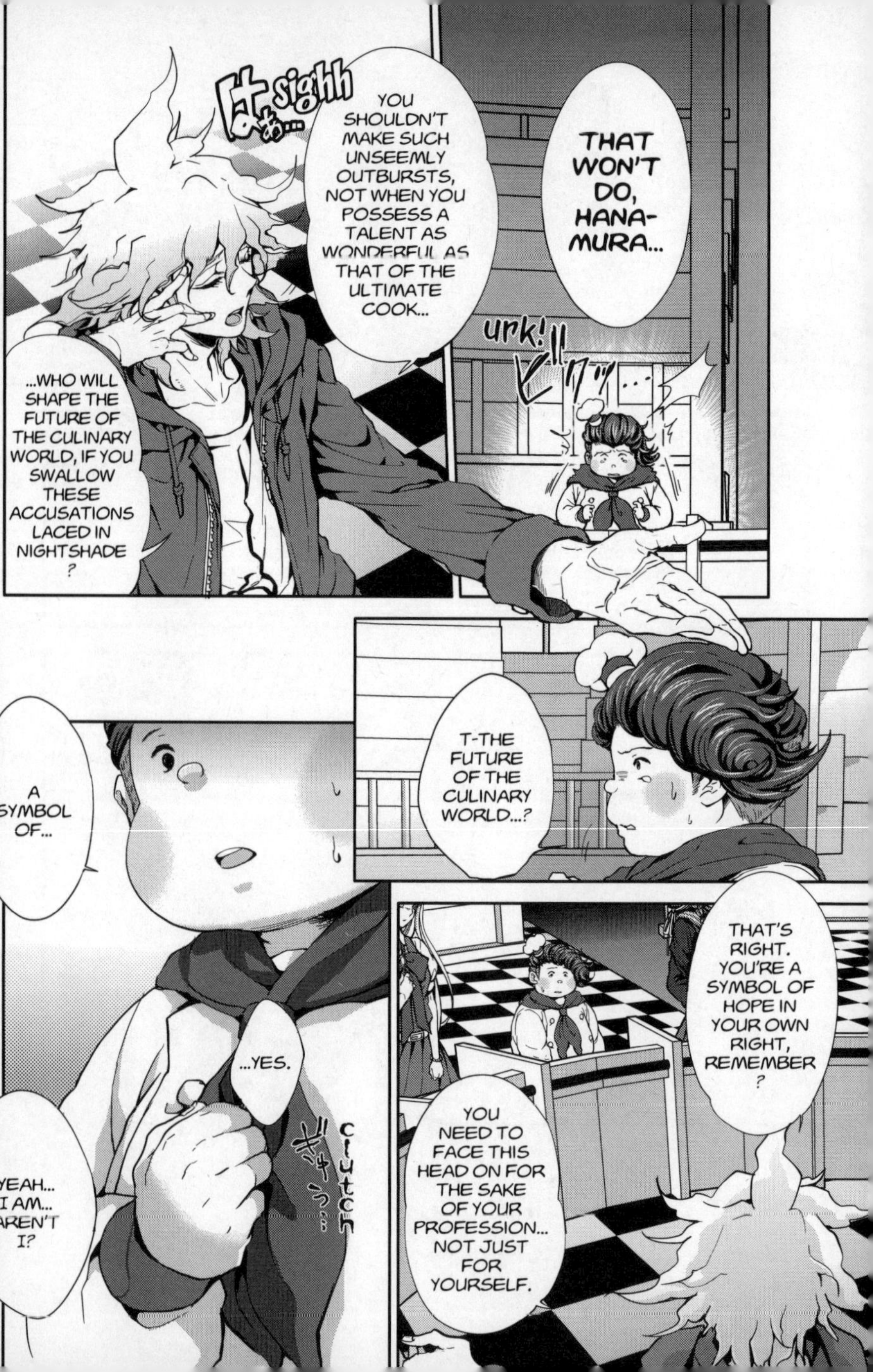
THAT WON'T DO, HANAMURA...
sighh
YOU SHOULDN'T MAKE SUCH UNSEEMLY OUTBURSTS, NOT WHEN YOU POSSESS A TALENT AS WONDERFUL AS THAT OF THE ULTIMATE COOK...
...WHO WILL SHAPE THE FUTURE OF THE CULINARY WORLD, IF YOU SWALLOW THESE ACCUSATIONS LACED IN NIGHTSHADE?
urk!!
T-THE FUTURE OF THE CULINARY WORLD...?
THAT'S RIGHT. YOU'RE A SYMBOL OF HOPE IN YOUR OWN RIGHT, REMEMBER?
YOU NEED TO FACE THIS HEAD ON FOR THE SAKE OF YOUR PROFESSION... NOT JUST FOR YOURSELF.
A SYMBOL OF...
...YES.
clutch
YEAH... I AM... AREN'T I?

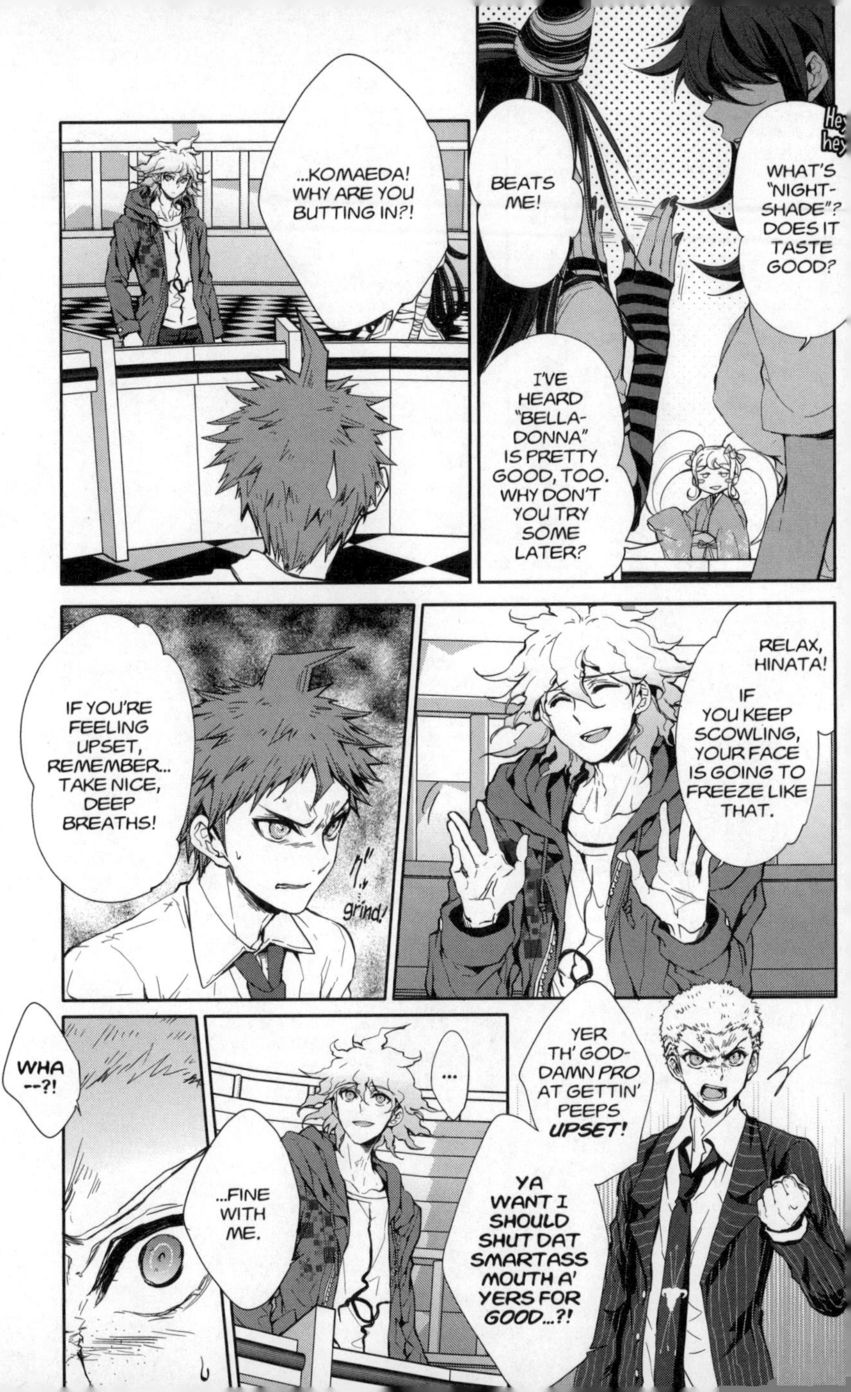

Hey hey
WHAT'S "NIGHT-SHADE"? DOES IT TASTE GOOD?
BEATS ME!
I'VE HEARD "BELLA-DONNA" IS PRETTY GOOD, TOO. WHY DON'T YOU TRY SOME LATER?
...KOMAEDA! WHY ARE YOU BUTTING IN?!
RELAX, HINATA!
IF YOU KEEP SCOWLING, YOUR FACE IS GOING TO FREEZE LIKE THAT.
IF YOU'RE FEELING UPSET, REMEMBER... TAKE NICE, DEEP BREATHS!
grind!
YER TH' GOD-DAMN *PRO* AT GETTIN' PEEPS ***UPSET!***
YA WANT I SHOULD SHUT DAT SMARTASS MOUTH A' YERS FOR ***GOOD...?!***
...
...FINE WITH ME.
WHA --?!

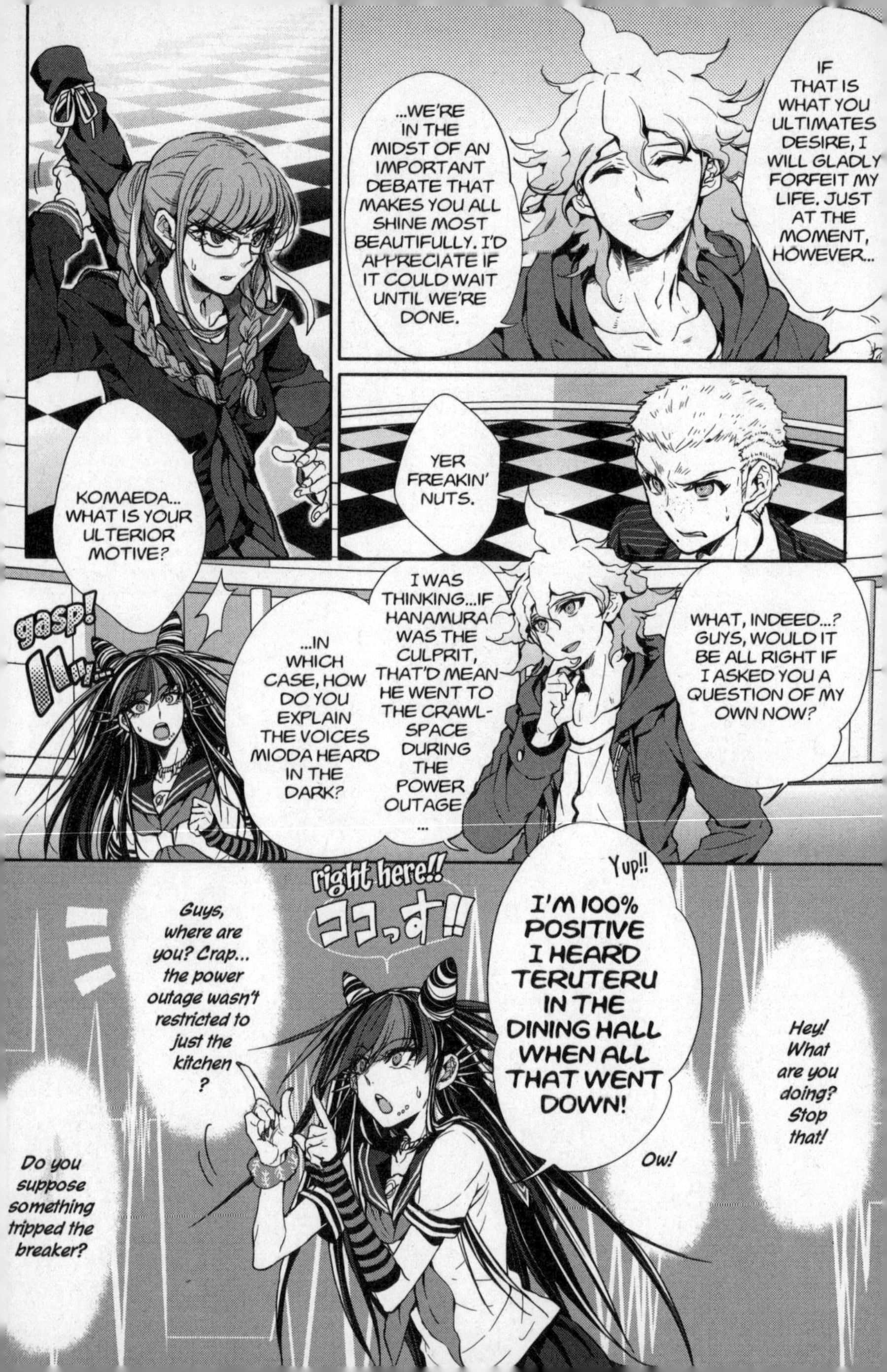
IF THAT IS WHAT YOU ULTIMATES DESIRE, I WILL GLADLY FORFEIT MY LIFE. JUST AT THE MOMENT, HOWEVER...
...WE'RE IN THE MIDST OF AN IMPORTANT DEBATE THAT MAKES YOU ALL SHINE MOST BEAUTIFULLY. I'D APPRECIATE IF IT COULD WAIT UNTIL WE'RE DONE.
YER FREAKIN' NUTS.
KOMAEDA... WHAT IS YOUR ULTERIOR MOTIVE?
WHAT, INDEED...? GUYS, WOULD IT BE ALL RIGHT IF I ASKED YOU A QUESTION OF MY OWN NOW?
I WAS THINKING...IF HANAMURA WAS THE CULPRIT, THAT'D MEAN HE WENT TO THE CRAWL-SPACE DURING THE POWER OUTAGE...
...IN WHICH CASE, HOW DO YOU EXPLAIN THE VOICES MIODA HEARD IN THE DARK?
gasp!
Yup!!
right here!! ココっす!!
I'M 100% POSITIVE I HEARD TERUTERU IN THE DINING HALL WHEN ALL THAT WENT DOWN!
Hey! What are you doing? Stop that!
Ow!
Guys, where are you? Crap... the power outage wasn't restricted to just the kitchen?
Do you suppose something tripped the breaker?

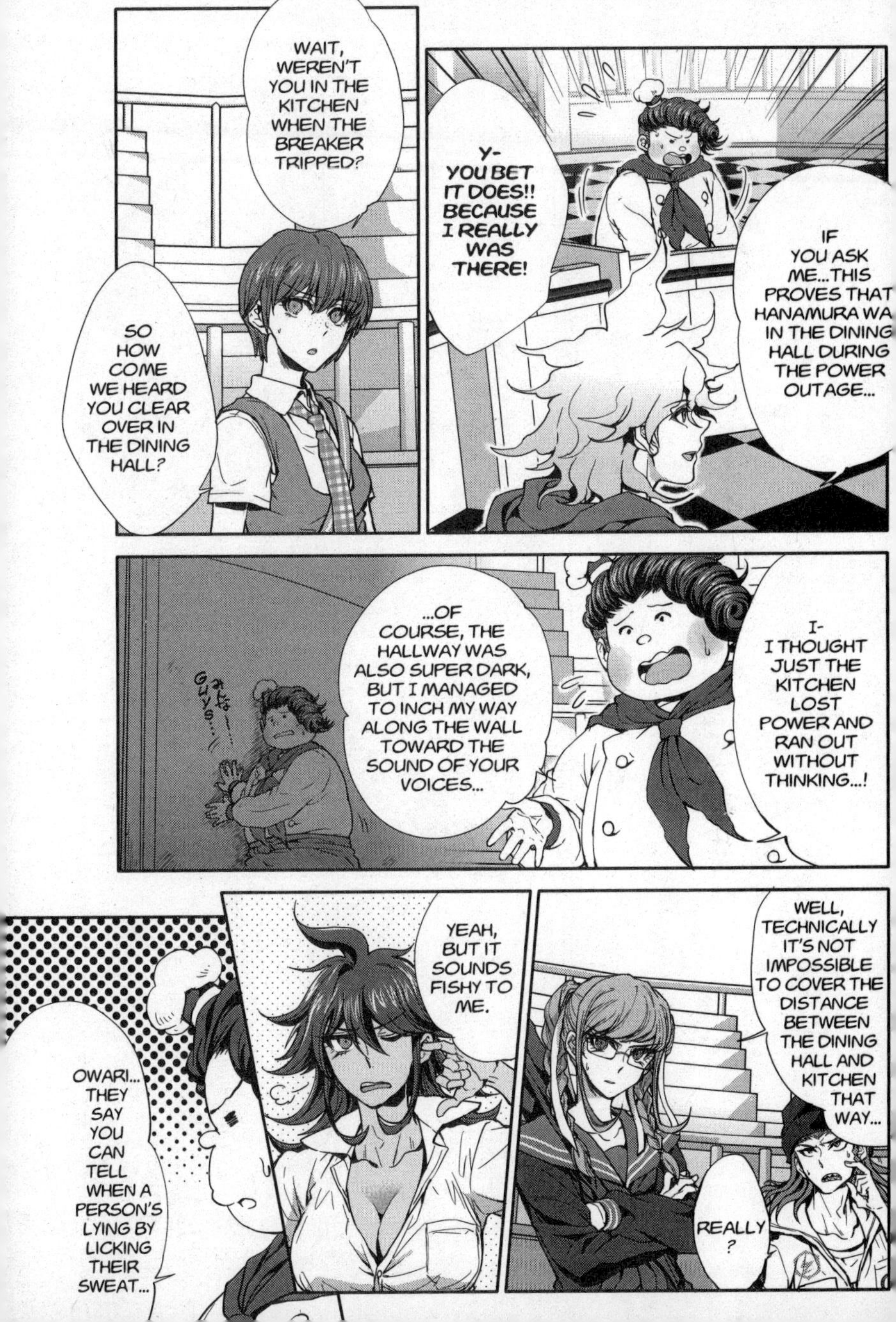
IF YOU ASK ME...THIS PROVES THAT HANAMURA WA IN THE DINING HALL DURING THE POWER OUTAGE...
Y- YOU BET IT DOES!! BECAUSE I REALLY WAS THERE!
WAIT, WEREN'T YOU IN THE KITCHEN WHEN THE BREAKER TRIPPED?
SO HOW COME WE HEARD YOU CLEAR OVER IN THE DINING HALL?
I- I THOUGHT JUST THE KITCHEN LOST POWER AND RAN OUT WITHOUT THINKING...!
...OF COURSE, THE HALLWAY WAS ALSO SUPER DARK, BUT I MANAGED TO INCH MY WAY ALONG THE WALL TOWARD THE SOUND OF YOUR VOICES...
みんな GUYS...!
WELL, TECHNICALLY IT'S NOT IMPOSSIBLE TO COVER THE DISTANCE BETWEEN THE DINING HALL AND KITCHEN THAT WAY...
REALLY?
YEAH, BUT IT SOUNDS FISHY TO ME.
OWARI... THEY SAY YOU CAN TELL WHEN A PERSON'S LYING BY LICKING THEIR SWEAT...

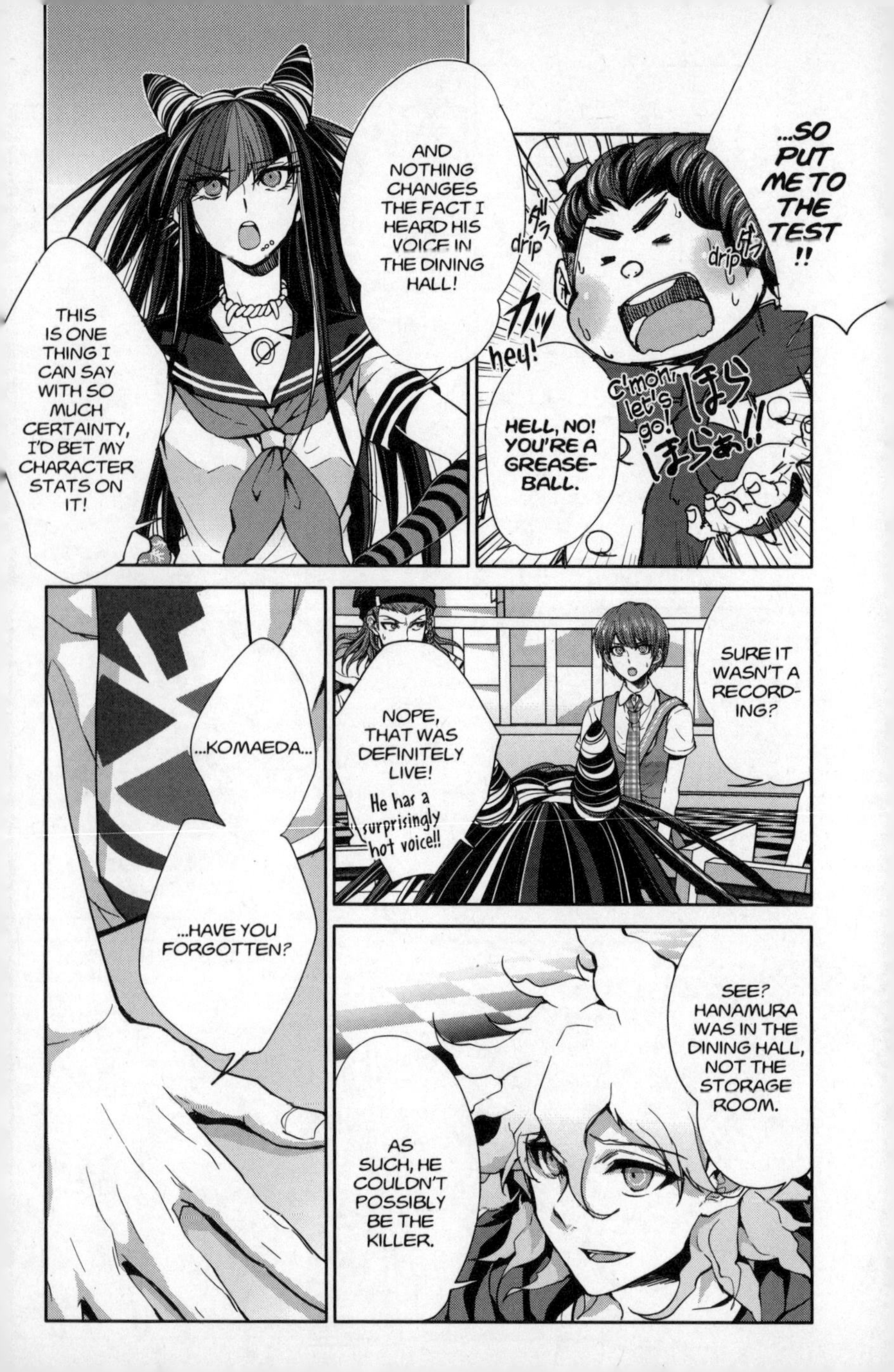
...SO PUT ME TO THE TEST!!
drip
drip
C'mon, let's go! ほら ほらぁ!!
hey!
HELL, NO! YOU'RE A GREASE-BALL.
AND NOTHING CHANGES THE FACT I HEARD HIS VOICE IN THE DINING HALL!
THIS IS ONE THING I CAN SAY WITH SO MUCH CERTAINTY, I'D BET MY CHARACTER STATS ON IT!
SURE IT WASN'T A RECORD-ING?
NOPE, THAT WAS DEFINITELY LIVE!
He has a surprisingly hot voice!!
SEE? HANAMURA WAS IN THE DINING HALL, NOT THE STORAGE ROOM.
AS SUCH, HE COULDN'T POSSIBLY BE THE KILLER.
...KOMAEDA...
...HAVE YOU FORGOTTEN?

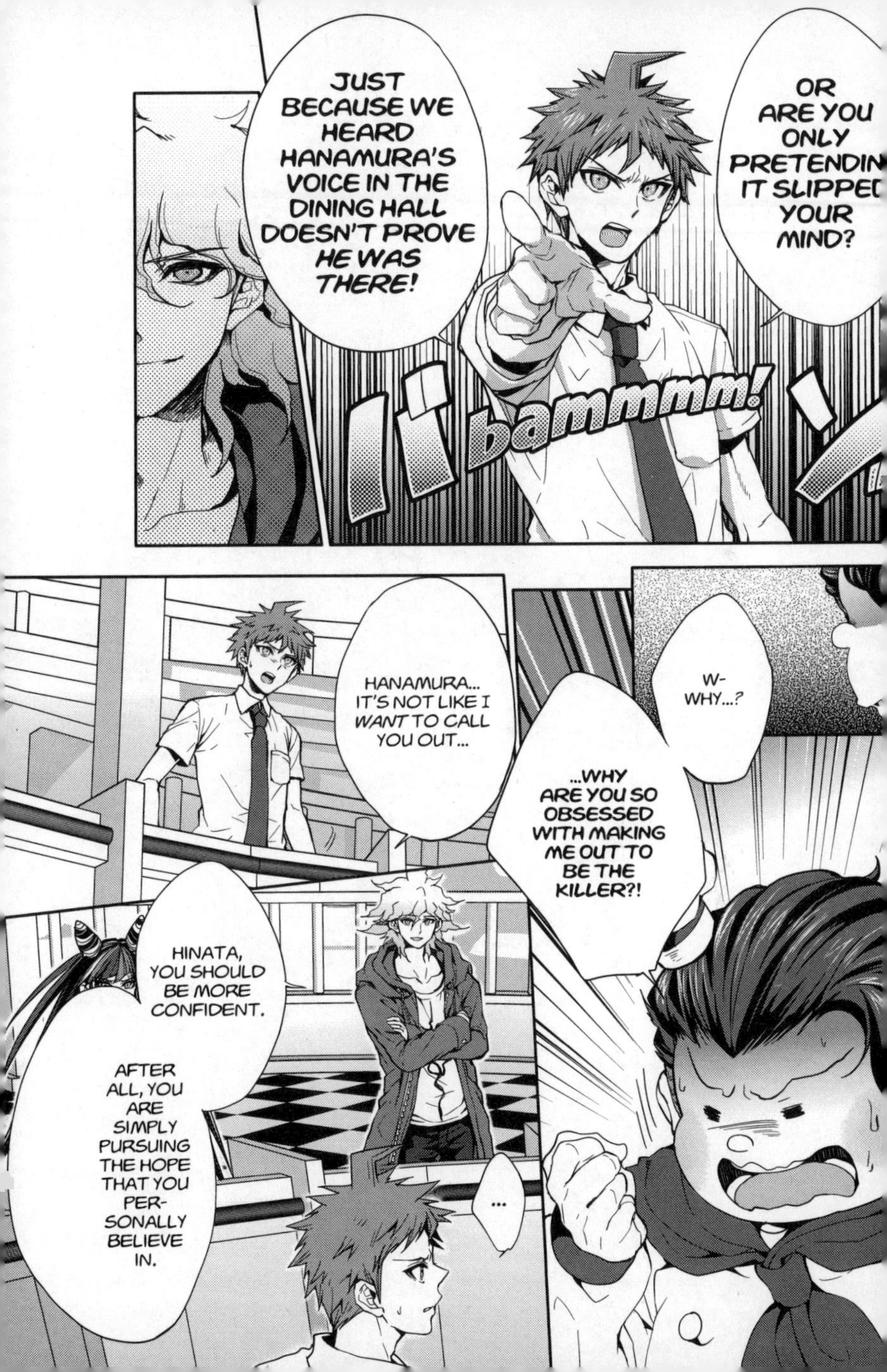
OR ARE YOU ONLY PRETENDIN IT SLIPPED YOUR MIND?
JUST BECAUSE WE HEARD HANAMURA'S VOICE IN THE DINING HALL DOESN'T PROVE HE WAS THERE!
bammmmm!
W- WHY...?
...WHY ARE YOU SO OBSESSED WITH MAKING ME OUT TO BE THE KILLER?!
HANAMURA... IT'S NOT LIKE I WANT TO CALL YOU OUT...
HINATA, YOU SHOULD BE MORE CONFIDENT.
AFTER ALL, YOU ARE SIMPLY PURSUING THE HOPE THAT YOU PERSONALLY BELIEVE IN.
...

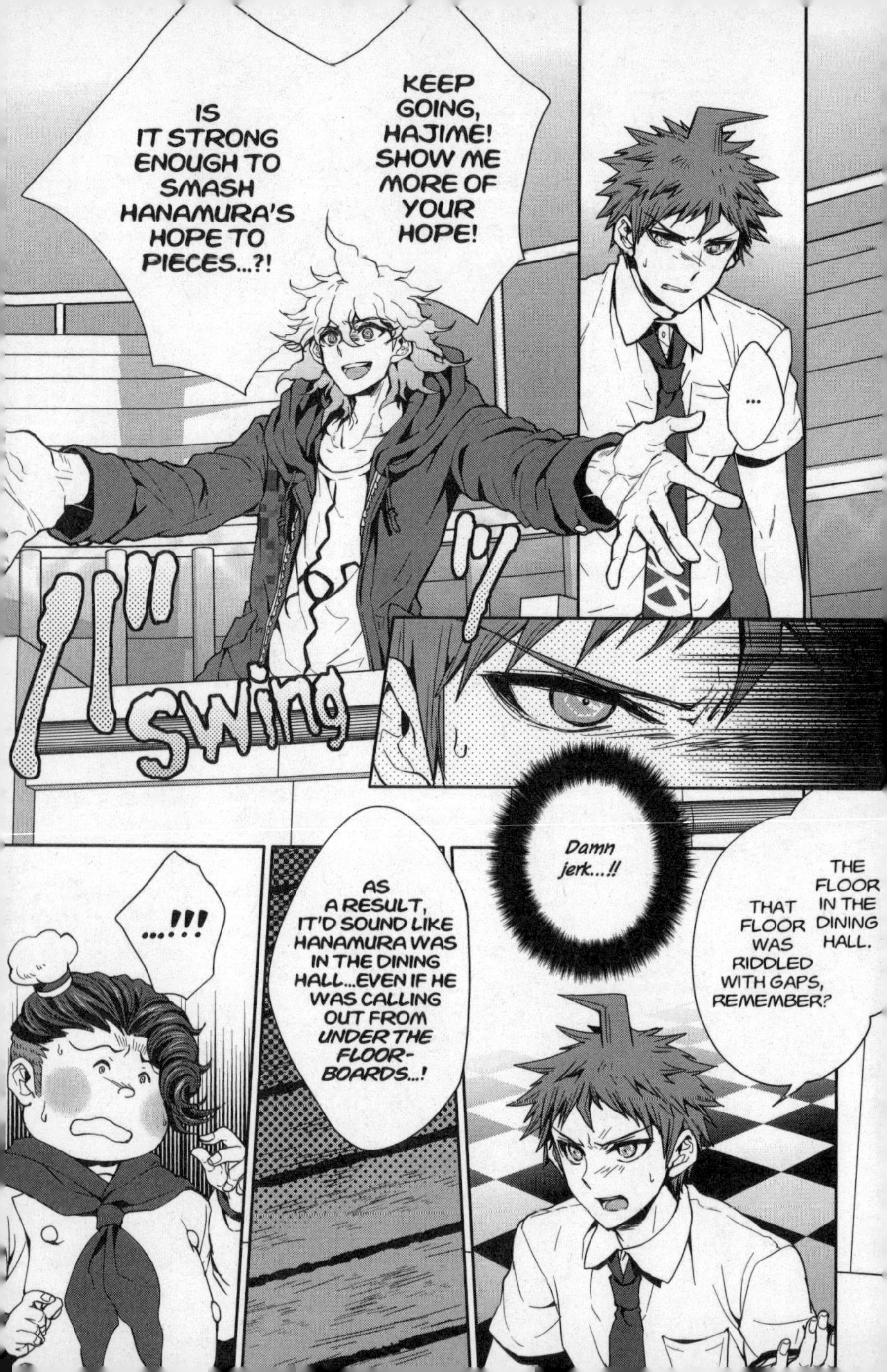
...
KEEP GOING, HAJIME! SHOW ME MORE OF YOUR HOPE!
IS IT STRONG ENOUGH TO SMASH HANAMURA'S HOPE TO PIECES...?!
Swing
Damn jerk...!!
THE FLOOR IN THE DINING HALL.
THAT FLOOR WAS RIDDLED WITH GAPS, REMEMBER?
AS A RESULT, IT'D SOUND LIKE HANAMURA WAS IN THE DINING HALL...EVEN IF HE WAS CALLING OUT FROM UNDER THE FLOOR-BOARDS...!
...!!!

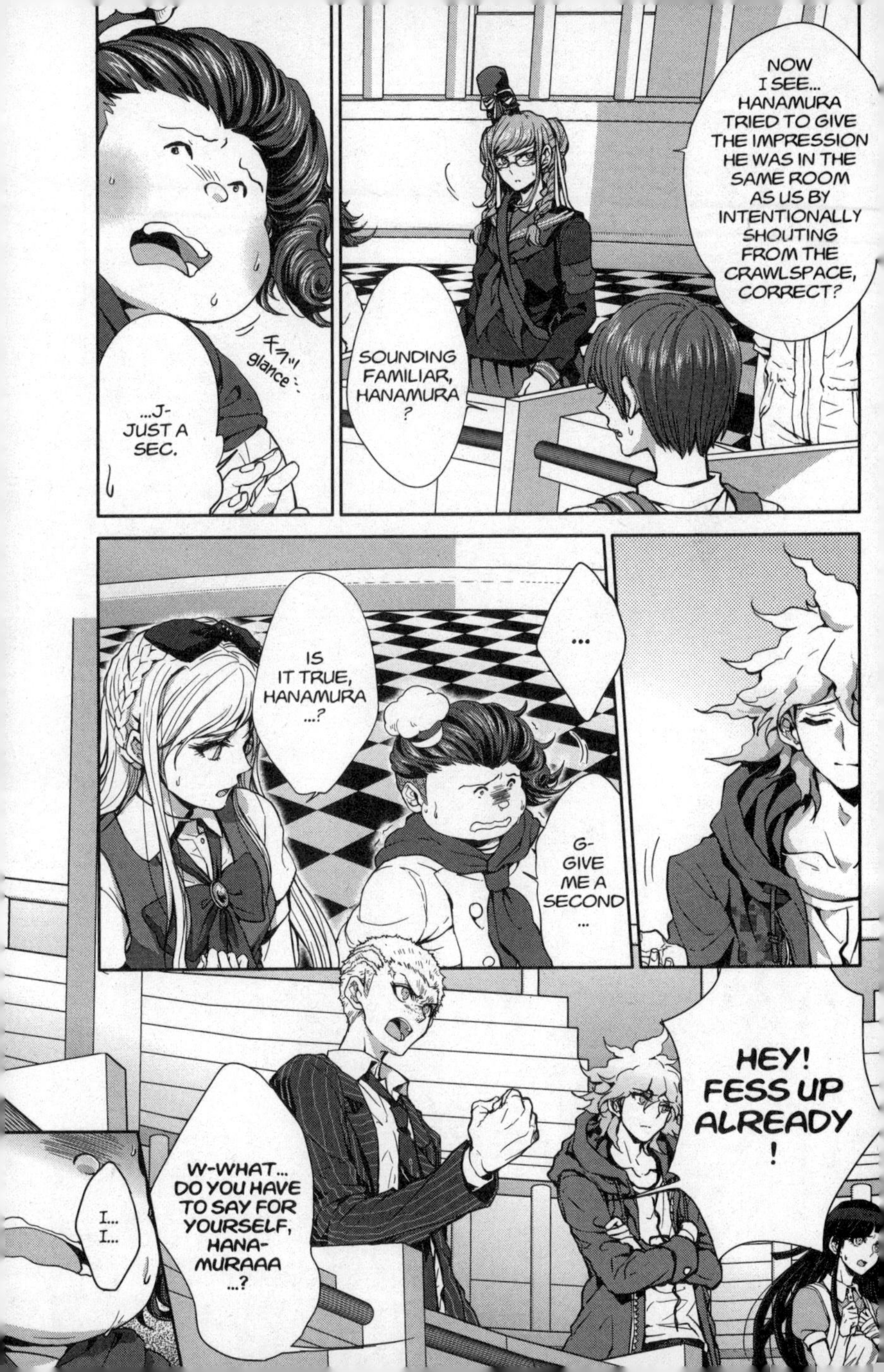
NOW I SEE... HANAMURA TRIED TO GIVE THE IMPRESSION HE WAS IN THE SAME ROOM AS US BY INTENTIONALLY SHOUTING FROM THE CRAWLSPACE, CORRECT?
SOUNDING FAMILIAR, HANAMURA?
チラッ glance
...J-JUST A SEC.
...
IS IT TRUE, HANAMURA...?
G-GIVE ME A SECOND...
HEY! FESS UP ALREADY!
W-WHAT... DO YOU HAVE TO SAY FOR YOURSELF, HANA-MURAAA...?
I... I...

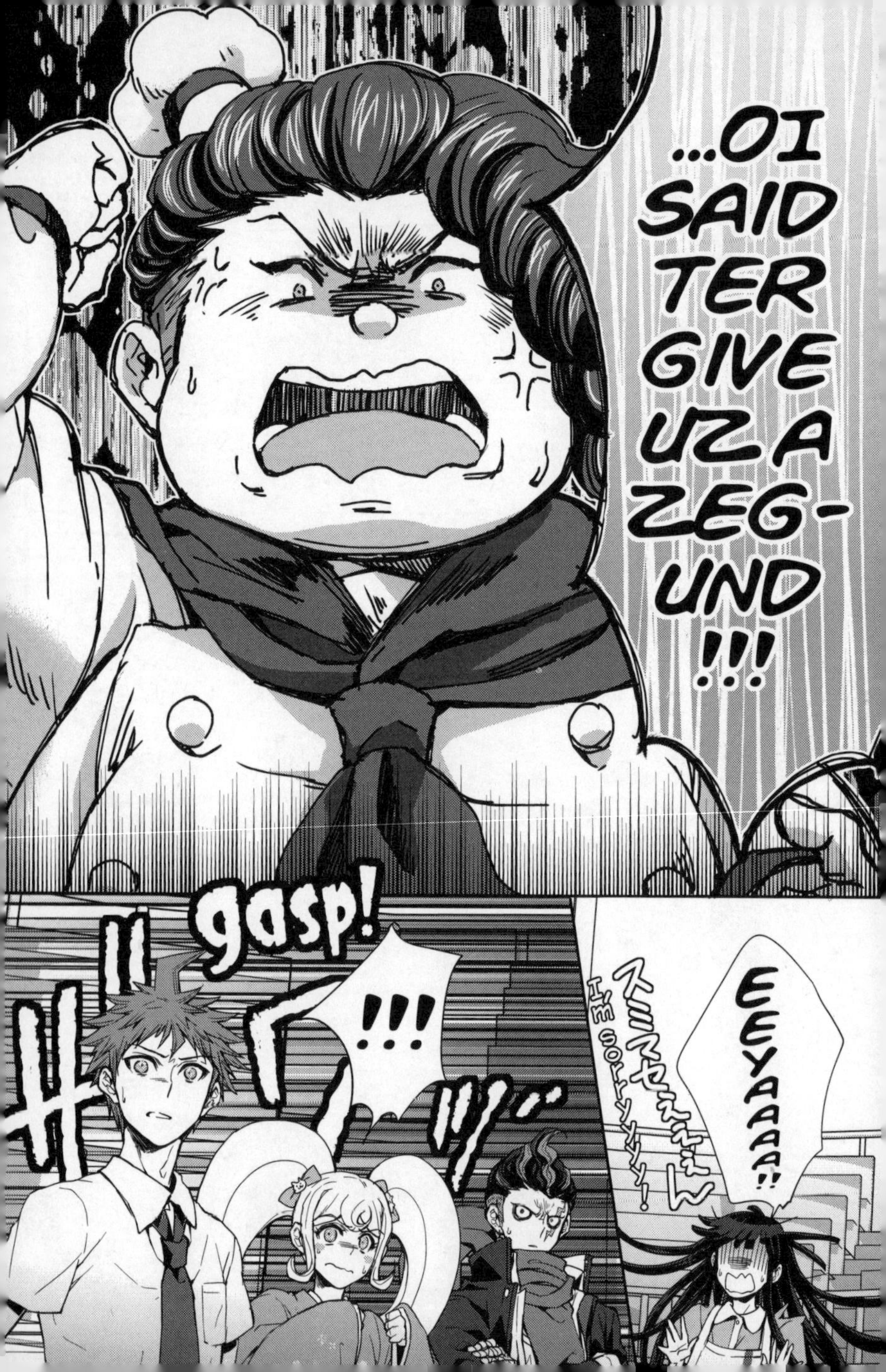
...OI SAID TER GIVE UZ A ZEG-UND!!!
EEYAAAAA!!
I'M SORRYYYYY!
!!!
gasp!

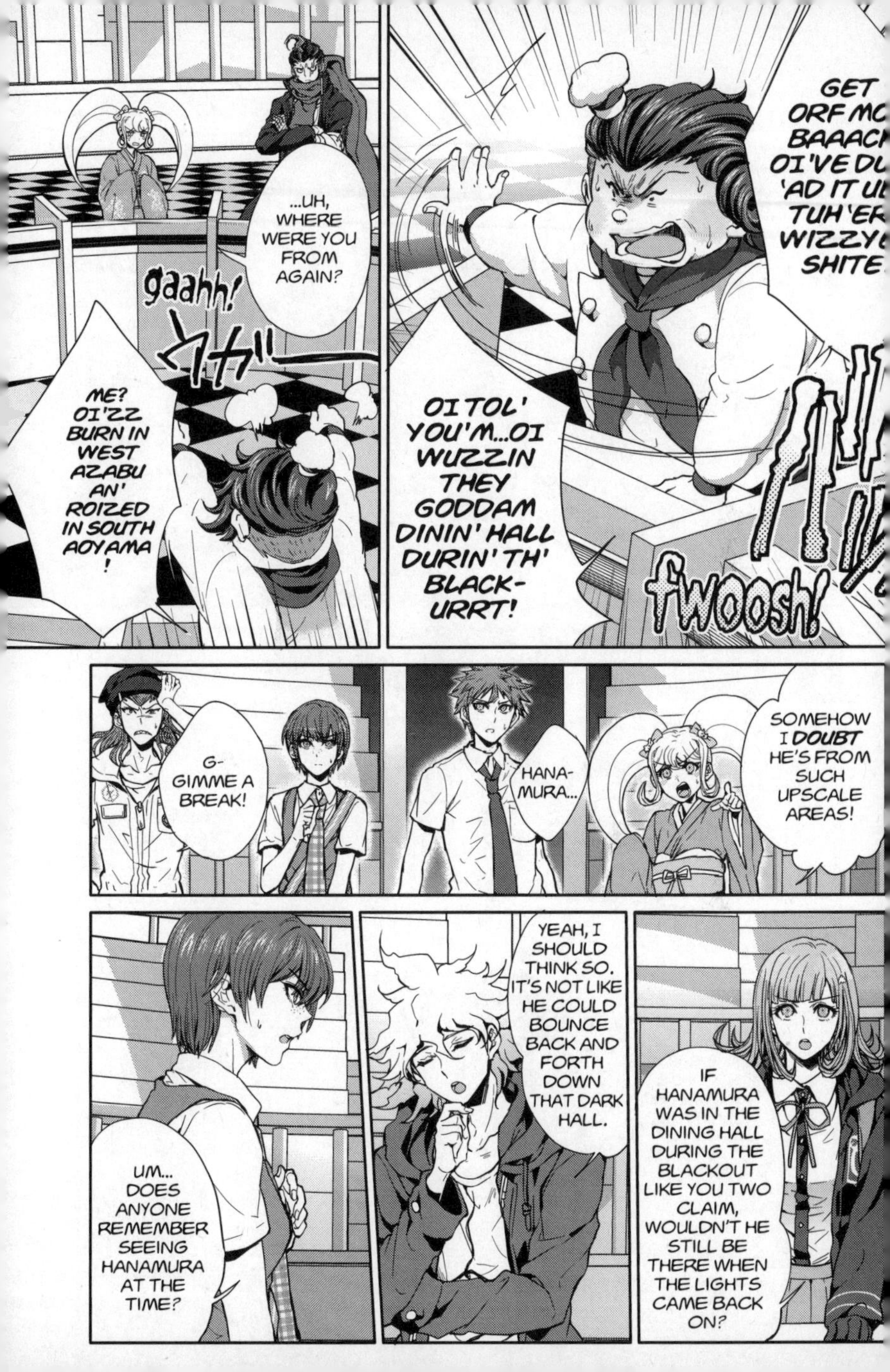
GET ORF MO BAAACK OI'VE DU 'AD IT U TUH 'ER WIZZY SHITE
OI TOL' YOU'M...OI WUZZIN THEY GODDAM DININ' HALL DURIN' TH' BLACK-URRT!
fwoosh!
...UH, WHERE WERE YOU FROM AGAIN?
gaahh!
ME? OI'ZZ BURN IN WEST AZABU AN' ROIZED IN SOUTH AOYAMA!
SOMEHOW I DOUBT HE'S FROM SUCH UPSCALE AREAS!
HANA-MURA...
G-GIMME A BREAK!
IF HANAMURA WAS IN THE DINING HALL DURING THE BLACKOUT LIKE YOU TWO CLAIM, WOULDN'T HE STILL BE THERE WHEN THE LIGHTS CAME BACK ON?
YEAH, I SHOULD THINK SO. IT'S NOT LIKE HE COULD BOUNCE BACK AND FORTH DOWN THAT DARK HALL.
UM... DOES ANYONE REMEMBER SEEING HANAMURA AT THE TIME?

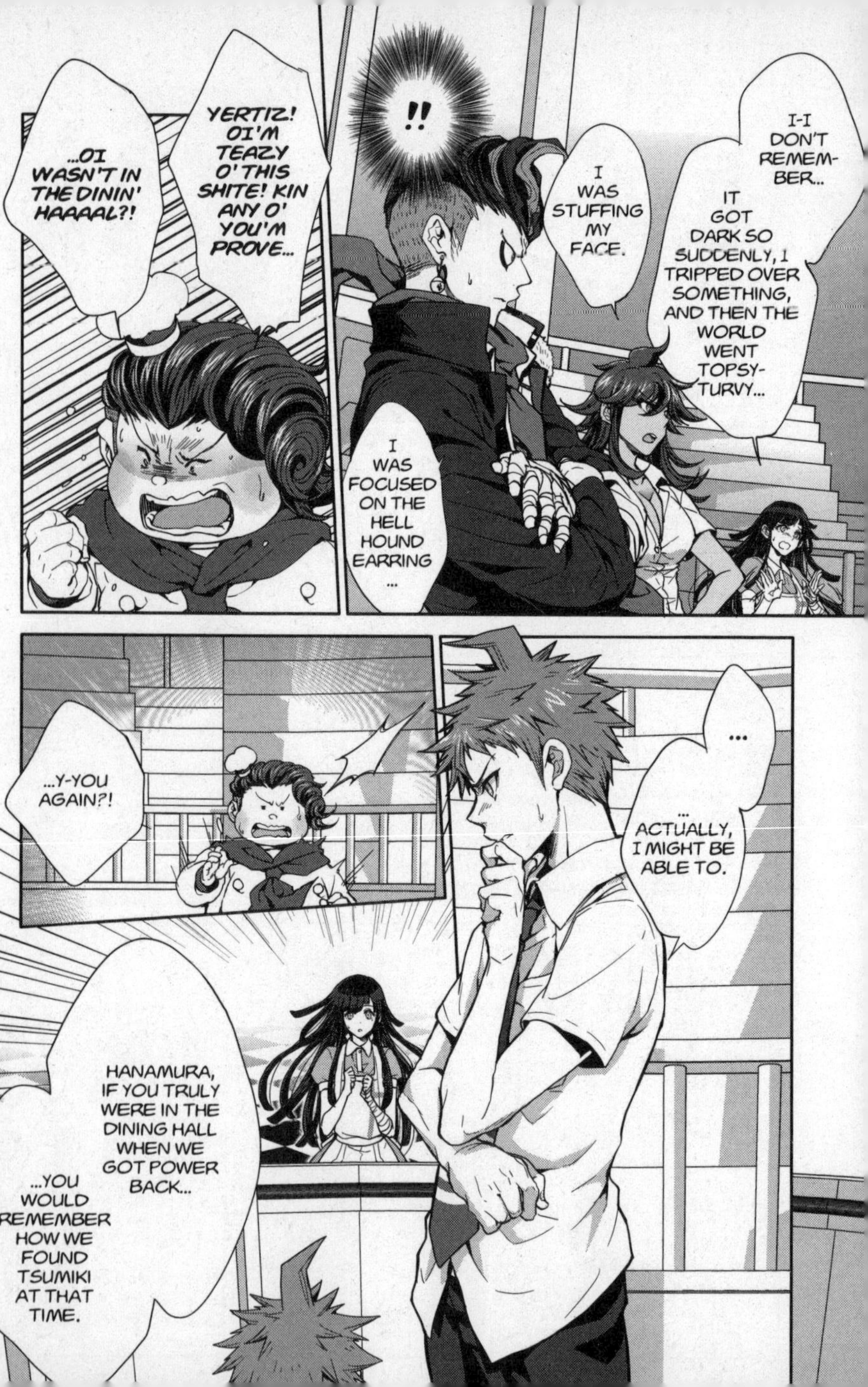
!!
I-I DON'T REMEMBER...
IT GOT DARK SO SUDDENLY, I TRIPPED OVER SOMETHING, AND THEN THE WORLD WENT TOPSY-TURVY...
I WAS STUFFING MY FACE.
I WAS FOCUSED ON THE HELL HOUND EARRING ...
YERTIZ! OI'M TEAZY O' THIS SHITE! KIN ANY O' YOU'M PROVE...
...OI WASN'T IN THE DININ' HAAAAL?!
...
... ACTUALLY, I MIGHT BE ABLE TO.
...Y-YOU AGAIN?!
HANAMURA, IF YOU TRULY WERE IN THE DINING HALL WHEN WE GOT POWER BACK...
...YOU WOULD REMEMBER HOW WE FOUND TSUMIKI AT THAT TIME.

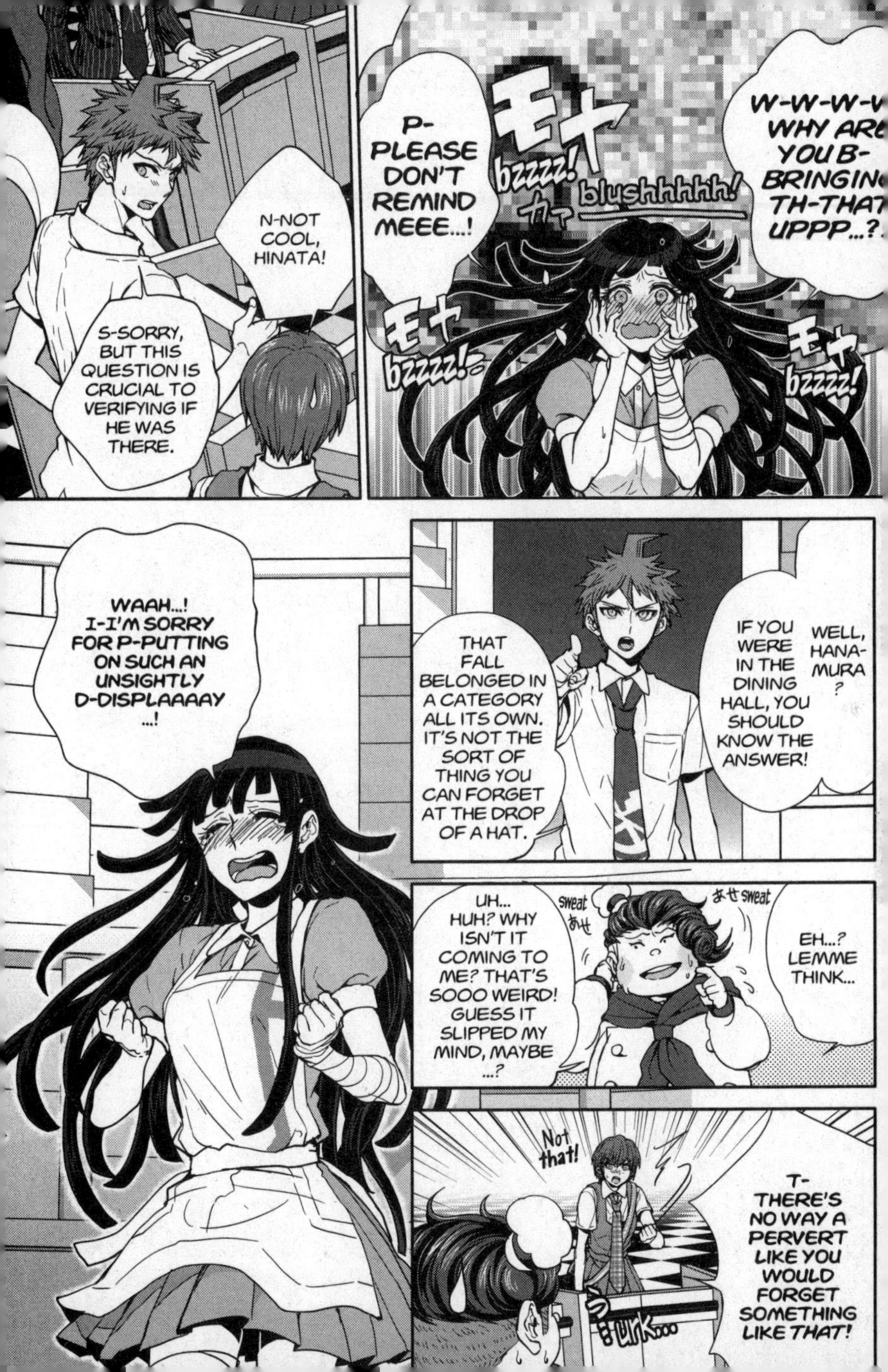
W-W-W-W WHY ARE YOU B-BRINGING TH-THAT UPPP...?
モヤ bzzzz!
カァ blushhhhh!
P-PLEASE DON'T REMIND MEEE...!
モヤ bzzzz!
モヤ bzzzz!
N-NOT COOL, HINATA!
S-SORRY, BUT THIS QUESTION IS CRUCIAL TO VERIFYING IF HE WAS THERE.
WELL, HANAMURA?
IF YOU WERE IN THE DINING HALL, YOU SHOULD KNOW THE ANSWER!
THAT FALL BELONGED IN A CATEGORY ALL ITS OWN. IT'S NOT THE SORT OF THING YOU CAN FORGET AT THE DROP OF A HAT.
EH...? LEMME THINK...
あせ sweat
sweat あせ
UH... HUH? WHY ISN'T IT COMING TO ME? THAT'S SOOO WEIRD! GUESS IT SLIPPED MY MIND, MAYBE...?
T-THERE'S NO WAY A PERVERT LIKE YOU WOULD FORGET SOMETHING LIKE THAT!
Not that!
urk...
WAAH...! I-I'M SORRY FOR P-PUTTING ON SUCH AN UNSIGHTLY D-DISPLAAAAY...!

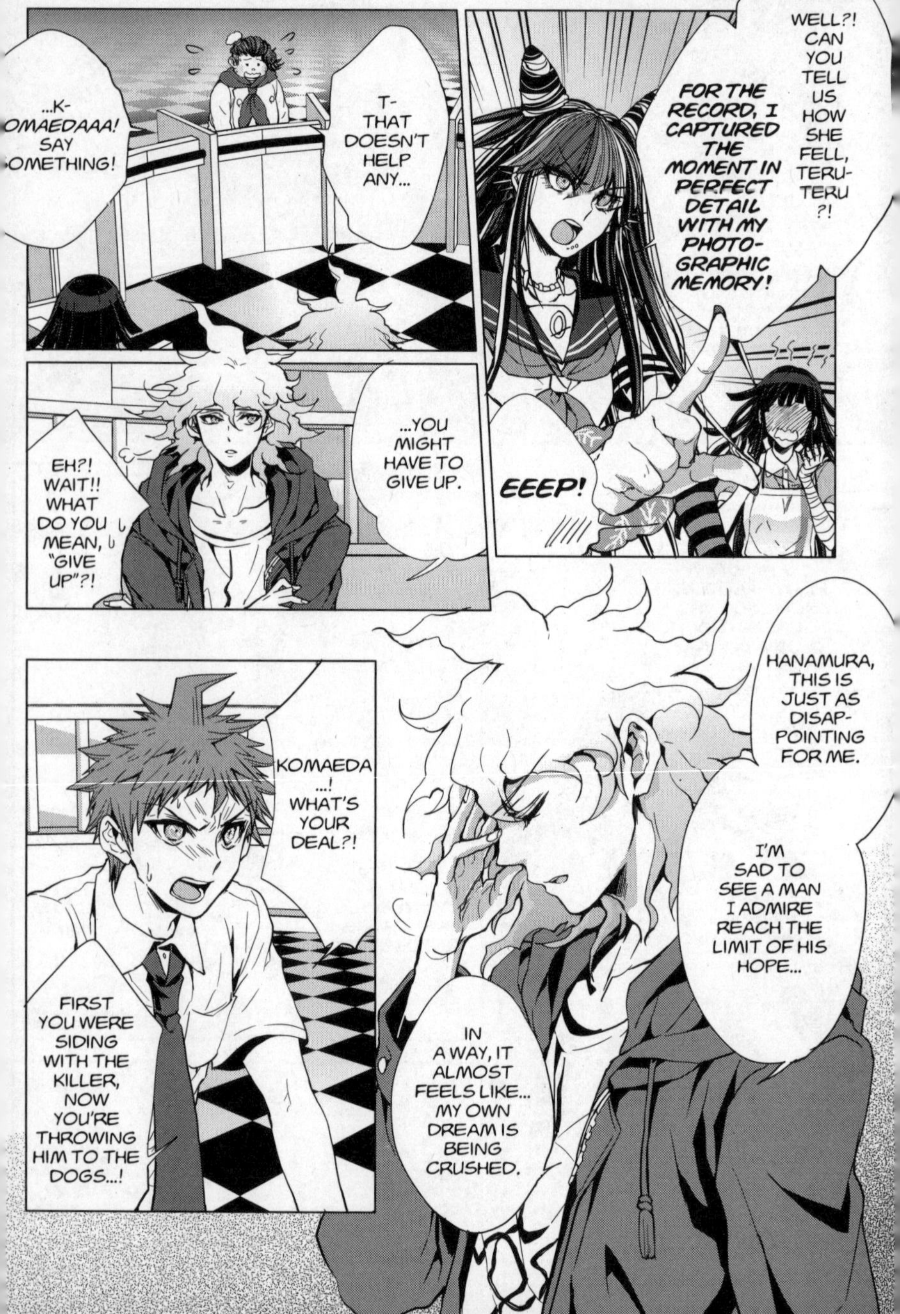
WELL?! CAN YOU TELL US HOW SHE FELL, TERU-TERU?!
FOR THE RECORD, I CAPTURED THE MOMENT IN PERFECT DETAIL WITH MY PHOTO-GRAPHIC MEMORY!
EEEP!
T-THAT DOESN'T HELP ANY...
...K-KOMAEDAAA! SAY SOMETHING!
...YOU MIGHT HAVE TO GIVE UP.
EH?! WAIT!! WHAT DO YOU MEAN, "GIVE UP"?!
HANAMURA, THIS IS JUST AS DISAP-POINTING FOR ME.
I'M SAD TO SEE A MAN I ADMIRE REACH THE LIMIT OF HIS HOPE...
IN A WAY, IT ALMOST FEELS LIKE... MY OWN DREAM IS BEING CRUSHED.
KOMAEDA...! WHAT'S YOUR DEAL?!
FIRST YOU WERE SIDING WITH THE KILLER, NOW YOU'RE THROWING HIM TO THE DOGS...!

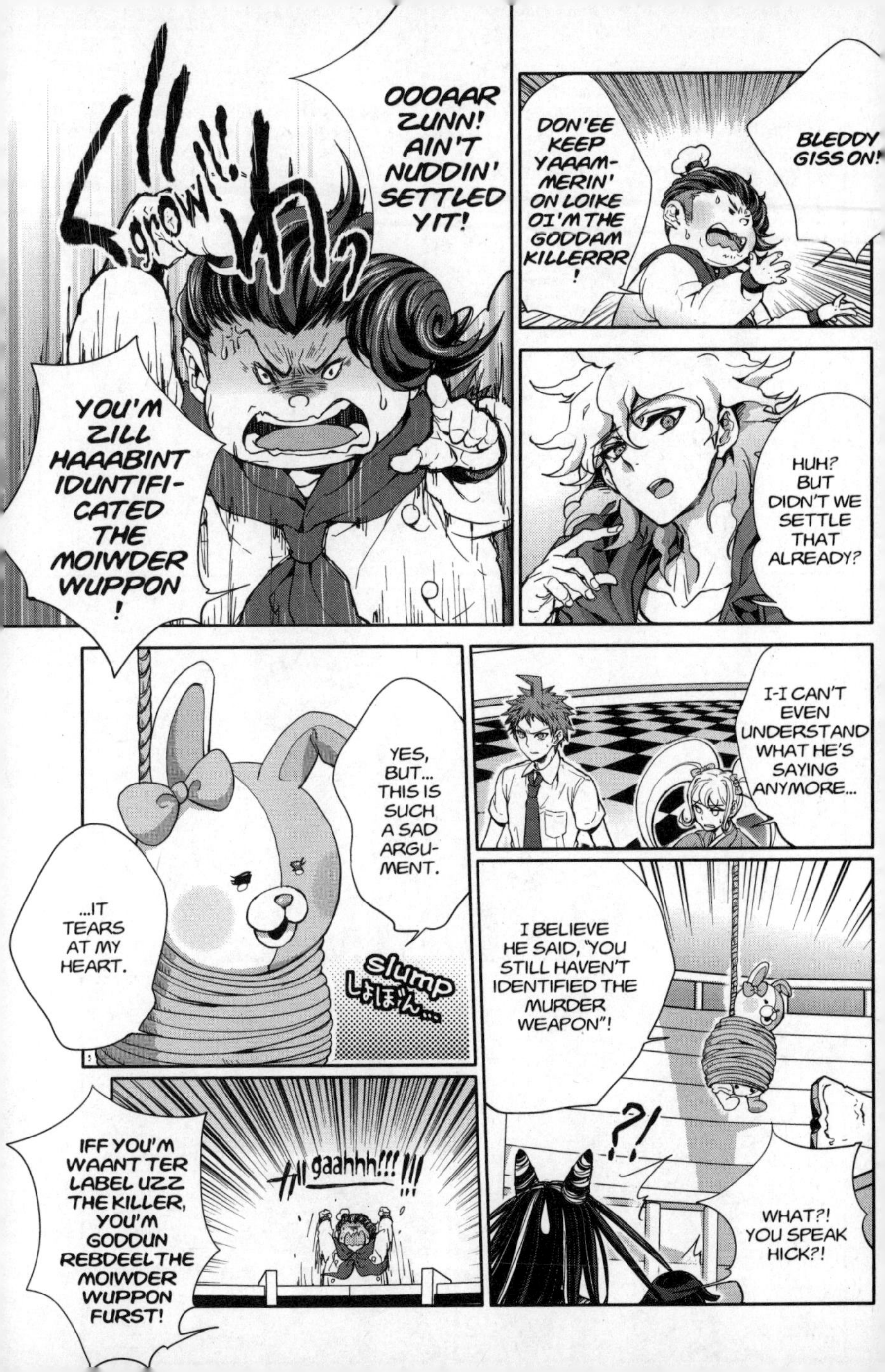
BLEDDY GISS ON!
DON'EE KEEP YAAAM-MERIN' ON LOIKE OI'M THE GODDAM KILLERRR!
HUH? BUT DIDN'T WE SETTLE THAT ALREADY?
OOOAAR ZUNN! AIN'T NUDDIN' SETTLED YIT!
growl!!
YOU'M ZILL HAAABINT IDUNTIFI-CATED THE MOIWDER WUPPON!
I-I CAN'T EVEN UNDERSTAND WHAT HE'S SAYING ANYMORE...
YES, BUT... THIS IS SUCH A SAD ARGU-MENT.
slump しょぼん...
...IT TEARS AT MY HEART.
I BELIEVE HE SAID, "YOU STILL HAVEN'T IDENTIFIED THE MURDER WEAPON"!
?!
WHAT?! YOU SPEAK HICK?!
IFF YOU'M WAANT TER LABEL UZZ THE KILLER, YOU'M GODDUN REBDEEL THE MOIWDER WUPPON FURST!
gaahhh!!!

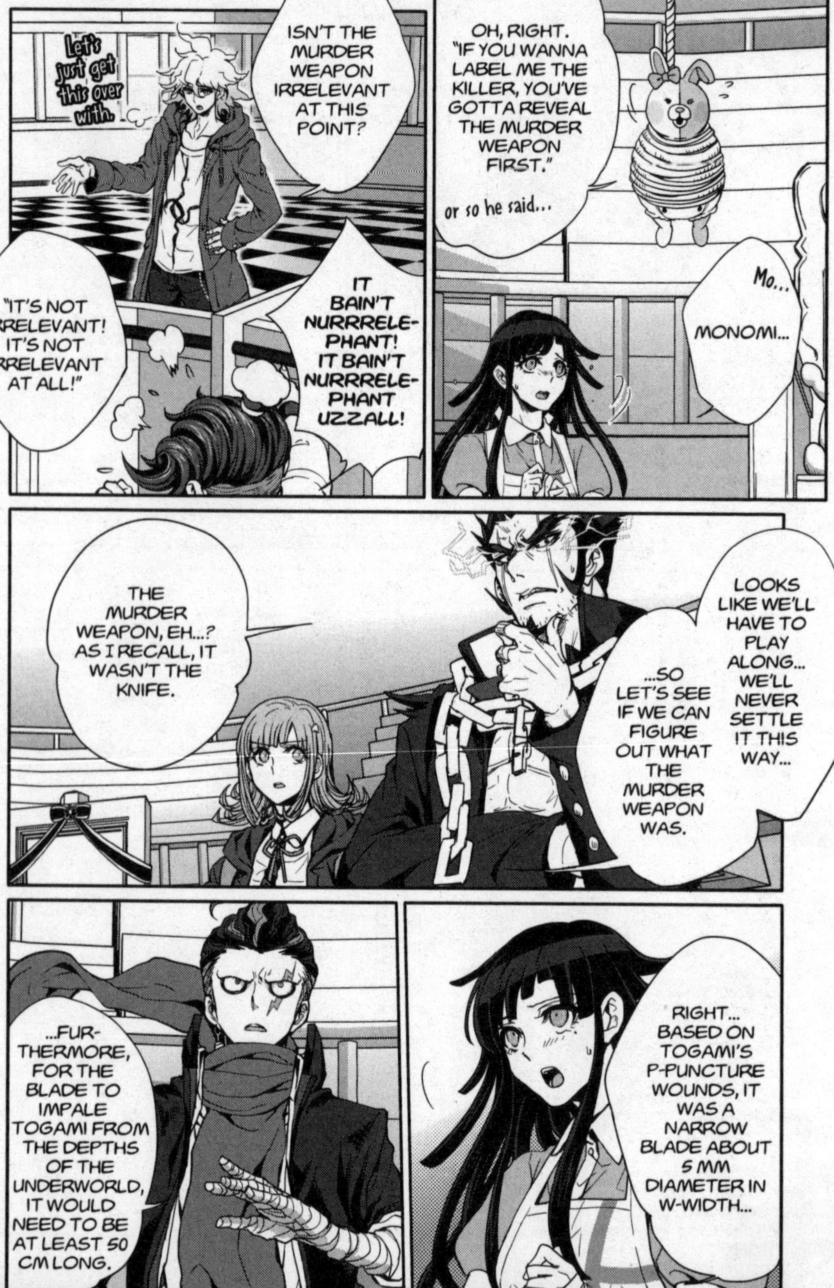
OH, RIGHT. "IF YOU WANNA LABEL ME THE KILLER, YOU'VE GOTTA REVEAL THE MURDER WEAPON FIRST."
or so he said...
Mo...
MONOMI...
ISN'T THE MURDER WEAPON IRRELEVANT AT THIS POINT?
Let's just get this over with.
IT BAIN'T NURRRELE-PHANT! IT BAIN'T NURRRELE-PHANT UZZALL!
"IT'S NOT IRRELEVANT! IT'S NOT IRRELEVANT AT ALL!"
LOOKS LIKE WE'LL HAVE TO PLAY ALONG... WE'LL NEVER SETTLE IT THIS WAY...
...SO LET'S SEE IF WE CAN FIGURE OUT WHAT THE MURDER WEAPON WAS.
THE MURDER WEAPON, EH...? AS I RECALL, IT WASN'T THE KNIFE.
RIGHT... BASED ON TOGAMI'S P-PUNCTURE WOUNDS, IT WAS A NARROW BLADE ABOUT 5 MM DIAMETER IN W-WIDTH...
...FUR-THERMORE, FOR THE BLADE TO IMPALE TOGAMI FROM THE DEPTHS OF THE UNDERWORLD, IT WOULD NEED TO BE AT LEAST 50 CM LONG.

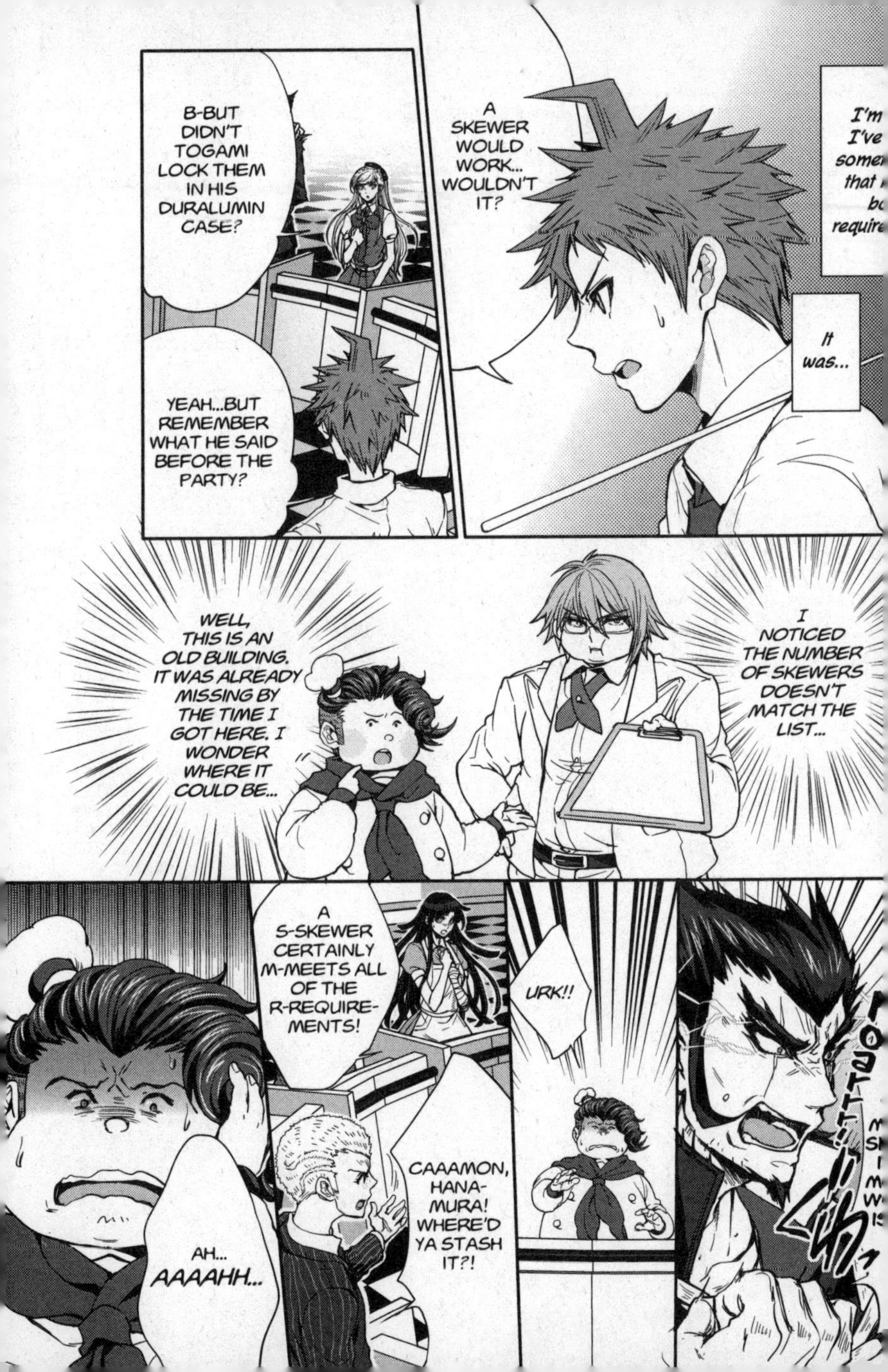
It was...
A SKEWER WOULD WORK... WOULDN'T IT?
B-BUT DIDN'T TOGAMI LOCK THEM IN HIS DURALUMIN CASE?
YEAH...BUT REMEMBER WHAT HE SAID BEFORE THE PARTY?
I NOTICED THE NUMBER OF SKEWERS DOESN'T MATCH THE LIST...
WELL, THIS IS AN OLD BUILDING. IT WAS ALREADY MISSING BY THE TIME I GOT HERE. I WONDER WHERE IT COULD BE...
URK!!
A S-SKEWER CERTAINLY M-MEETS ALL OF THE R-REQUIRE-MENTS!
CAAAMON, HANA-MURA! WHERE'D YA STASH IT?!
AH... AAAAAHH...

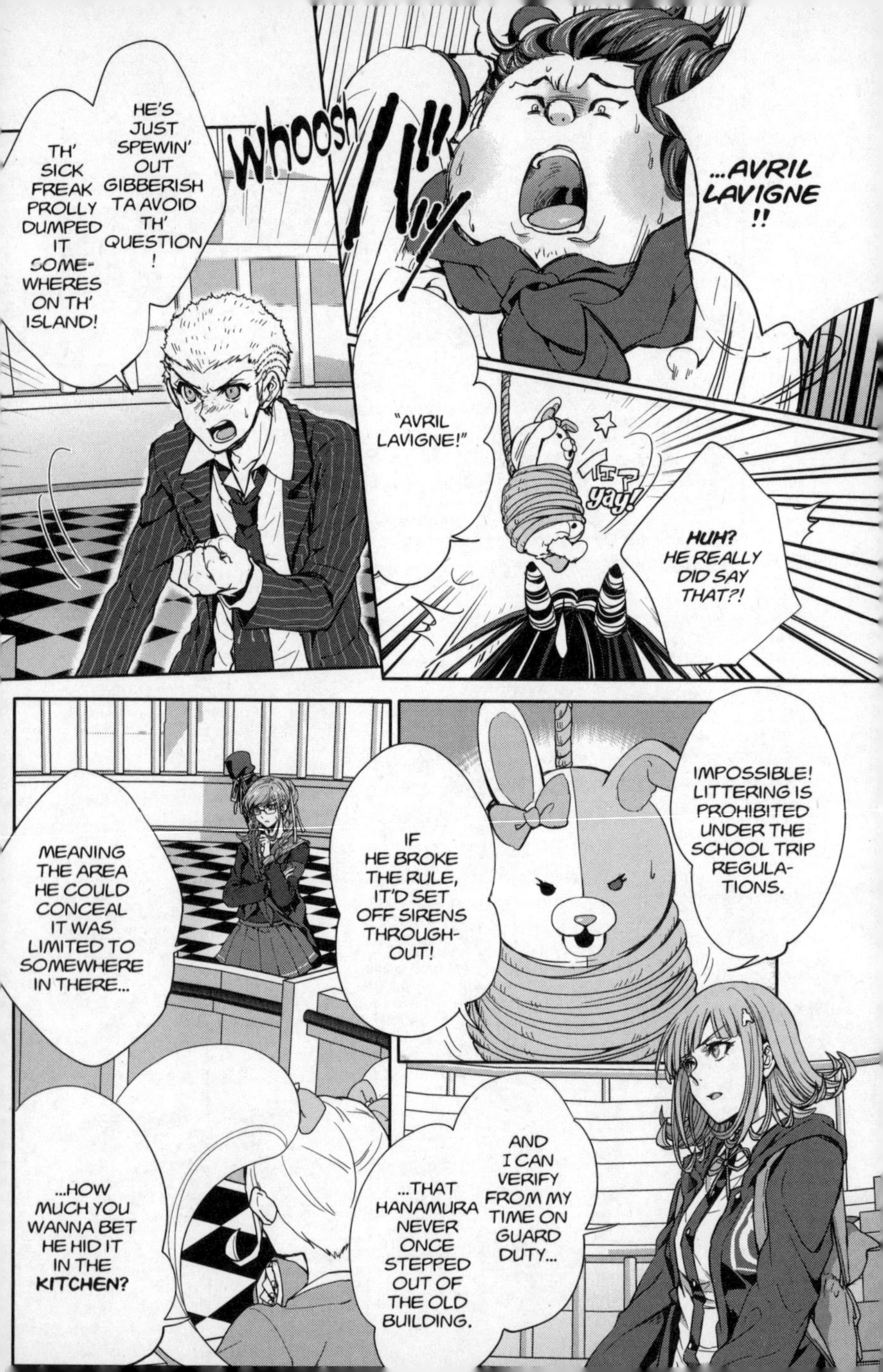

Whoosh
...AVRIL LAVIGNE!!
"AVRIL LAVIGNE!"
イエア yay!
HUH? HE REALLY DID SAY THAT?!
HE'S JUST SPEWIN' OUT GIBBERISH TA AVOID TH' QUESTION!
TH' SICK FREAK PROLLY DUMPED IT SOME-WHERES ON TH' ISLAND!
IMPOSSIBLE! LITTERING IS PROHIBITED UNDER THE SCHOOL TRIP REGULA-TIONS.
IF HE BROKE THE RULE, IT'D SET OFF SIRENS THROUGH-OUT!
AND I CAN VERIFY FROM MY TIME ON GUARD DUTY...
...THAT HANAMURA NEVER ONCE STEPPED OUT OF THE OLD BUILDING.
MEANING THE AREA HE COULD CONCEAL IT WAS LIMITED TO SOMEWHERE IN THERE...
...HOW MUCH YOU WANNA BET HE HID IT IN THE KITCHEN?

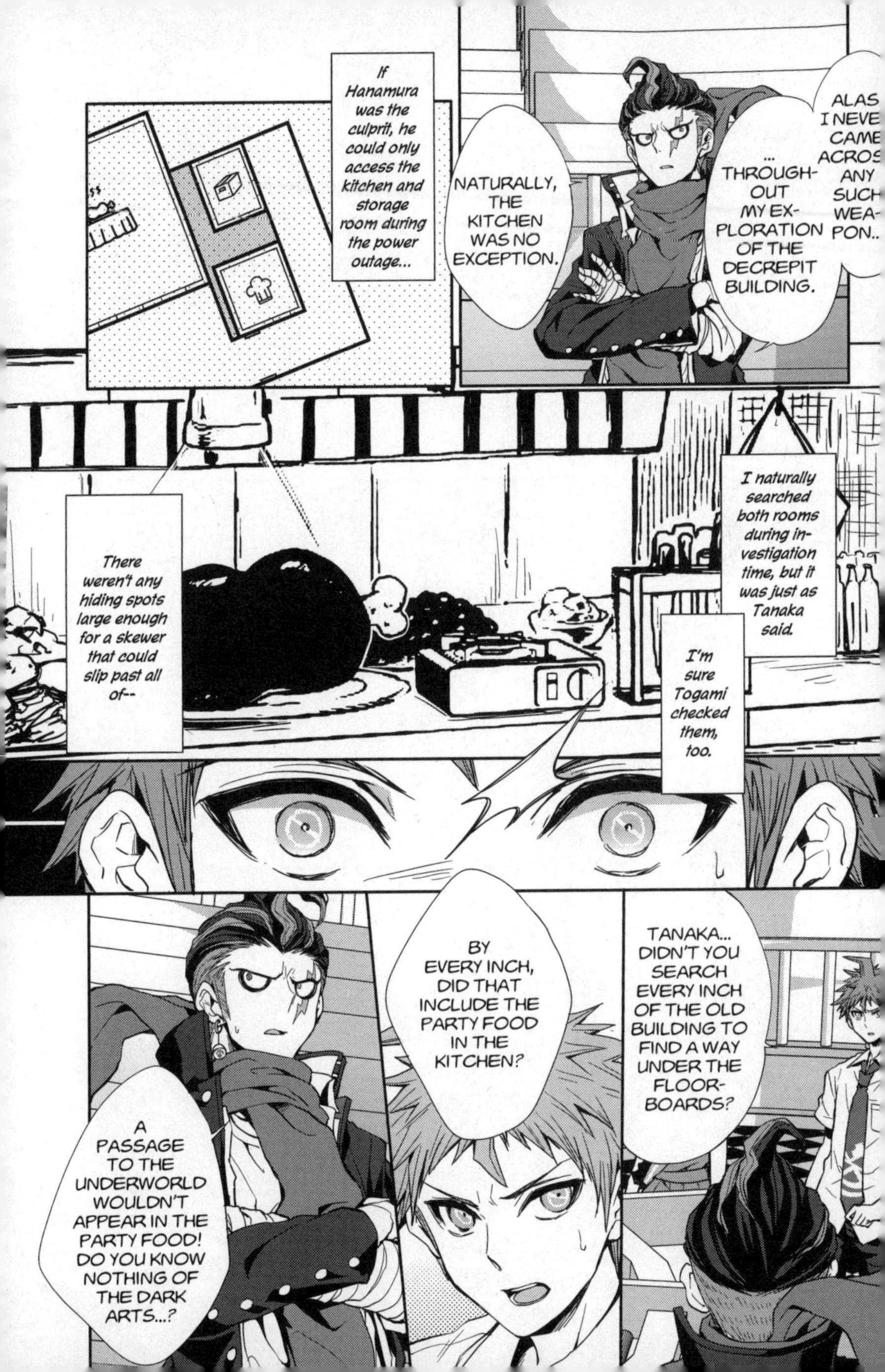
ALAS I NEVE CAME ACROS ANY SUCH WEA- PON..
... THROUGH- OUT MY EX- PLORATION OF THE DECREPIT BUILDING.
NATURALLY, THE KITCHEN WAS NO EXCEPTION.
If Hanamura was the culprit, he could only access the kitchen and storage room during the power outage...
I naturally searched both rooms during in- vestigation time, but it was just as Tanaka said.
I'm sure Togami checked them, too.
There weren't any hiding spots large enough for a skewer that could slip past all of--
TANAKA... DIDN'T YOU SEARCH EVERY INCH OF THE OLD BUILDING TO FIND A WAY UNDER THE FLOOR- BOARDS?
BY EVERY INCH, DID THAT INCLUDE THE PARTY FOOD IN THE KITCHEN?
A PASSAGE TO THE UNDERWORLD WOULDN'T APPEAR IN THE PARTY FOOD! DO YOU KNOW NOTHING OF THE DARK ARTS...?

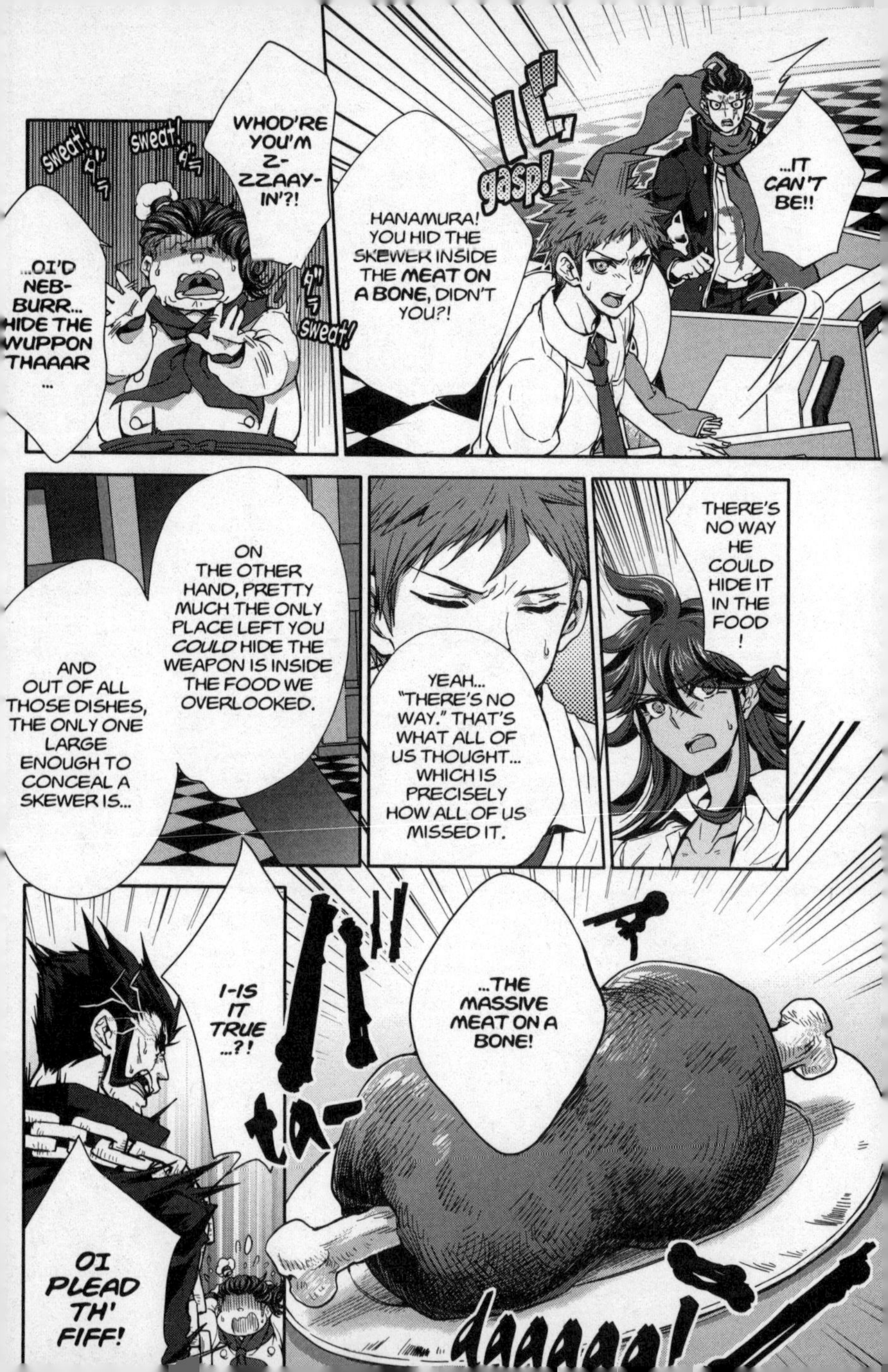
...IT CAN'T BE!!
gasp!
HANAMURA! YOU HID THE SKEWER INSIDE THE MEAT ON A BONE, DIDN'T YOU?!
WHOD'RE YOU'M Z-ZZAAY-IN'?!
sweat!
sweat!
sweat!
...OI'D NEB-BURR... HIDE THE WUPPON THAAAR ...
THERE'S NO WAY HE COULD HIDE IT IN THE FOOD!
YEAH... "THERE'S NO WAY." THAT'S WHAT ALL OF US THOUGHT... WHICH IS PRECISELY HOW ALL OF US MISSED IT.
ON THE OTHER HAND, PRETTY MUCH THE ONLY PLACE LEFT YOU *COULD* HIDE THE WEAPON IS INSIDE THE FOOD WE OVERLOOKED.
AND OUT OF ALL THOSE DISHES, THE ONLY ONE LARGE ENOUGH TO CONCEAL A SKEWER IS...
...THE MASSIVE MEAT ON A BONE!
ta-
daaaaa!
I-IS IT TRUE ...?!
OI PLEAD TH' FIFF!

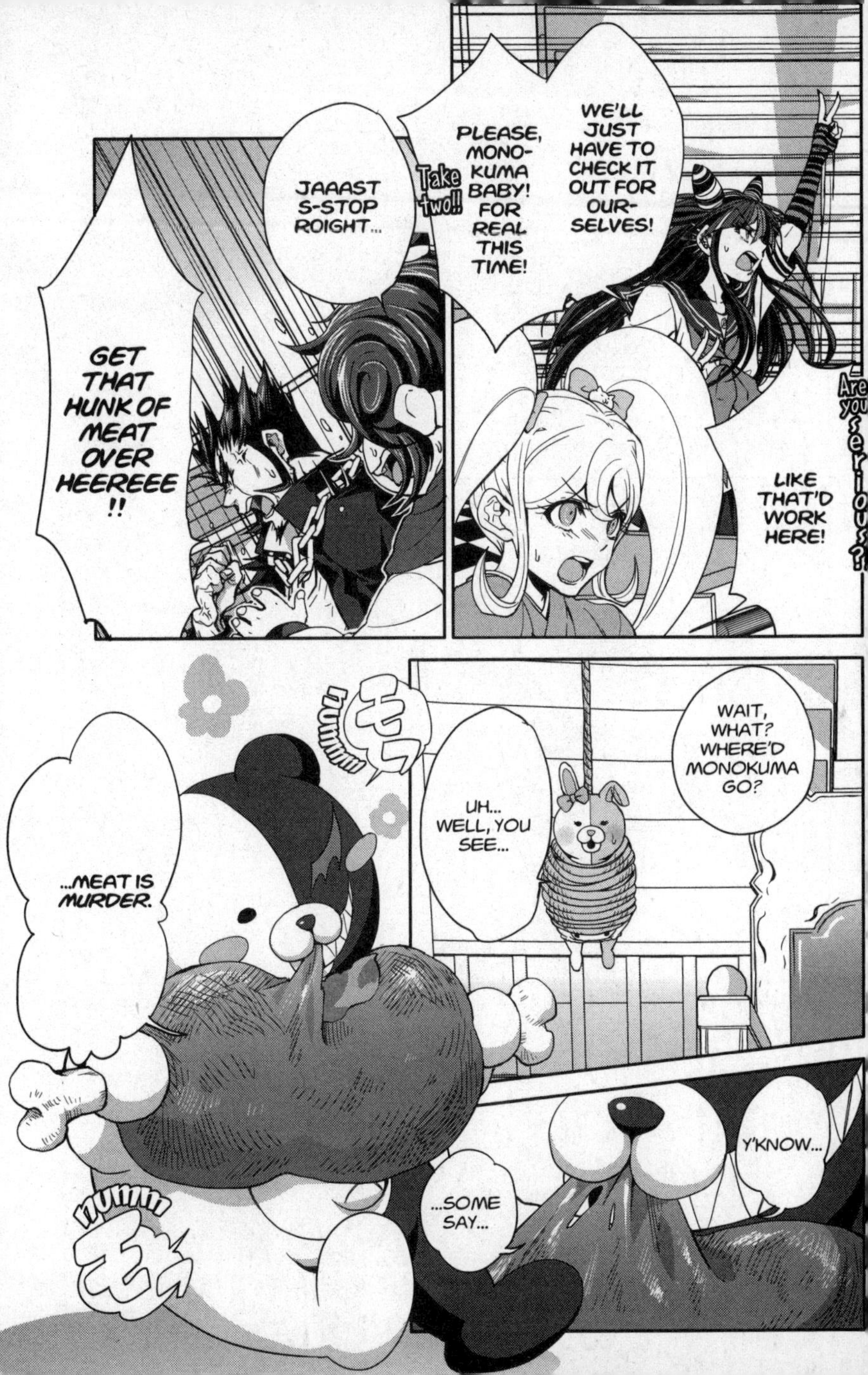

WE'LL JUST HAVE TO CHECK IT OUT FOR OUR-SELVES!
PLEASE, MONO-KUMA BABY! FOR REAL THIS TIME!
Take two!!
LIKE THAT'D WORK HERE!
Are you serious?!
JAAAST S-STOP ROIGHT...
GET THAT HUNK OF MEAT OVER HEEREEE!!
WAIT, WHAT? WHERE'D MONOKUMA GO?
UH... WELL, YOU SEE...
Y'KNOW...
...SOME SAY...
nummm
...MEAT IS MURDER.
nummm

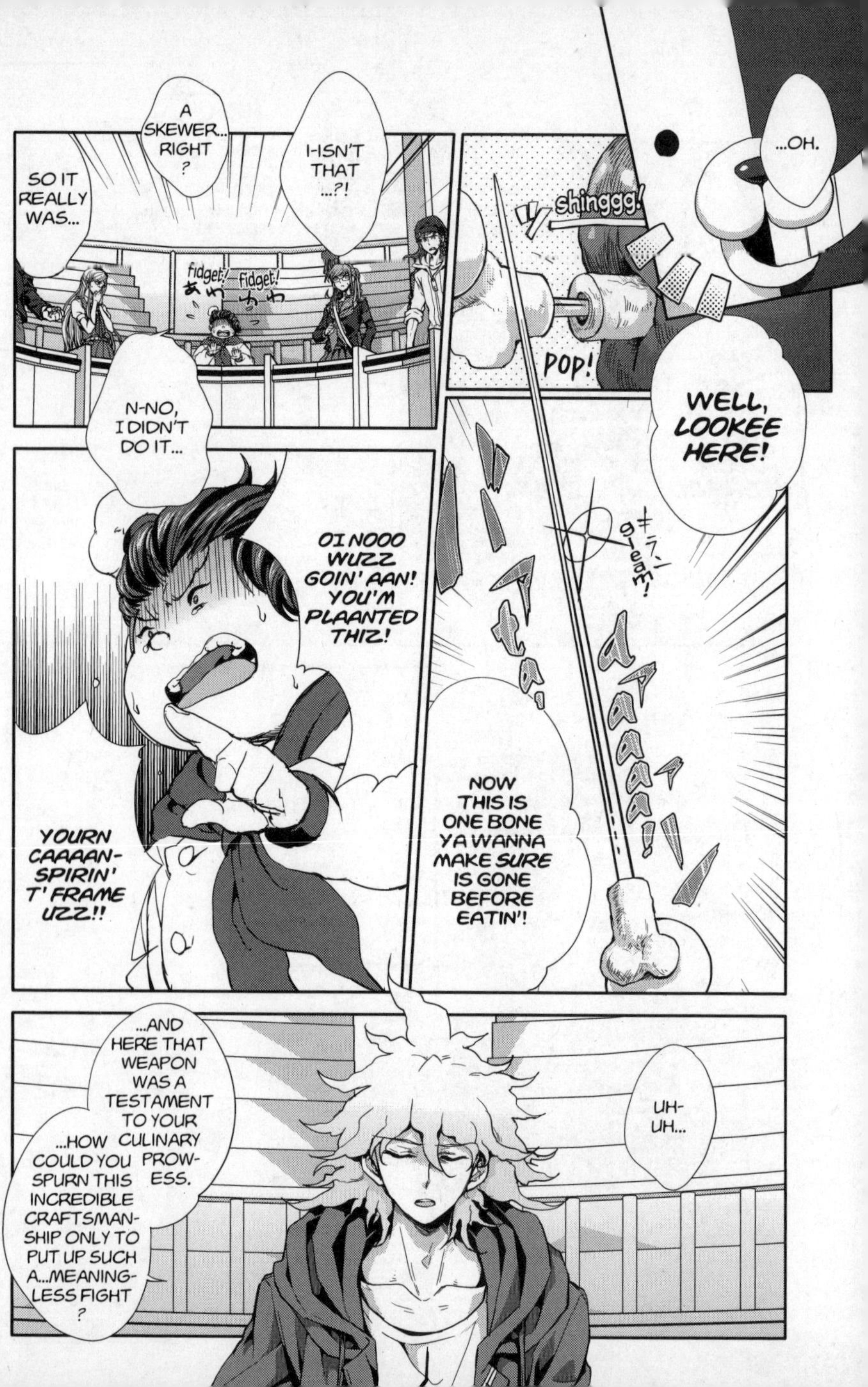
...OH.
Shinggg!
POP!
I-ISN'T THAT ...?!
A SKEWER... RIGHT?
SO IT REALLY WAS...
fidget!
fidget!
N-NO, I DIDN'T DO IT...
WELL, LOOKEE HERE!
gleam!
NOW THIS IS ONE BONE YA WANNA MAKE SURE IS GONE BEFORE EATIN'!
OI NOOO WUZZ GOIN' AAN! YOU'M PLAANTED THIZ!
YOURN CAAAAN-SPIRIN' T' FRAME UZZ!!
UH-UH...
...AND HERE THAT WEAPON WAS A TESTAMENT TO YOUR CULINARY PROW-ESS.
...HOW COULD YOU SPURN THIS INCREDIBLE CRAFTSMAN-SHIP ONLY TO PUT UP SUCH A...MEANING-LESS FIGHT?

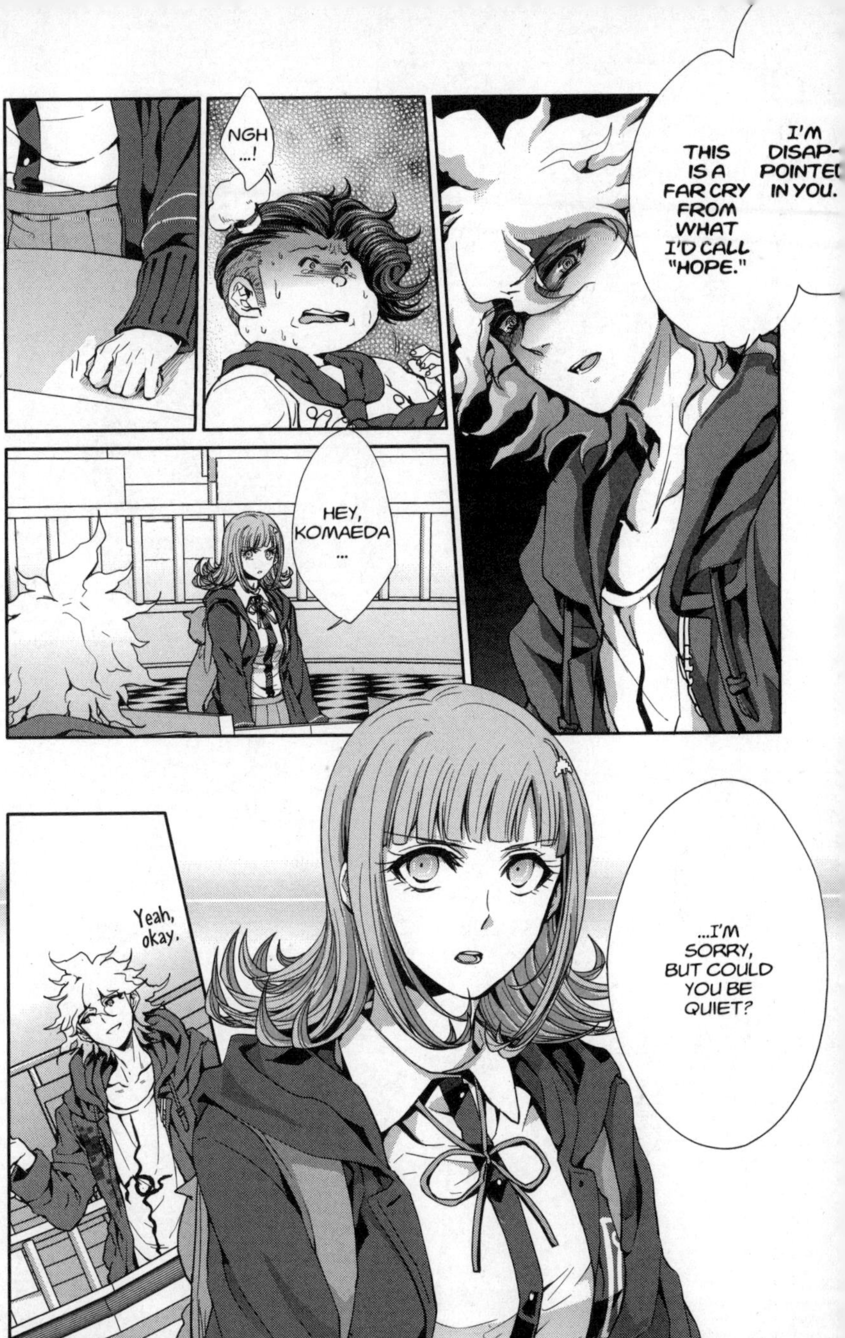
THIS IS A FAR CRY FROM WHAT I'D CALL "HOPE."
I'M DISAP-POINTED IN YOU.
NGH ...!
HEY, KOMAEDA ...
...I'M SORRY, BUT COULD YOU BE QUIET?
Yeah, okay.

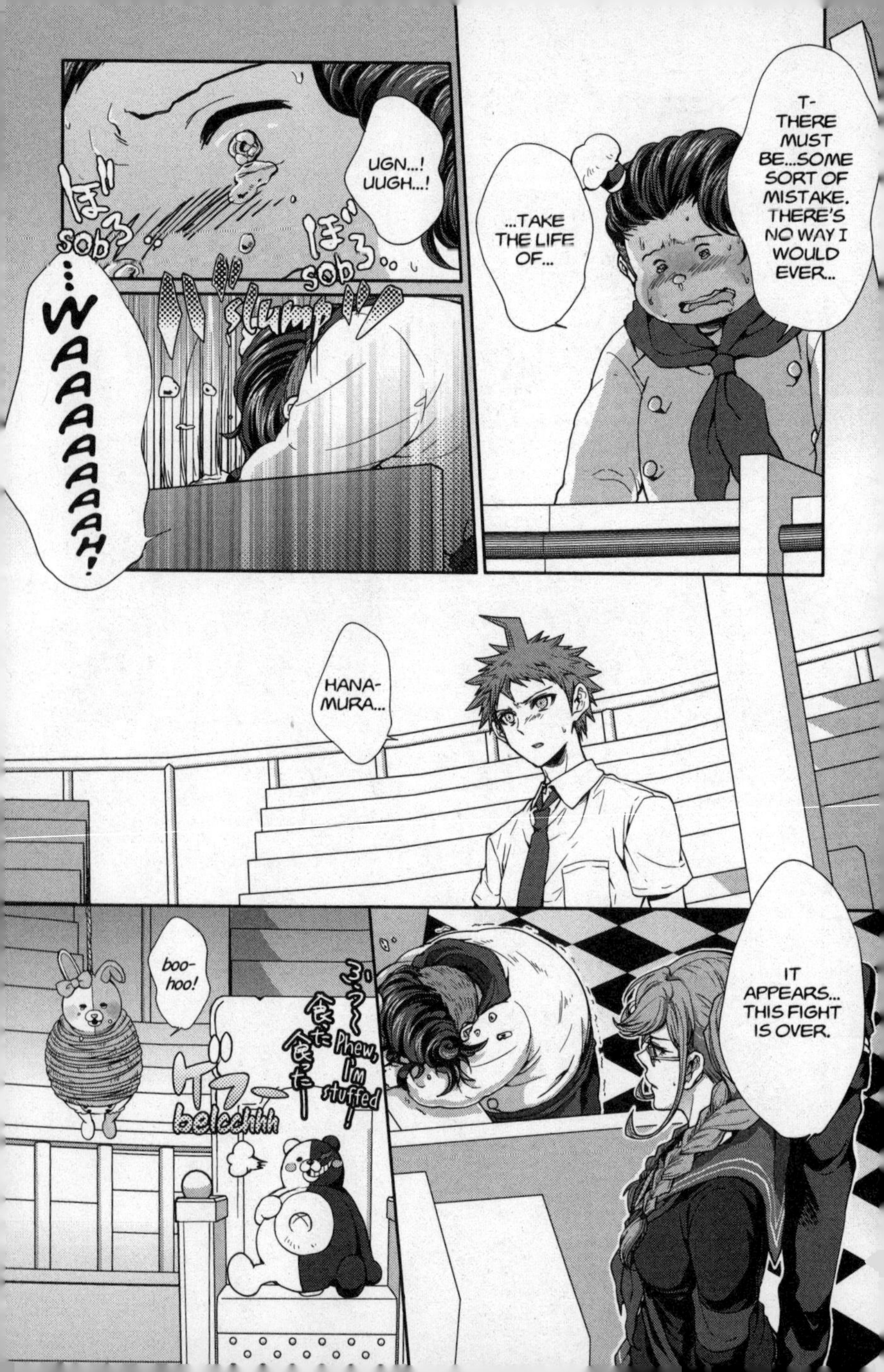
T-THERE MUST BE...SOME SORT OF MISTAKE. THERE'S NO WAY I WOULD EVER...
...TAKE THE LIFE OF...
UGN...! UUGH...!
sob
sob
slump
...WAAAAAAAAAH!
HANA-MURA...
IT APPEARS... THIS FIGHT IS OVER.
boo-hoo!
Phew, I'm stuffed!
belechhh

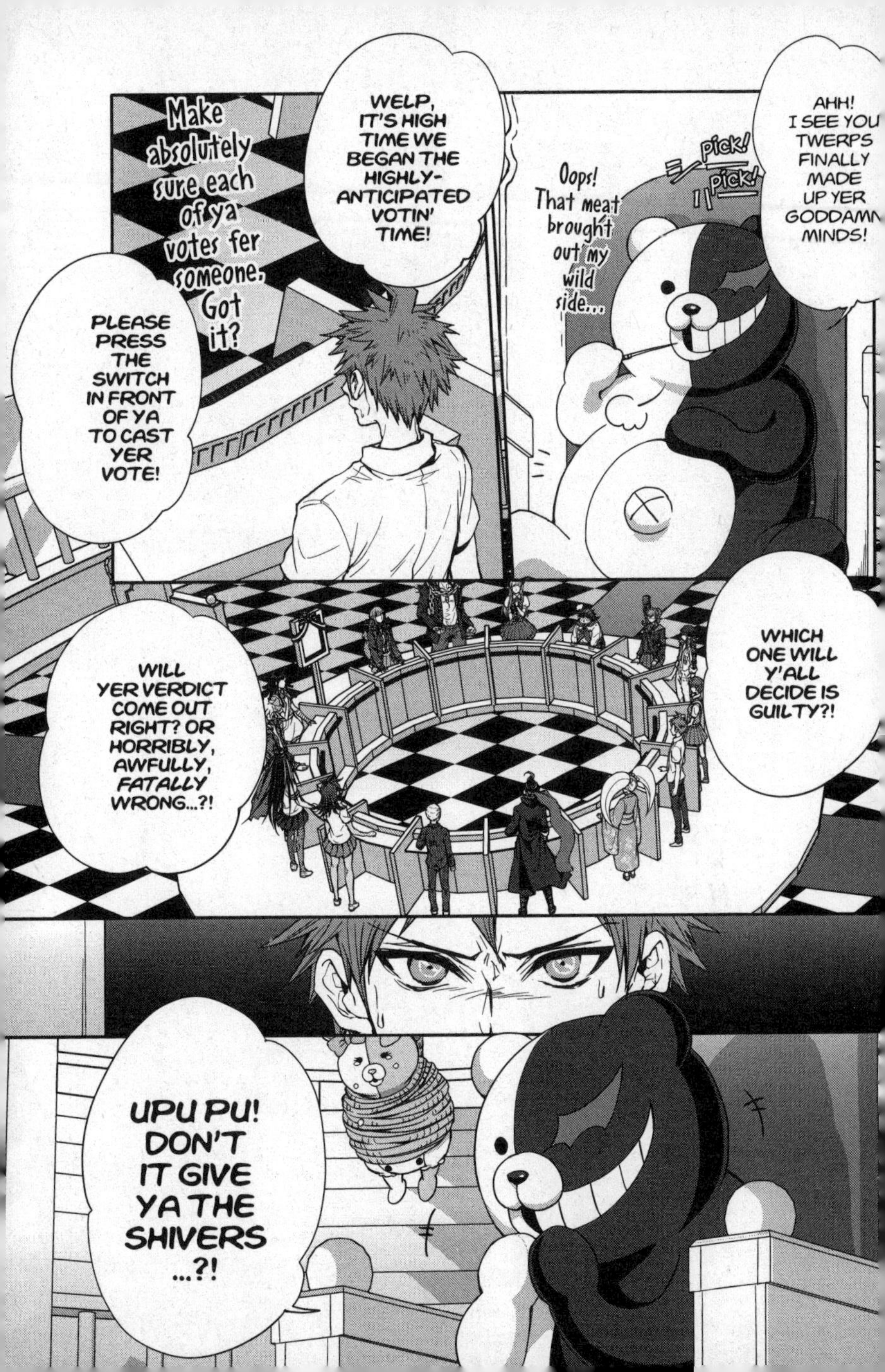
AHH! I SEE YOU TWERPS FINALLY MADE UP YER GODDAMN MINDS!
pick! pick!
Oops! That meat brought out my wild side...
WELP, IT'S HIGH TIME WE BEGAN THE HIGHLY-ANTICIPATED VOTIN' TIME!
Make absolutely sure each of ya votes fer someone. Got it?
PLEASE PRESS THE SWITCH IN FRONT OF YA TO CAST YER VOTE!
WHICH ONE WILL Y'ALL DECIDE IS GUILTY?!
WILL YER VERDICT COME OUT RIGHT? OR HORRIBLY, AWFULLY, FATALLY WRONG...?!
UPU PU! DON'T IT GIVE YA THE SHIVERS ...?!

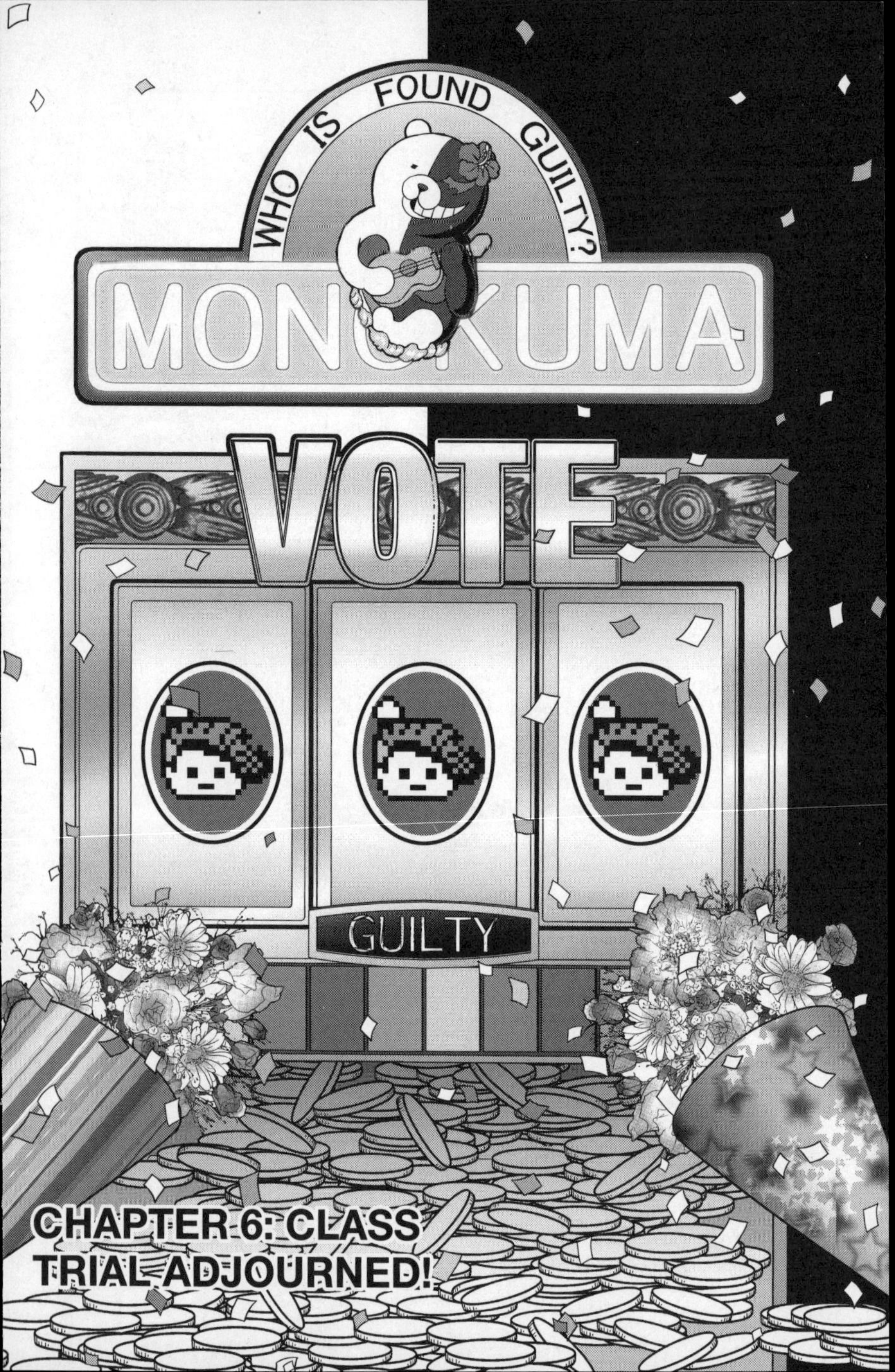
WHO IS FOUND GUILTY?
MONOKUMA
VOTE
GUILTY

CHAPTER 6: CLASS TRIAL ADJOURNED!

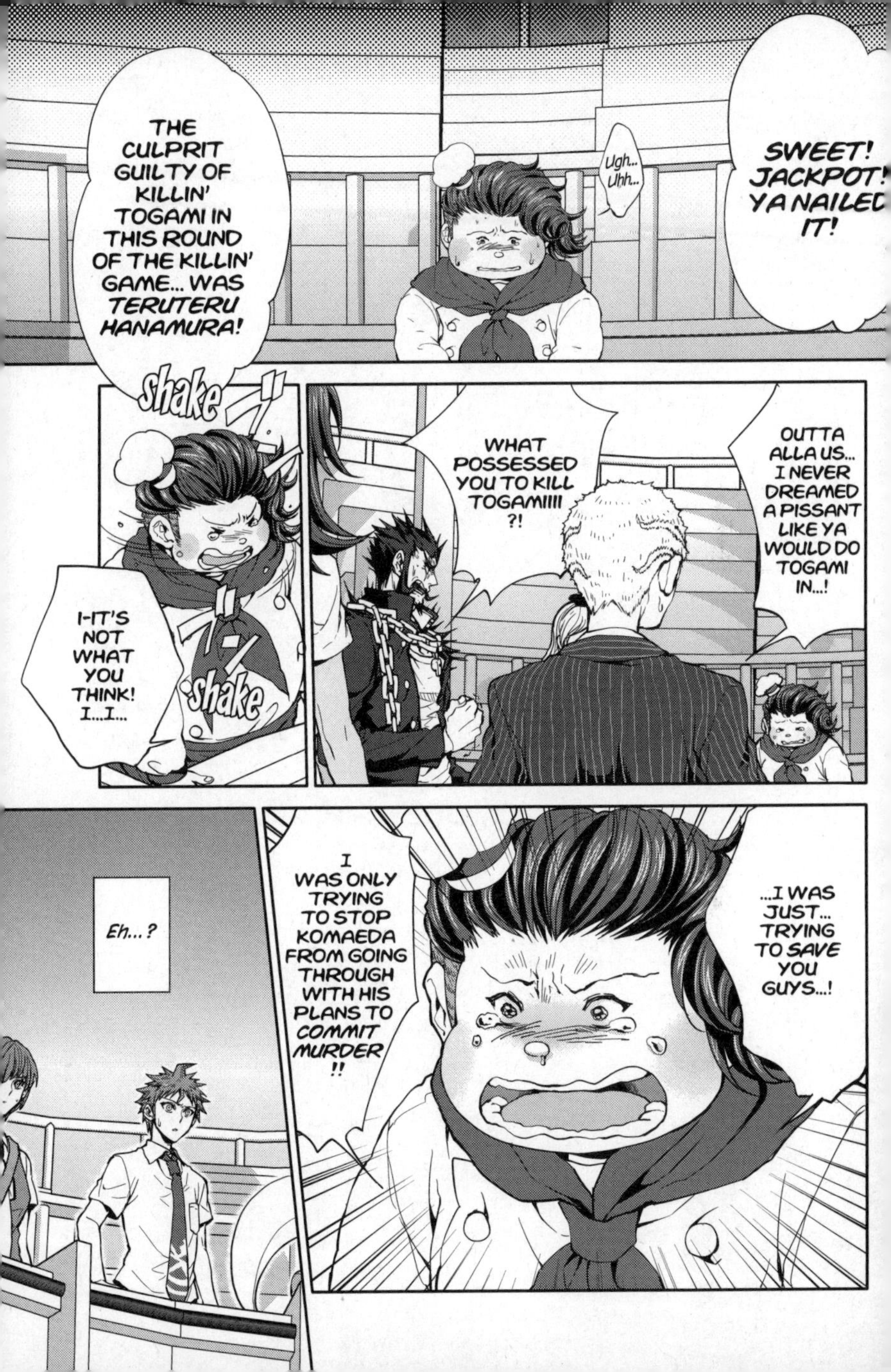
SWEET! JACKPOT! YA NAILED IT!
Ugh... Uhh...
THE CULPRIT GUILTY OF KILLIN' TOGAMI IN THIS ROUND OF THE KILLIN' GAME... WAS TERUTERU HANAMURA!
OUTTA ALLA US... I NEVER DREAMED A PISSANT LIKE YA WOULD DO TOGAMI IN...!
WHAT POSSESSED YOU TO KILL TOGAMIIII?!
shake
I-IT'S NOT WHAT YOU THINK! I...I...
shake
...I WAS JUST... TRYING TO SAVE YOU GUYS...!
I WAS ONLY TRYING TO STOP KOMAEDA FROM GOING THROUGH WITH HIS PLANS TO COMMIT MURDER!!
Eh...?

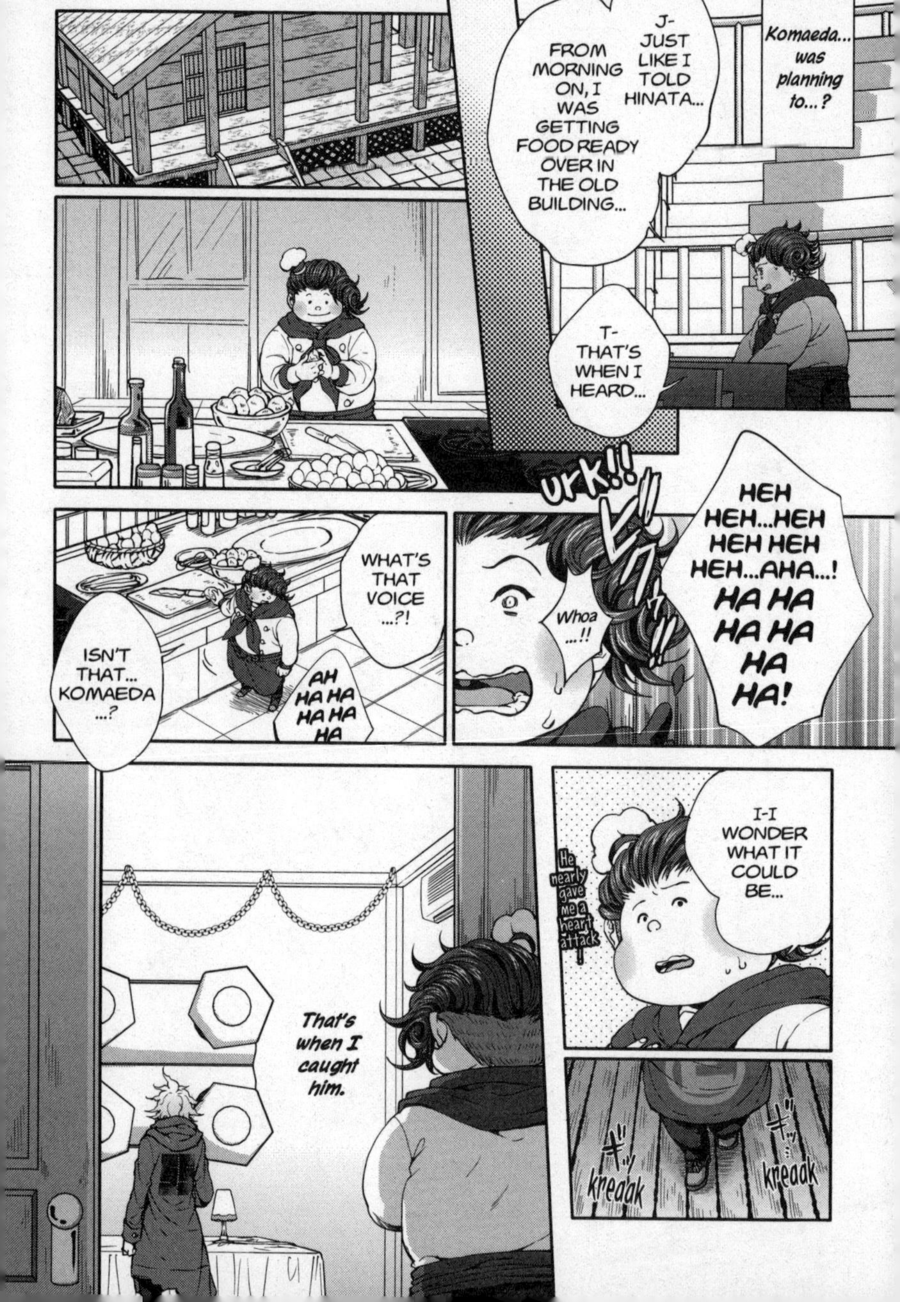
Komaeda... was planning to...?
J- JUST LIKE I TOLD HINATA... FROM MORNING ON, I WAS GETTING FOOD READY OVER IN THE OLD BUILDING...
T- THAT'S WHEN I HEARD...
HEH HEH...HEH HEH HEH HEH...AHA...! HA HA HA HA HA HA!
URK!!
Whoa ...!!
WHAT'S THAT VOICE ...?!
AH HA HA HA HA HA
ISN'T THAT... KOMAEDA ...?
I-I WONDER WHAT IT COULD BE...
He nearly gave me a heart attack!
kreaak
kreaak
That's when I caught him.

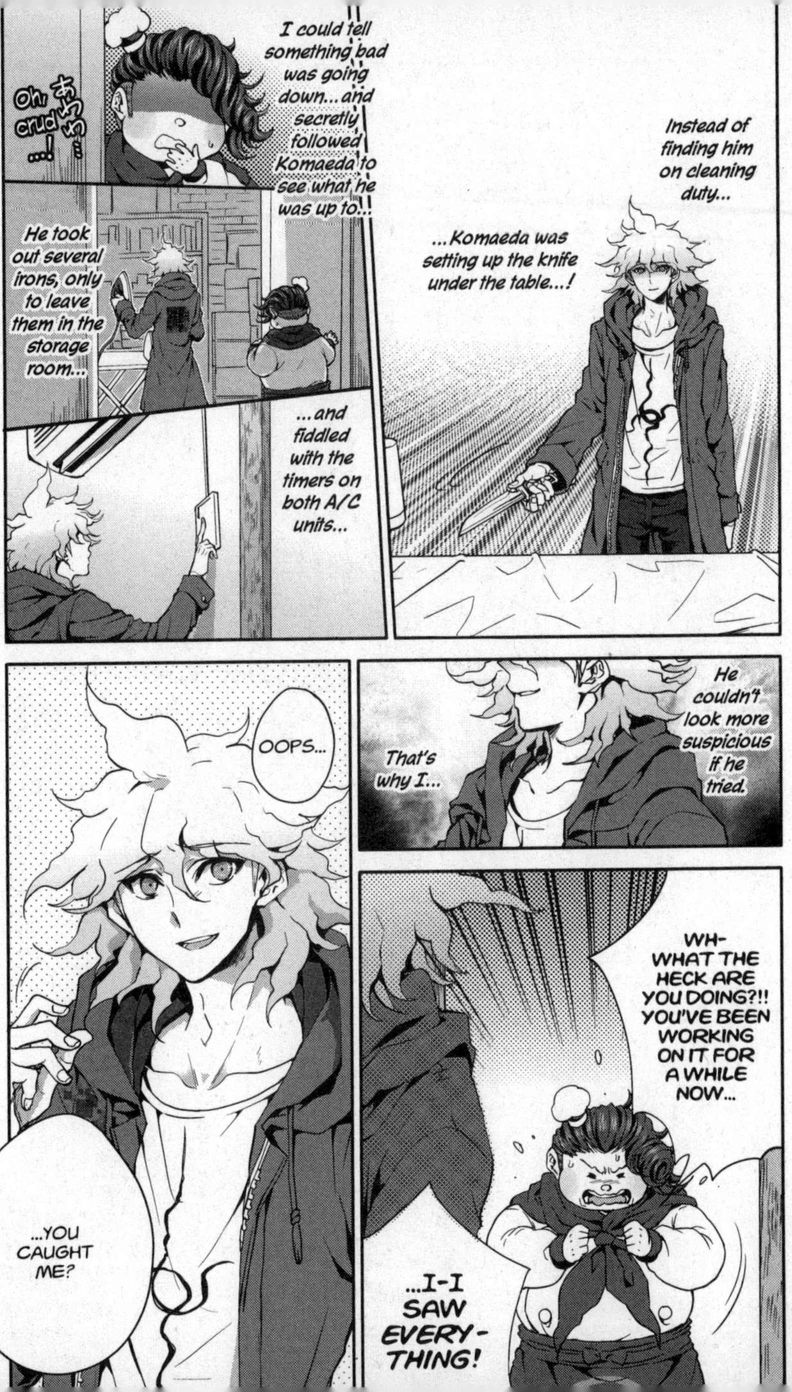

I could tell something bad was going down... and secretly followed Komaeda to see what he was up to...
Instead of finding him on cleaning duty...
...Komaeda was setting up the knife under the table...!
あわわ…
Oh, crud...!
He took out several irons, only to leave them in the storage room...
...and fiddled with the timers on both A/C units...
He couldn't look more suspicious if he tried.
That's why I...
WH- WHAT THE HECK ARE YOU DOING?!! YOU'VE BEEN WORKING ON IT FOR A WHILE NOW...
...I-I SAW EVERY-THING!
OOPS...
...YOU CAUGHT ME?

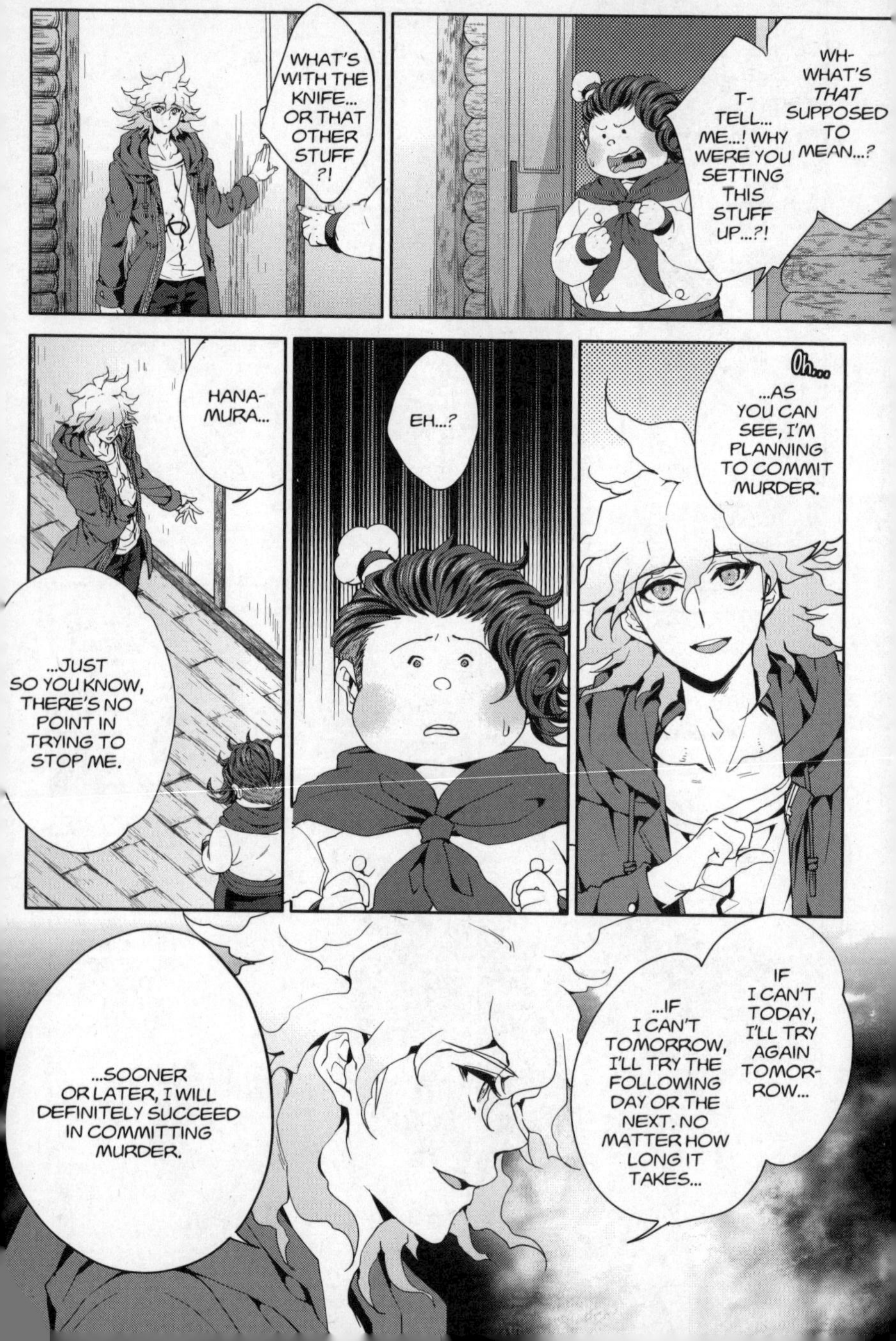
WH- WHAT'S THAT SUPPOSED TO MEAN...?
T- TELL... ME...! WHY WERE YOU SETTING THIS STUFF UP...?!
WHAT'S WITH THE KNIFE... OR THAT OTHER STUFF ?!
Oh...
...AS YOU CAN SEE, I'M PLANNING TO COMMIT MURDER.
EH...?
HANA-MURA...
...JUST SO YOU KNOW, THERE'S NO POINT IN TRYING TO STOP ME.
IF I CAN'T TODAY, I'LL TRY AGAIN TOMOR-ROW...
...IF I CAN'T TOMORROW, I'LL TRY THE FOLLOWING DAY OR THE NEXT. NO MATTER HOW LONG IT TAKES...
...SOONER OR LATER, I WILL DEFINITELY SUCCEED IN COMMITTING MURDER.

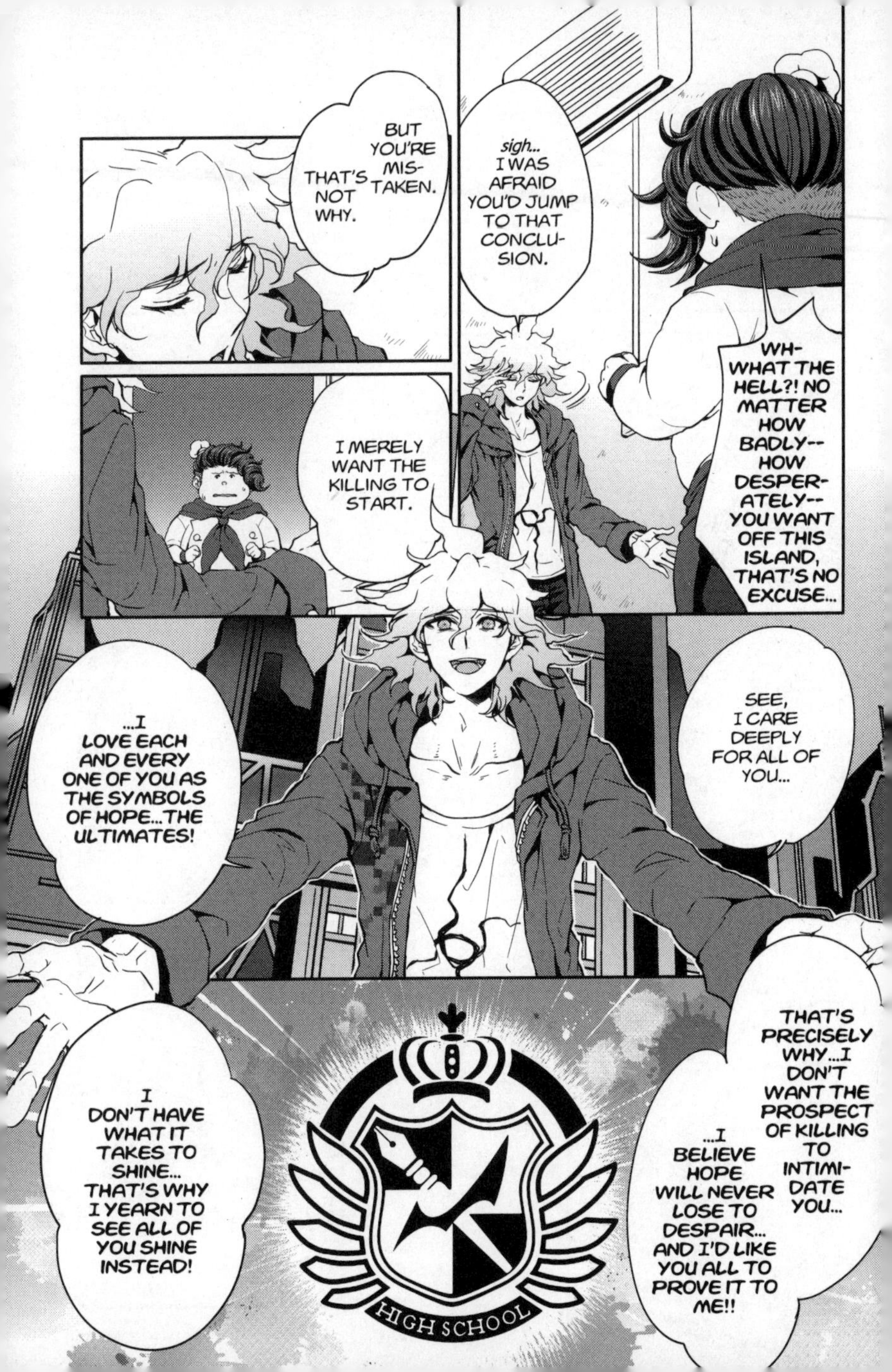
WH- WHAT THE HELL?! NO MATTER HOW BADLY-- HOW DESPERATELY-- YOU WANT OFF THIS ISLAND, THAT'S NO EXCUSE...
sigh... I WAS AFRAID YOU'D JUMP TO THAT CONCLUSION.
BUT YOU'RE MISTAKEN.
THAT'S NOT WHY.
I MERELY WANT THE KILLING TO START.
SEE, I CARE DEEPLY FOR ALL OF YOU...
...I LOVE EACH AND EVERY ONE OF YOU AS THE SYMBOLS OF HOPE...THE ULTIMATES!
THAT'S PRECISELY WHY...I DON'T WANT THE PROSPECT OF KILLING TO INTIMIDATE YOU...
...I BELIEVE HOPE WILL NEVER LOSE TO DESPAIR... AND I'D LIKE YOU ALL TO PROVE IT TO ME!!
HIGH SCHOOL
I DON'T HAVE WHAT IT TAKES TO SHINE... THAT'S WHY I YEARN TO SEE ALL OF YOU SHINE INSTEAD!

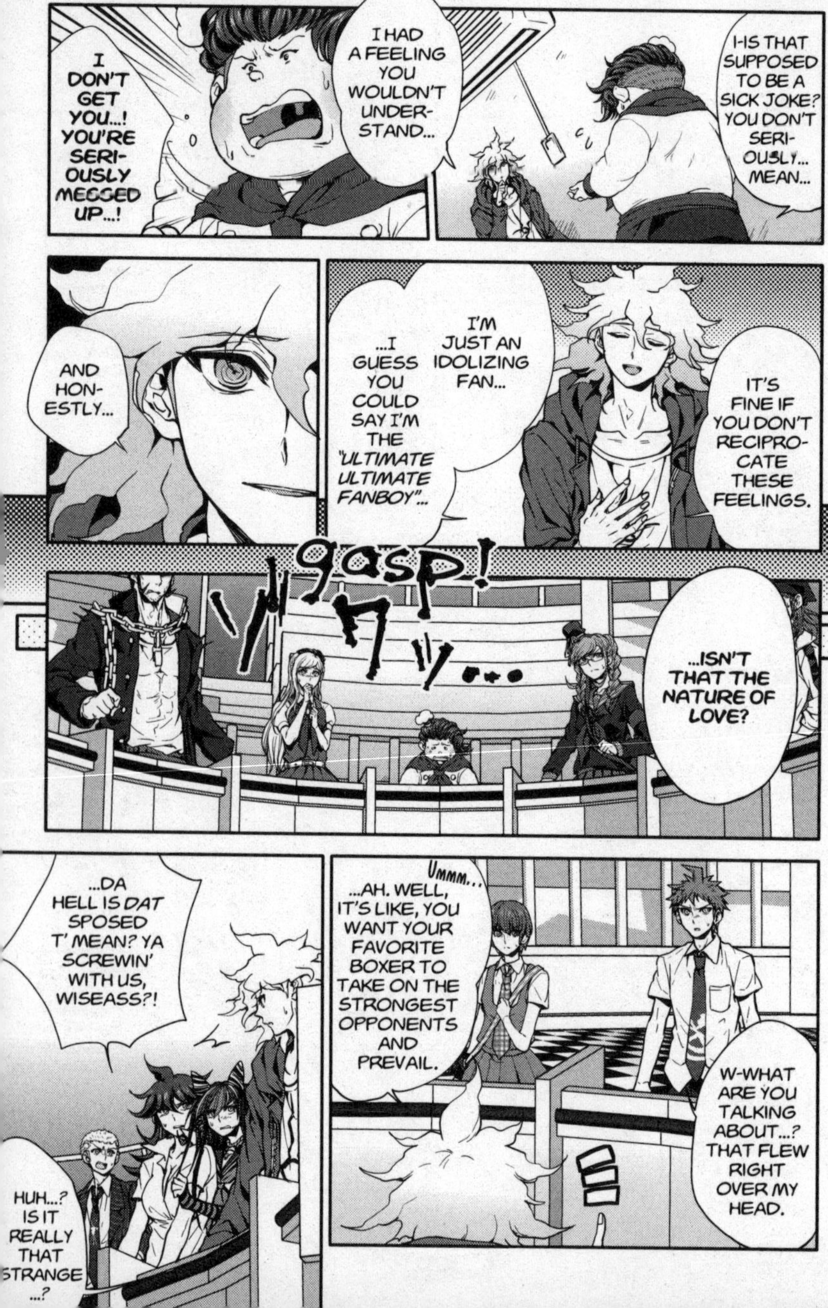
I-IS THAT SUPPOSED TO BE A SICK JOKE? YOU DON'T SERI-OUSLY... MEAN...
I HAD A FEELING YOU WOULDN'T UNDER-STAND...
I DON'T GET YOU...! YOU'RE SERI-OUSLY MESSED UP...!
IT'S FINE IF YOU DON'T RECIPRO-CATE THESE FEELINGS.
I'M JUST AN IDOLIZING FAN...
...I GUESS YOU COULD SAY I'M THE "ULTIMATE ULTIMATE FANBOY"...
AND HON-ESTLY...
...ISN'T THAT THE NATURE OF LOVE?
gasp!
ワッ...
UMMM...
...AH. WELL, IT'S LIKE, YOU WANT YOUR FAVORITE BOXER TO TAKE ON THE STRONGEST OPPONENTS AND PREVAIL.
W-WHAT ARE YOU TALKING ABOUT...? THAT FLEW RIGHT OVER MY HEAD.
...DA HELL IS DAT SPOSED T' MEAN? YA SCREWIN' WITH US, WISEASS?!
HUH...? IS IT REALLY THAT STRANGE...?

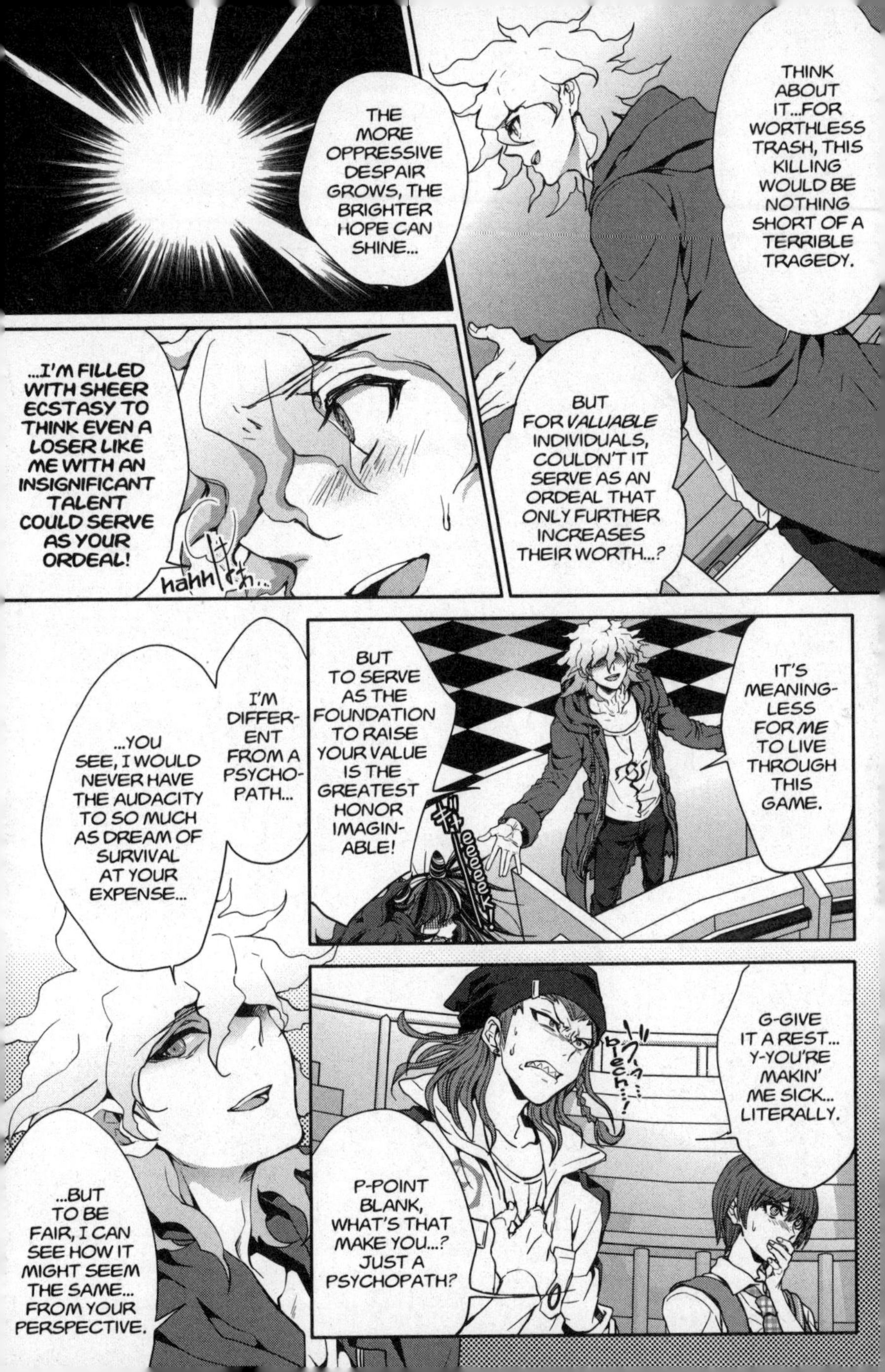
THINK ABOUT IT...FOR WORTHLESS TRASH, THIS KILLING WOULD BE NOTHING SHORT OF A TERRIBLE TRAGEDY.
BUT FOR *VALUABLE* INDIVIDUALS, COULDN'T IT SERVE AS AN ORDEAL THAT ONLY FURTHER INCREASES THEIR WORTH...?
THE MORE OPPRESSIVE DESPAIR GROWS, THE BRIGHTER HOPE CAN SHINE...
...I'M FILLED WITH SHEER ECSTASY TO THINK EVEN A LOSER LIKE ME WITH AN INSIGNIFICANT TALENT COULD SERVE AS YOUR ORDEAL!
hahh
IT'S MEANING-LESS FOR *ME* TO LIVE THROUGH THIS GAME.
BUT TO SERVE AS THE FOUNDATION TO RAISE YOUR VALUE IS THE GREATEST HONOR IMAGINABLE!
eeeeek!
G-GIVE IT A REST... Y-YOU'RE MAKIN' ME SICK... LITERALLY.
blech...!
P-POINT BLANK, WHAT'S THAT MAKE YOU...? JUST A PSYCHOPATH?
I'M DIFFERENT FROM A PSYCHOPATH...
...YOU SEE, I WOULD NEVER HAVE THE AUDACITY TO SO MUCH AS DREAM OF SURVIVAL AT YOUR EXPENSE...
...BUT TO BE FAIR, I CAN SEE HOW IT MIGHT SEEM THE SAME... FROM YOUR PERSPECTIVE.

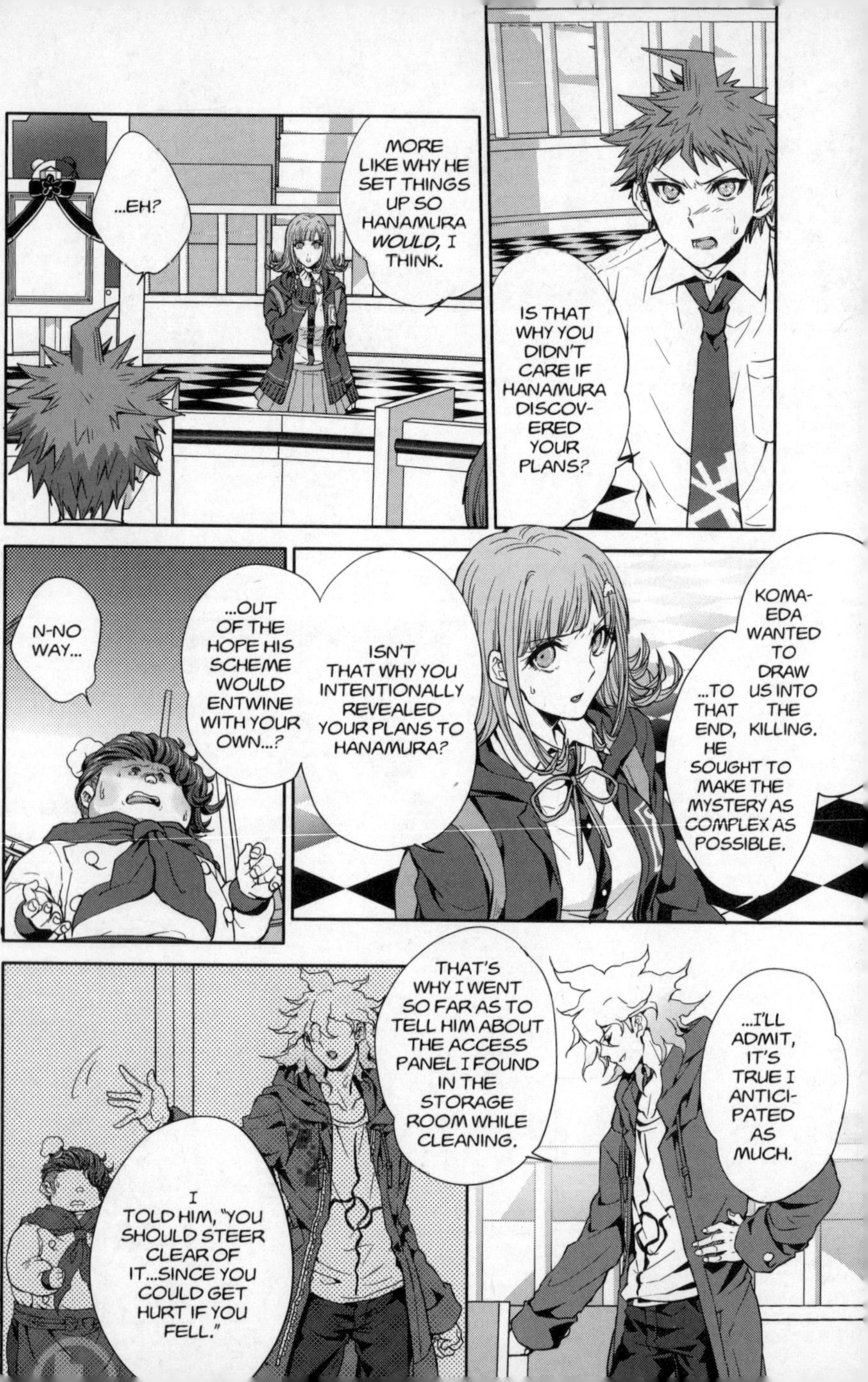
IS THAT WHY YOU DIDN'T CARE IF HANAMURA DISCOVERED YOUR PLANS?
MORE LIKE WHY HE SET THINGS UP SO HANAMURA *WOULD*, I THINK.
...EH?
KOMAEDA WANTED TO DRAW US INTO THE KILLING.
...TO THAT END, HE SOUGHT TO MAKE THE MYSTERY AS COMPLEX AS POSSIBLE.
ISN'T THAT WHY YOU INTENTIONALLY REVEALED YOUR PLANS TO HANAMURA?
...OUT OF THE HOPE HIS SCHEME WOULD ENTWINE WITH YOUR OWN...?
N-NO WAY...
...I'LL ADMIT, IT'S TRUE I ANTICIPATED AS MUCH.
THAT'S WHY I WENT SO FAR AS TO TELL HIM ABOUT THE ACCESS PANEL I FOUND IN THE STORAGE ROOM WHILE CLEANING.
I TOLD HIM, "YOU SHOULD STEER CLEAR OF IT...SINCE YOU COULD GET HURT IF YOU FELL."

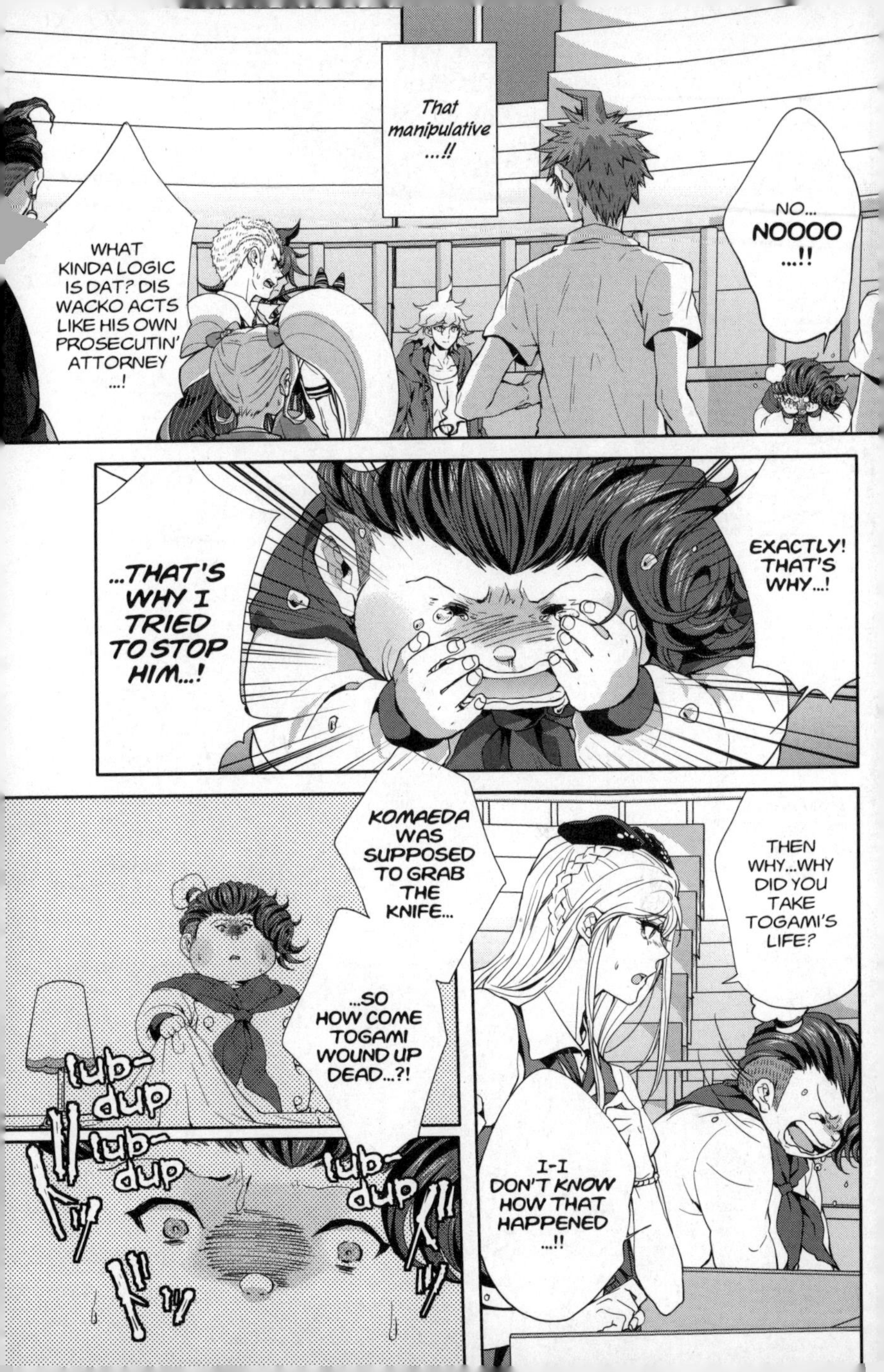
NO... NOOOO ...!!
That manipulative ...!!
WHAT KINDA LOGIC IS DAT? DIS WACKO ACTS LIKE HIS OWN PROSECUTIN' ATTORNEY ...!
EXACTLY! THAT'S WHY...!
...THAT'S WHY I TRIED TO STOP HIM...!
THEN WHY...WHY DID YOU TAKE TOGAMI'S LIFE?
I-I DON'T KNOW HOW THAT HAPPENED ...!!
KOMAEDA WAS SUPPOSED TO GRAB THE KNIFE...
...SO HOW COME TOGAMI WOUND UP DEAD...?!
tub-dup
tub-dup
tub-dup

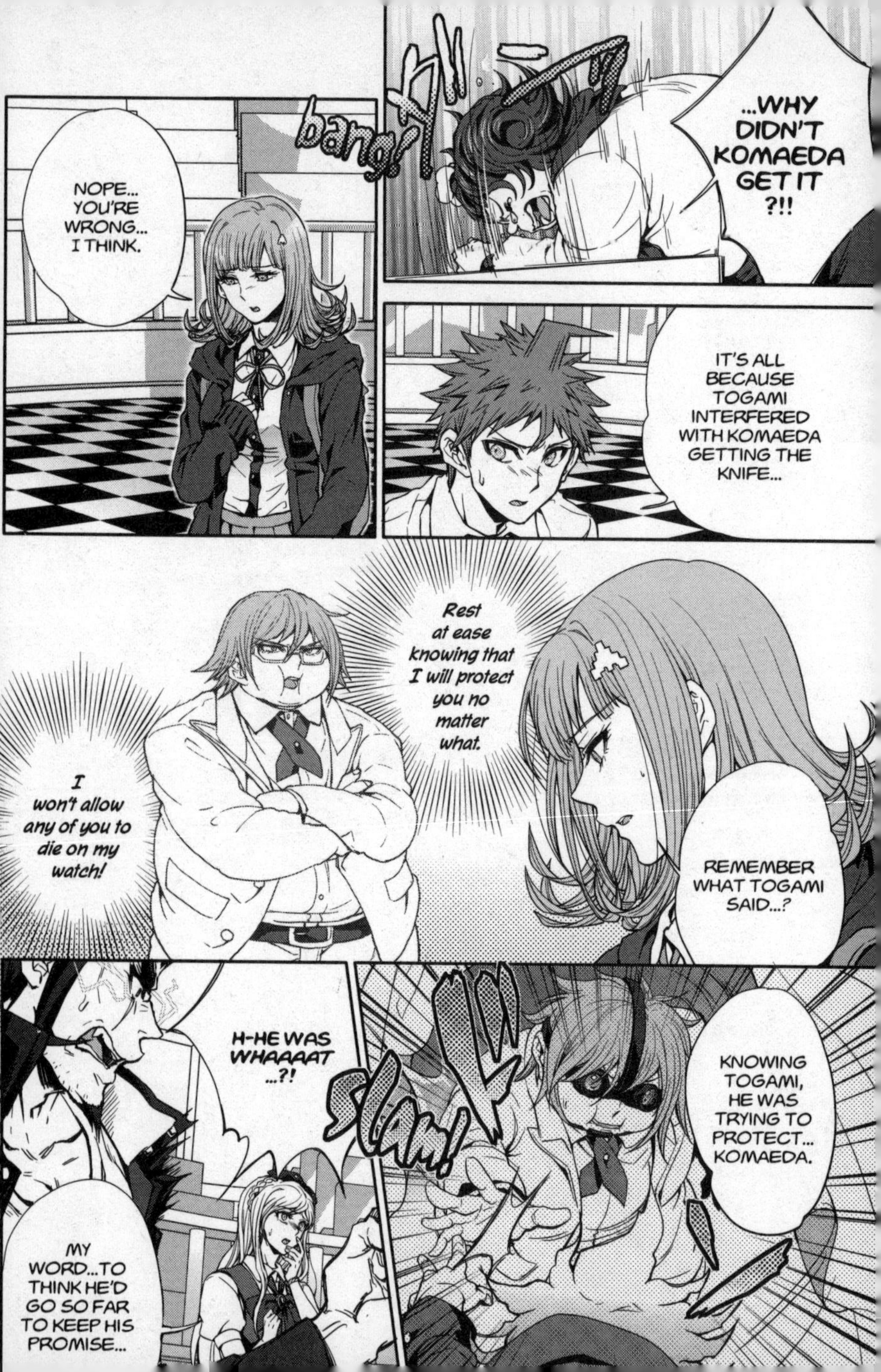
bang!
...WHY DIDN'T KOMAEDA GET IT ?!!
IT'S ALL BECAUSE TOGAMI INTERFERED WITH KOMAEDA GETTING THE KNIFE...
NOPE... YOU'RE WRONG... I THINK.
REMEMBER WHAT TOGAMI SAID...?
Rest at ease knowing that I will protect you no matter what.
I won't allow any of you to die on my watch!
SLAM!
KNOWING TOGAMI, HE WAS TRYING TO PROTECT... KOMAEDA.
H-HE WAS WHAAAAT ...?!
MY WORD...TO THINK HE'D GO SO FAR TO KEEP HIS PROMISE...

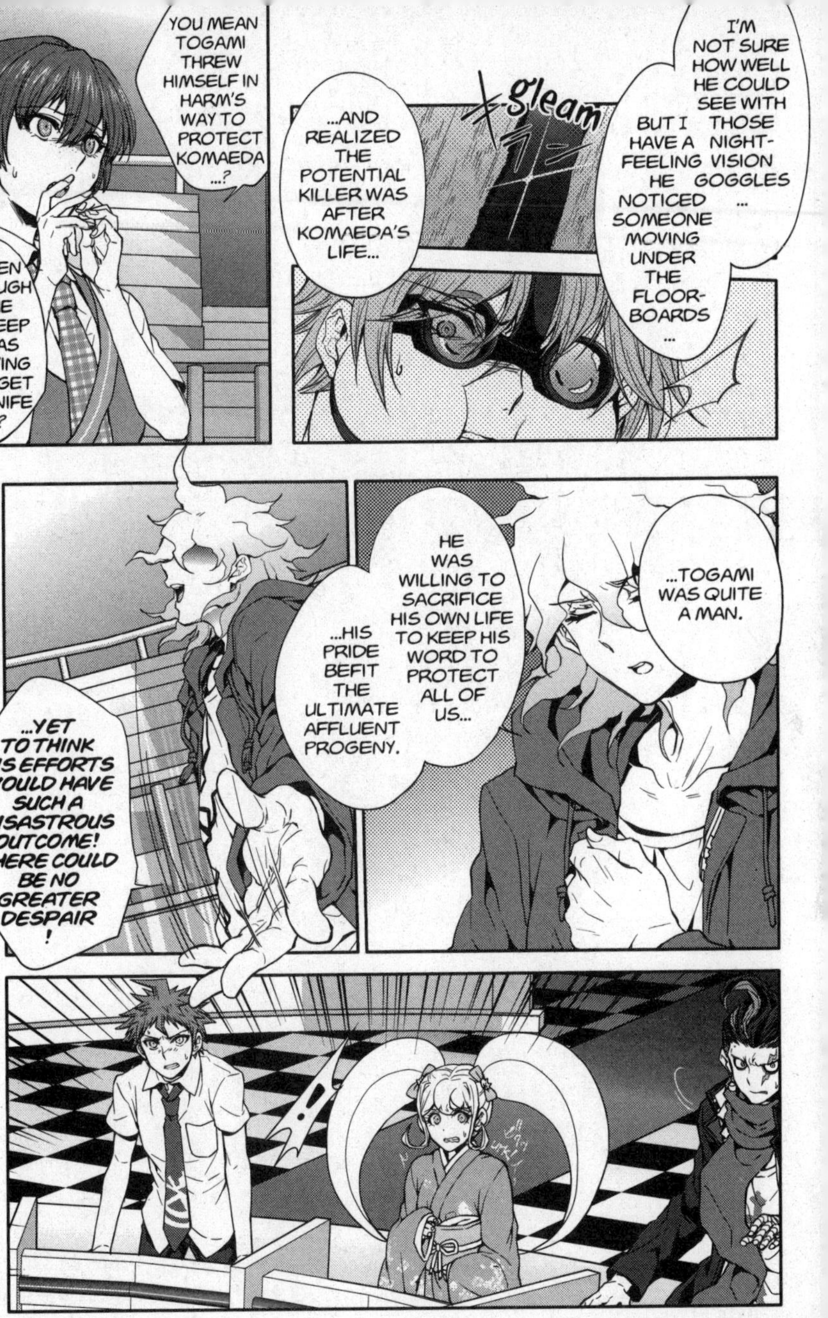
I'M NOT SURE HOW WELL HE COULD SEE WITH THOSE NIGHT-VISION GOGGLES...
gleam
BUT I HAVE A FEELING HE NOTICED SOMEONE MOVING UNDER THE FLOOR-BOARDS...
...AND REALIZED THE POTENTIAL KILLER WAS AFTER KOMAEDA'S LIFE...
YOU MEAN TOGAMI THREW HIMSELF IN HARM'S WAY TO PROTECT KOMAEDA...?
...EVEN THOUGH THE CREEP WAS TRYING TO GET A KNIFE...?
...TOGAMI WAS QUITE A MAN.
HE WAS WILLING TO SACRIFICE HIS OWN LIFE TO KEEP HIS WORD TO PROTECT ALL OF US...
...HIS PRIDE BEFIT THE ULTIMATE AFFLUENT PROGENY.
...YET TO THINK HIS EFFORTS WOULD HAVE SUCH A DISASTROUS OUTCOME! THERE COULD BE NO GREATER DESPAIR!

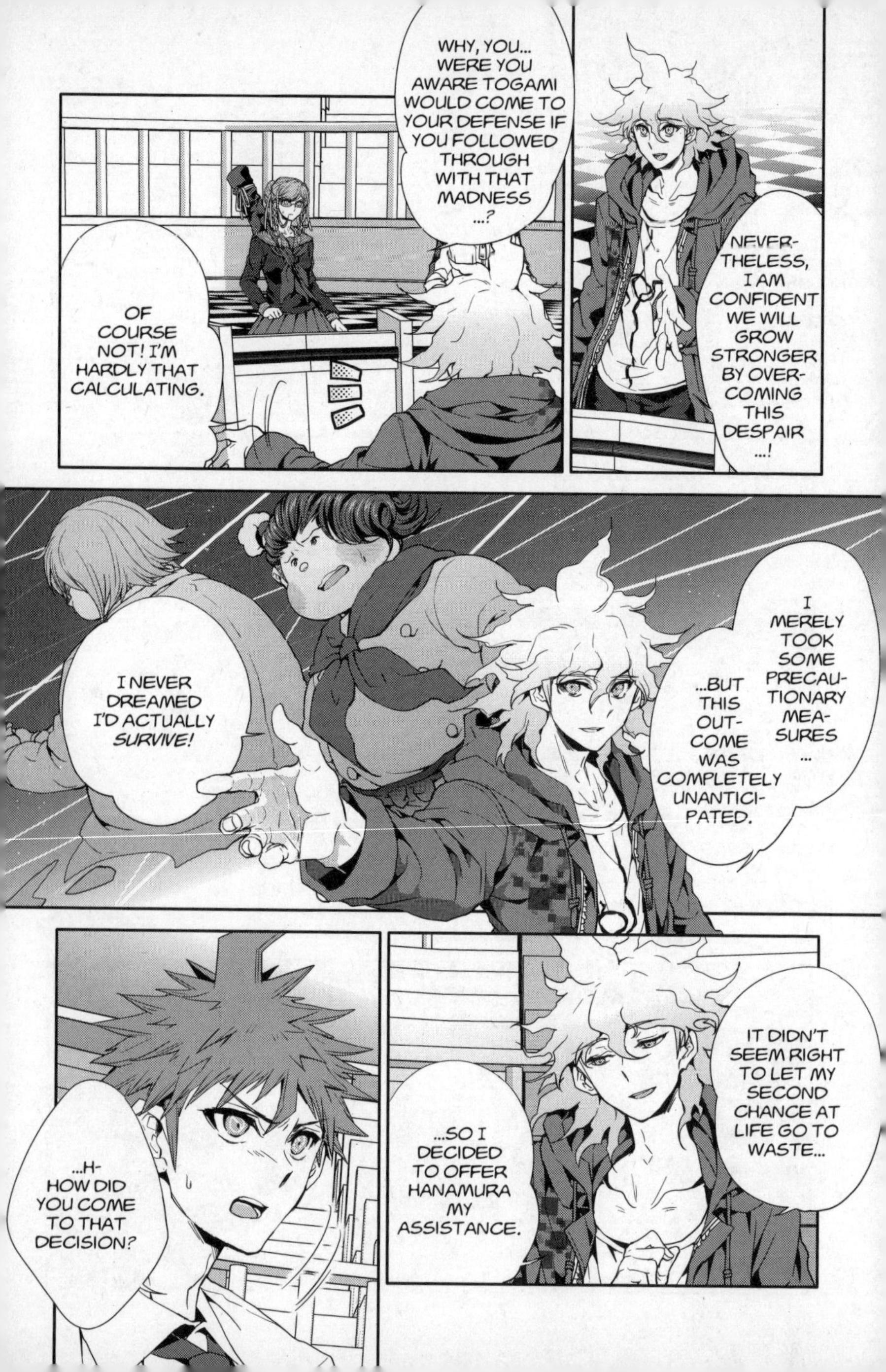
WHY, YOU... WERE YOU AWARE TOGAMI WOULD COME TO YOUR DEFENSE IF YOU FOLLOWED THROUGH WITH THAT MADNESS ...?
OF COURSE NOT! I'M HARDLY THAT CALCULATING.
NEVERTHELESS, I AM CONFIDENT WE WILL GROW STRONGER BY OVERCOMING THIS DESPAIR ...!
I MERELY TOOK SOME PRECAUTIONARY MEASURES ...
...BUT THIS OUTCOME WAS COMPLETELY UNANTICIPATED.
I NEVER DREAMED I'D ACTUALLY SURVIVE!
IT DIDN'T SEEM RIGHT TO LET MY SECOND CHANCE AT LIFE GO TO WASTE...
...SO I DECIDED TO OFFER HANAMURA MY ASSISTANCE.
...H-HOW DID YOU COME TO THAT DECISION?

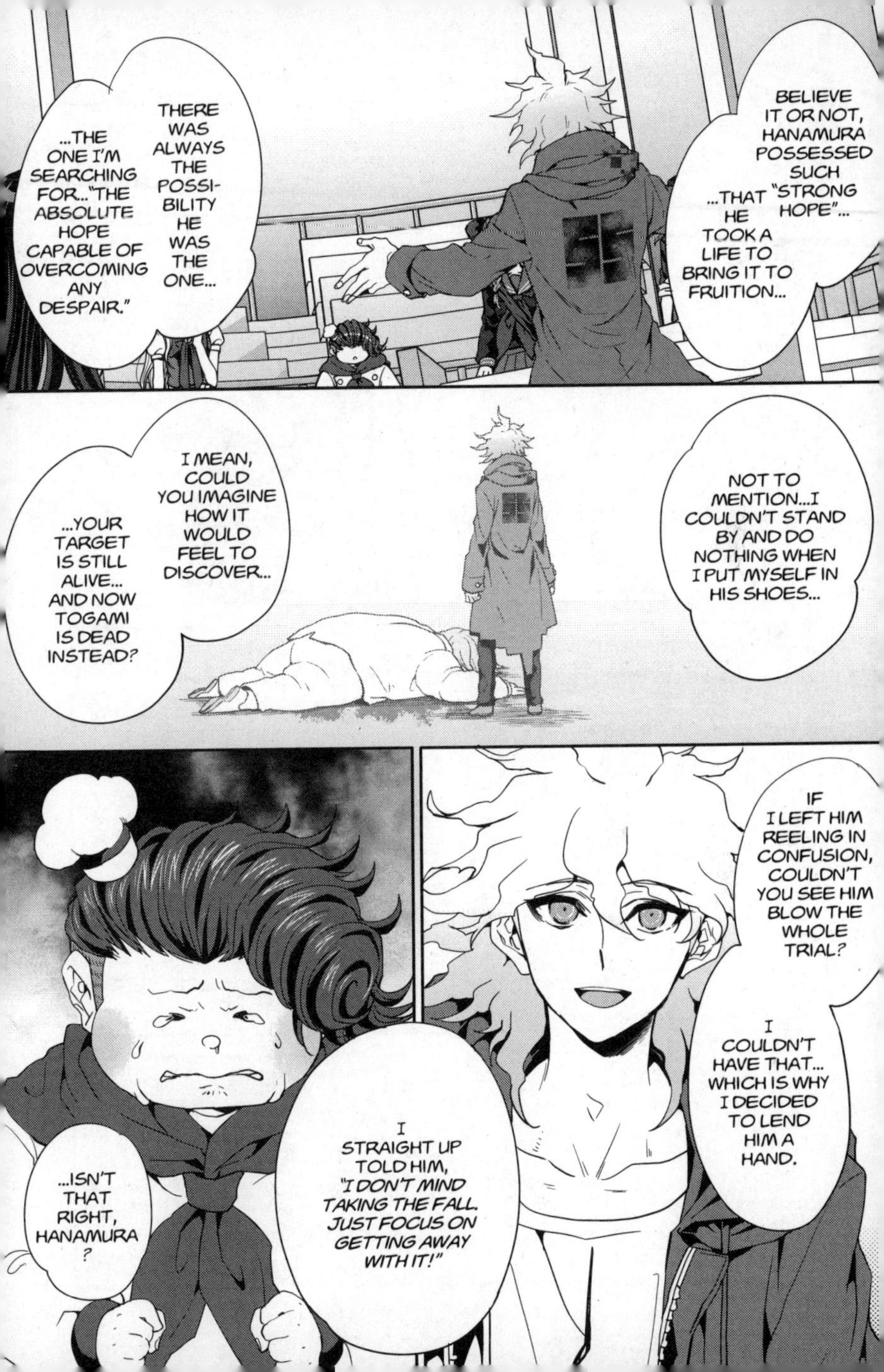
BELIEVE IT OR NOT, HANAMURA POSSESSED SUCH "STRONG HOPE"...
...THAT HE TOOK A LIFE TO BRING IT TO FRUITION...
THERE WAS ALWAYS THE POSSIBILITY HE WAS THE ONE...
...THE ONE I'M SEARCHING FOR..."THE ABSOLUTE HOPE CAPABLE OF OVERCOMING ANY DESPAIR."
NOT TO MENTION...I COULDN'T STAND BY AND DO NOTHING WHEN I PUT MYSELF IN HIS SHOES...
I MEAN, COULD YOU IMAGINE HOW IT WOULD FEEL TO DISCOVER...
...YOUR TARGET IS STILL ALIVE... AND NOW TOGAMI IS DEAD INSTEAD?
IF I LEFT HIM REELING IN CONFUSION, COULDN'T YOU SEE HIM BLOW THE WHOLE TRIAL?
I COULDN'T HAVE THAT... WHICH IS WHY I DECIDED TO LEND HIM A HAND.
I STRAIGHT UP TOLD HIM, "I DON'T MIND TAKING THE FALL. JUST FOCUS ON GETTING AWAY WITH IT!"
...ISN'T THAT RIGHT, HANAMURA?

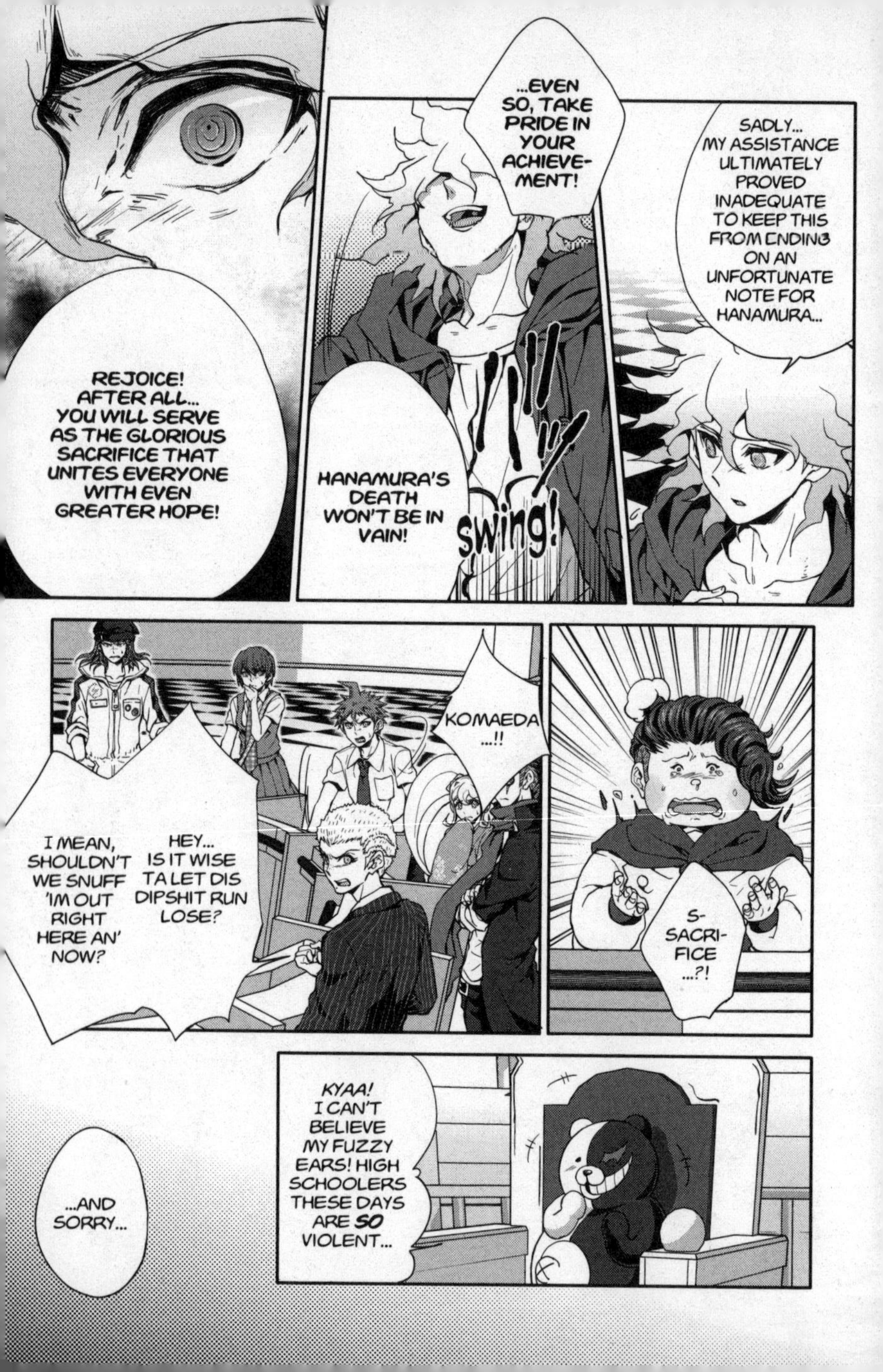
SADLY... MY ASSISTANCE ULTIMATELY PROVED INADEQUATE TO KEEP THIS FROM ENDING ON AN UNFORTUNATE NOTE FOR HANAMURA...
...EVEN SO, TAKE PRIDE IN YOUR ACHIEVEMENT!
HANAMURA'S DEATH WON'T BE IN VAIN!
swing!
REJOICE! AFTER ALL... YOU WILL SERVE AS THE GLORIOUS SACRIFICE THAT UNITES EVERYONE WITH EVEN GREATER HOPE!
S-SACRIFICE ...?!
KOMAEDA ...!!
HEY... IS IT WISE TA LET DIS DIPSHIT RUN LOSE?
I MEAN, SHOULDN'T WE SNUFF 'IM OUT RIGHT HERE AN' NOW?
KYAA! I CAN'T BELIEVE MY FUZZY EARS! HIGH SCHOOLERS THESE DAYS ARE *SO* VIOLENT...
...AND SORRY...

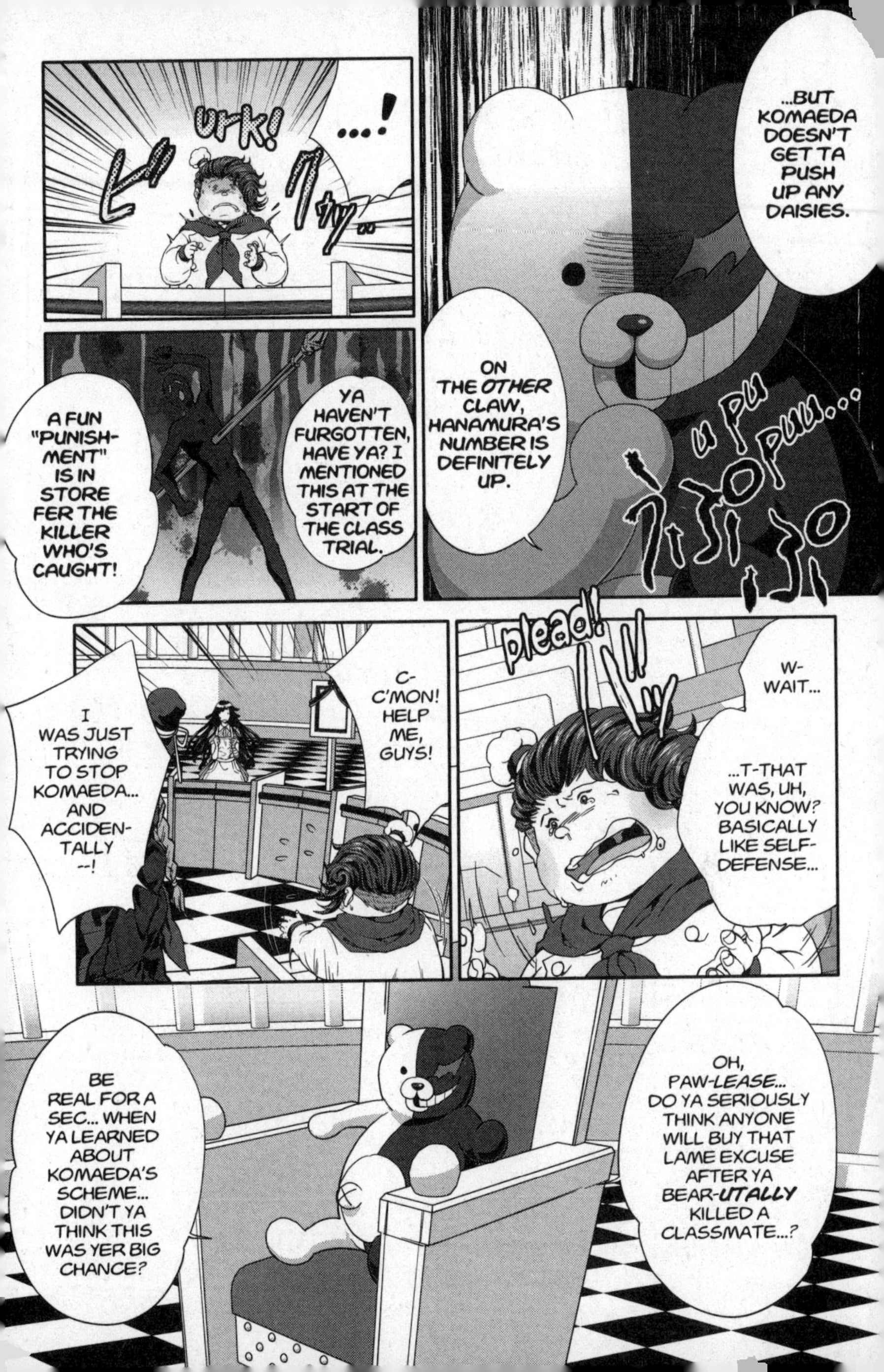
...BUT KOMAEDA DOESN'T GET TA PUSH UP ANY DAISIES.
ON THE *OTHER* CLAW, HANAMURA'S NUMBER IS DEFINITELY UP.
U PU PU PUU...
...!
urk!
YA HAVEN'T FURGOTTEN, HAVE YA? I MENTIONED THIS AT THE START OF THE CLASS TRIAL.
A FUN "PUNISH-MENT" IS IN STORE FER THE KILLER WHO'S CAUGHT!
plead!
W-WAIT...
...T-THAT WAS, UH, YOU KNOW? BASICALLY LIKE SELF-DEFENSE...
C-C'MON! HELP ME, GUYS!
I WAS JUST TRYING TO STOP KOMAEDA... AND ACCIDEN-TALLY --!
OH, PAW-*LEASE*... DO YA SERIOUSLY THINK ANYONE WILL BUY THAT LAME EXCUSE AFTER YA BEAR-***UTALLY*** KILLED A CLASSMATE...?
BE REAL FOR A SEC... WHEN YA LEARNED ABOUT KOMAEDA'S SCHEME... DIDN'T YA THINK THIS WAS YER BIG CHANCE?

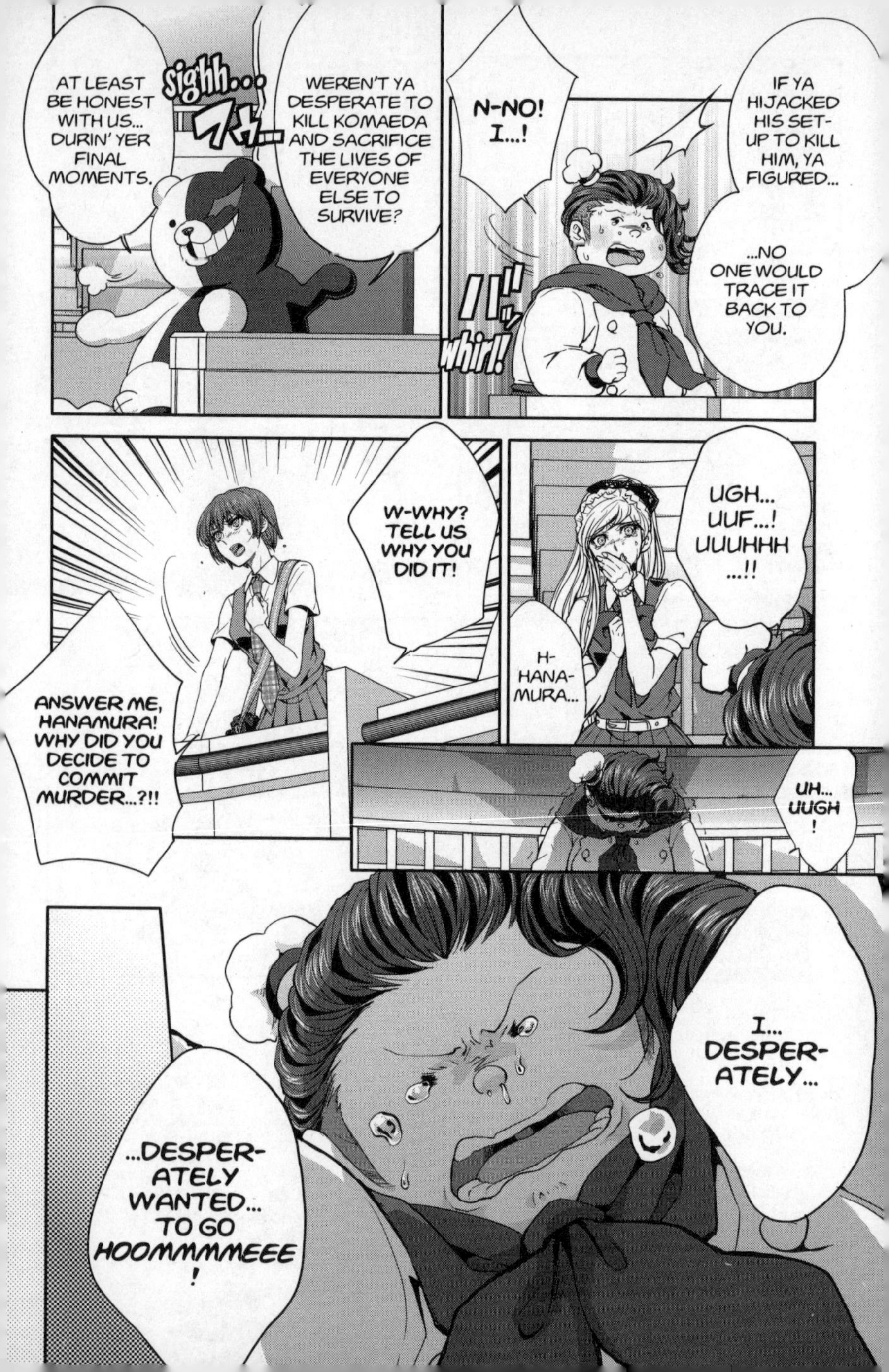

IF YA HIJACKED HIS SET-UP TO KILL HIM, YA FIGURED...
N-NO! I...!
...NO ONE WOULD TRACE IT BACK TO YOU.
whirl!!
WEREN'T YA DESPERATE TO KILL KOMAEDA AND SACRIFICE THE LIVES OF EVERYONE ELSE TO SURVIVE?
sighh...
AT LEAST BE HONEST WITH US... DURIN' YER FINAL MOMENTS.
UGH... UUF...! UUUHHH ...!!
H-HANAMURA...
W-WHY? TELL US WHY YOU DID IT!
ANSWER ME, HANAMURA! WHY DID YOU DECIDE TO COMMIT MURDER...?!!
UH... UUGH!
I... DESPERATELY...
...DESPERATELY WANTED... TO GO HOOMMMMEEE!

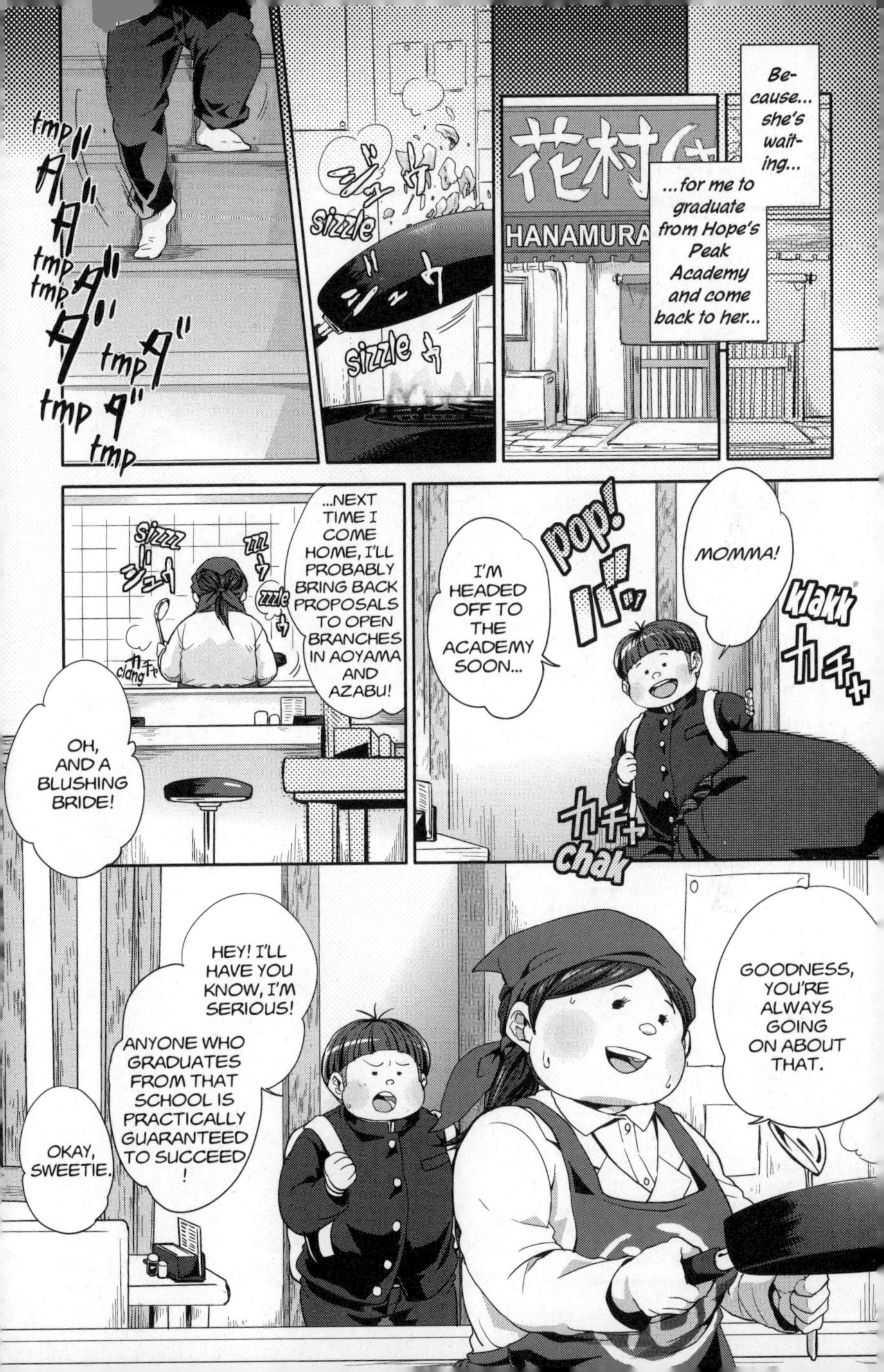

Be-cause... she's wait-ing...
...for me to graduate from Hope's Peak Academy and come back to her...
花村
HANAMURA
sizzle
sizzle
tmp
tmp
tmp
tmp
tmp
tmp
klakk
カチャ
MOMMA!
pop!
I'M HEADED OFF TO THE ACADEMY SOON...
カチャ
Chak
...NEXT TIME I COME HOME, I'LL PROBABLY BRING BACK PROPOSALS TO OPEN BRANCHES IN AOYAMA AND AZABU!
sizzz
zzz
zzzle
clang
OH, AND A BLUSHING BRIDE!
GOODNESS, YOU'RE ALWAYS GOING ON ABOUT THAT.
HEY! I'LL HAVE YOU KNOW, I'M SERIOUS!
ANYONE WHO GRADUATES FROM THAT SCHOOL IS PRACTICALLY GUARANTEED TO SUCCEED!
OKAY, SWEETIE.

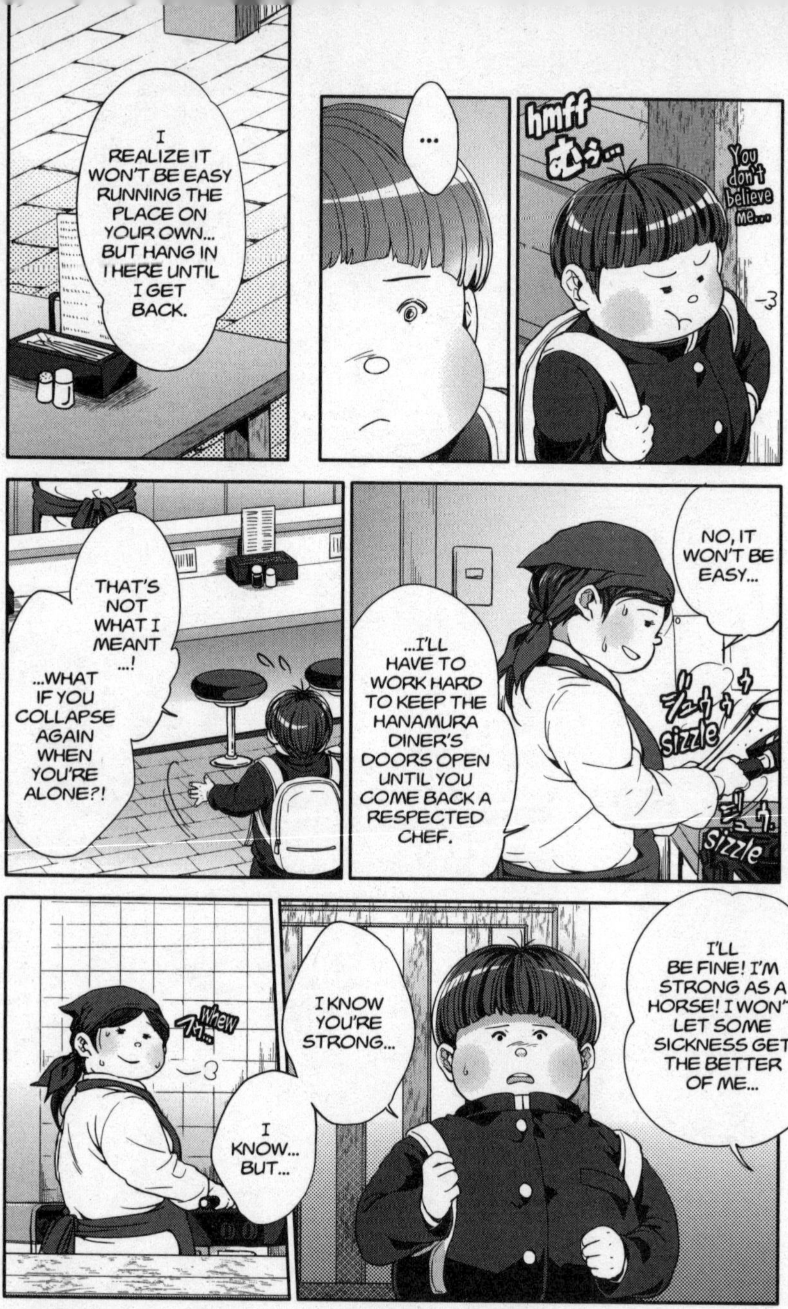
hmff
むぅ...
You don't believe me...
...
I REALIZE IT WON'T BE EASY RUNNING THE PLACE ON YOUR OWN... BUT HANG IN THERE UNTIL I GET BACK.
NO, IT WON'T BE EASY...
...I'LL HAVE TO WORK HARD TO KEEP THE HANAMURA DINER'S DOORS OPEN UNTIL YOU COME BACK A RESPECTED CHEF.
sizzle
sizzle
THAT'S NOT WHAT I MEANT...!
...WHAT IF YOU COLLAPSE AGAIN WHEN YOU'RE ALONE?!
I'LL BE FINE! I'M STRONG AS A HORSE! I WON'T LET SOME SICKNESS GET THE BETTER OF ME...
I KNOW YOU'RE STRONG...
I KNOW... BUT...
whew

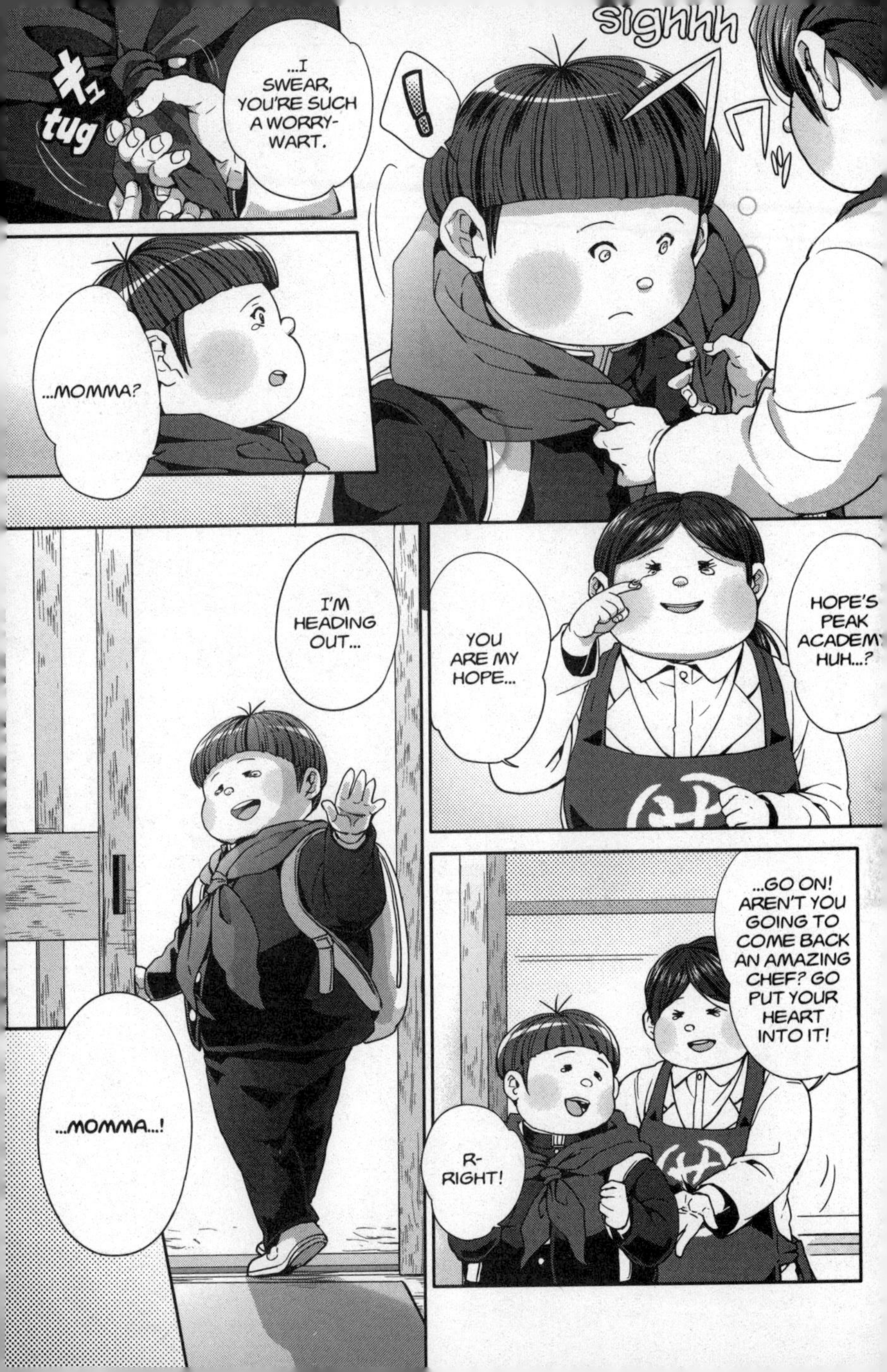
sighhh
!
キュ
tug
...I SWEAR, YOU'RE SUCH A WORRY-WART.
...MOMMA?
HOPE'S PEAK ACADEM HUH...?
YOU ARE MY HOPE...
...GO ON! AREN'T YOU GOING TO COME BACK AN AMAZING CHEF? GO PUT YOUR HEART INTO IT!
R-RIGHT!
I'M HEADING OUT...
...MOMMA...!

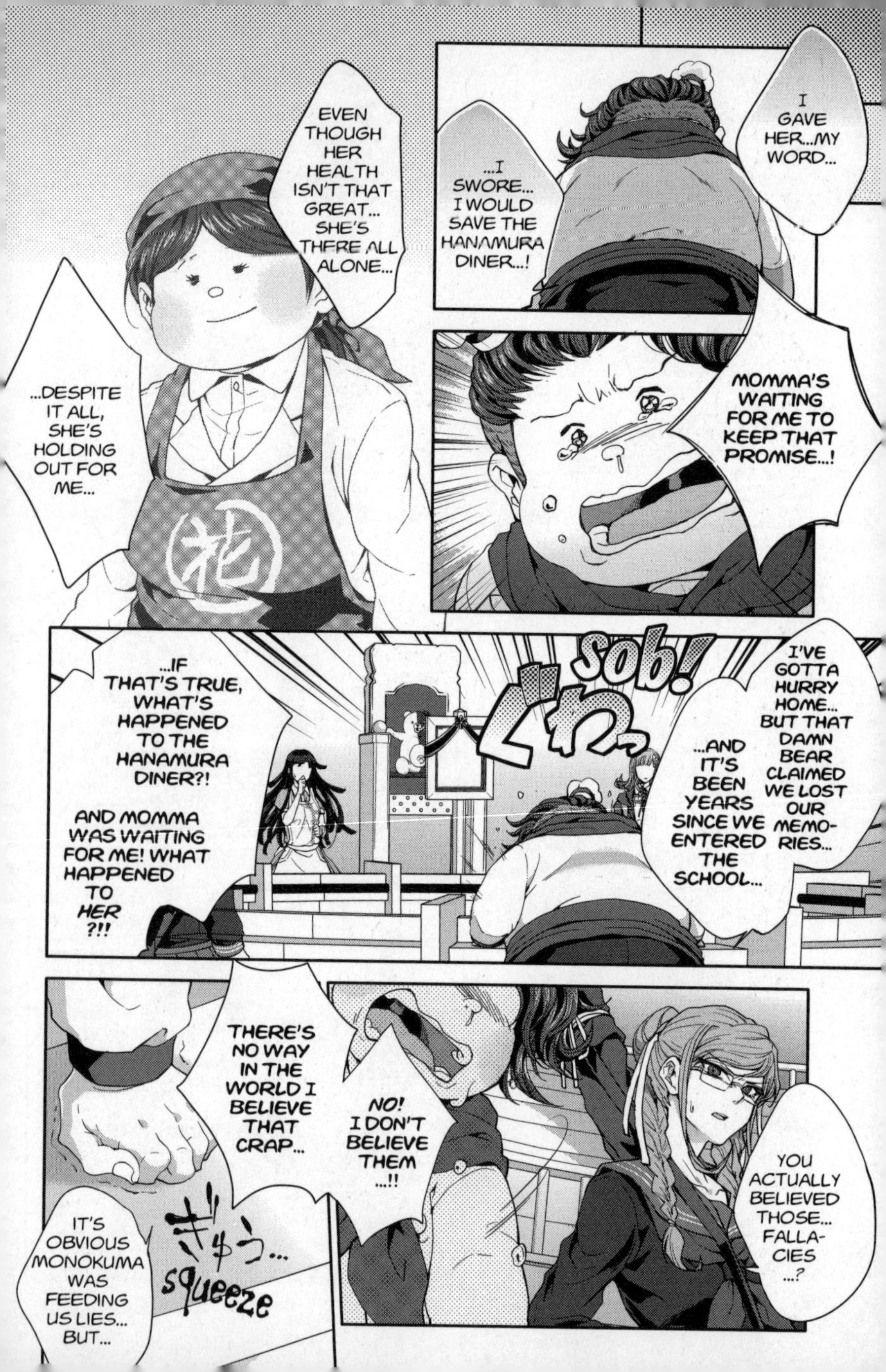
I GAVE HER...MY WORD...
...I SWORE... I WOULD SAVE THE HANAMURA DINER...!
MOMMA'S WAITING FOR ME TO KEEP THAT PROMISE...!
EVEN THOUGH HER HEALTH ISN'T THAT GREAT... SHE'S THERE ALL ALONE...
...DESPITE IT ALL, SHE'S HOLDING OUT FOR ME...
I'VE GOTTA HURRY HOME... BUT THAT DAMN BEAR CLAIMED WE LOST OUR MEMORIES...
...AND IT'S BEEN YEARS SINCE WE ENTERED THE SCHOOL...
sob!
...IF THAT'S TRUE, WHAT'S HAPPENED TO THE HANAMURA DINER?!
AND MOMMA WAS WAITING FOR ME! WHAT HAPPENED TO HER?!!
YOU ACTUALLY BELIEVED THOSE... FALLACIES...?
NO! I DON'T BELIEVE THEM...!!
THERE'S NO WAY IN THE WORLD I BELIEVE THAT CRAP...
squeeze
IT'S OBVIOUS MONOKUMA WAS FEEDING US LIES... BUT...

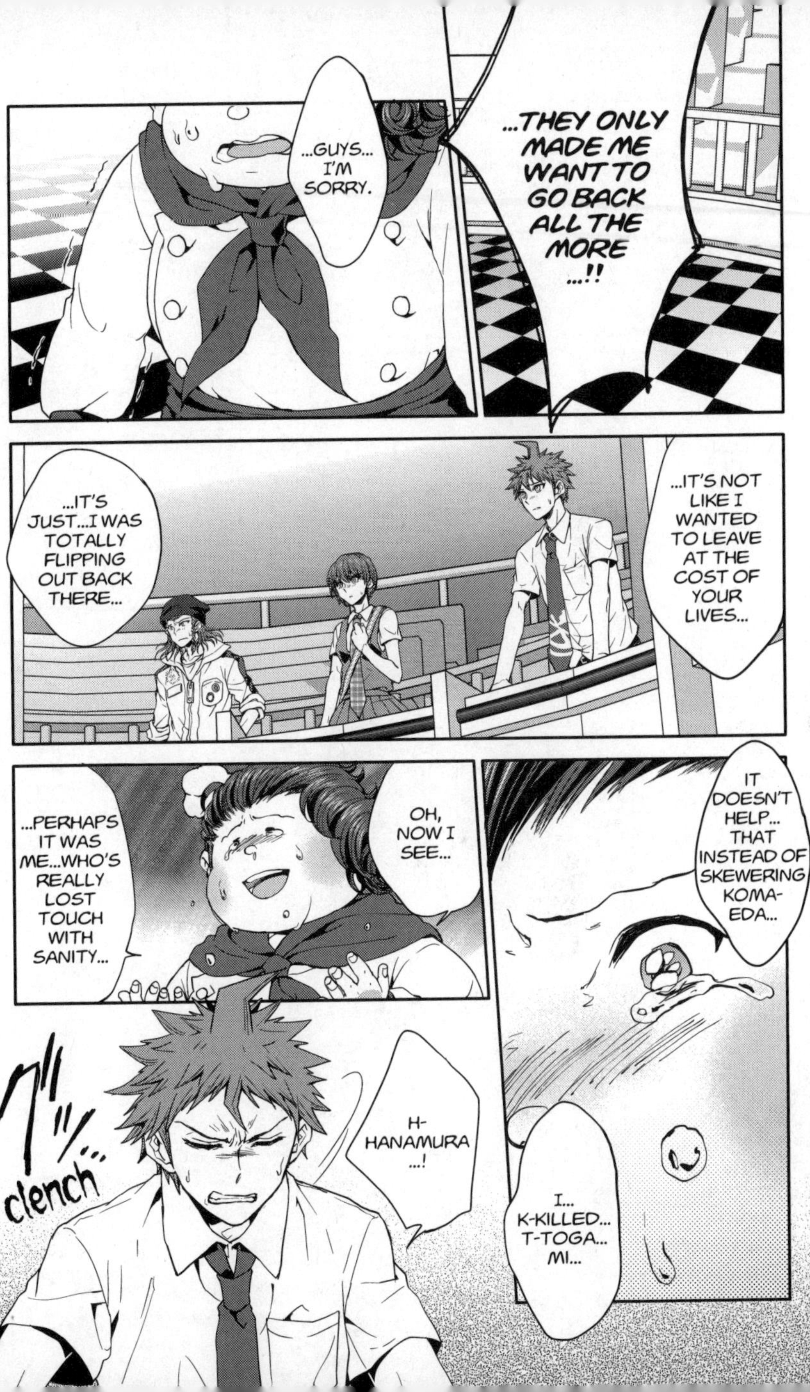
...THEY ONLY MADE ME WANT TO GO BACK ALL THE MORE ...!!
...GUYS... I'M SORRY.
...IT'S NOT LIKE I WANTED TO LEAVE AT THE COST OF YOUR LIVES...
...IT'S JUST...I WAS TOTALLY FLIPPING OUT BACK THERE...
IT DOESN'T HELP... THAT INSTEAD OF SKEWERING KOMA-EDA...
I... K-KILLED... T-TOGA... MI...
OH, NOW I SEE...
...PERHAPS IT WAS ME...WHO'S REALLY LOST TOUCH WITH SANITY...
H-HANAMURA ...!
clench

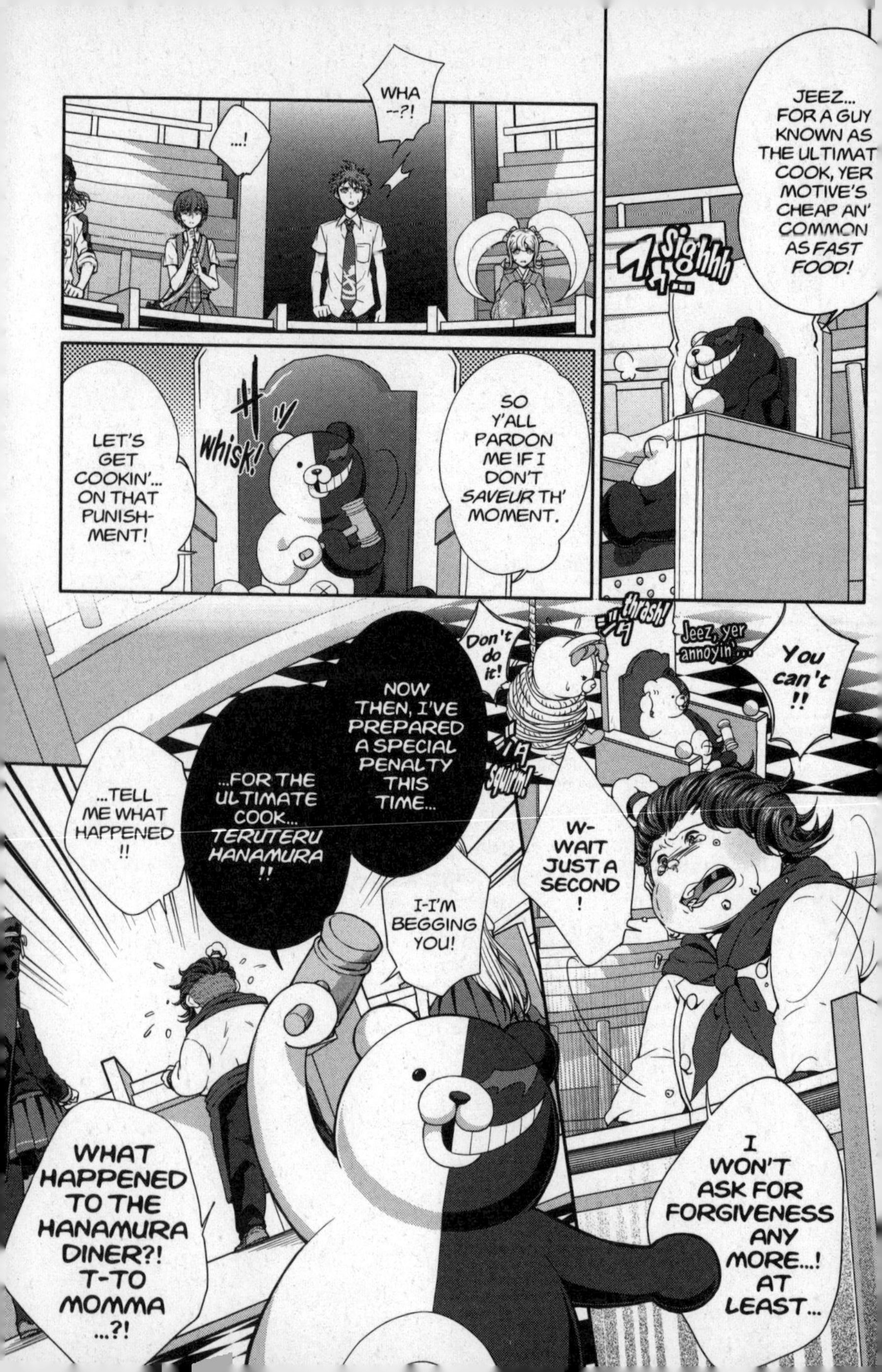
JEEZ... FOR A GUY KNOWN AS THE ULTIMAT COOK, YER MOTIVE'S CHEAP AN' COMMON AS FAST FOOD!
Sighhh
WHA --?!
...!
SO Y'ALL PARDON ME IF I DON'T SAVEUR TH' MOMENT.
whisk!
LET'S GET COOKIN'... ON THAT PUNISHMENT!
You can't!!
Jeez, yer annoyin'...
thrash!
Don't do it!
squirm!
NOW THEN, I'VE PREPARED A SPECIAL PENALTY THIS TIME...
...FOR THE ULTIMATE COOK... TERUTERU HANAMURA!!
W-WAIT JUST A SECOND!
I-I'M BEGGING YOU!
...TELL ME WHAT HAPPENED!!
I WON'T ASK FOR FORGIVENESS ANY MORE...! AT LEAST...
WHAT HAPPENED TO THE HANAMURA DINER?! T-TO MOMMA...?!

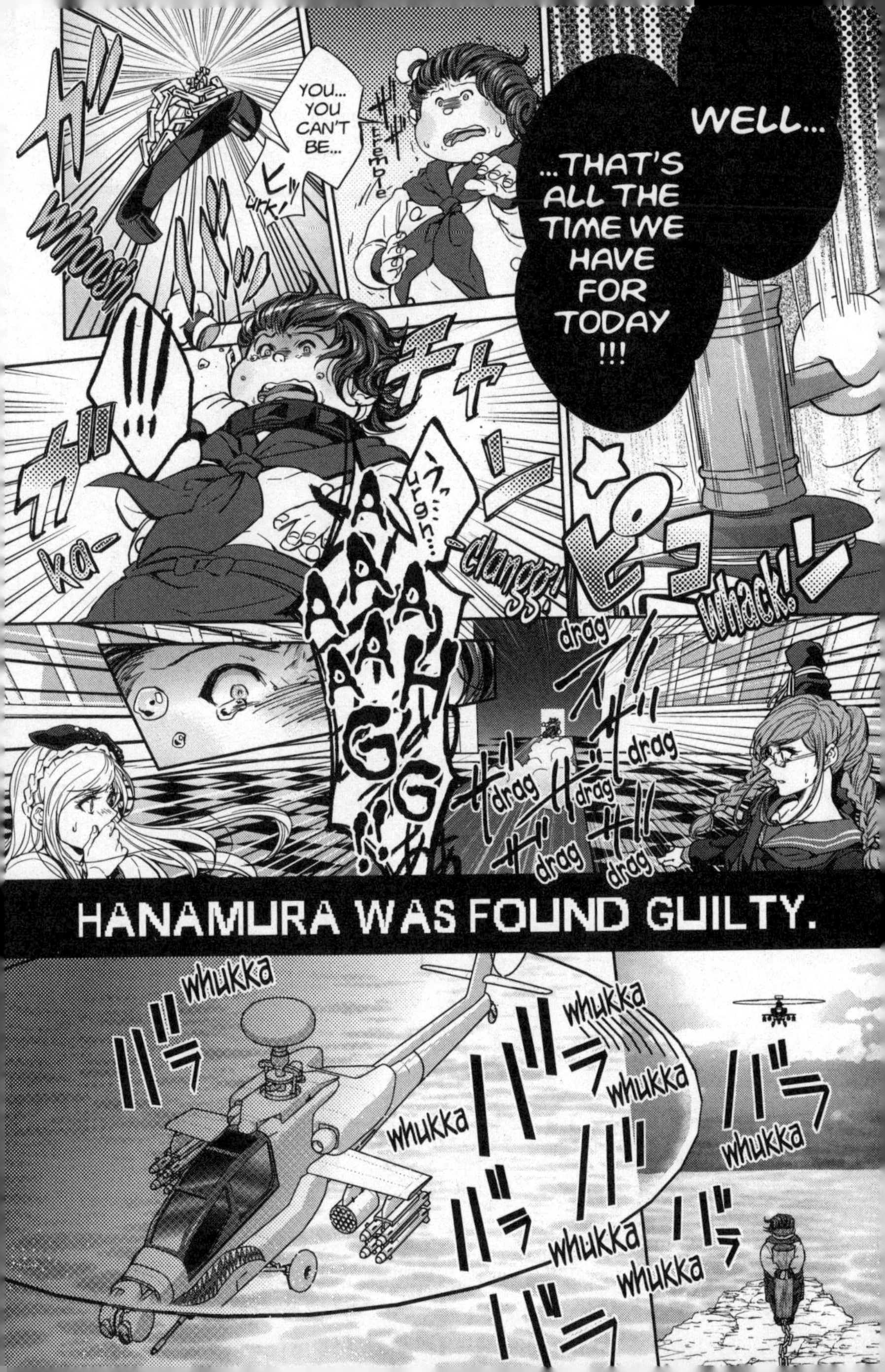
WELL...
...THAT'S ALL THE TIME WE HAVE FOR TODAY !!!
whack!
YOU... YOU CAN'T BE...
tremble
urk!
whoosh
!!!
urgh...
clangg!
ka-
AAAAAAHGGG!!
drag
drag
drag
drag
drag
drag
HANAMURA WAS FOUND GUILTY.
whukka
whukka
whukka
whukka
whukka
whukka
whukka

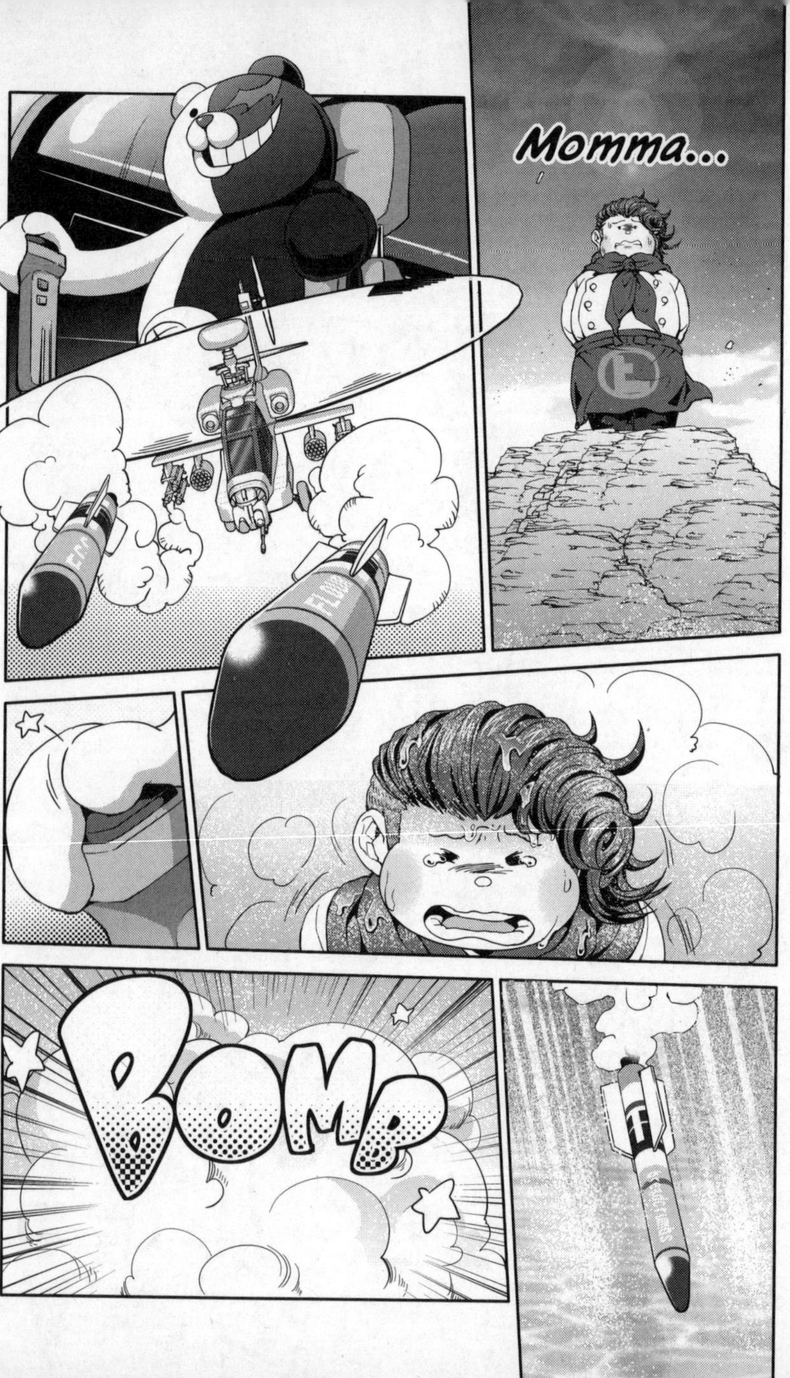
Momma...
BOMB

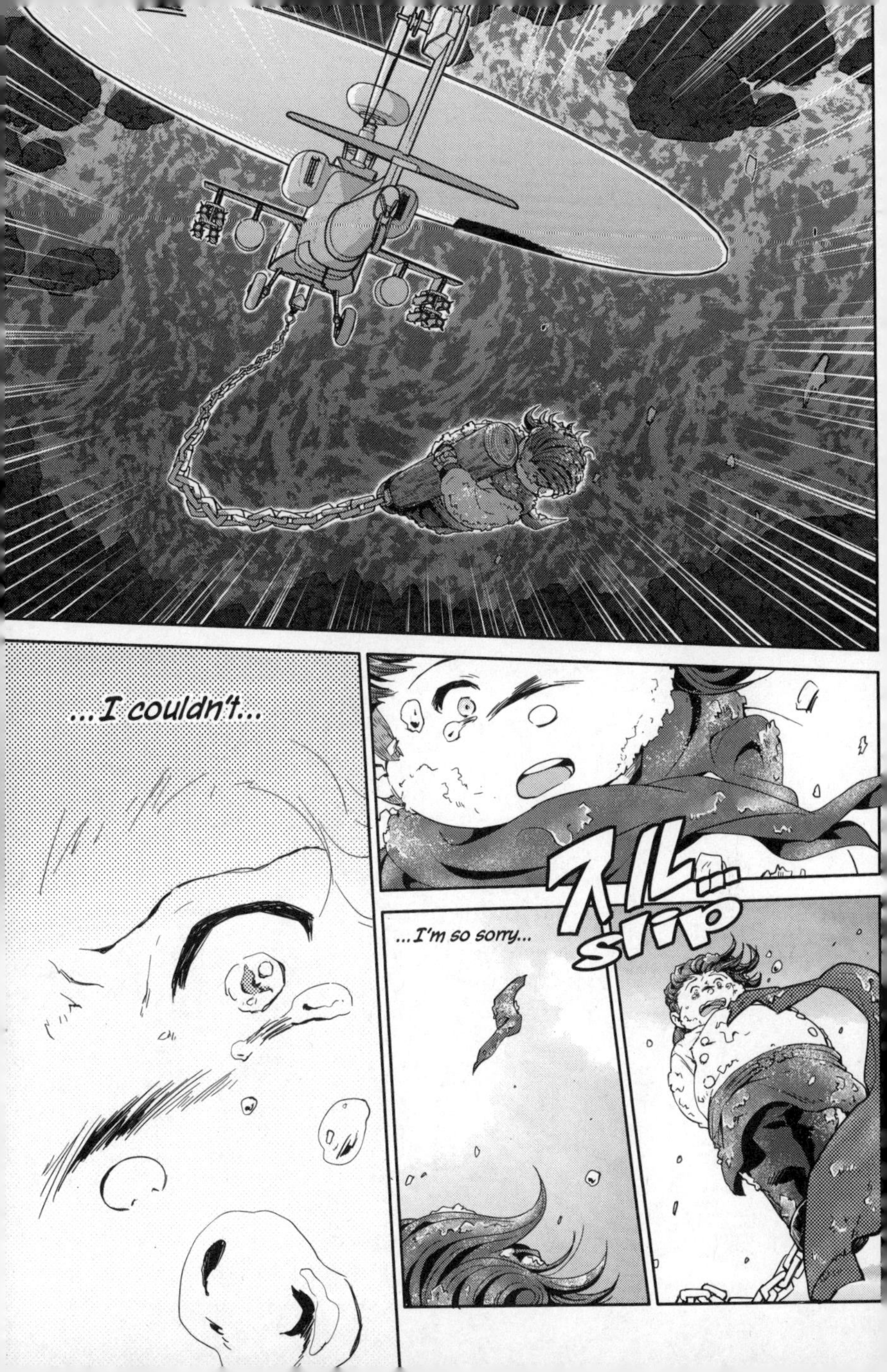
スル...
SLIP
...I'm so sorry...
...I couldn't...

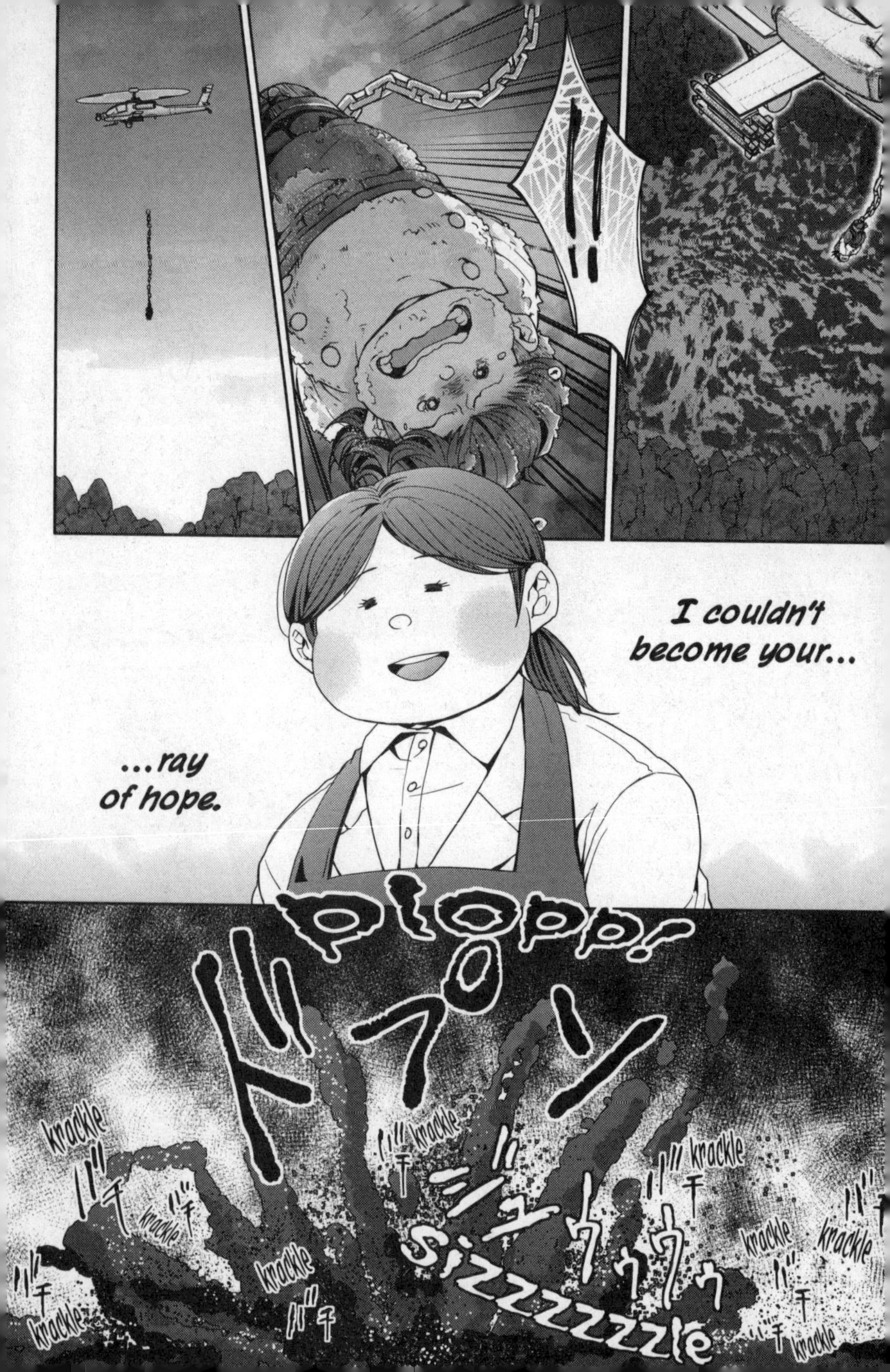

!!
I couldn't become your...
...ray of hope.
ドプン
plopp!
ジュウウウウ
sizzzzzzzle
バチ krackle
バチ krackle
バチ krackle
バチ krackle
バチ krackle
バチ krackle
バチ krackle
バチ krackle

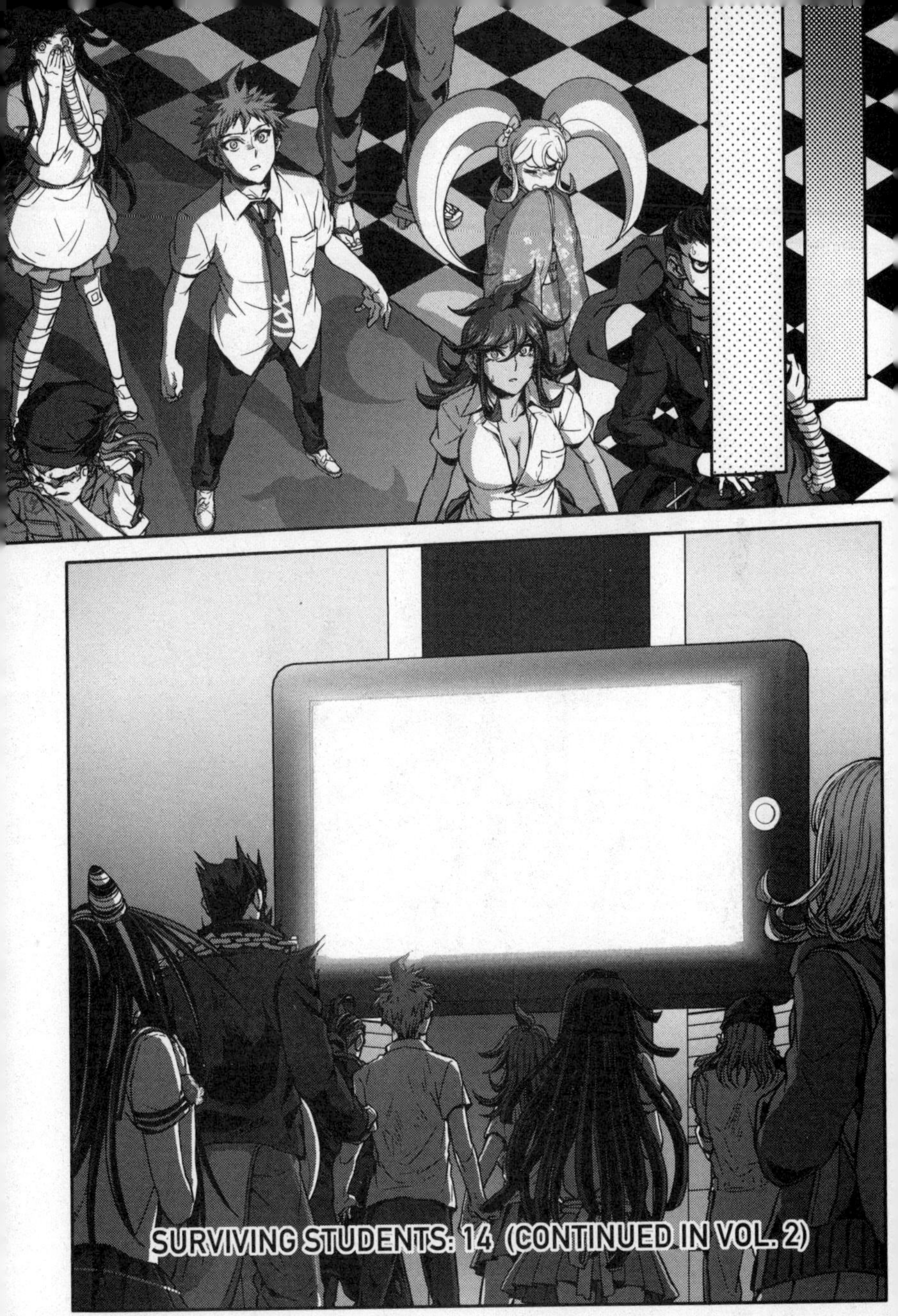
SURVIVING STUDENTS: 14 (CONTINUED IN VOL. 2)

DR2: SPECIAL ILLUSTRATIONS

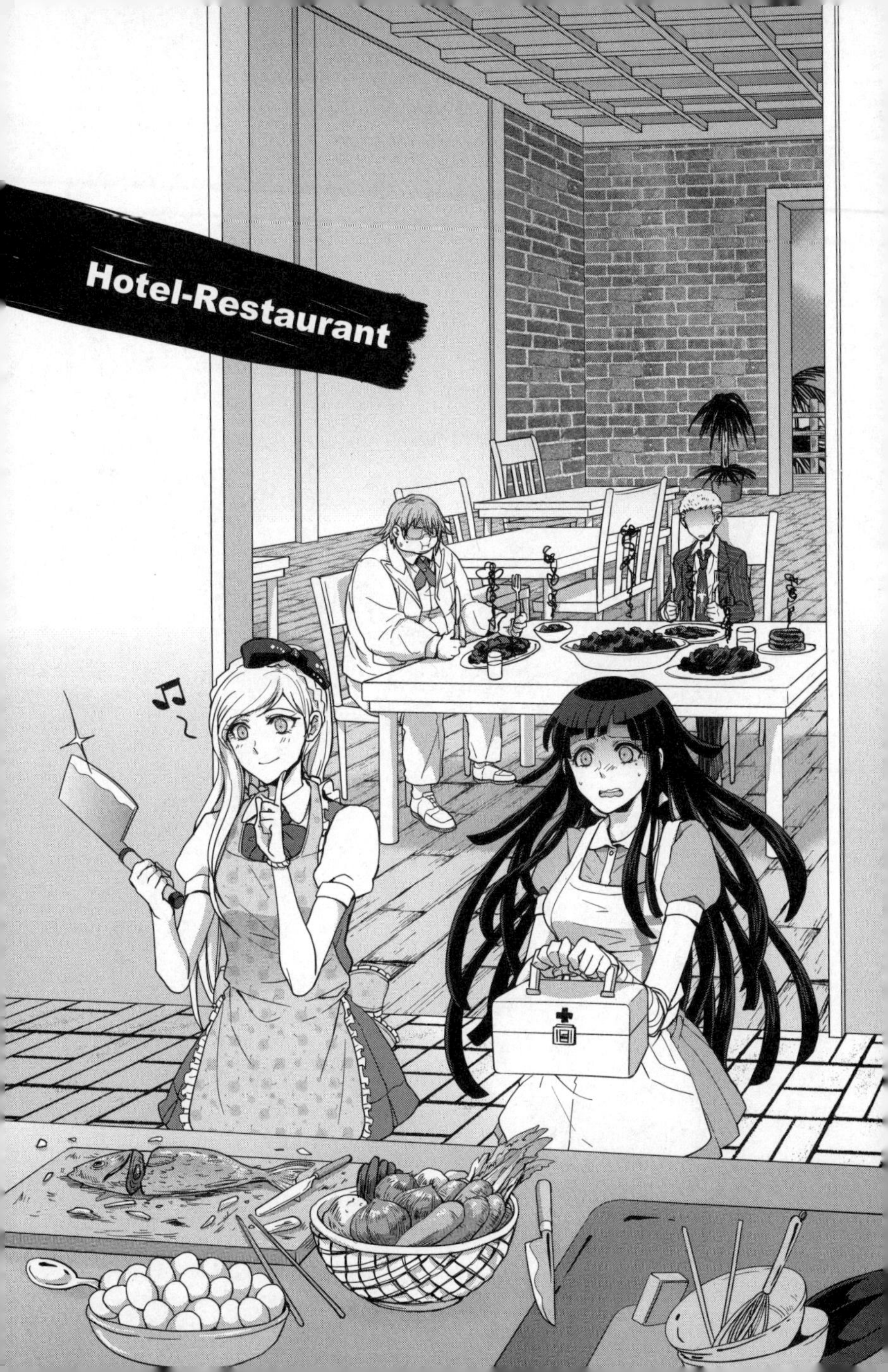
Hotel-Restaurant

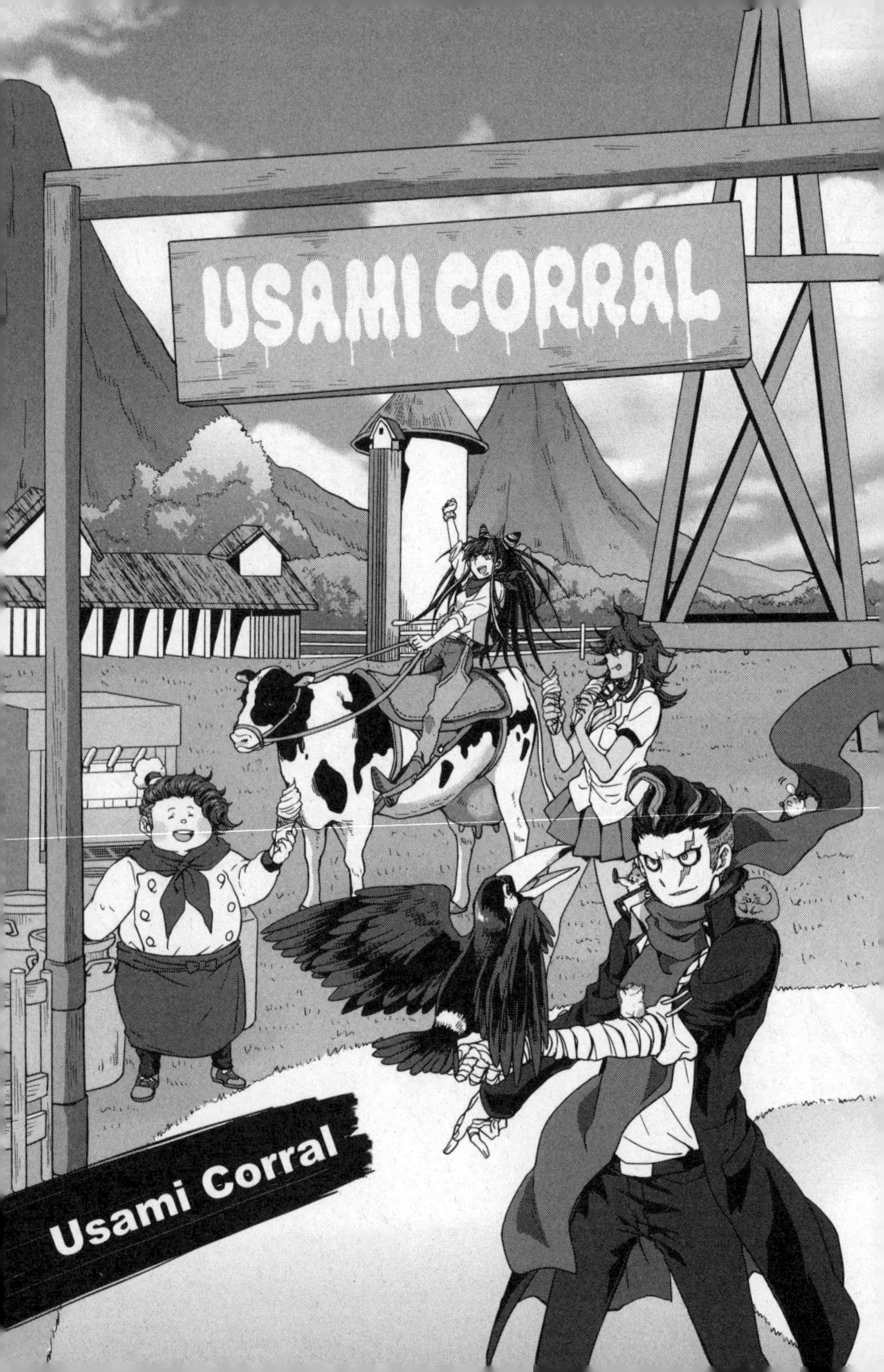
USAMI CORRAL
Usami Corral

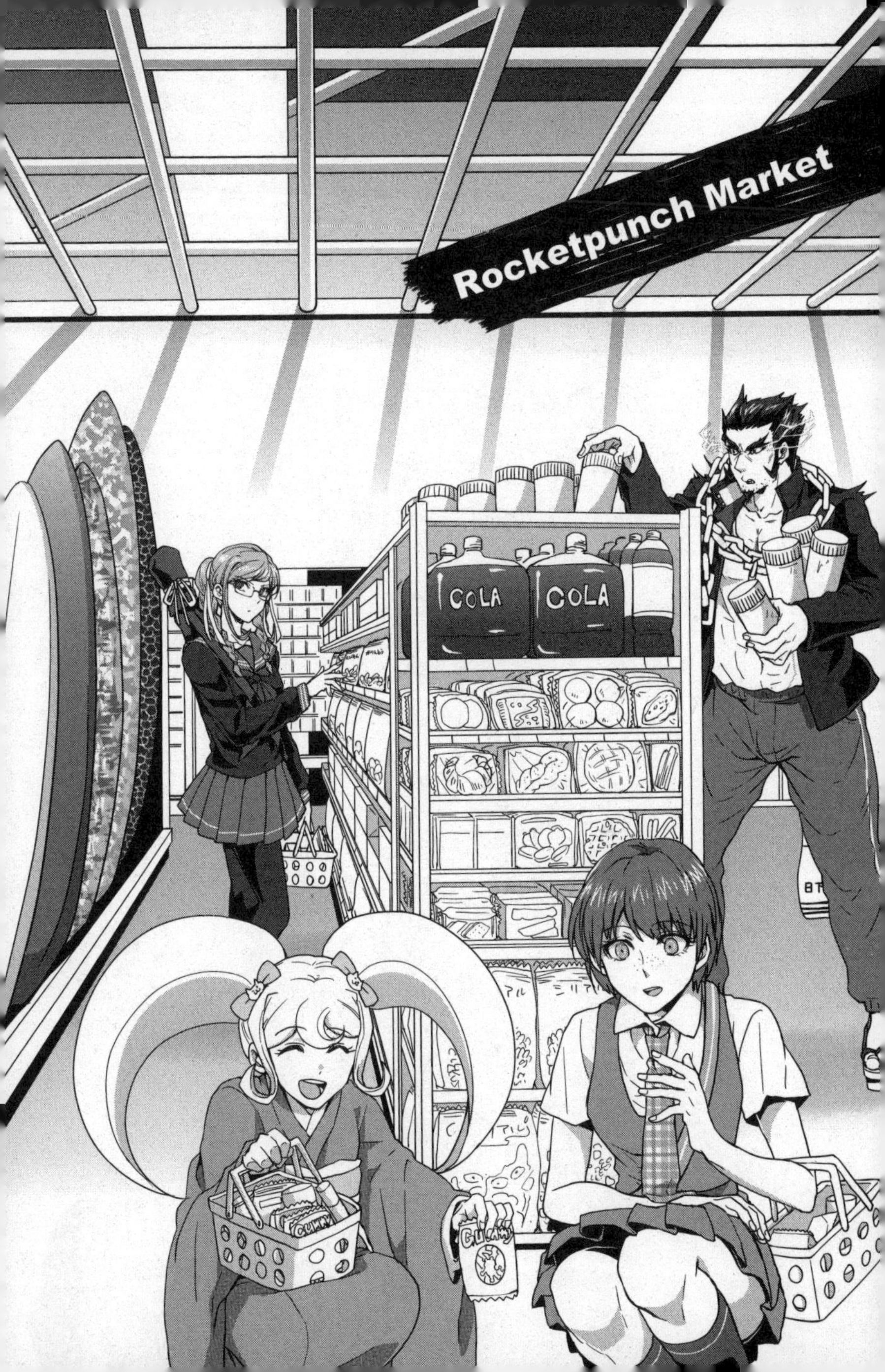
Rocketpunch Market
COLA
COLA

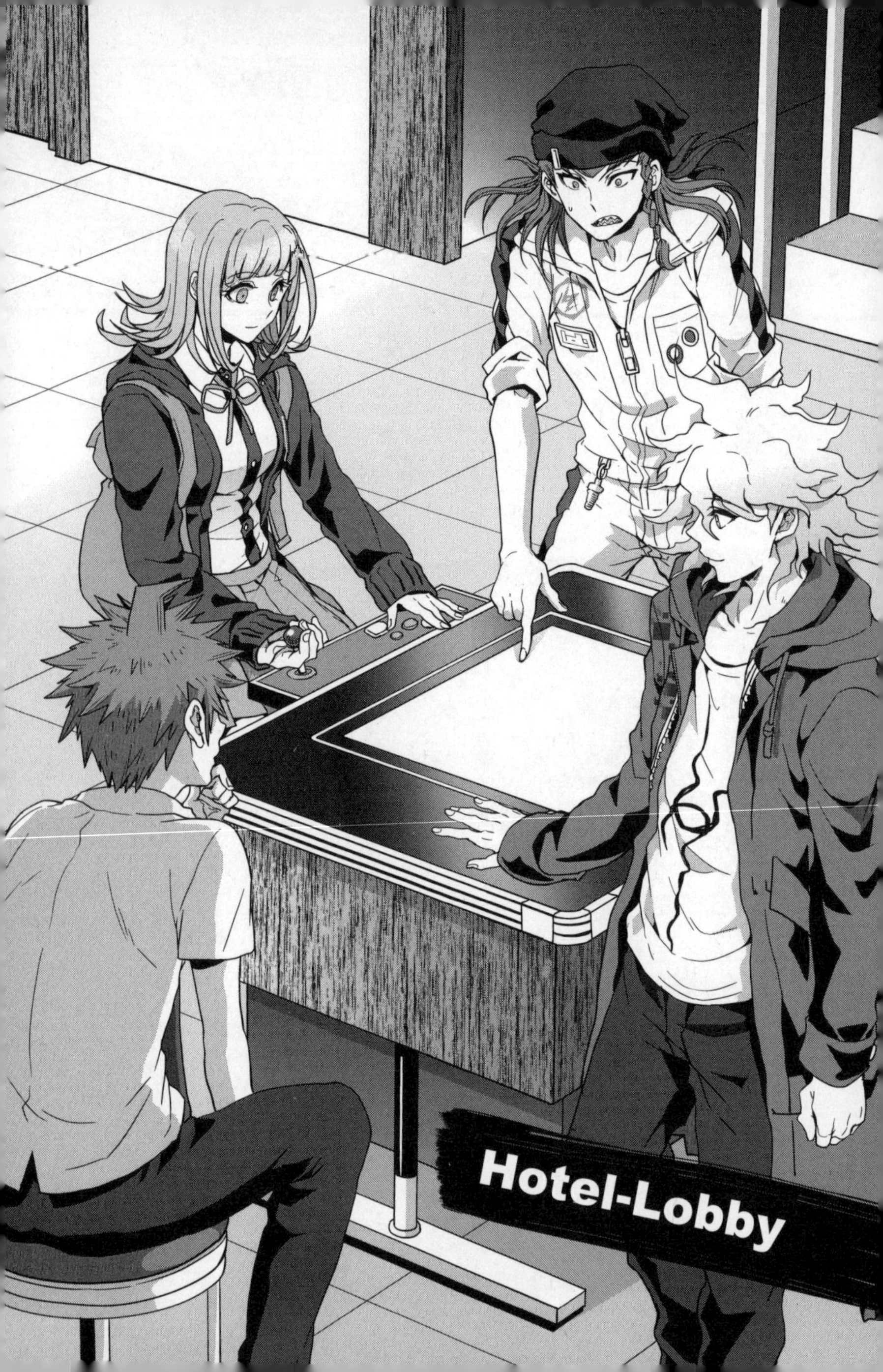
Hotel-Lobby

Hello, everyone. I'm Kuroki Q. I'm truly excited to be part of this manga publication! I first started playing **Danganronpa** about this time last year. A friend introduced me to the game when I had some down time. Something of a gamer to begin with, I quickly got immersed in the unique story and gameplay and played it the whole way through. Now jump forward to the release of **Danganronpa 2: Goodbye Despair.** Right when I was thinking about buying a copy, I just so happened to receive the offer to work on this manga series. I'll never forget how shocked I was. As a personal **Danganronpa** fan, I never dreamed I'd get to work on it like this... It's the Ultimate Twist of Fate! ^_^

Both **Danganronpa: Trigger Happy Havoc** and **Danganronpa 2: Goodbye Despair** are extremely captivating, so I've taken great pains to capture the overall flow of the game with this manga adaption. Nevertheless, I believe the manga and video game are each fun and unique in their own right. I'm sure you'll be able to enjoy this adaption whether you're familiar with the game or new to the series. That having been said, I hope you continue to support the manga!

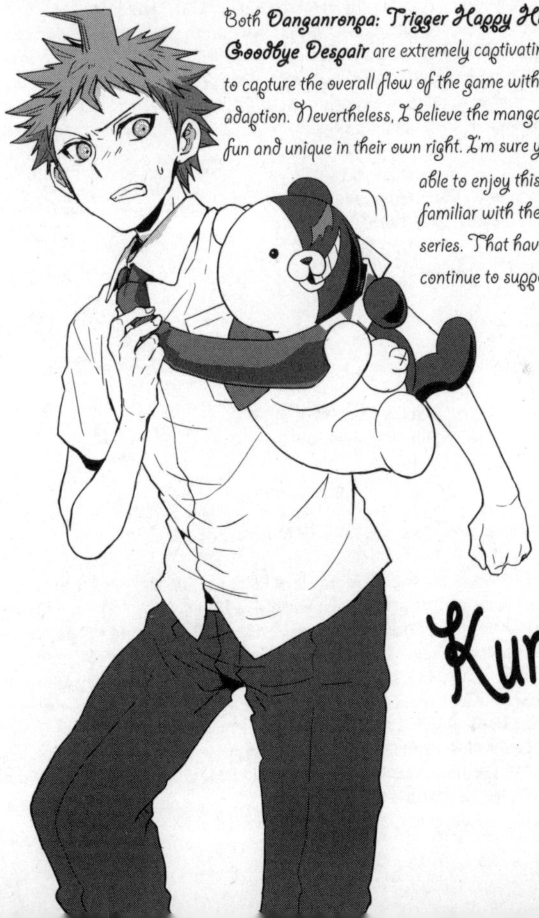

Kuroki Q

President and Publisher // **Mike Richardson**

Designer // **Skyler Weissenfluh**

Ultimate Digital Art Technician // **Samantha Hummer**

English-language version produced by Dark Horse Comics

DANGANRONPA 2: GOODBYE DESPAIR VOLUME 1

Published by
Dark Horse Manga
A division of Dark Horse Comics LLC.
10956 SE Main Street
Milwaukie, OR 97222

DarkHorse.com

To find a comics shop in your area, visit comicshoplocator.com

First edition: March 2020
ISBN 978-1-50671-359-5

1 3 5 7 9 10 8 6 4 2

Printed in the United States of America.

DESPAIR MAIL

c/o Dark Horse Comics | 10956 SE Main St. | Milwaukie, OR 97222 | danganronpa@darkhorse.com

Welcome to Dark Horse's next Danganronpa series, Danganronpa 2: Goodbye Despair! Well…we say "next," but events may seem eerily reminiscent of, well, Danganronpa 2: Ultimate Luck and Hope and Despair ^_^ It might seem a little strange at first two publish two different manga series based on the same game in the series, but apparently they didn't think it was that strange in Japan :) so a weeb like myself must follow their lead.

Of course, Danganronpa 2 is many people's favorite game in the series, so it's not entirely surprising that there's more than one manga based on it. And not only is Danganronpa 2: Goodbye Despair framed quite differently from Ultimate Luck and Hope and Despair (which is really Nagito's point of view), but the art style is quite different, as is the staging of the scenes. The large cast and the varying decision paths of the Danganronpa games gives many different possibilities for how to tell the story, so we hope you will like this one. By the way, we are looking into doing manga from the other Danganronpa games/stories as well!

By the way, thanks to all the Danganronpa cosplayers I ran into at MomoCon in Atlanta last May. I was doing a Dark Horse manga panel and was asked to take some cosplay pictures for our Instagram, but I feel I was being kind of lazy about it, because while I did take half a dozen pics, there were easily three times as many people there cosplaying Danganronpa (and maybe I'm still underestimating—I didn't even think to see if there was a photo meet-up during the con, and there probably was ^_^)

Anyway! Fortunately, YOU send in your photos and drawings, and we'd always like to see more! Remember to use high resolution if possible (300 dpi or better) for your photos or images, so it'll look its best in print. Also remember that even if you don't draw or cosplay, and just want to express your thoughts as a Danganronpa fan, it's OK to send those in too—you don't need a visual :-) As Remy Shimada once said in an entirely different series, see you again!

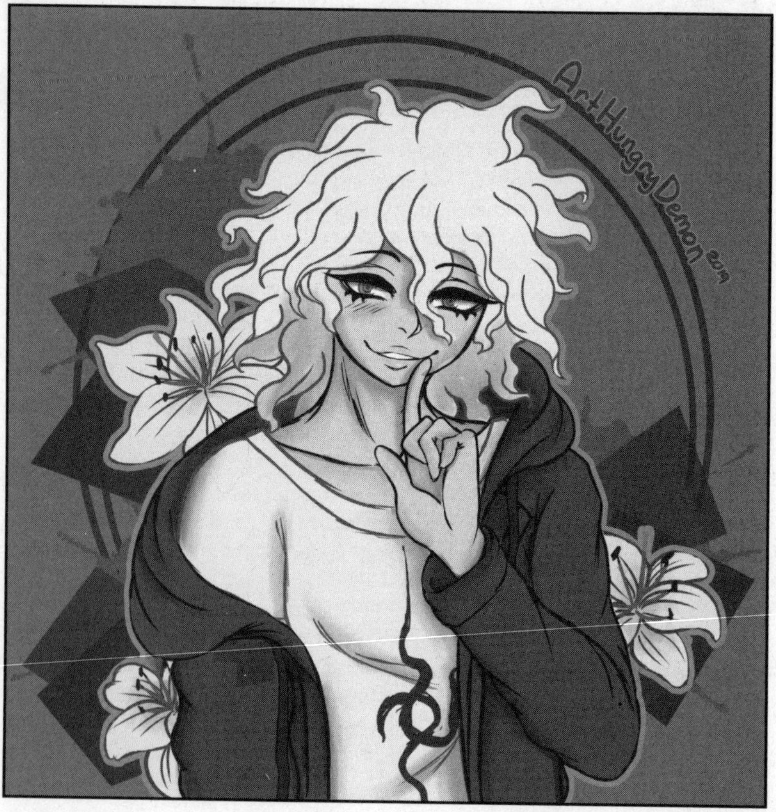
ArtHungryDemon 2019

Kiga, a.k.a. ArtHungryDemon, writes in to say "Hiya! I was really happy when I read volumes 1 & 2 of the Danganronpa 2: Ultimate Luck and Hope and Despair *manga, as I've been wishing to have it in my hands ever since I knew about it! Thank you so much for taking the time to translate and publish this manga and hopefully this fanart evokes both despair and happiness :>"*

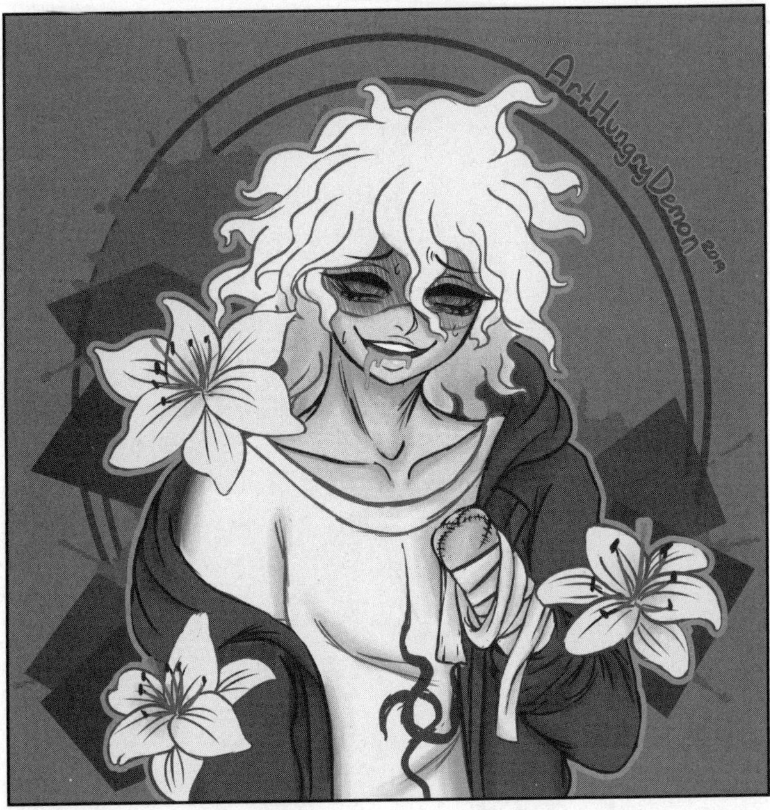
ArtHungryDemon
2019

Nagito is always willing to lend a hand to support the cause of hope for his fellow students. Are those lilies? As Steven Rainey reported for TheThinAir.net, when Kurt Cobain gave instructions on how to decorate the stage for Nirvana's MTV Unplugged *performance, he specified stargazer lilies: "'You mean like a funeral?' asked the producer. To which Cobain replied, 'Exactly. Like a funeral.'" Serve the servant(s).*

And he continues to spread joy, mirth, and of course, insane laughter (is that a straitjacket?) for us through this illustration by Corinth from Texas, who says, "I'm absolutely in love with the Ultimate Luck and Hope and Despair manga! After finishing Vol. 2, I decided it was only right that I draw our boy Nagito!"

*Dankcidueye returns with a cosplay, saying, "I offer you a dabbing Monokuma."
Uh-huh, yeah, I can see that, but what I want to know is...are his eyebrows
on fleek? The answer is probably no, as Monokuma doesn't have any.*

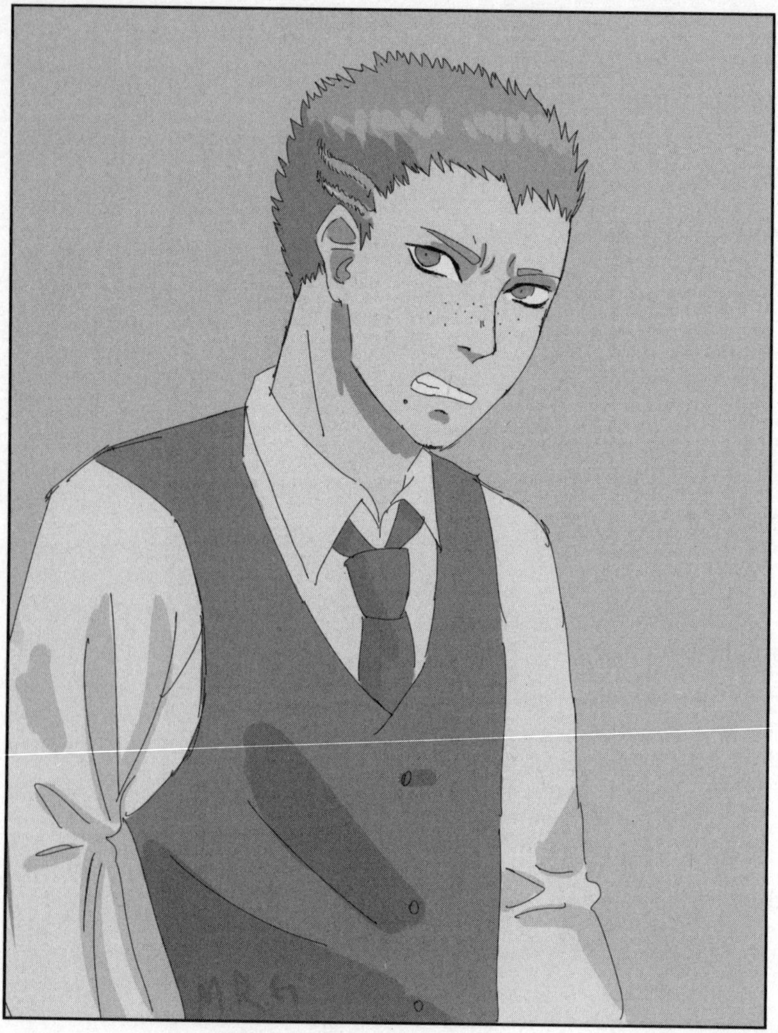

Matthew, a.k.a. sslugmoth, writes: "I love Danganronpa 2, *it's my favorite game in the series. It was hard to choose who to draw, but I had to go with Fuyuhiko." For some reason his style here reminds me a little of the gangsters in* Boardwalk Empire. *Hmm, imagine a version of* Danganronpa *set in the 1920s, with an Ultimate Flapper and Ultimate Bootlegger . . . ^_^*

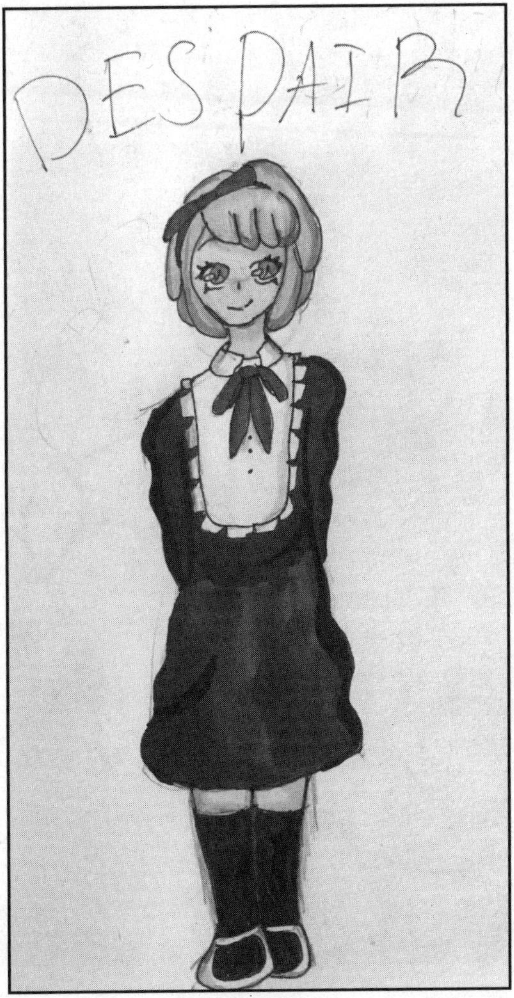
DESPAIR

Hailey writes in to say, "Here is a drawing of Monaca Towa! She is my favorite character in the Warriors of Hope. I just wanted to say thank you for making the manga for Danganronpa V2!*" Monaca, naturally (we already said her last name was Towa in a previous volume, which someone pointed out is a spoiler, but what the heck) is in the other* Danganronpa *series Dark Horse is currently running,* Danganronpa Another Episode: Ultra Despair Girls.

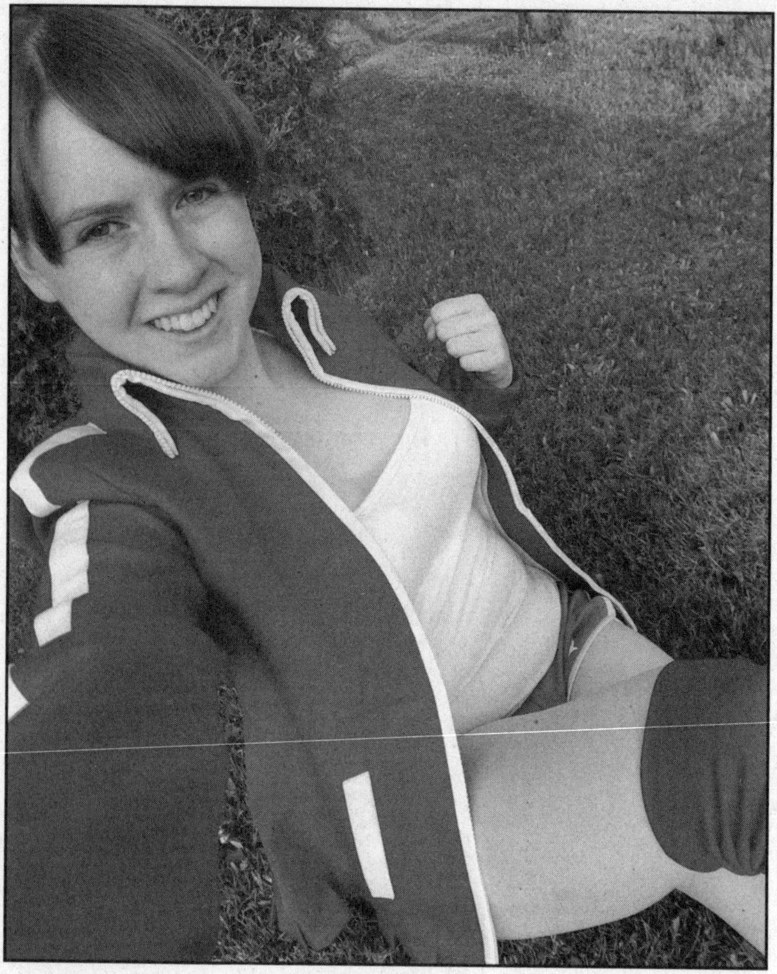

Gillian (@gillybellycosplays on Instagram) sends in this and the next three images, taken at Animaritime in Fredericton, New Brunswick. Canada has a strong tradition when it comes to anime and manga fans, but Animaritime, as its name might suggest, is said to be the first Japanese fan con to be established in the Canadian Maritime provinces. Gillian says, "Hello! Danganronpa is the first series to bring me together with a whole ton of other amazing cosplayers who love the games and anime just as much as I do!"

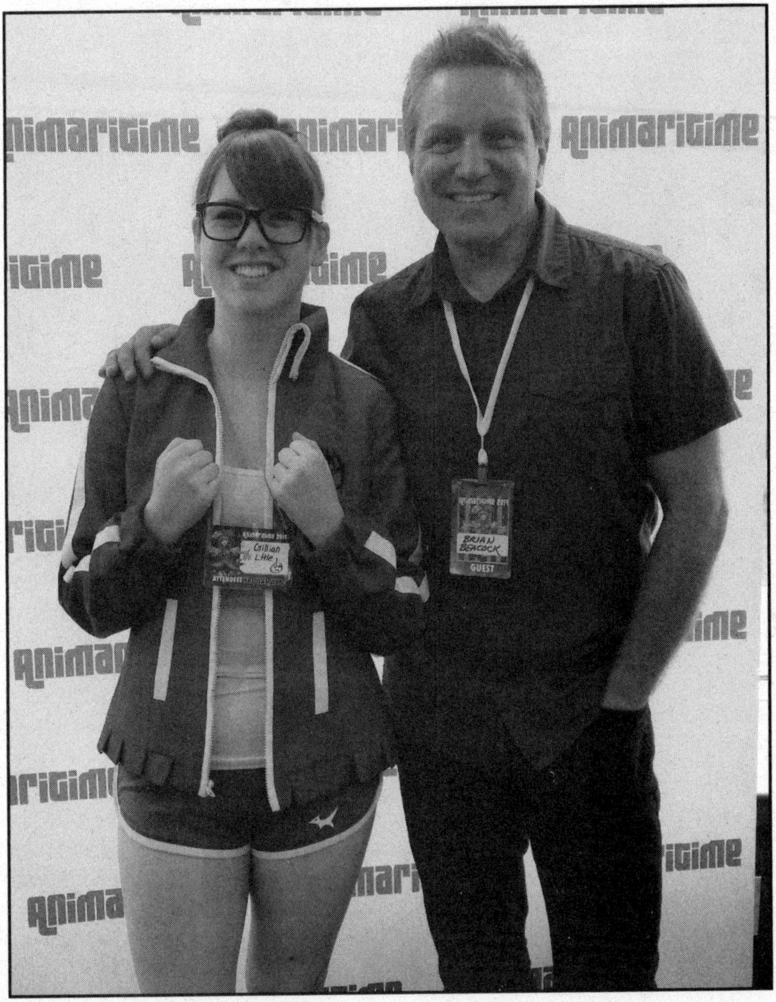
Animaritime
Gillian Little
ATTENDEE
BRIAN BEACOCK
GUEST

"Not only was I invited to participate in my first ever photoshoot (which you can see the results of above), I also got the chance to meet Brian Beacock, the voice of Monokuma in the video games! I absolutely adore cosplaying best girl Aoi Asahina and I had a blast giving out donuts to other attendees at the convention! My fellow cosplayers pictured made that convention the best one I ever attended, and I have Danganronpa to thank for the memories!"

This group shot was taken on the steps of the Legislative Building in Fredericton, which was constructed in 1882 in the so-called Second Empire style that arose in France and was associated with the reign of Napoleon III (he was the nephew of the original Napoleon, whose son, Napoleon II, never actually got to rule—that's why III's reign is called the Second Empire, and not the third as would seem more logical).

I think it's cool when people use an unexpected location as a cosplay backdrop, such as an historic building. Some anime cons in Europe are even held in historic buildings, including Connichi in Germany, which takes place in the elegant Kongress Palais Kassel.

Well, I didn't hear anything in the news about a tragedy at an anime con in New Brunswick, so I'm just going to assume that everyone was all right.

We'll say goodbye for now with this picture from Isa uwu, who says, *"Clown Nagito is kind of a huge joke in the American side of the fanbase, so I decided to cosplay it :> (My Instagram is @ grapekinnie)."* I'm suddenly having a vision of not only Nagito, but the entire *Danganronpa 2* cast as clowns, having a big rumble in the manner of Arctic Monkeys' "Fluorescent Adolescent."

But *Goodbye Despair* Vol. 2 is on the way (and we've also got our other current *Danganronpa* manga, *Danganronpa Another Episode: Ultra Despair Girls*), so we'd love to receive more of your thoughts, fan art, cosplay, etc., on all things *Danganronpa*!

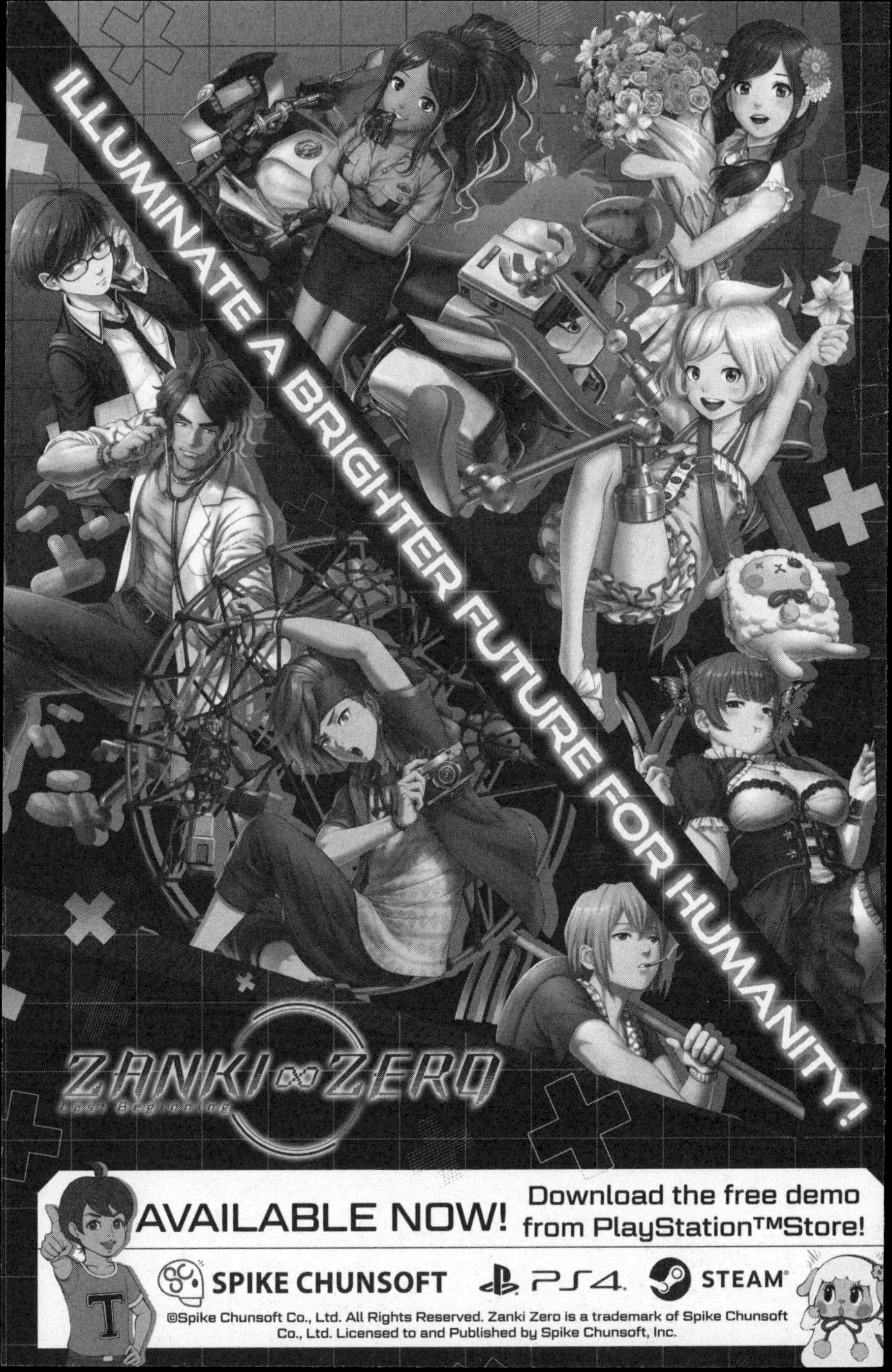
ILLUMINATE A BRIGHTER FUTURE FOR HUMANITY!
ZANKI ZERO
Last Beginning
AVAILABLE NOW!
Download the free demo from PlayStation™Store!
SPIKE CHUNSOFT
PS4
STEAM
©Spike Chunsoft Co., Ltd. All Rights Reserved. Zanki Zero is a trademark of Spike Chunsoft Co., Ltd. Licensed to and Published by Spike Chunsoft, Inc.

REPENT, SINNERS! THEY'RE BACK!

Miss the anime?
Try the *Panty & Stocking with Garterbelt* manga! Nine ALL-NEW stories of your favorite filthy fallen angels, written and drawn by TAGRO, with a special afterword by *Kill La Kill* director Hiroyuki Imaishi!
978-1-61655-735-5 | $9.99

MAY I HAVE YOUR, ATTENTION, PLEASE?

Your powers of observation will be vital if you want to survive the courtroom drama (or never mind courtroom—the just plain drama) of *Danganronpa*. So remember that this book reads right-to-left, because that's just the kind of detail that might REFUTE! someone's trial testimony. Also, remember that this book reads right-to-left, because if you read it left-to-right, the murder victims will seem to rise up off the floor and come back to life, which may be a little disconcerting.

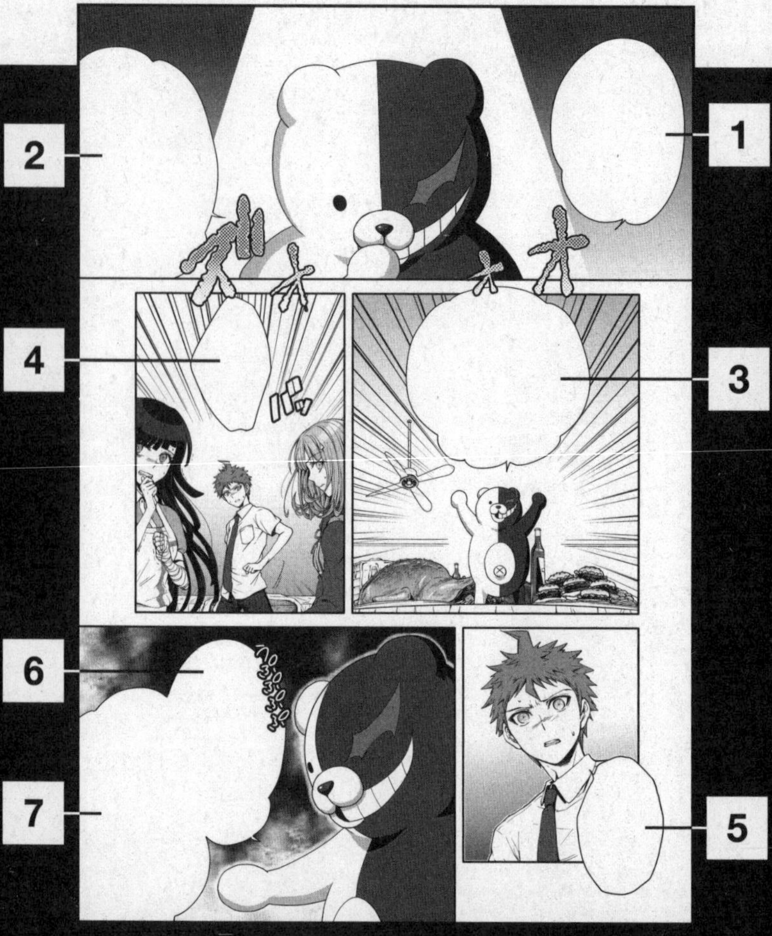
1
2
3
4
5
6
7